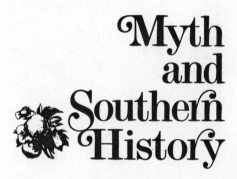

Myth and Southern History

Myth and Southern History

Edited by **PATRICK GERSTER**
and **NICHOLAS CORDS**

LAKEWOOD COMMUNITY COLLEGE

 RAND McNALLY COLLEGE PUBLISHING COMPANY • Chicago

For
Mark, Jennifer, Jason
James and John

Acknowledgments

As is the case with any project based on secondary sources, we have incurred many debts. Because this work is thematic, we are indebted to all those historians whose works have contributed either directly or indirectly to our developing interest in the relationship between myth and history. The work being regional in focus, we are particularly indebted to southern historians' contributions, and most particularly to those whose works are included herein. We are impressed that they represent the historical profession at its finest. We also extend our thanks to Lawrence Malley, Robert Erhart, and Margaret L. Boberschmidt of Rand McNally; to Neil R. McMillen for strategic aid and valuable suggestions; and to our typist, Mrs. Van Johnson. Finally, we express deep gratitude to our wives and families for their support and forebearance.

It's all *now* you see. Yesterday won't be over until tomorrow and tomorrow began ten thousand years ago. For every Southern boy fourteen years old, not once but whenever he wants it, there is the instant when it's still not yet two o'clock on that July afternoon in 1863, the brigades are in position behind the rail fence, the guns are laid and ready in the woods and the furled flags are already loosened to break out and Pickett himself with his long oiled ringlets and his hat in one hand probably and his sword in the other looking up the hill waiting for Longstreet to give the word and it's all in the balance, it hasn't happened yet, it hasn't even begun yet, it not only hasn't begun yet but there is still time for it not to begin against that position and those circumstances which made more men than Garnett and Kemper and Armstead and Wilcox look grave yet it's going to begin, we all know that, we have come too far with too much at stake and that moment doesn't even need a fourteen-year-old boy to think *This time. Maybe this time* with all this much to lose and all this much to gain: Pennsylvania, Maryland, the world, the golden dome of Washington itself to crown with desperate and unbelievable victory the desperate gamble, the cast made two years ago; or to anyone who ever sailed even a skiff under a quilt sail, the moment in 1492 when somebody thought *This is it:* the absolute edge of no return, to turn back now and make home or sail irrevocably on and either find land or plunge over the world's roaring rim.

WILLIAM FAULKNER, *Intruder in the Dust*

Contents

Introduction

Students of the southern past have long sought to identify a central theme in southern history. It was out of such a concern, for example, that historian Ulrich B. Phillips spoke of the sustained southern commitment to white supremacy; journalist Wilbur J. Cash sought to tap the inner workings of "the mind" of the South; and others have concluded the inner logic of southern history to be climate, geography, or its seemingly distinctive economic, political, social, or religious patterns. Indeed the debate over the central theme of southern history is a continuing one, with the only consensus being that there does exist a common thread of experience somewhere in the deep recesses of the southern past.

In 1964, while in pursuit of this central theme, George B. Tindall isolated "mythology" as a "new frontier" in southern history.[1] Acknowledging the work of earlier historians such as Francis Pendelton Gaines (*The Southern Plantation: A Study in the Development and Accuracy of a Tradition,* 1925), and anticipating the verdict of southern historians to come, Tindall's essay enthusiastically endorsed mythology as a tool for analyzing the rather blatant ambiguities, ironies, and paradoxes inherent in the southern past. The lens of myth had indeed been applied to the South before Professor Tindall's seminal work, but it was left for him to suggest that such an approach might well result in a new synthesis and a perspective worthy of sustained application. In short, Tindall's article posed the question: Is myth indeed one of the more important psychological determinants of southernism?

To what extent George B. Tindall's suggested approach to southern history will withstand the long-term erosion of historical scholarship is a question only future generations of scholars can answer with any full degree of certitude. It is the opinion of the editors, however, that an affirmative yet tentative judgment is now possible given the body of historical literature which has arisen clearly vindicating the Tindall thesis. An impressive array of southern scholars prior to and since Tindall's seminal essay have sought to determine the parameters of myth within what C. Vann Woodward has labeled "that twilight zone between living memory and written history." This volume brings together a sampling of their findings. Such scholars

---

[1] George B. Tindall, "Mythology: A New Frontier in Southern History," in *The Idea of the South: Pursuit of a Central Theme,* ed. Frank E. Vandiver (Chicago, 1964).

are representative of an expanding and distinguished group of American historians who have come to see important distinctions between what might be termed "history as actuality" and "history as perceived."[2]

But perhaps further clarification and explanation are needed before this work can indeed provide the measure of historical insight which the "new frontier of mythology" potentially holds. The term "myth," as presented in this set of readings, is viewed in two ways. In the first instance, some of the authors seem to have Thomas A. Bailey's definition in mind as they speak of the myths of southern history: "a historical myth is . . . an account or belief that is demonstrably untrue, in whole or substantial part."[3] Those reflecting this definition tend to emphasize the negative aspects of myth, to isolate, and when the occasion warrants to debunk the results of misguided scholarship. Second, others appear more consistent with Henry Nash Smith's view of myth as "an intellectual construction that fuses concept and emotion into an image."[4] Briefly stated, one school seeks to emphasize historical inaccuracies while the other approaches the problem from the vantage point of social psychology. One sees myth as the by-product of historical scholarship (or lack of it), while the other shows a marked concern for the ways in which myth serves the decidedly positive function of unifying experience providing, in the words of Mark Schorer, "a large controlling image that gives philosophical meaning to the facts of ordinary life. . . ."[5] Certainly, at times both definitions are present—on occasion they tend to blend to the point of becoming almost indistinguishable. Both notions of myth are germane to the South and its history.

It is also important to note that the existence of a southern mythology in no way sets the South apart as distinctive or unique. It has been demonstrated in other quarters that much behavior and belief based on myth survives, and in fact thrives, in the contemporary world. The preeminent mythic scholar, Mircea Eliade, has observed that "certain aspects and functions of mythical thought are constituents of the human being."[6] Fundamental to the "human condition," myths in their infinite variety and complexity serve a supportive role to the dreams, ideals, and values of every society. Accordingly, "southern mythology" must be seen as differing from

[2] For a view of myth in its larger American context see Nicholas Cords and Patrick Gerster (eds.), *Myth and the American Experience*, 2 vols. (New York and Beverly Hills, 1973).

[3] Thomas A. Bailey, "The Mythmakers of American History," *The Journal of American History*, 55 (June 1968), p. 5.

[4] Henry Nash Smith, *Virgin Land: The American West as Symbol and Myth* (New York, 1950), p. v.

[5] Mark Schorer, "The Necessity of Myth," in Henry A. Murray (ed.), *Myth and Mythmaking* (New York, 1960), p. 355.

[6] Mircea Eliade, "Survivals and Camouflages of Myth," *Diogenes*, 41 (Spring 1963), p. 1.

its American equivalent only in degree not in kind, just as "American mythology" stands in relation to that of the world at large. Paul M. Gaston concurred with this judgment in his recent work, *The New South Creed: A Study in Southern Mythmaking:*

> What does distinguish the South, at least from other parts of the United States, is the degree to which myths have been spawned and the extent to which they have asserted their hegemony over the Southern mind.[7]

In this sense, at least, the American South has successfully transcended the strictures of regionalism.

Finally, the identification of myth as an important element in the historical process demonstrates anew that history is the dual product of documentation and imagination—both the record of the past *and* the dialogue among historians. The basic documents and the personal and professional prejudices of the historian (for Wendell H. Stephenson, "the fallacies of assumptions and methods") all find their way into the historical "record." The historian cannot dismiss the controlling images or myths of the society within which he writes. Because the serious historian must factor for all of these as he engages his discipline, this volume is as much a commentary on the writing of southern history—that is to say historiography—as it is on the viability of myth in the historical process. In these pages there is much support of the observation that "myth[s] have been used for centuries in writing history as well as making it."[8] The reader will find that "mythology" has provided, as well as suggests, new realms of scholarly speculation. More specifically, it becomes evident that such an approach applied to the South has come of age. It is an approach to southern history both relevant and exciting, deserving to *take its stand* beside the more traditional and validated perspectives long provided by historians of the marketplace, the political and diplomatic arenas, and the social record.

Some years ago Wilbur Cash wrote of the importance of the South's frontier experience: ". . . the history of the roll of frontier upon frontier— and on to the frontier beyond."[9] Given George B. Tindall's scholarly directive and the focus provided by the following selections, perhaps the South's enigmatic frontiers of the past—even that elusive central theme—can now find clearer explanation and synthesis in terms of her "new frontier of mythology."

[7] Paul M. Gaston, *The New South Creed: A Study in Southern Mythmaking* (New York, 1970), p. 8.

[8] Alfred Stern, "Fiction and Myth in History," *Diogenes,* 42 (Summer 1963), p. 98.

[9] Wilbur Cash, *The Mind of the South* (New York, 1941), p. 4.

1

Mythology: A New Frontier in Southern History

George B. Tindall

The "reality" of history, irrespective of time or place, remains an
elusive commodity, especially as regards the American South. Indeed, as George B. Tindall, Professor of History at the University
of North Carolina, Chapel Hill, argues in the selection which follows, the basic problem of distinguishing *objective reality* from *perceived reality* is ever present for the historian. Historical reality
involves not only that which is demonstrably true but also that
which one believes to be true. As such, the historian has a dual
role: he remains at once a "custodian of the past and keeper of the
public memory." The role of the historian involves both countering
misguided scholarship and identifying the public dreams which do
so much to orchestrate human behavior. Both of these facets of the
historical enterprise inevitably lead the historian into the province
of myth. Thus, in determining the dimensions of the southern experience, the historian must reckon not only with peculiar regional
characteristics but also the myths which have conditioned them. As
a significant unit of the region's experience, myth supplies an internal structure and a sustaining symmetry to our understanding
of the South. Professor Tindall's exploration of this new frontier of
mythology does much to establish the context—the perspective and
technique—for this entire work.

From George Tindall, "Mythology: A New Frontier in Southern History," in Frank
E. Vandiver (ed.), *The Idea of the South: Pursuit of a Central Theme,* pp. 1–15.
Reprinted by permission of the author and the University of Chicago Press. Copyright © 1964 by William Rice University. All rights reserved. Published 1964. Composed and printed by the University of Chicago Press, Chicago, Illinois, U.S.A.

The idea of the South—or more appropriately, the ideas of the South—
belong in large part to the order of social myth. There are few areas of the
modern world that have bred a regional mythology so potent, so profuse
and diverse, even so paradoxical, as the American South. But the various
mythical images of the South that have so significantly affected American
history have yet to be subjected to the kind of broad and imaginative historical analysis that has been applied to the idea of the American West,
particularly in Henry Nash Smith's *Virgin Land: The American West as
Symbol and Myth*. The idea of the South has yet to be fully examined in
the context of mythology, as essentially a problem of intellectual history.

To place the ideas of the South in the context of mythology, of course,
is not necessarily to pass judgment upon them as illusions. The game of
debunking myths, Harry Levin has warned us, starts "in the denunciation
of myth as falsehood from the vantage-point of a rival myth."[1] Mythology
has other meanings, not all of them pejorative, and myths have a life of
their own which to some degree renders irrelevant the question of their
correlation to empirical fact. Setting aside for the moment the multiple
connotations of the term, we may say that social myths in general, including those of the South, are simply mental pictures that portray the pattern
of what a people think they are (or ought to be) or what somebody else
thinks they are. They tend to develop abstract ideas in more or less concrete and dramatic terms. In the words of Henry Nash Smith, they fuse
"concept and emotion into an image."[2]

They may serve a variety of functions. "A myth," Mark Schorer has
observed, "is a large, controlling image that gives philosophical meaning
to the facts of ordinary life; that is, which has organizing value for experience."[3] It may offer useful generalizations by which data may be tested.
But being also "charged with values, aspirations, ideals and meanings,"[4]
myths may become the ground for belief, for either loyalty and defense on
the one hand or hostility and opposition on the other. In such circumstances a myth itself becomes one of the realities of history, significantly
influencing the course of human action, for good or ill. There is, of course,
always a danger of illusion, a danger that in ordering one's vision of reality,
the myth may predetermine the categories of perception, rendering one
blind to things that do not fit into the mental image.

[1] Harry Levin, "Some Meanings of Myth," in Henry A. Murray (ed.), *Myth and
Mythmakers* (New York, 1960), p. 106.

[2] Henry Nash Smith, *Virgin Land: The American West as Symbol and Myth* (Vintage ed., New York, 1957), p. v.

[3] Mark Schorer, "The Necessity for Myth," in Murray (ed.), *Myth and Mythmakers*, p. 355.

[4] C. Vann Woodward, "The Antislavery Myth," *American Scholar*, XXXI (Spring,
1962), 325.

Since the Southern mind is reputed to be peculiarly resistant to pure abstraction and more receptive to the concrete and dramatic image, it may be unusually susceptible to mythology. Perhaps for the same reason our subject can best be approached through reference to the contrasting experiences of two Southerners—one recent, the other about forty-five years ago.

The first is the experience of a contemporary Louisiana writer, John T. Westbrook.

During the thirties and early forties [Westbrook has written] when I was an English instructor at the University of Missouri, I was often mildly irritated by the average northerner's Jeeter-Lester-and-potlikker idea of the South. Even today the northern visitor inertia-headedly maintains his misconception: he hankers to see eroded hills and rednecks, scrub cotton and sharecropper shacks.

It little profits me to drive him through Baton Rouge, show him the oil-ethyl-rubber-aluminum-chemical miles of industry along the Mississippi River, and say, "This . . . is the fastest-growing city of over 100,-000 in America. We can amply substantiate our claim that we are atomic target number one, that in the next war the Russians will obliterate us first. . . ."

Our northerner is suspicious of all this crass evidence presented to his senses. It bewilders and befuddles him. He is too deeply steeped in William Faulkner and Robert Penn Warren. The fumes of progress are in his nose and the bright steel of industry towers before his eyes, but his heart is away in Yoknapatawpha County with razorback hogs and night riders. On this trip to the South he wants, above all else, to sniff the effluvium of backwoods-and-sand-hill subhumanity and to see at least one barn burn at midnight. So he looks at me with crafty misgiving, as if to say, "Well, you *do* drive a Cadillac, talk rather glibly about Kierkegaard and Sartre . . . but, after all, you *are* only fooling, aren't you? You do, don't you, sometimes, go out secretly by owl-light to drink swamp water and feed on sowbelly and collard greens?"[5]

The other story was the experience of a Southern historian, Frank L. Owsley, who traveled during World War I from Chicago via Cincinnati to Montgomery with a group of young ladies on the way to visit their menfolk at an army camp. He wrote later that, "despite everything which had ever been said to the contrary," the young ladies had a romantic conception of the "Sunny South" and looked forward to the journey with considerable ex-

John T. Westbrook, "Twilight of Southern Regionalism," *Southwest Review,* XLII (Summer, 1957), 231.

citement. "They expected to enter a pleasant land of white columned mansions, green pastures, expansive cotton and tobacco fields where negroes sang spirituals all the day through." Except in the bluegrass basins of central Kentucky and Tennessee, what they actually found "were gutted hillsides; scrub oak and pine; bramble and blackberry thickets, bottom lands once fertile now senile and exhausted, with spindling tobacco, corn, or cotton stalks . . . ; unpainted houses which were hardly more than shacks or here and there the crumbling ruins of old mansions covered with briars, the homes of snakes and lizards."[6] The disappointment of Dr. Owsley's ladies was, no doubt, even greater than that of Mr. Westbrook's friend in Baton Rouge.

There is a striking contrast between these two episodes, both in the picture of Southern reality and in the differing popular images that they present. The fact that they are four decades apart helps to account for the discrepancies, but what is not apparent at first is the common ancestry of the two images. They are not very distant cousins, collateral descendants from the standard image of the Old South, the plantation myth. The version of Owsley's lady friends is closer to the original primogenitor, which despite its advancing age and debility, still lives amid a flourishing progeny of legendary Southern gentility. According to Francis Pendleton Gaines, author of *The Southern Plantation,* the pattern appeared full-blown at least as early as 1832 in John Pendleton Kennedy's romance, *Swallow Barn.*[7] It has had a long career in story and novel and song, in the drama and motion picture. The corrosions of age seem to have ended its Hollywood career, although the old films still turn up on the late late. It may still be found in the tourist bait of shapely beauties in hoop skirts posed against the backdrop of white columns at Natchez, Orton, or a hundred other places.

These pictures are enough to trigger in the mind the whole euphoric pattern of kindly old marster with his mint julep; happy darkies singing in fields perpetually white to the harvest or, as the case may be, sadly recalling the long lost days of old; coquettish belles wooed by slender gallants in gray underneath the moonlight and magnolias. It is a pattern that yields all too easily to caricature and ridicule, for in its more sophisticated versions the figure of the planter carries a heavy freight of the aristocratic virtues: courtliness, grace, hospitality, honor, *noblesse oblige,* as well as many no less charming aristocratic vices: a lordly indifference to the balance sheet, hot temper, profanity, overindulgence, a certain stubborn obstinacy. The old-time Negro, when not a figure of comedy, is the very embodiment of

[6] Frank L. Owsley, "The Old South and the New," *American Review,* VI (February, 1936), 475.

[7] Francis Pendleton Gaines, *The Southern Plantation: A Study in the Development and Accuracy of a Tradition* (New York, 1925), p. 23.

loyalty. And the Southern belle: "Beautiful, graceful, accomplished in social charm, bewitching in coquetry, yet strangely steadfast in soul," Gaines has written, "she is perhaps the most winsome figure in the whole field of our fancy."[8] "The plantation romance," Gaines says, "remains our chief social idyl of the past; of an Arcadian scheme of existence, less material, less hurried, less prosaically equalitarian, less futile, richer in picturesqueness, festivity, in realized pleasure that recked not of hope or fear or unrejoicing labor."[9]

But there is still more to the traditional pattern. Somewhere off in the piney woods and erosion-gutted clay hills, away from the white columns and gentility, there existed Po' White Trash: the crackers; hillbillies; sandhillers; rag, tag, and bobtail; squatters; "po' buckra" to the Negroes; the Ransy Sniffle of A. B. Longstreet's *Georgia Scenes* and his literary descendants like Jeeter Lester and Ab Snopes, abandoned to poverty and degeneracy—the victims, it was later discovered, of hookworm, malaria, and pellagra. Somewhere in the pattern the respectable small farmer was lost from sight. He seemed to be neither romantic nor outrageous enough to fit in. His neglect provides the classic example in Southern history of the blind spots engendered by the power of mythology. It was not until the 1930's that Frank L. Owsley and his students at Vanderbilt rediscovered the Southern yeoman farmer as the characteristic, or at least the most numerous, ante bellum white Southerner.[10] More about the yeoman presently; neglected in the plantation myth, he was in the foreground of another.

In contrast to the legitimate heirs of the plantation myth, the image of John T. Westbrook's Yankee visitor in Baton Rouge seems to be descended from what might be called the illegitimate line of the plantation myth, out of abolition. It is one of the ironies of our history that, as Gaines put it, the "two opposing sides of the fiercest controversy that ever shook national thought agreed concerning certain picturesque elements of plantation life and joined hands to set the conception unforgettably in public consciousness."[11] The abolitionists found it difficult, or even undesirable, to escape the standard image. It was pretty fully developed even in *Uncle Tom's Cabin*. Harriet Beecher Stowe made her villain a Yankee overseer, and has been accused by at least one latter-day abolitionist of implanting deeply in the American mind the stereotype of the faithful darkey. For others the plantation myth simply appeared in reverse, as a pattern of corrupt opulence resting upon human exploitation. Gentle old marster became the ar-

[8] *Ibid.*, p. 16.
[9] *Ibid.*, p. 4.
[10] Frank L. Owsley, *Plain Folk of the Old South* (Baton Rouge, 1949).
[11] Gaines, *The Southern Plantation*, p. 30.

rogant, haughty, imperious potentate, the very embodiment of sin, the central target of the antislavery attack. He maintained a seraglio in the slave quarters; he bred Negroes like cattle and sold them down the river to certain death in the sugar mills, separating families if that served his purpose, while Southern women suffered in silence the guilty knowledge of their men's infidelity. The happy darkies in this picture became white men in black skins, an oppressed people longing for freedom, the victims of countless atrocities so ghastly as to be unbelievable except for undeniable evidence, forever seeking an opportunity to follow the North Star to freedom. The masses of the white folks were simply poor whites, relegated to ignorance and degeneracy by the slavocracy.

Both lines of the plantation myth have been remarkably prolific, but the more adaptable one has been that of the abolitionists. It has repeatedly readjusted to new conditions while the more legitimate line has courted extinction, running out finally into the decadence perpetrated by Tennessee Williams. Meanwhile, the abolitionist image of brutality persisted through and beyond Reconstruction in the Republican outrage mills and bloody shirt political campaigns. For several decades it was more than overbalanced by the Southern image of Reconstruction horrors, disarmed by prophets of a New South created in the image of the North, and almost completely submerged under the popularity of plantation romances in the generation before Owsley's trainload of ladies ventured into their "Sunny South" of the teens. At about that time, however, the undercurrents began to emerge once again into the mainstream of American thought. In the clever decade of the twenties a kind of neoabolitionist myth of the Savage South was compounded. It seemed that the benighted South, after a period of relative neglect, suddenly became an object of concern to every publicist in the country. One Southern abomination after another was ground through their mills: child labor, peonage, lynching, hookworm, pellagra, the Scopes trial, the Fundamentalist crusade against Al Smith. The guiding genius was Henry L. Mencken, the hatchet man from Baltimore who developed the game of South-baiting into a national pastime, a fine art at which he had no peer. In 1917, when he started constructing his image of "Baptist and Methodist barbarism" below the Potomac, he began with the sterility of Southern literature and went on from there. With characteristic glee he anointed one J. Gordon Coogler of South Carolina "the last bard of Dixie" and quoted his immortal couplet:

> Alas, for the South! Her books have grown fewer—
> She never was much given to literature.

"Down there," Mencken wrote, "a poet is now almost as rare as an oboe-player, a dry-point etcher or a metaphysician." As for "critics, musical composers, painters, sculptors, architects . . . there is not even a bad one between the Potomac mud-flats and the Gulf. Nor an historian. Nor a sociologist. Nor a philosopher. Nor a theologian. Nor a scientist. In all these fields the south is an awe-inspiring blank. . . ."[12] It was as complete a vacuity as the interstellar spaces, the "Sahara of the Bozart," "The Bible Belt." He summed it all up in one basic catalogue of Southern grotesqueries: "Fundamentalism, Ku Kluxry, revivals, lynchings, hog wallow politics—these are the things that always occur to a northerner when he thinks of the south."[13] The South, in short, had fallen prey to its poor whites, who would soon achieve apotheosis in the Snopes family.

It did not end with the twenties. The image was reinforced by a variety of episodes: the Scottsboro trials, chain gang exposés, Bilbo and Rankin, Senate filibusters, labor wars; much later by Central High and Orval Faubus, Emmett Till and Autherine Lucy and James Meredith, bus boycotts and Freedom Riders; and not least of all by the lush growth of literature that covered Mencken's Sahara, with Caldwell's *Tobacco Road* and Faulkner's *Sanctuary* and various other products of what Ellen Glasgow labeled the Southern Gothic and a less elegant Mississippi editor called the "privy school" of literature. In the words of Faulkner's character, Gavin Stevens, the North suffered from a curious "gullibility: a volitionless, almost helpless capacity and eagerness to believe anything about the South not even provided it be derogatory but merely bizarre enough and strange enough."[14] And Faulkner, to be sure, did not altogether neglect that market. Not surprisingly, he was taken in some quarters for a realist, and the image of Southern savagery long obscured the critics' recognition of his manifold merits.

The family line of the plantation myth can be traced only so far in the legendary gentility and savagery of the South. Other family lines seem to be entirely independent—if sometimes on friendly terms. In an excellent study, "The New South Creed, 1865–1900," soon to be published, Paul M. Gaston has traced the evolution of the creed into a genuine myth. In the aftermath of the Civil War, apostles of a "New South," led by Henry W. Grady, preached with almost evangelical fervor the gospel of industry. Their dream, Gaston writes, "was essentially a promise of American life for the South. It proffered all the glitter and glory and freedom from guilt that inhered in the American ideal."[15] From advocacy, from this vision of

[12] Henry L. Mencken, "The Sahara of the Bozart," in *Prejudices: Second Series* (New York, 1920), pp. 136, 137, 139.

[13] Henry L. Mencken, "The South Rebels Again," in Robert McHugh (ed.), *The Bathtub Hoax and Other Blasts & Bravos from the Chicago Tribune* (New York, 1958), p. 249. From a column in the Chicago *Tribune,* December 7, 1924.

[14] William Faulkner, *Intruder in the Dust* (New York, 1948), p. 153.

[15] Paul Morton Gaston, "The New South Creed, 1865–1900" (Ph.D. dissertation, Department of History, University of North Carolina, 1961), p. 193.

the future, the prophets soon advanced to the belief that "their promised land [was] at hand, no longer merely a gleaming goal." "By the twentieth century . . . there was established for many in the South a pattern of belief within which they could see themselves and their section as rich, success-oriented, and just . . . opulence and power were at hand . . . the Negro lived in the best of all possible worlds."[16]

As the twentieth century advanced, and wealth did in fact increase, the creed of the New South took on an additional burden of crusades for good roads and education, blending them into what Francis B. Simkins has called the "trinity of Southern progress": industrial growth, good roads, and schools. When the American Historical Association went to Durham in 1929 for its annual meeting, Robert D. W. Connor of the University of North Carolina presented the picture of a rehabilitated South that had "shaken itself free from its heritage of war and Reconstruction. Its self-confidence restored, its political stability assured, its prosperity regained, its social problems on the way to solution. . . ."[17] Two months before Connor spoke, the New York Stock Exchange had broken badly, and in the aftermath the image he described was seriously blurred, but before the end of the thirties it was being brought back into focus by renewed industrial expansion that received increased momentum from World War II and postwar prosperity.

Two new and disparate images emerged in the depression years, both with the altogether novel feature of academic trappings and affiliations. One was the burgeoning school of sociological regionalism led by Howard W. Odum and Rupert B. Vance at the University of North Carolina. It was neither altogether the image of the Savage South nor that of industrial progress, although both entered into the compound. It was rather a concept of the "Problem South," which Franklin D. Roosevelt labeled "the Nation's Economic Problem No. 1," a region with indisputable shortcomings but with potentialities that needed constructive attention and the application of rational social planning. Through the disciples of Odum as well as the agencies of the New Deal, the vision issued in a flood of social science monographs and programs for reform and development. To one undergraduate in Chapel Hill at the time, it seemed in retrospect that "we had more of an attitude of service to the South as the South than was true later. . . ."[18]

The regionalists were challenged by the Vanderbilt Agrarians, who de-

[16] *Ibid.,* pp. 195, 216.

[17] Robert D. W. Connor, "The Rehabilitation of a Rural Commonwealth," *American Historical Review,* XXXVI (October, 1930), 62.

[18] Alexander Heard, quoted in Wilma Dykeman and James Stokely, *Seeds of Southern Change: The Life of Will Alexander* (Chicago, 1962), p. 303.

veloped a myth of the traditional South. Their manifesto, *I'll Take My Stand,* by Twelve Southerners, appeared by fortuitous circumstance in 1930 when industrial capitalism seemed on the verge of collapse. In reaction against both the progressive New South and Mencken's image of savagery they championed, in Donald Davidson's words, a "traditional society . . . that is stable, religious, more rural than urban, and politically conservative," in which human needs were supplied by "Family, bloodkinship, clanship, folkways, custom, community. . . ."[19] The ideal of the traditional virtues took on the texture of myth in their image of the agrarian South. Of course, in the end, their agrarianism proved less important as a social-economic force than as a context for creative literature. The central figures in the movement were the Fugitive poets John Crowe Ransom, Donald Davidson, Allen Tate, and Robert Penn Warren. But, as Professor Louis Rubin has emphasized, "Through their vision of an agrarian community, the authors of *I'll Take My Stand* presented a critique of the modern world. In contrast to the hurried, nervous life of cities, the image of the agrarian South was of a life in which human beings existed serenely and harmoniously." Their critique of the modern frenzy "has since been echoed by commentator after commentator."[20]

While it never became altogether clear whether the Agrarians were celebrating the aristocratic graces or following the old Jeffersonian dictum that "Those who labor in the earth are the chosen people of God . . . ," most of them seemed to come down eventually on the side of the farmer rather than the planter. Frank L. Owsley, who rediscovered the ante bellum yeoman farmer, was one of them. Insofar as they extolled the yeoman farmer, the Agrarians laid hold upon an image older than any of the others—the Jeffersonian South. David M. Potter, a Southerner in exile at Stanford University, has remarked how difficult it is for many people to realize that the benighted South "was, until recently, regarded by many liberals as the birthplace and the natural bulwark of the Jeffersonian ideal. . . ."[21] The theme has long had an appeal for historians as well as others, Frederick Jackson Turner developed it for the West and William E. Dodd for the South. According to Dodd the democratic, equalitarian South of the Jeffersonian image was the norm; the plantation slavocracy was the great aberration. Dodd's theme has been reflected in the writing of other his-

[19] Donald Davidson, "Why the Modern South Has a Great Literature," *Vanderbilt Studies in the Humanities,* I (1951), 12.

[20] Louis D. Rubin, Jr., "Introduction to the Torchbook Edition," in Twelve Southerners, *I'll Take My Stand* (Torchbook ed.; New York, 1962), pp. xiv, xvii. See also Herman Clarence Nixon, "A Thirty Years' Personal View," *Mississippi Quarterly,* XIII (Spring, 1960), 79, for parallels in recent social criticism.

[21] David M. Potter, "The Enigma of the South," *Yale Review,* LI (Autumn, 1961), 143.

torians, largely in terms of a region subjected to economic colonialism by an imperial Northeast: Charles A. Beard, for example, who saw the sectional conflict as a struggle between agrarianism and industrialism; Howard K. Beale, who interpreted Reconstruction in similar terms; C. Vann Woodward, defender of Populism; Arthur S. Link, who first rediscovered the Southern progressives; and Walter Prescott Webb, who found the nation divided between an exploited South and West on the one hand, and a predatory Northeast on the other. Jefferson, like the South, it sometimes seems, can mean all things to all men, and the Jefferson image of agrarian democracy has been a favorite recourse of Southern liberals, just as his state-rights doctrines have nourished conservatism.

In stark contrast to radical agrarianism there stands the concept of monolithic conservatism in Southern politics. It seems to be a proposition generally taken for granted now that the South is, by definition, conservative—and always has been. Yet the South in the late nineteenth century produced some of the most radical Populists and in the twentieth was a bulwark of Wilsonian progressivism and Roosevelt's New Deal, at least up to a point. A good case has been made out by Arthur S. Link that Southern agrarian radicals pushed Wilson further into progressivism than he intended to go.[22] During the twenties Southern minority leadership in Congress kept up such a running battle against the conservative tax policies of Andrew Mellon that, believe it or not, there was real fear among some Northern businessmen during the 1932 campaign that Franklin D. Roosevelt might be succeeded by that radical Southern income-taxer, John Nance Garner![23] The conservative image of course has considerable validity, but it obscures understanding of such phenomena as Albert Gore, Russell Long, Lister Hill, John Sparkman, Olin D. Johnston, William Fulbright, the Yarboroughs of Texas, or the late Estes Kefauver. In the 1960 campaign the conservative image seriously victimized Lyndon B. Johnson, who started in politics as a vigorous New Dealer and later maneuvered through the Senate the first civil rights legislation since Reconstruction.

The infinite variety of Southern mythology could be catalogued and analyzed endlessly. A suggestive list would include the Proslavery South; the Confederate South; the Demagogic South; the State Rights South; the Fighting South; the Lazy South; the Folklore South; the South of jazz and the blues; the Booster South; the Rapacious South running away with Northern industries; the Liberal South of the interracial movement; the White Supremacy South of racial segregation, which seems to be for some

[22] Arthur S. Link, "The South and the 'New Freedom': An Interpretation," *American Scholar*, XX (Summer, 1951), 314–24.

[23] A. G. Hopkins to Sam Rayburn, July 29, 1932; Rayburn to J. Andrew West, October 26, 1932, in Sam Rayburn Library, Bonham, Texas.

the all-encompassing "Southern way of life"; the Anglo-Saxon (or was it the Scotch-Irish?) South, the most American of all regions because of its native population; or the Internationalist South, a mainstay of the Wilson, Roosevelt, and Truman foreign policies.

The South, then, has been the seedbed for a proliferation of paradoxical myths, all of which have some basis in empirical fact and all of which doubtlessly have, or have had, their true believers. The result has been, in David Potter's words, that the South has become an enigma, "a kind of Sphinx on the American land."[24] What is really the answer to the riddle, what is at bottom the foundation of Southern distinctiveness has never been established with finality, but the quest for a central theme of Southern history has repeatedly engaged the region's historians. Like Frederick Jackson Turner, who extracted the essential West in his frontier thesis, Southern historians have sought to distill the quintessence of the South into some kind of central theme.

In a recent survey of these efforts David L. Smiley of Wake Forest College has concluded that they turn upon two basic lines of thought: "the causal effects of environment, and the development of certain acquired characteristics of the people called Southern."[25] The distinctive climate and weather of the South, it has been argued, slowed the pace of life, tempered the speech of the South, dictated the system of staple crops and Negro slavery—in short, predetermined the plantation economy. The more persuasive suggestions have resulted from concentration upon human factors and causation. The best known is that set forth by U. B. Phillips. The quintessence of Southernism, he wrote in 1928, was "a common resolve indomitably maintained" that the South "shall be and remain a white man's country." Whether "expressed with the frenzy of a demagogue or maintained with a patrician's quietude," this was "the cardinal test of a Southerner and the central theme of Southern history."[26] Other historians have pointed to the rural nature of Southern society as the basic conditioning factor, to the prevalence of the country gentleman ideal imported from England, to the experience of the South as a conscious minority unified by criticism and attack from outside, to the fundamental piety of the Bible Belt, and to various other factors. It has even been suggested by one writer that a chart of the mule population would determine the boundaries of the South.

More recently, two historians have attempted new explanations. In his

---

[24] Potter, "The Enigma of the South," p. 142.

[25] David L. Smiley, "The Quest for the Central Theme in Southern History," paper read before the Southern Historical Association, Miami Beach, Florida, November 8, 1962, p. 2.

[26] Ulrich B. Phillips, "The Central Theme of Southern History," in E. Merton Coulter (ed.), *The Course of the South to Secession* (New York, 1939), p. 152.

search for a Southern identity, C. Vann Woodward advances several crucial factors: the experience of poverty in a land of plenty; failure and defeat
in a land that glorifies success; sin and guilt amid the legend of American
innocence; and a sense of place and belonging among a people given to
abstraction.[27] David M. Potter, probing the enigma of the South, has found
the key to the riddle in the prevalence of a folk society. "This folk culture,
we know, was far from being ideal or utopian," he writes, "and was in fact
full of inequality and wrong, but if the nostalgia persists was it because
even the inequality and wrong were parts of a life that still had a relatedness and meaning which our more bountiful life in the mass culture seems
to lack?"[28]

It is significant that both explanations are expressed largely in the past
tense, Potter's explicitly in terms of nostalgia. They recognize, by implication at least, still another image—that of the Dynamic or the Changing
South. The image may be rather nebulous and the ultimate ends unclear,
but the fact of change is written inescapably across the Southern scene. The
consciousness of change has been present so long as to become in itself
one of the abiding facts of Southern life. Surely, it was a part of the inspiration for the symposium that resulted in this volume. As far back as the
twenties it was the consciousness of change that quickened the imaginations
of a cultivated and sensitive minority, giving us the Southern renaissance
in literature. The peculiar historical consciousness of the Southern writer,
Allen Tate has suggested, "made possible the curious burst of intelligence
that we get at a crossing of the ways, not unlike, on an infinitesmal scale,
the outburst of poetic genius at the end of the sixteenth century when commercial England had already begun to crush feudal England."[29] Trace it
through modern Southern writing, and at the center—in Ellen Glasgow, in
Faulkner, Wolfe, Caldwell, the Fugitive-Agrarian poets, and all the others
—there is the consciousness of change, of suspension between two worlds, a
double focus looking both backward and forward.

The Southerner of the present generation has seen the old landmarks
crumble·with great rapidity: the one-crop agriculture and the very predominance of agriculture itself, the one-party system, the white primary,
the poll tax, racial segregation, the poor white (at least in his classic connotations), the provincial isolation—virtually all the foundations of the
established order. Yet, sometimes, the old traditions endure in surprising
new forms. Southern folkways have been carried even into the factory,

[27] C. Vann Woodward, "The Search for a Southern Identity," in *The Burden of
Southern History* (Baton Rouge, 1960), pp. 3–25.

[28] Potter, "The Enigma of the South," p. 151.

[29] Allen Tate, "The New Provincialism," *Virginia Quarterly Review,* XXI (Spring,
1945), 272.

and the Bible Belt has revealed resources undreamed of in Mencken's philosophy—but who, in the twenties, could have anticipated Martin Luther King?

One wonders what new images, what new myths, might be nurtured by the emerging South. Some, like Harry Ashmore, have merely written *An Epitaph for Dixie*. It is the conclusion of two Southern sociologists, John M. Maclachlan and Joe S. Floyd, Jr., that present trends "might well hasten the day when the South, once perhaps the most distinctively 'different' American region, will have become . . . virtually indistinguishable from the other urban-industrial areas of the nation."[30] U. B. Phillips long ago suggested that the disappearance of race as a major issue would end Southern distinctiveness. One may wonder if Southern distinctiveness might even be preserved in new conditions entirely antithetic to his image. Charles L. Black, Jr., another *émigré* Southerner (at Yale Law School) has confessed to a fantastic dream that Southern whites and Negroes, bound in a special bond of common tragedy, may come to recognize their kinship. There is not the slightest warrant for it, he admits, in history, sociology, or common sense. But if it should come to pass, he suggests, "The South, which has always felt itself reserved for a high destiny, would have found it, and would have come to flower at last. And the fragrance of it would spread, beyond calculation, over the world."[31]

Despite the consciousness of change, perhaps even more because of it, Southerners still feel a persistent pull toward identification with their native region as a ground for belief and loyalty. Is there not yet something more than nostalgia to the idea of the South? Is there not some living heritage with which the modern Southerner can identify? Is there not, in short, a viable myth of the South? The quest for myth has been a powerful factor in recent Southern literature, and the suspicion is strong that it will irresistibly affect any historian's quest for the central theme of Southern history. It has all too clearly happened before—in the climatic theory, for example, which operated through its geographical determinism to justify the social order of the plantation, or the Phillips thesis of white supremacy, which has become almost a touchstone of the historian's attitude toward the whole contemporary issue of race. "To elaborate a central theme," David L. Smiley has asserted, is "but to reduce a multi-faceted story to a single aspect, and its result . . . but to find new footnotes to confirm revealed truths and prescribed views."[32] The trouble is that the quest for the central

[30] John M. Maclachlan and Joe S. Floyd, Jr., *This Changing South* (Gainesville, Fla., 1956), p. 151.

[31] Charles L. Black, Jr., "Paths to Desegregation," *New Republic,* CXXXVII (October 21, 1957), 15.

[32] Smiley, "The Quest for the Central Theme in Southern History," p. 1.

theme, like Turner's frontier thesis, becomes absorbed willy-nilly into the process of myth making.

To pursue the Turner analogy a little further, the conviction grows that the frontier thesis, with all its elaborations and critiques, has been exhausted (and in part exploded) as a source of new historical insight. It is no derogation of insights already gained to suggest that the same thing has happened to the quest for the central theme, and that the historian, *as historian,* may be better able to illuminate our understanding of the South now by turning to a new focus upon the regional mythology.

To undertake the analysis of mythology will no longer require him to venture into uncharted wilderness. A substantial conceptual framework of mythology has already been developed by anthropologists, philosophers, psychologists, theologians, and literary critics. The historian, while his field has always been closely related to mythology, has come only lately to the critique of it. But there now exists a considerable body of historical literature on the American national mythology and the related subject of the national character, and Smith's stimulating *Virgin Land* suggests the trails that may be followed into the idea of the South.

Several trails, in fact, have already been blazed. Nearly forty years ago, Francis Pendleton Gaines successfully traced the rise and progress of the plantation myth, and two recent authors have belatedly taken to the same trail. Howard R. Floan has considerably increased our knowledge of the abolitionist version in his study of Northern writers, *The South in Northern Eyes,* while William R. Taylor has approached the subject from an entirely new perspective in his *Cavalier and Yankee.* Shields McIlwaine has traced the literary image of the poor white, while Stanley Elkins' *Slavery* has broken sharply from established concepts on both sides of that controversial question.[33] One foray into the New South has been made in Paul Gaston's "The New South Creed, 1865–1900." Yet many important areas —the Confederate and Reconstruction myths, for example—still remain almost untouched.

Some of the basic questions that need to be answered have been attacked in these studies; some have not. It is significant that students of literature have led the way and have pointed up the value of even third-rate creative literature in the critique of myth. The historian, however, should be able to contribute other perspectives. With his peculiar time perspective he can seek to unravel the tangled genealogy of myth that runs back from the modern Changing South to Jefferson's yeoman and Kennedy's plantation.

---

[33] Howard R. Floan, *The South in Northern Eyes, 1831–1860* (Austin, 1958); William R. Taylor, *Cavalier and Yankee: The Old South and American National Character* (New York, 1961); Shields McIlwaine, *The Southern Poor White from Lubberland to Tobacco Road* (Norman, Okla., 1939); Stanley M. Elkins, *Slavery: A Problem in American Institutional and Intellectual Life* (Chicago, 1959).

Along the way he should investigate the possibility that some obscure dialectic may be at work in the pairing of obverse images: the two versions of the plantation, New South and Old, Cavalier and Yankee, genteel and savage, regionalist and agrarian, nativist and internationalist.

What, the historian may ask, have been the historical origins and functions of the myths? The plantation myth, according to Gaines and Floan, was born in the controversy and emotion of the struggle over slavery. It had polemical uses for both sides. Taylor, on the other hand, finds it origin in the psychological need, both North and South, to find a corrective for the grasping, materialistic, rootless society symbolized by the image of the Yankee. Vann Woodward and Gaston have noted its later psychological uses in bolstering the morale of the New South. The image of the Savage South has obvious polemical uses, but has it not others? Has it not served the function of national catharsis? Has it not created for many Americans a convenient scapegoat upon which the sins of all may be symbolically laid and thereby expiated—a most convenient escape from problem solving?[34] To what extent, indeed, has the mythology of the South in general welled up from the subconscious depths? Taylor, especially, has emphasized this question, but the skeptical historian will also be concerned with the degree to which it has been the product or the device of deliberate manipulation by propagandists and vested interests seeking identification with the "real" South.

Certainly any effort to delineate the unique character of a people must take into account its mythology. "Poets," James G. Randall suggested, "have done better in expressing this oneness of the South than historians in explaining it."[35] Can it be that the historians have been looking in the wrong places, that they have failed to seek the key to the enigma where the poets have so readily found it—in the mythology that has had so much to do with shaping character, unifying society, developing a sense of community, of common ideals and shared goals, making the region conscious of its distinctiveness?[36] Perhaps by turning to different and untrodden paths we shall encounter the central theme of Southern history at last on the new frontier of mythology.

[34] "In a sense, the southern writer has been a scapegoat for his fellow Americans, for in taking his guilt upon himself and dramatizing it he has borne the sins of us all." C. Hugh Holman, "The Southerner as American Writer," in Charles Grier Sellers, Jr. (ed.), *The Southerner as American* (Chapel Hill, 1960), p. 199.

[35] James G. Randall, *The Civil War and Reconstruction* (Boston, 1937), pp. 3–4.

[36] Josiah Royce's definition of a "province" is pertinent here: ". . . any one part of a national domain which is geographically and socially sufficiently unified to have a true consciousness of its own ideals and customs and to possess a sense of its distinction from other parts of the country." Quoted in Frederick Jackson Turner, *The Significance of Sections in American History* (New York, 1932), p. 45.

2

The Colonial Search for a Southern Eden

Louis B. Wright

It is commonly accepted among historians that America has been, to a large degree, an extension of the European imagination—"the dream of Europe." Perhaps less tenable, but nevertheless widely accepted, is the belief that the English were more motivated by imaginative, edenic, even utopian strains of thought than other Europeans. In this article, Louis B. Wright, recently retired Director of the Folger Shakespeare Library in Washington, D.C., and currently History Consultant to the National Geographic Society, focuses on the edenic impulse prompting colonial settlement to the south of Virginia. As settlement proceeded, Mr. Wright argues, and although imaginative visions would at times be altered greatly by economic realities, a highly favorable and temperate climate together with the development of lucrative overseas trade worked to sustain lingering dreams of prosperity. It would seem that The South was fast becoming a state of mind. Indeed, as myth and reality repeatedly intersected in these formative years, many southerners learned that the latter could be as elusive and uncontrollable as the former. Viewed within a wider historical context, however, this utopian thrust carried with it even greater implications for the future. Born of such an impulse, and despite the fiction and delusion often involved, the southern colonies were thus intellectually conditioned to becoming a land at ease with myth and legend. Professor Wright's article supports the premise that within the matrix of myth is to be discovered the soil in which southern history found its roots.

From "Eden and Utopia South of Virginia" in *The Colonial Search for a Southern Eden,* by Louis B. Wright. University, Alabama: University of Alabama Press, 1953. Reprinted by permission of the author.

The notion that the earthly paradise, similar to if not the veritable site of the Scriptural Eden, might be found in some southern region of the New World was widely held in the seventeenth and early eighteenth centuries. Explorers from Virginia expected to find the Great South Sea somewhere to the southwest and they believed its shores would be a land like Eden. In the summer of 1650, Edward Bland, an English merchant resident in Virginia, and Abraham Wood, a militia captain and Indian trader, led an expedition from the site of Petersburg to a point in southwest Virginia where they discovered a river which they believed ran west into the South Sea.[1] The next year Bland printed in London *The Discovery of New Britain* (1651), which carried a preface extolling the land and urging all who desired "the advancement of God's glory by the conversion of the Indians [and] the augmentation of the English commonwealth in extending its liberties" to consider "the present benefit and future profits" of settling the new territory lying between thirty-five and thirty-seven degrees of north latitude.

This geographical position carried a mystical significance. Bland's book reprinted a passage attributed to Sir Walter Raleigh's *Marrow of History*, pointing out that God had placed Eden on the thirty-fifth parallel of north latitude.[2] This location guaranteed an ideal climate of perpetual spring and summer, a garden shaded by palm trees, described by Raleigh as the greatest blessing and wonder of nature. Other earthly paradises, the passage implied, would be found along the thirty-fifth parallel, presumably also shaded by palm trees and producing dates, raisins, spices, and everything else which Adam had had for his comfort. This location would put paradise along a line connecting Newbern and Fayetteville, North Carolina, with Chattanooga and Memphis, Tennessee.

When Lieutenant Governor Alexander Spotswood of Virginia in 1716 led an exploring expedition across the Blue Ridge Mountains, he discovered a river which we now call the Shenandoah but which Spotswood and his company named the Euphrates, after one of the four rivers of Eden, because the country looked to them like paradise. The explanation of why this spot appeared so rosy at that time may be found, however, in an account of the expedition, which must have been one of the most convivial on record. On the very crest of the ridge, the explorers stopped to drink the health of King George I, and the opportunity seemed appropriate to celebrate still further. "We had a good dinner," reported John Fontaine, chronicler of the expedition, "and after it we got the men together, and

[1] A part of this first appeared in Louis B. Wright, "The Westward Advance of the Atlantic Frontier," *The Huntington Library Quarterly*, XI (1948), 261–275.

[2] *The First Explorations of the Trans-Allegheny Region by the Virginians, 1650–1674*, ed. Clarence W. Alvord and Lee Bidgood (Cleveland, Ohio, 1912), pp. 112–113.

loaded all their arms, and we drank the King's health in champagne, and fired a volley; the Princess' health in burgundy, and fired a volley; and all the rest of the royal family in claret, and fired a volley. We drank the Governor's health and fired another volley: We had several sorts of liquor, viz., Virginia red wine and white wine, Irish usquebaugh, brandy, shrub, two sorts of rum, champagne, canary, cherry punch, water, cider, etc."[3] After these potations, the driest river bed in Arizona, much less the Valley of Virginia, would have seemed a land flowing with milk and honey.

When William Byrd II of Westover, Virginia, set out to promote the sale of a large tract of land which he had acquired on the Dan River near the border between North Carolina and Virginia, he called his property the Land of Eden and supplied notes to a German-Swiss land agent named Jenner who published in Switzerland in 1737 an alluring promotional tract under the title of *Neu-gefundenes Eden* [New Found Eden]. The description of Byrd's property was intended to leave no doubt in the reader's mind that here indeed was the earthly paradise.

Because promoters had lately been recommending South Carolina and Georgia to hopeful Swiss emigrants as lands of fertility and felicity, Byrd's agent goes to some pains to prove that this particular Eden far surpasses any other. "I am pleased to have the opportunity to make it known to my fellow countrymen, the Swiss," Jenner remarks with an air of objectivity, "that they [may] turn their thoughts to this beautiful, healthful and fertile land, and renounce miserable and unhealthful South Carolina, since [there] they will find after all nothing but poverty, sickness, and early death. . . ." South Carolina, Jenner argues, is trying to create a fortress on its southern border, or Georgia, and wants settlers in that unwholesome spot. And he cites what he says is an English proverb, "Whoever desires to die soon, just go to Carolina."[4]

The exact reverse is Byrd's Land of Eden. There the climate is perfect, the air is pure, the water is as sweet as milk, and the sun shines every day of the year. When it rains, it rains gently at night sufficient to keep the heavenly place well-watered. In this mild and beneficent land, disease is practically unknown and Europeans who come ailing soon find themselves restored to health, and "what is much more miraculous, the old people receive quite new strength, feel as if they were wholly born anew, that is, much stronger, much more light-footed, and in every way much more comfortable than before. . . ."[5]

[3] *Memoirs of a Huguenot Family,* ed. Ann Maury (New York, 1872), pp. 288–289.

[4] Richmond C. Beatty and William J. Mulloy (eds.), *William Byrd's Natural History of Virginia or The Newly Discovered Eden* (Richmond, Va., 1940), pp. 11, 14.

[5] *Ibid.,* pp. 2–3.

The products of this Eden, we will not be surprised to learn, are practically all those which a settler—or the British Board of Trade—might desire. At last, in the Dan River bottoms, if one believes this tract, the production of silk and wine is assured, along with other good things. "One could make silk also very easily," the author asserts, "because the land is full of mulberry trees, and requires little exertion. People have already tried this, and obtained very beautiful silk. The English, however, do not want to go to any trouble in this. Cotton grows in sufficiency in this land. One can merely pick it and spin it, and make all kinds of materials from it for use. It is also a very good ware in trade." Flax, hemp, indigo, grains, fruits, and herbs of all descriptions flourish. Grapes grow in great abundance and have already proved their utility and "therefore nothing is lacking but good grape people."[6] Especially valuable is the sugar maple tree: "This is the most useful tree in the whole world, because one makes wine, spirits, vinegar, honey, and sugar from it, which comes from its juice."[7] Verily nothing was lacking in Eden but a happy people to consume its products. Unfortunately the ship loaded with the Swiss emigrants who heeded the siren words of the promoter wrecked off the coast of North Carolina and only a handful survived to reach the promised land. For all the fine promises, William Byrd never succeeded in turning the rich bottom lands along the Dan River into the paradise his agent pictured. To this day the land is reasonably fertile but its products have always been such prosaic things as corn, cotton, and tobacco.

Notwithstanding William Byrd's low opinion of South Carolina, as indicated in the *New Found Eden,* and an equally low opinion of North Carolina, which he had expressed in *The History of the Dividing Line,* the Carolinas proved highly profitable to the empire and won the approval of merchants, bankers, and politicians in London. Although their products were not precisely the ones which the mercantilists had originally intended, they fulfilled perfectly the current idea of the proper relation between colony and mother country. Even that irascible and hard-to-please agent of the Crown, Edward Randolph, surveyor-general of His Majesty's Customs for North America, had only words of praise in a report which he made to the Board of Trade in London on March 16, 1699. "The great improvement made in this Province is wholly owing to the industry and labour of the Inhabitants," he wrote. "They have applied themselves to make such commodities as might increase the revenue of the Crown, as Cotton, Wool, Ginger, Indigo, etc. But finding them not to answer the end, they are set upon making Pitch, Tar, and Turpentine, and planting of rice, and can

---

[6] *Ibid.,* p. 33.
[7] *Ibid.,* p. 35.

send over great quantityes yearly, if they had encouragement from England, . . ."[8]

The Carolinas, Randolph reported, are a much better source for naval stores than New England: "My Lords, I did formerly present Your Lordships with proposals for supplying England with Pitch and Tar, Masts and all our Naval Stores from New England. . . . But since my arrival here I find I am come into the only place for such commodities upon the Continent of America."[9] By this statement he meant the *best* place, not literally the only place. The value of the tar, pitch, masts, and other supplies helped to bring prosperity to the Carolinas and security to the Royal Navy.

In other ways the Carolinas, especially South Carolina, pleased the mercantilists. A constant stream of raw materials poured out of Charleston and into English channels of industry and commerce. For instance, South Carolina developed a great trade in deerskins needed by the leathermakers and glovers. Furs from the backcountry also added to the revenue. Unlike the Chesapeake Bay colonies, which depended upon tobacco for their money crop, the Southeast developed a diverse commerce centered in Charleston, and of this commerce, the deerskin and fur trade contributed much to colonial and imperial prosperity.

So much attention has been lavished on the fur trade of other regions that we forget the importance of the South in this connection. Louisiana is still the largest fur-producing region in North America. Throughout the eighteenth century Charleston, South Carolina, was the great skin and fur market. Some of the toughest characters in all North America brought their pack trains of deerskins and furs to Charleston each spring. The tinkle of the packhorse bells and the clatter of hoofs on the cobble stones of the Battery brought Charlestonians to their windows to view picturesque traders, some well-known and famous as Indian fighters.

The caravans often brought long strings of Indian captives to be sold as slaves to Barbádos and other islands of the West Indies. We must also remember this dark chapter in the history of commerce. Charleston was an important slaving port. Captured Indians by the hundreds were sold to ship captains headed for the West Indies, and Negroes by the thousands were brought into Charleston from Africa. Indian slaves were not dependable in the Carolinas, for they might escape to the forests and make their way back to their tribes, but African Negroes had no such hope. They proved useful laborers in the pine forests and hot fields of the coastal plain. The traffic in slaves and the commodities which they produced made rich

[8] Alexander S. Salley, Jr. (ed.), *Narratives of Early Carolina, 1650–1708* (New York, 1911), p. 207.
[9] *Ibid.,* p. 208.

the merchants and shipowners of London and Bristol as well as their agents in Charleston.

South Carolina gave promise late in the seventeenth century of becoming the dream colony of the English mercantilists. Some of the inhabitants wrote to London in the year 1691 that "We are encouraged with severall new rich Comodityes as Silck, Cotton, Rice and Indigo, which are naturally produced here."[10] Silk remained a delusion, but rice, indigo, and eventually cotton became indeed "rich commodities." The first of these to be grown extensively was rice, which flourished in the alluvial swamp lands of the coastal region. Although colonists even in Virginia had experimented with rice, not until the last decade of the seventeenth century, in South Carolina, was it grown extensively. The legend that a shipmaster from Madagascar, accidentally touching at Charleston in 1696, left a half-bushel of rice seed from which grew the Carolina rice industry, is apparently only a half-truth,[11] but from that date until the mid-nineteenth century rice was an increasingly important article of commerce with England.

To an extraordinary woman, Eliza Lucas, South Carolina owed the development of the production of indigo, a vegetable dye much in demand in the eighteenth century when clothing of this hue was especially fashionable. In the year 1739, Eliza Lucas, then just sixteen, found herself established as manager of a plantation on the west side of the Ashley River above Charleston. Her father, Lieutenant Colonel George Lucas, was stationed at Antigua in the West Indies, but since his wife was sickly and could not endure that climate, he moved his family to South Carolina and put this remarkable girl in charge of the family plantation. In a letter to her father written in July 1739, she reported that she was trying "to bring the Indigo, Ginger, Cotton, and Lucern and Casada [cassava] to perfection and had greater hopes from the Indigo (if I could have the seed earlier next year from the West Indies) than of ye rest of ye things I had try'd."[12] After many discouragements, not only in raising the plants, but in producing the dye, Eliza achieved success. By 1747–48, the production was such that the port of Charleston exported 138,334 pounds of the dyestuff. When the British government offered a bounty in 1748 for the production of the dye in the British-American colonies, some growers found it so profitable that they doubled their capital every three or four years.[13]

The production of indigo within the empire was important, for the

---

[10] Lewis C. Gray and Esther K. Thompson, *History of Agriculture in the Southern United States* (Washington, D. C., 1933), I, 278; quoted from the *Calendar of State Papers, America and West Indies, 1677–1680*, p. 59.

[11] *Ibid.*, I, 278–279.

[12] *Ibid.*, I, 290.

[13] *Ibid.*, I, 292.

source of most of the dye would otherwise have been the French West Indies. Since England was at war with France through a good part of the eighteenth century, it was imperative that she not buy this useful commodity from the enemy. The power of fashion was such, however, that the clothiers and dyers would have obtained the dye even if they had been obliged to deal in the enemy's black market. The solution of course was to stimulate production in the tropical and semi-tropical areas of the British dominions, an operation which proved highly successful.

The production of cotton, another article which England had bought outside the empire, was less successful than indigo and rice, but some cotton was produced in the various Southern colonies and in the West Indies in the period before the Revolution. Few of us stop to realize the importance of cotton in the social progress of mankind. The importation into England of cheap cotton textiles from India, brought about by the expansion of the East India Company's activities in the seventeenth century, for the first time made it possible for Englishmen of average means to be reasonably clean. Up to that time linen was the only available fabric for undergarments, and linen, then as now, was expensive.[14]

The East India Company brought in chintzes, muslins, calicoes, and other fabrics. The word calico comes from the name of an Indian town, Calicut. Though the importation of cotton from India gave English merchants an article of trade much in demand on the continent of Europe, the East India Company had to pay out cash for its textiles. If raw cotton could be produced within the empire and woven at home, this would be an advantage to both the industry and commerce of Great Britain.

Although efforts continued throughout the colonial period to stimulate the production of raw cotton, only small amounts reached the markets. In the year 1768, Virginia led the South by exporting 43,350 pounds of ginned cotton. In the same year South Carolina exported only 3,000 pounds, and Georgia, only 300 pounds.[15] During most of the period, planters lacked confidence in the stability of cotton prices—an old complaint—and they found other crops more profitable. The separation of the lint from the seed was also a troublesome problem. Although roller gins were known and used in the colonial period, not until Eli Whitney invented the saw gin in the last decade of the eighteenth century was this problem solved.

By the end of the century South Carolina and Georgia were producing several million pounds of cotton. Although the colonies were now politically free of Great Britain, trade retained many of its old characteristics. The South continued to supply raw materials for English industry; and of

[14] James A. Williamson, *The Ocean in English History* (Oxford, 1941), p. 107.
[15] Gray & Thompson, *History of Agriculture*, I, 184. See also *Ibid.*, II, 680 ff.

these raw materials, cotton rapidly increased in importance. By the mid-nineteenth century, cotton spinning and weaving had become one of Great Britain's most valuable industries, and raw cotton from the plantations of the Southern states was an essential of international trade. By a curious irony of history, cotton textiles of English manufacture in the nineteenth century ruined the native weaving industry of India, which had first supplied cottons to Britain. And by another reversal of the process, the cheap labor in the Indian cotton mills in the twentieth century ruined the English textile industry by destroying its Asiatic market for cotton goods.

Paralleling the British emphasis on trade in the eighteenth century was a growing spirit of humanitarianism. As in the United States in the twentieth century, the brotherhood of man and the acquisition of material property were somehow equated. As humanitarians and mercantilists, often one and the same, viewed the southern American colonies, they warmed with enthusiasm over the prospect of discovering there at last the perfect paradise where all men could be happy and prosperous as they produced the commodities which served the best interests of the British Empire. Occasionally the humanitarians contemplated the institution of slavery, which seemed to be necessary for prosperity, and found it disturbing; but usually they salved their consciences by thinking of the boon of Christianity which slavery had brought to the heathen whom they imported from Africa. George Whitefield, the evangelist, for example, wept over man's sins and distress, but he recommended slavery for Georgia and helped pay the expenses of Bethesda, his orphan home, from the profits of a South Carolina plantation worked with slaves.

As the humanitarian planners contemplated the opportunities in the South, they had visions of new Edens in which the poor and oppressed of England would find a refuge; there the erstwhile indigents would work out their salvation and keep a steady stream of profitable raw materials pouring into the home ports. Some of the planners had read More's *Utopia,* Bacon's essay "Of Plantations," James Harrington's *The Commonwealth of Oceana* (1656), or some other treatise on ideal commonwealths. The spirit of social experiment was in the air. Furthermore the atmosphere was also heavily charged with the excitement of speculation. During 1719 and the early part of 1720, men and women rushed to buy stock in the South Sea Company which doubled, trebled, quadrupled and further multiplied in value as they watched it. Before the bubble burst in August 1720, other speculations promised similar incredible profits. It was an age of "projectors," or promoters, some of whom picked the region embracing this very spot as the scene of their activities. No scheme seemed impossible, not even Swift's satirical project to extract sunbeams from cucumbers.

For reasons not difficult to comprehend, the hope of finding a fruitful land in the South appealed strongly to Scots. No country could have been more unlike the hills of Scotland than the coastal plains and river bottoms of the Carolinas and Georgia. Perhaps that was its greatest attraction. During the eighteenth century Scots were among the most important immigrant groups received in the Southern colonies. Because we usually think of the Scots as a practical and thrifty people, convinced that destiny has already settled the affairs of man in accordance with the theology of John Calvin, it may be a surprise to find that some of the most fantastic of the Utopian projects were dreamed up by Scots.

One of the better known and most colorful schemes was hatched in the mind of a Scottish baronet, Sir Robert Montgomery of Skelmorly, who in 1717 published *A Discourse Concerning the design'd Establishment Of a New Colony To The South of Carolina, In The Most delightful Country of the Universe*. This was a plan to establish a colony in the country embraced between the mouths of the Savannah and Altamaha rivers and extending westward to the Great South Sea [the Pacific Ocean]. That included most of the present state of Alabama, not to mention the states westward to the California coast.

Sir Robert described this country, which he named Azilia, as "our future Eden," and he further declared that English writers "universally agree that Carolina, and especially in its Southern Bounds, is the most amiable Country in the Universe: that Nature has not bless'd the World with any Tract, which can be preferable to it, that Paradise, with all her Virgin Beauties, may be modestly suppos'd at most but equal to its Native Excellencies."[16] This territory which exceeded Paradise itself in excellence was claimed by South Carolina, but the Lords Proprietors were more than glad to encourage Scottish settlers who would serve as a protection against the Spaniards in Florida and the French in Louisiana. Accordingly they granted permission to Sir Robert and his colleagues to settle Azilia.

In a literary genre characterized by optimism, Sir Robert Montgomery's *Discourse* is surely one of the most hopeful ever printed. Azilia, as he describes it, "lies in the same Latitude with Palestine Herself, That promis'd Canaan, which was pointed out by God's own Choice, to bless the Labours of a favourite People. It abounds with Rivers, Woods, and Meadows. Its gentle Hills are full of Mines, Lead, Copper, Iron, and even some of Silver. 'Tis beautified with odiferous Plants, green all the Year. ... The Air is healthy, and the Soil in general fruitful, and of infinite Variety; Vines, naturally flourishing upon the Hills, bear Grapes in most luxuriant Plenty. They have every Growth which we possess in England, and almost every Thing that England wants besides. The Orange and the

[16] J. Max Patrick (ed.), *Azilia: A Discourse by Sir Robert Montgomery, 1717, Projecting a Settlement in the Colony Later Known as Georgia*, Emory University Publications: Sources and Reprints, Series IV (Atlanta, 1948), p. 18.

Limon thrive in the same common Orchard with the Apple, and the Pear-Tree, Plumbs, Peaches, Apricots, and Nectarins bear from Stones in three years growing. The Planters raise large Orchards of these Fruits to feed their Hogs with."[17] To Scots and Englishmen, who knew oranges from Seville and lemons from Portugal merely as symbols of luxury, this country, in the same latitude as Palestine, must have appeared indeed as a new Canaan.

To help him in the colonization of Azilia, Montgomery had as associates Aaron Hill, a theatrical poet who claimed to have an invention for making potash, and Amos Kettleby, merchant and politician of London, whom the South Carolina Assembly had dismissed in the previous year from his post as colonial agent. Montgomery was to have the title of Margrave, with a great palace at the exact center of the district where he would reside. There he would live in splendor and rule over a feudal principality peopled with a hierarchy of gentry, tenants, and slaves. Aaron Hill and Amos Kettleby appear to have been more concerned with the financial returns from the venture than with the glories of title.

The chapter in Montgomery's tract headed "Of some Designs in View for making Profit" assures the reader that at long last imperial and mercantilist ambitions are about to be realized in Azilia. "Our Prospects in this Point are more extensive than we think it needful to discover," Montgomery remarks with an air of mystery. "It were a shame shou'd we confine the Fruitfulness of such a rich and lovely Country to some single Product, which Example first makes common, and the being common robs of Benefit. Thus Sugar in Barbadoes, Rice in Carolina, and Tobacco in Virginia take up all the Labours of their People, overstock the Markets, stifle the Demand, and make their Industry their Ruin, . . ." Azilia, however, will not be a one-crop country. Instead it will produce the very commodities which England still has had to buy from foreigners. Montgomery makes this explicit: "Coffee, Tea, Figs, Raisins, Currants, Almonds, Olives, Silk, Wine, Cochineal, and a great Variety of still more rich Commodities which we are forc'd to buy at mighty Rates from Countries lying in the very Latitude of our Plantations: All these we certainly shall Propagate, . . . mean while we shall confine our first Endeavours to such easy Benefits as will (without the smallest waiting for the Growth of Plants) be offer'd to our Industry from the spontaneous Wealth which overruns the Country."[18] With Aaron Hill's alleged invention in mind, Montgomery promises that potash will be a source of immediate profit.

The happy Margravate of Azilia, alas, was doomed to be a delusion. To transport colonists, to clear land, to build a palace, and even to make

---

[17] *Ibid.*, p. 18.
[18] *Ibid.*, p. 23.

potash required capital. There were also political complications. Discouraged at frustrations and delays, Sir Robert Montgomery sold his interest late in 1718 to Aaron Hill the poet. But after the failure of the South Sea Company in 1720, not even Aaron Hill's literary style was sufficiently purple to lure investors in Azilia, and the scheme collapsed. Yet such was the hopefulness of the projectors that one of them, possibly Hill, published two further pamphlets late in 1720, one of which was entitled *A Description of the Golden Islands, with an Account of the Undertaking Now on Foot for Making a Settlement There.* This tract outlined a plan for making a paradise of the sea islands along the coast of Georgia and producing there not only silk and almonds, but "many more Fruits and Drugs, growing in Persia, in India about Lahore, in China, and in Japan."[19] But the public had its fingers too thoroughly burned on the South Sea Company stock to take an interest in the Golden Islands. The Azilian project is worth detailed consideration, however, because it epitomizes the search for Eden which had obsessed British thinking since the beginning of the colonial effort and which was to continue to the end.

Another Scottish baronet, Sir Alexander Cuming of Coulter, even more erratic than Sir Robert Montgomery, conceived a project to settle three hundred thousand Jews on the Cherokee tribal lands in the backcountry of South Carolina. This proposal for a Zion on the Carolina frontier had as its object the relief of oppressed Jewish families in Europe by taking them out of crowded ghettos and establishing them on the land where they could turn their talents and industry to farming and the production of commodities useful to the British Empire. If the government would underwrite the enterprise, Sir Alexander promised, it would presently be able to retire a large portion of the national debt from the profits.

Sir Alexander attributed his zeal for colonial affairs to a vision of his wife's which suggested that he make a journey to the backcountry of South Carolina. Considering the Scot's peculiarities, we cannot escape the suspicion that his wife's vision was a clever ruse to procure a little peace at home. But whatever the motive, Sir Alexander set out in 1729 on a self-appointed mission to Carolina and the Cherokees. Surely the Scottish baronet had read books similar to those which had sent Cervantes' good knight of La Mancha on his adventures, for his travels read like a chapter from *Don Quixote.* Leaving Charleston on March 13, 1730, Sir Alexander travelled during the following month nearly a thousand miles through the Cherokee tribes. Armed to the teeth and boasting of the power and brilliance of his King, George II, the baronet astonished his Indian hearers and persuaded them that he was a great chief representing a king whose power reached even to the hills of South Carolina. At a tribal council he

[19] *Ibid.,* p. 12.

persuaded the chiefs to kneel and swear allegiance to King George—or so he thought—and he had himself acclaimed the King's viceroy. So persuasive was Sir Alexander's eloquence that he induced six Cherokees, a minor chief and five warriors, to set out with him for London and the King's court. Near Charleston they picked up another stray Indian. When they all reached England, the chief was a king and the other Indians were described as generals or chiefs. On June 18, 1730, King George received the Scot and his Indian protegés. During the next three months the Cherokee "king" and his fellow "chiefs" were the sensation of London. They were entertained, feted, and taught English vices. On September 28, the play of *Orinoco* was performed in their honor at Lincoln's Inn Fields, and so great was the public excitement over the Indians that the theatre's box office receipts trebled that night. When they returned to their tribesmen, the Indians' report of the glories of the English nation probably helped to keep the Cherokees loyal to England in the succeeding wars with France.[20]

Fantastic as were Sir Alexander Cuming's schemes for Cherokee-Jewish Utopias in the foothills of Carolina, the publicity which they received helped to focus further interest on the Southern colonies. The settlement of Georgia itself was a manifestation of the freshly aroused humanitarian, mercantilist, and imperialistic interest in expansion south of the Carolina settlements.

During the summer of 1730, about the time the Cherokees were exciting the London populace, General James Oglethorpe and some of his friends were petitioning the King to make them a grant of land south of the Carolina border "for settling poor persons of London."[21] The plan, as every school child knows, was prompted by a desire on the part of this philanthropic group to provide relief for imprisoned debtors. It received favorable consideration from the government for other reasons. The need for a bulwark against Spain and France from the South and southwest was greater than ever. And once more the merchants and bankers of London were dreaming of a source for those raw materials which they still found it necessary to buy from their enemies. Moved by so many worthy reasons, the King granted a charter to Oglethorpe and his fellow trustees on June 9, 1732. This time a Utopian scheme was to succeed, but not precisely as Oglethorpe or the government planned it. For few debtors ever came to Georgia and once more the vision of exotic produce was a mirage. Nevertheless Georgia did become a useful colony and an element in the imperial organization.

[20] Verner W. Crane, *The Southern Frontier, 1670–1732* (Durham, N. C., 1928), p. 280.

[21] E. Merton Coulter, *Georgia: A Short History* (Chapel Hill, N. C., 1947), pp. 17–18.

The Trustees tried earnestly to make Georgia the combination of Eden and Utopia which they had envisioned. They opened the country to oppressed folk not only of England but of the Continent as well. They passed regulations aimed at keeping the commonwealth pure by excluding rum and forbidding slavery. And they were determined to produce silk, wine, olives, and other good things which had always eluded Englishmen. A poet writing in the *South Carolina Gazette* in 1733 pictured the new colony as a garden of Hesperides. Its silks would clothe England's beauties; its wine would flow unstinted, "refreshing Labour and dispelling Woe"; and its orchards and groves would be fruitful with dates, lemons, oranges, citrons, limes, almonds, tea and coffee.[22] The trustees included some hard-headed businessmen who knew such beneficence would not be spontaneous, even in Paradise, in the rational eighteenth century. They therefore encouraged Swiss and other Continental silkworkers to come to Georgia; they ordered every recipient of a grant of land to plant mulberry trees; and they encouraged experimentation with other exotic commodities. But it was all to no avail. Georgia followed South Carolina in depending upon rice, the skin and fur trade, and upon naval stores for the basis of its economy.

The search for an exotic Eden did not end with the settlement of Georgia. The ink on the Treaty of Paris was hardly dry in 1763 before Archibald Menzies of Megerny Castle, Perthshire, devised a plan to people Florida with Armenians, Greeks, and Minorcans, who would be expert in growing olives, grapes, and silk worms. Nothing came of his proposal but four years later a brother Scot, Dr. Andrew Turnbull, and two English associates, Sir William Duncan and Sir Richard Temple, formed a partnership to settle other Greeks, Italians, and Minorcans in Florida. They succeeded actually in establishing a group at New Smyrna on the coast below St. Augustine, but quarreling and fighting among the settlers quickly ruined the enterprises in which the promoters had pinned such hope. When a Scot takes leave of practical matters and begins to spin ingenious plans, the extent of his fantasy is illimitable

The faith in a Southern Utopia persisted and manifested itself in numerous projects throughout the colonial period and afterward. Time will not permit even the mention of various schemes to create a paradise in the lands south of Virginia. Perhaps the most visionary of all was a project of a sentimental and mystical German from Saxony, one Christian Gottlieb Priber, who devised a plan for a Utopia among the Cherokees on the headwaters of the Tennessee River. A precursor of Rousseau, Priber's state represented a fusion of ideas from Plato's *Republic,* current doctrines of humanitarianism, and concepts of the noble savage which

[22] *Ibid.*

had cropped up from time to time. His efforts to found a communistic state among the Cherokees and to teach them to resist the inroads of the whites and the knavery of traders aroused the antagonism of Georgians who succeeded in arresting Priber in 1743. He was kept a political prisoner and died at Frederica on St. Simon's Island a few years later. Among his manuscripts was one describing his projected Utopian state as the "Kingdom of Paradise." In the opinion of his captors it was "extremely wicked" because "he enumerates many whimsical privileges and natural rights, as he calls them, which his citizens are to be entitled to, particularly dissolving marriages and allowing community of women, and all kinds of licentiousness."[23] His greatest sin, however, lay in his success in winning the friendship of the Indians and developing an organization which threatened the expansion of the British.

The British Empire profited immensely from the Southern colonies, but the mercantilists never succeeded in making these colonies the source of all the exotic commodities they yearned to produce within the empire. The economic planners, then as now, never grasped all of the factors involved in their schemes. For example, they never realized that silk production required both skilled and cheap labor, which the colonies always lacked, a lack which indeed has always been a serious problem in the New World.

The dream of making the South the source of many of the luxuries which mankind requires has never died. In modern times we have seen a certain realization of these hopes in the expansion of the textile industry. If we do not produce worm silk in the South, we at least have manufactories of rayon, nylon, and other chemical substitutes. A Japanese economist was in my office recently lamenting the shift in fashion and production, which had ruined the silk industry of Japan.

Not far from where Swiss and Italian colonists in the eighteenth century sought to establish new industries on the upper Savannah River the United States government is today building a great plant to transform hydrogen into energy. The end product of that effort is yet unknown. Some believe that ultimately the release of energy from such an abundant source will solve most of the problems of mankind. Others, more gloomy, see in it the destruction of civilization. But we are witnessing one more effort to establish Utopia, even at the risk of universal destruction.

---

[23] Verner W. Crane, "A Lost Utopia of the First American Frontier," *Sewanee Review*, XXVII (1919), pp. 48–61.

3

The Southern Ethic in a Puritan World

C. Vann Woodward

Of those forces said to have been instrumental in forging the American character, "Puritanism" and its concomitant the Protestant Ethic are generally granted singular importance. Though subject to considerable myth in its own right, not all have come to grant Puritanism such exalted status. Arguments in favor of seeing the distinctiveness of a southern culture quite at odds with "Puritan" theory and practice have long prevailed on both sides of the Mason-Dixon line. While speaking of the entire range of the southern experience, C. Vann Woodward, Sterling Professor of History at Yale, here attempts to analyze the Puritan ethic and its southern counterpart, and to judge their relationship. By isolating the leisure-laziness myth, a basic ingredient of the "southern ethic," Professor Woodward attempts not its destruction but rather a serious critique. While essentially a review article examining the impact of recent historical scholarship as it relates to this theme, it remains as well a status report on a staple of southern mythology: leisure as a mythical element which continues to pervade the "real life" of the South. Finally, the article suggests that the southern inclination toward a leisured and mannered society had sufficient grounding in the colonial era to allow southerners largely to escape the extremes of the Puritan ethic.

Myths that support the notion of a distinctive Southern culture tend to be Janus-faced, presenting both an attractive and an unattractive countenance. The side they present depends on which way they are turned and

From C. Vann Woodward, "The Southern Ethic in a Puritan World," *William and Mary Quarterly*, 25 (1968). Reprinted by permission of the author and publisher.

who is manipulating them. The reverse side of Chivalry is Arrogance, and the other side of Paternalism is Racism. The Plantation myth is similarly coupled with the Poor White myth, the myth of Honor with that of Violence. Graciousness, Harmony, and Hospitality also have their less appealing faces. And for Leisure there is its long-standing counterpart, Laziness—together with the synonyms, idleness, indolence, slothfulness, languor, lethargy, and dissipation.

Early and late Southerners and their friends and critics have worried the Leisure-Laziness myth. It began with Captain John Smith's jeremiad against "idleness and sloth" at Jamestown and continued with Robert Beverley's disquisition on industrious beavers and William Byrd's lamentations on the slothful Carolinians of "Lubberland." An impressive literature on the subject has proliferated over the centuries. Leisure, the brighter side of the coin, has been repeatedly praised as an ideal, a redeeming quality of the Southern way that sets it off against the ant-like busyness and grubby materialism of the Northern way, another adornment of the Cavalier to shame the Yankee. Laziness, the darker face of the legend, has been deplored, denied, lamented, and endlessly explained. The explanations include climate, geography, slavery, and the staple crop economy, not to mention pellagra and a formidable list of parasites. No matter which face of the myth is favored and which explanation is stressed, agreement is general that this is a fundamental aspect of Southern distinctiveness.

As much as they deplored laziness, even exponents of the New South and the Northern way of bustle and enterprise often retained a fondness for the reverse side of the stereotype and clung to leisureliness as an essential mark of regional identity. Although Walter Hines Page scorned many characteristics of the old regime and urged a program of industrialization for the South, he cherished "the inestimable boon of leisure," hoped that "in the march of industrialism these qualities of fellowship and leisure may be retained in the mass of people," and thought that "no man who knows the gentleness and dignity and the leisure of the old Southern life would like to see these qualities blunted by too rude a growth of sheer industrialism."[1]

At the opposite pole from Page on the matter of industrialization for the South, John Crowe Ransom, arch-champion of agrarianism and "the old-time life," also fixed upon leisure as the essence of the Southern Ethic. Whatever the shortcomings of the Old South, "the fault of being intemperately addicted to work and to gross material prosperity" was hardly among them, he says. "The South never conceded that the whole

[1] Walter Hines Page, *The Rebuilding of Old Commonwealths* (New York, 1902), 111, 114, 141.

duty of man was to increase material production, or that the index to the degree of his culture was the volume of his material production." The arts of the South were "arts of living and not arts of escape." All classes participated in these arts and their participation created the solid sense of community in the South. "It is my thesis," he writes, "that all were committed to a form of leisure, and that their labor itself was leisurely."[2]

Between Page and Ransom, though much closer in ideology to the former than the latter, W. J. Cash was more ambivalent than either about leisure. Conceding that the South's "ancient leisureliness—the assumption that the first end of life is living itself . . . is surely one of its greatest virtues," he thought that "all the elaborately built-up pattern of leisure and hedonistic *drift;* all the slow, cool, gracious and graceful gesturing of movement . . . was plainly marked out for abandonment as incompatible with success" and the ethic of the new industrial order. This was not to be written off as pure loss. The lot of the poor white had been a "void of pointless leisure," and for that matter, "in every rank men lolled much on their verandas or under their oaks, sat much on fences, dreaming." Leisure easily degenerated into laziness. Both leisure and laziness perpetuated frontier conditions and neither produced cities or a real sense of community. Cash leaned to the Northern view that culture and community are largely developed in towns, "and usually in great towns."[3]

When one gets down to modern economists and the theory of under-developed countries and regions like the South, ambivalence about leisure and laziness tends to disappear. The two become almost indistinguishable and equally reprehensible. In the opinion of one Southern economist, leisure becomes "a cover-up for lack of enterprise and even sheer laziness among Southerners." For the mass of them, in fact, "leisure was probably from early days a virtue by necessity rather than by choice. If they were small landowners they lacked sufficient resources to keep them busy more than half of the year. If they were slaves or sharecroppers the near impossibility of advancing themselves by their own efforts bred inefficiency, lassitude, and improvidence." The phenomenon of television aerials over rural slums "may clearly make (through its positive effect on incentives) its own substantial contribution to regional economic progress." But the tradition of leisure has been a major cause of underdevelopment.[4]

---

[2] Twelve Southerners, *I'll Take My Stand: The South and the Agrarian Tradition* (New York, 1930), 12–14.

[3] W. J. Cash, *The Mind of the South* (New York, 1941), 384, 150, 50, 95.

[4] William H. Nicholls, *Southern Tradition and Regional Progress* (Chapel Hill, 1960), 34–39.

I

New light on this ancient dispute comes from a number of sources—
new works on moral, intellectual, economic, and slavery history—and a
reconsideration of the debate would seem to be in order. One of these
new sources is a work by David Bertelson, whose preference between the
Janus faces is clearly announced by the title of his book, *The Lazy South.*
The informality of the title might suggest to some that this is another
light-hearted and genial essay on regional foibles. Nothing could be
further from the author's intentions. He is fully conscious of the "strong
volitional and moral connotations" of the word "laziness" and never
flinches in his employment of it. This presumes to be the history of a
failure, the moral failure of a whole society.

Mr. Bertelson is not one to borrow support casually from conventional
assumptions and traditional explanations. Much has been written of
geographical determinants of Southern history. "But geography did not
create the South," he writes. Pennsylvania, with its waterways and its soil,
was as easily adaptable to a tobacco staple culture as Virginia. Nor will
he seek an out in economic determinism: rather he asks what determined
the economy. He scarcely pauses over the old climatic and ethnic chestnuts.
As for the uses of the Peculiar Institution, he is simply not in the market.
"Negro servitude did not make the southern colonies different from New
England and Pennsylvania. They were different first. That is why slavery
became so widespread there. The presence of a small number of slaves
in the northern colonies did not change the essential conditions of life
in these either. That is why the number remained so small." He has little
space for the familiar biological determinants—pellagra, malaria, hookworm, and the rest. They were the accompaniments of poverty and laziness,
not their causes. Laziness afflicted the affluent as often as the parasites
afflicted the indigent.[5]

What then does account for this distinctive trait of the South? "The
difference lay not in the land but in the people," we are told, "and that
difference was ultimately due to the different attitudes and assumptions
which they brought with them and their descendants perpetuated." The
attitudes and assumptions derive ultimately from values, in other words
morals, ethics. "To get at what lies behind poverty, slavery, staple crops,
and stressing personal enjoyment one must consider historically the
meaning of work in the South." It all boils down to an analysis of the
Southern Ethic—though that is not a term the author uses.[6]

Virginia existed first in the minds of Englishmen as an answer to the

[5] David Bertelson, *The Lazy South* (New York, 1967), 244, 104.
[6] *Ibid.*, 244, viii.

problem of idleness in England. The cure for idleness, it was thought, lay in the allurements of material gain in the New World which would induce men to work without the necessity of violating their freedom. Spokesmen of Virginia were sometimes vague about personal responsibility to society and a sense of community. Puritans, on the other hand, "thought of themselves as small societies before they established communities."[7] Authoritarians failed in Virginia, and no prophet of a godly community prevailed, no Chesapeake Zion appeared. The same was true of Maryland, the Carolinas, and after abortive experiments, Georgia.

Without coercion and community, Southern colonists established societies based on the exploitation of natural resources. The motive force was individual aggrandizement, we are told, not social purpose or community aims. They established plantations, not cities, and cultivated staples, not trade. The result was dispersion, fragmentation, and chaotic self-aggrandizement. The meaning of work in the Southern colonies thus came to have no social dimension or content. Work there *was,* hard work, but it produced idleness with plenty and was intermittent according to seasonal necessities.

"The problem then is," it seems to Mr. Bertelson, "to explain why most men in the southern colonies *seemed* to lead idle lives while in actuality they were often very busy. The answer lies in the fact that they were not busy all of the time." When crops were laid by they tended to go fishing. Max Weber, to whom the author attributes the conception of his study, associated with "the spirit of capitalism" a pattern of industry and diligence that was not based on economic considerations. This pattern is found to be conspicuously absent in the South, along with "the intellectual climate to favor diligence." As a figure of contrast the author pictures "young Benjamin Franklin trudging the streets of Philadelphia in the early morning and his remark that he took care not only to be industrious but to appear industrious." It is conceded that the South was "not without examples of industrious people like Franklin, but . . . most of them were recently arrived foreign Protestants." Your genuine Southerner did not even bother to *appear* industrious.[8]

Yet we are told that the Southerners were deeply troubled with guilt about laziness and took extreme measures to overcome an oppressive sense of purposelessness with sheer "busyness." Thus William Byrd, for all his pre-dawn vigils with Hebrew, Greek, and Latin, was desperately driven by the specter of laziness and futility. Even that model of methodical industriousness Thomas Jefferson, in advising his daughter about work

[7] *Ibid.,* 40–41.
[8] *Ibid.,* 75–77.

habits, "was advocating simply keeping busy rather than purposefulness." Anyway, Jefferson and James Madison "expressed very little of the South" in the way, presumably, that Cotton Mather expressed New England and Benjamin Franklin, New England and Pennsylvania. As for George Washington, he proves to have had very rational and Yankeefied notions about work (though the evidence offered is not very persuasive), notions shared by Patrick Henry and Richard Henry Lee. Apart from these unrepresentative deviants, the pattern of Virginia prevailed among Southerners generally. James Winthrop, a Massachusetts Federalist, is quoted as distinguishing sharply between the "idle and dissolute inhabitants of the South" and "the sober and active people of the North."[9]

The trouble with the South, one of the many troubles perceived, was its total inability to conceptualize social unity in terms other than personal relationships, to achieve any real sense of community, or to define industry in social terms. The plantation as community is written off as "imaginary." Southerners, it seems, proved unable to derive social unity "from a community of belief in God and love for one another as it had been for early Puritans."[10] Their efforts to define community in terms of home, personal affections, and local loyalties, the very essence of patriarchal community in the South, are summarily dismissed as futile. Southerners are also said to have been incapable of any real sense of loyalty. Unlike charity, loyalty does not appear to begin at home.[11] "While many Southerners doubtless had great affection for family and friends," he concedes, "and for the localities in which they lived, this did not involve any larger social unity nor any sense of loyalty to the South as a whole—but rather a pervasive particularism."[12]

Personalism and persistent local attachments have been offered by David M. Potter as evidence of the survival of an authentic folk culture in the South long after it had disappeared in urban culture elsewhere.[13] While Mr. Bertelson concedes that "at times in the past or in certain

[9] *Ibid.*, 166, 161.

[10] *Ibid.*, 65.

[11] In a strongly contrasting analysis of the roots of loyalty, David M. Potter writes, "The strength of the whole is not enhanced by destroying the parts, but is made up of the sum of the parts. The only citizens who are capable of strong national loyalty are those who are capable of strong group loyalty, and such people are likely to express this capacity in their devotion to their religion, their community, and their families, as well as in their love of country." "The Historian's Use of Nationalism and Vice Versa," *American Historical Review*, LXVII (1961–1962), 932.

[12] Bertelson, *The Lazy South*, 210.

[13] David M. Potter, "The Enigma of the South," *Yale Review*, LI (1961–1962), 150–151.

limited areas of the South people's lives did attain relatedness and mean-ing," in the region as a whole disruptive economic forces, pursuit of gain, and chaotic mobility have made impossible "the kind of stability which one usually associates with folk culture." Far from constituting evidence of a sense of community, "courtesy, hospitality, graciousness—is simply a series of devices for minimizing friction only to create the appearance of intimacy or affection."[14] If these particular myths *are* indeed Janus-faced, one face would seem to be effectively veiled from the author's vision.

The emphasis throughout is on the want of any meaningful sense of community in the South. The essence of community is tacitly assumed to be urban, something associated with cities—preferably built on a hill or in a wilderness. "Both the Quakers and to an even greater degree the Puritans in New England founded societies based on communities of consent and common goals. Imbued with a sense of community and social purposeful-ness, these people were truly able to build cities in the wilderness."[15] It is perhaps inevitable and even appropriate that the myths of an urban society should attach symbolic significance to cities, and it is understandable that these symbols should retain their appeal long after the metropolis has become something less than the ideal embodiment of community, has become in fact the symbol of anti-community. What is surprising is the total unconsciousness of the mythic quality of these symbols and the faith that they embody.

Harry Levin has commented on the "mythoclastic rigors" of the early Christians. "Myths were pagan," he writes, "and therefore false in the light of true belief—albeit that true belief might today be considered merely another variety of mythopoeic faith. Here is where the game of debunking starts in the denunciation of myth as falsehood from the vantage point of a rival myth."[16]

Mr. Bertelson erects at least one guard against the charge of drawing a geographical line between virtue and vice. He concedes that "Northern society only imperfectly exemplified a sense of community," and that personal aggrandizement, anarchic individualism, and maybe Old Adam himself have been known to break out at times above the Potomac. "The South," he nevertheless maintains, "represents the logical extreme of this tendency. To the degree that America has meant economic opportunity without social obligations or limitations, Southerners are Americans and Americans are Southerners."[17] Some comfort is gratefully derived

[14] Bertelson, *The Lazy South,* 242–243.
[15] *Ibid.,* 244.
[16] Harry Levin, "Some Meanings of Myth," *Daedalus,* LXXXVIII (1959), 225.
[17] Bertelson, *The Lazy South,* 245.

from this remarkable concession, even if it is the comfort the poor white derives in Southern myth as repository of the less fortunate traits: at least he belongs.

II

It is, however, just on this score of Southern distinctiveness that a vulnerable spot occurs in the thesis. In a recent analysis of what he calls "the Puritan Ethic," Edmund S. Morgan addresses himself to many of the traditional values that Mr. Bertelson denies the South.[18] Yet in Mr. Morgan's analysis these were "the values that all Americans held," even though the claim upon them varied in authenticity, and adherence to them differed in consistency and tenacity. And in spite of the name assigned to the ethic, he disavows any proprietary regional exclusiveness about it and holds that "it prevailed widely among Americans of different times and places," and that "most Americans made adherence to the Puritan ethic an article of faith."[19] Indeed, leaders of North and South found "room for agreement in the shared values of the Puritan Ethic" until the break over slavery. Thomas Jefferson was "devoted to the values of the Puritan Ethic," and Mr. Morgan quotes the identical letters containing Jefferson's advice to his daughter that Mr. Bertelson presents as evidence of the Southern syndrome about idleness and remarks that they "sound as though they were written by Cotton Mather."[20] In a mood of generosity he makes honorary Puritans of numerous Southerners: Richard Henry Lee of Virginia was "a New Englander manqué," Henry Laurens of South Carolina had characteristics that made him "sound like a Puritan," Hugh Williamson of North Carolina was forever "drawing upon another precept of the Puritan Ethic," and the thousands of Southerners who poured into Kentucky and Tennessee in the 1780's "carried the values of the Puritan Ethic with them," whence they presumably suffused the Cotton Belt.[21]

These references are undoubtedly of generous intent, and there are rules about looking a gift horse in the mouth. Mr. Morgan is careful to say that " 'The Puritan Ethic' is used here simply as an appropriate shorthand term" to designate widely held American ideas and attitudes. And perhaps he is right that "it matters little by what name we call them or where they came from."[22] What's in a name? Yet there is *something* about

---

[18] Edmund S. Morgan, "The Puritan Ethic and the American Revolution," *William and Mary Quarterly*, 3d Ser., XXIV (1967), 3–43.

[19] *Ibid.*, 7, 23, 24, 33, 42.

[20] *Ibid.*, 7, 24, 42.

[21] *Ibid.*, 21–22, 28–29, 38.

[22] *Ibid.*, 6.

the name that does raise questions. One cannot help wondering at times how some of those Southern mavericks, sinners that they were, might have reacted to being branded with the Puritan iron. It might have brought out the recalcitrance, or laziness, or orneriness in them—or whatever it was that was Southern and not Puritan. There are in fact, as will later appear, certain limits to the indiscriminate applicability of the Puritan Ethic down South.

By whatever name, however, Mr. Morgan's insights provide needed help in understanding the polemical uses of regional myth and the study of regional character. And he does have a point that in sectional disputes, each side often tended to appeal to the same values. He notes that in the sectional conflict between East and West that followed the Revolution and was accompanied by talk of secession of the lower Mississippi and Ohio Valley, "each side tended to see the other as deficient in the same virtues": "To westerners the eastern-dominated governments seemed to be in the grip of speculators and merchants determined to satisfy their own avarice by sacrificing the interests of the industrious farmers of the West. To easterners, or at least to some easterners, the West seemed to be filled up with shiftless adventurers, as lazy and lawless and unconcerned with the values of the Puritan Ethic as were the native Indians." In this confrontation of East and West the tendency of each to accuse the other of deficiencies in the same virtues and delinquencies in the same code, Mr. Morgan holds that "the role of the Puritan Ethic in the situation was characteristic."[23]

This sectional encounter of the 1780's recalls another one a century later when the Populists were the spokesmen of Southern (and Western) grievances against the East. The Populist Ethic—perhaps I had better say myth—the Populist Myth had much in common with this Puritan Ethic. According to Populist doctrine, labor was the source of all values, and work to be productive had to have social meaning. Productive labor was the index to the health of a society. Populists swore by producer values. Farmers and laborers were "producers." Merchants were the favored symbol of non-productive labor. They were "middle men" who merely moved things around. With them were classified bankers and "monopolists" and "speculators." Their work was not socially useful and served only selfish ends. They exploited the industrious farmers and laborers of the South and West. They deprived men of the just fruits of their labors and removed one of the main motives of industry and frugality. Their gains were ill-gotten, and they could be justly deprived of such gains by the state for the welfare of the community, for their profits were not the fruit of virtuous industry and frugality.

Populists were by and large an inner-directed lot, geared to austerity by

[23] Ibid., 20.

necessity, suspicious of affluence, and fearful of prosperity. They were the children of a life-long depression. They looked with baleful eye upon the city as productive of idleness, luxury, extravagance, and avarice. If the city was an appropriate symbol of community for the Puritan Myth, it was just as naturally a symbol of anti-community for the Populist Myth. Cities were full of non-producers—merchants, bankers, usurers, monopolists. Merchants and cities were concentrated in the East and particularly in New England. A great deal of Populist animus therefore had a regional target.

The Populists believed they had a direct line of inspiration and continuity from the American Revolution, that Thomas Jefferson was its true spokesman, and that their creed of agrarian radicalism was authentically blessed. They harked back continually to the Revolutionary period for fundamental principles and lamented with traditional jeremiads the expiring of republican virtue. It was their historic mission, they believed, to restore virtue and ideals and drive out those who had fouled the temple.[24]

True to tradition, spokesmen of the urban East in the 1890's replied in kind. They pronounced the Populists deficient in virtue and wholly given over to shiftlessness, laziness, and greed. It was the Populists who had defected from the code, not the Eastern capitalist. It was their own deficiencies and lapses from virtue and not exploitation by the East or hostile policies of the government that had brought the farmers to their unhappy plight. Populist resort to government aid and monetary manipulation for relief instead of reliance on frugality and the sweat of their brows was further evidence of shiftlessness and moral delinquency.

Sectional confrontation between the South and other parts of the country in the 1960's has hinged more on moral than on economic issues, but these encounters nevertheless have called forth many familiar recriminations and echoes of the traditional rhetoric of sectional polemics, including those of the 1860's, and their deep moral cleavages. Once again, each side has tended to view the other as deficient in similar virtues while proclaiming its own undeviating adherence. It is, however, perhaps the first instance in the annals of sectional recrimination (not even excepting the 1860's) in which one region has been seriously denied any allegiance to a common ethic, in which historic violations have been treated not as defections but as the promptings of an alien code. For in this instance the delinquencies have been attributed not to some institutional peculiarity that could be eradicated at a cost, nor to some impersonal force of nature or economics for which allowance might be made, but to indigenous,

[24] For examples from Populist literature see Norman Pollack, ed., *The Populist Mind* (Indianapolis, 1967), 51, 66–69, 211–221, 501–519, and *passim*.

ineradicable attitudes of a whole people "which they brought with them and their descendants perpetuated." This introduces a modern use for an ancient concept resembling the tragic flaw that cursed families in Greek tragedy, something inexorable and fatefully ineluctable.

III

Nothing in this vein of critical evaluation, however, is intended as endorsement of the concept of an undifferentiated national ethic, whether it is called Puritan, Protestant, or by any other name. To be sure, there do exist deep ethical commitments that override barriers of section, class, religion, or race. Otherwise there is no accounting for such limited success as the country has enjoyed in achieving national unity. Mr. Morgan and other historians have served their calling well in bringing these commitments to light. But there still remain sectional differences to be accounted for, and the distinctiveness of the South in this respect is especially unavoidable. The evidence of this distinctiveness, however unsatisfactory the explanations for it may be, is too massive to deny. Where there is so much smoke—whether the superficial stereotypes of the Leisure-Laziness sort, or the bulky literature of lamentation, denial, or celebration that runs back to the seventeenth century, or the analytical monographs of the present day—there must be fire. It remains to find a satisfactory explanation for this aspect of Southern distinctiveness.

Before exploring some explanatory approaches to this problem it would be well to start with an underpinning of agreement, if possible. First there is the question of the foundations of settlement and what the settlers brought with them. Perhaps we could do no better for this purpose than to quote the views of Perry Miller. He pointed out that "however much Virginia and New England differed in ecclesiastical politics, they were both recruited from the same type of Englishmen, pious, hard-working, middle-class, accepting literally and solemnly the tenets of Puritanism—original sin, predestination, and election—who could conceive of the society they were erecting in America only within a religious framework." It is true, he went on to say, that even before Massachusetts was settled, "Virginia had already gone through the cycle of exploration, religious dedication, disillusionment, and then reconciliation to a world in which making a living was the ultimate reality." But even after "the glorious mission of Virginia came down to growing a weed," and even though there were never any Winthrop-type "saints" hanging around Jamestown, the religious underpinnings remained.[25]

[25] Perry Miller, *Errand into the Wilderness* (Cambridge, Mass., 1956), 108, 138, 139.

In her exhaustive study of Puritanism in the Southern colonies, Babette
M. Levy avoids estimates of percentage, but her investigation suggests
that a majority of the original settlers were Puritans or Calvinists of
some persuasion. Of Virginia she writes that "their presence was felt
throughout the colony," and that it was felt extensively in the other
Southern colonies as well.[26] Southern colonies sustained two further in-
fusions of Puritans, the Huguenots in the seventeenth century and the
Scotch-Irish in the eighteenth. They were assimilated in the evolving
Southern Ethic, but not without leaving their mark. Then there were the
Methodists. Quoting John Wesley to the effect that "the Methodists in
every place grow diligent and frugal," Max Weber comments that "the
idea of duty in one's calling prowls about in our lives like the ghost of
dead religious beliefs."[27] Even after the Enlightenment and the cotton gin
those ghosts continued to prowl under the magnolias and, perhaps more
wanly, even in the Spanish-moss and cabbage-palm latitudes. Doubtless
they were less at home under the palm than under the pine, but their
presence was felt nonetheless.

Yet it is Weber who points out "the difference between the Puritan
North, where, on account of the ascetic compulsion to save, capital in
search of investment was always available" and "the condition in the
South," where such compulsions were inoperative and such capital was
not forthcoming.[28] He goes further to compare religio-cultural contrasts in
England with those in America. "Through the whole of English society
in the time since the seventeenth century," he writes, "goes the conflict
between the squirearchy . . . and the Puritan circles of widely varying social
influence. . . . Similarly, the early history of the North American Colonies
is dominated by the sharp contrast of the adventurers, who wanted to set
up plantations with the labour of indentured servants, and live as feudal
lords, and the specifically middle-class outlook of the Puritans."[29] Weber
was conscious of the paradox that the New England colonies, founded in
the interest of religion, became a seedbed of the capitalist spirit, while the
Southern colonies, developed in the interest of business, generated a climate
uncongenial to that spirit.

This is not the place to enter the "scholarly meleé"[30] over the validity of
Max Weber's thesis regarding the influence of the Protestant Ethic in the

[26] Babette M. Levy, "Early Puritanism in the Southern and Island Colonies," in
American Antiquarian Society, *Proceedings,* LXX (1960), Pt. i, 60–348, esp. 86, 119,
308.

[27] Max Weber, *The Protestant Ethic and the Spirit of Capitalism,* trans. Talcott
Parsons (London, 1930), 175, 182.

[28] *Ibid.,* 278n. But see Gabriel Kolko, "Max Weber on America: Theory and
Evidence," *History and Theory,* I (1960–1961), 243–260.

[29] Weber, *The Protestant Ethic,* trans. Parsons, 173–174.

[30] For examples see Robert W. Green, ed., *Protestantism and Capitalism: The
Weber Thesis and Its Critics* (Boston, 1959), *passim.*

development of modern capitalism. But here is Weber's delineation of the Puritan Ethic based on his gloss of Richard Baxter's *Saints' Everlasting Rest* (London, 1650) and *Christian Directory* (London, 1673), which he describes as "the most complete compendium of Puritan ethics":

> Not leisure and enjoyment, but only activity serves to increase the glory of God, according to the definite manifestations of His will.
>
> Waste of time is thus the first and in principle the deadliest of sins. The span of human life is infinitely short and precious to make sure of one's own election. Loss of time through sociability, idle talk, luxury, even more sleep than is necessary for health, six to at most eight hours, is worthy of absolute moral condemnation. It does not yet hold, with Franklin, that time is money, but the proposition is true in a certain spiritual sense. It is infinitely valuable because every hour lost is lost to labour for the glory of God. Thus inactive contemplation is also valueless, or even directly reprehensible if it is at the expense of one's daily work.[31]

With regard to "the Puritan aversion to sport," unless it "served a rational purpose" or was "necessary for physical efficiency," Weber observes that "impulsive enjoyment of life, which leads away both from work in a calling and from religion, was as such the enemy of rational asceticism, whether in the form of seigneurial sports, or the enjoyment of the dance-hall or the public-house of the common man."[32]

The precise relation of Puritan asceticism to the "spirit of capitalism" is disputed, but in his characterization of the latter, Weber's friend Ernst Troeltsch makes apparent the affinity between the two:

> For this spirit displays an untiring activity, a boundlessness of grasp, quite contrary to the natural impulse to enjoyment and ease, and contentment with the mere necessaries of existence; it makes work and gain an end in themselves, and makes men the slaves of work for work's sake; it brings the whole of life and action within the sphere of an absolutely rationalised and systematic calculation, combines all means to its end, uses every minute to the full, employs every kind of force, and in the alliance with scientific technology and the calculus which unites all these things together, gives to life a clear calculability and abstract exactness.[33]

[31] Weber, *The Protestant Ethic*, trans. Parsons, 157–158.

[32] *Ibid.*, 167–168.

[33] Ernst Troeltsch, *Protestantism and Progress, A Historical Study of the Relation of Protestantism to the Modern World*, trans. W. Montgomery (Boston, 1958), 133–134.

Commenting upon the influence of the Puritan Ethic on "the development of a capitalistic way of life," Weber adds that "this asceticism turned with all its force against one thing: the spontaneous enjoyment of life and all it had to offer."[34]

With all deference to Weber's reputation, this would seem to be an excessively harsh characterization of the Puritan Ethic. He does remind us that "Puritanism included a world of contradictions."[35] Surely the code must have been honored in the breach as well as in the observance, and even Puritans in good standing must have had occasional moments of "the spontaneous enjoyment of life." One would hope so, and one is comforted by assurances of modern authorities on the subject that they in fact occasionally did. If not, then it is obvious that "a capitalistic way of life," even with a couple of industrial revolutions thrown in for good measure, came at much too high a cost.

The views of Max Weber, nevertheless, still carry weight.[36] And if his delineation of the Puritan Ethic bears any resemblance to the real thing, then it is abundantly clear that no appreciable number of Southerners came up to scratch. There are to be found, of course, authentic instances of Puritan-like behavior in various periods down South. And no doubt a genuine deviant occasionally appeared, some "New Englander manqué," just as a Southerner manqué might, more rarely, turn up in the valleys of Vermont or even on State Street. By and large, however, the great majority of Southerners, including those concerned about their "election," shamelessly and notoriously stole time for sociability and idle talk, and the few who could afford it stole time, and sometimes more than time, for luxury. It is likely that a statistically significant number of them of a given Sunday morning stole more than their allotted eight hours of sleep. It is extremely unlikely that a sports event—horse race, fox hunt, cock fight, or gander pulling anywhere from the Tidewater to the Delta—was typically preceded by a prayerful debate over whether it "served a rational purpose" or was "necessary for physical efficiency." It was more likely to be contaminated with "the spontaneous expression of undisciplined impulses." Such "inactive contemplation" as went on below the Potomac does not appear to have altered the mainstream of western civilization, but the temptation to indulge the impulse would rarely have struck the inactive contemplator as morally reprehensible.

A regional propensity for living it up had tangible manifestations of more practical consequence than habits of sociability, sleeping, and sports.

---

[34] Weber, *The Protestant Ethic*, trans. Parsons, 166.

[35] *Ibid.*, 169.

[36] For a spirited and persuasive defense of Weber from a recent critic, see Edmund S. Morgan's review of Kurt Samuelsson, *Religion and Economic Action* (New York, 1961), in *Wm. and Mary Qtly.*, 3d Ser., XX (1963), 135–140.

Modern economists have often sought to explain why a region of such abundant natural and human resources as the South should have remained economically underdeveloped in a nation of highly developed regional economies—some with poorer natural resources—and suffered the attendant penalties of strikingly lower levels of per capita wealth and income. The Southern scene as of 1930 could be described as "an almost classic picture of an underdeveloped society."[37] Many explanations are offered and no one alone is adequate, but of prime importance in modern theory on the subject is the factor of capital formation. Apart from sheer productivity, the ability to produce more than enough to support the population, the key variable in the rate of capital growth is the willingness to save, or the other side of the coin, the propensity to consume. "Any difference among regions," one economist writes, "in their tendency to consume rather than to save will probably be reflected in their respective rates of capital formation."[38]

Economic and social historians have long remarked on distinctive spending habits, not to say extravagance, of Southerners—the Populist Myth to the contrary notwithstanding. Most often such habits have been attributed to antebellum planters and their tastes for fast horses, fine furniture, and expensive houses. The flaunting of wealth in an aristocratic society was, according to Weber, a weapon in the struggle for power. These generalizations of historians about extravagance in the South have been based on more or less well-founded impressions and random samples. The only comprehensive statistical study of regional spending habits of which I am aware is one made by several agencies of the federal government covering the years 1935 and 1936 and embracing thousands of families analyzed by population segments and income groups. The limited samples studied indicate that "people in the South did spend, in given income classes, a larger amount for consumption than did residents of other regions"; that in small-city samples low-income groups saved less in the South than in other parts of the country; that at higher income levels in this urban sector "southerners showed a tendency towards higher levels of consumption and less saving"; and that among high farm-income groups in the South "the proportion spent for consumption was significantly higher than that for the same farm income levels elsewhere."[39]

Thus the differences between the Puritan North and the Southern

[37] Douglas F. Dowd, "A Comparative Analysis of Economic Development in the American West and South," *Journal of Economic History,* XVI (1956), 563, and *passim.*

[38] W. H. Baughn, "Capital Formation and Entrepreneurship in the South," *Southern Economic Journal,* XVI (1949–1950), 162.

[39] *Ibid.,* 165–166. Since no allowance was made in these computations for the lower living costs in the South, according to Mr. Baughn, they tend to understate the extent of Southern spending.

colonies over "the ascetic compulsion to save" that Weber saw operating to influence the availability of capital for investment in the 1600's appeared to be still operative in the 1930's. If the ascetic compulsion is rightly attributed to the Puritan Ethic, then the absence or remission of that compulsion might be another indication of a distinctive Southern Ethic.

IV

The real question then is not whether Southerners fell under the discipline of the Puritan Ethic, but rather—given their heritage and the extent of their exposure—how it was they managed to escape it, in so far as they did. To attribute their deliverance to attitudes they brought with them to America seems rather unhelpful in view of the fact that they brought so many of the same attitudes the New Englanders brought and that these were reinforced by massive transfusions of Puritan blood in later years. Their escape would seem to be more plausibly derived from something that happened to them after they arrived. An acceptable explanation would probably turn out to be plural rather than singular, complex rather than simple, and rather more "environmental" than ideological. To explore and test all the reasonably eligible hypotheses would be the work of elaborate researches and much *active* contemplation. Here it is only possible to suggest a few hypotheses that would appear worth such attention.

Slavery would not come first in any chronological ordering of causal determinants of Southern attitudes toward work, but it hardly seems wise to brush it off entirely into the category of consequences. Granting that some distinctive Southern attitudes on work appeared before slavery attained very much importance in the economy, and conceding that these attitudes played a certain part in the spread of the institution, it would be willful blindness to deny the influence it had, once entrenched, in the evolution of the Southern Ethic. The causes of slavery are another subject—a very large one. But once the system became rooted in the land in the seventeenth century, its influence was all-pervasive, and the impact it had on the status of important categories of necessary work and on white and black attitudes toward them was profound and lasting. For not only were these types of work associated firmly with a degraded status, but also fatefully linked with a despised race that continued to perform the same types of work, with no appreciable improvement in racial status, long after slavery disappeared. The testimony of white Southerners themselves, ranging in authority and prestige from Thomas Jefferson to Hinton Rowan Helper, is impressive on the effect that slavery had upon the honor and esteem accorded work in the South. Statistical analysis of the comparative figures on employment might be effectively used in testing these impressions.

Regional variations in the nature of work might also deserve attention as determinants of the Southern Ethic. Much of the work required of men in all parts of early America was crude and hard, and little of it anywhere could honestly be characterized as stimulating, creative, or inherently enjoyable. Those who wrote of its joys and rewards probably had a larger share of work that could be so characterized than those who failed to record their impressions. Perhaps it was somewhat easier to surround the labors of shop, countinghouse, and trade with the aura of honor and glamor. That type of work was in short supply in the South.

The agrarian myth of yeoman farmers as "the chosen people of God" certainly did bestow honor and a literary aura of dignity, even glamor, upon a way of making a living, but not necessarily on work itself. No other class of Americans was so persistently and assiduously flattered. The qualities for which the hero of the myth was admired, however, were his independence, his republican virtues, his purifying communion with nature. It was the political and public qualities of the yeomanry that Jefferson had in mind when he wrote that "the small land holders are the most precious part of the state." Work itself was not the essential thing, and certainly not the religion-driven, compulsive, ascetic work of the Puritan Ethic. In fact, neither the hired man nor the slave who did the same work (and probably more of it) shared the dignity and honor conferred by the myth on the yeoman, while the employer or owner of such labor might do little work by himself and yet enjoy the blessings of the myth. In its full flower in the late eighteenth century the agrarian myth, in fact, stressed escape from the bustle of the world and celebrated pastoral contentment and ease, the blandishments and pleasures of the simple life—the very "impulsive enjoyment of life" held up by Puritan divines as "the deadliest of sins." Never did the agrarian myth regard yeomen as "slaves of work for work's sake." The myth of the happy yeoman was much more congenial to the Southern Ethic than it was to the Puritan Ethic.[40]

As for the black slaves, their very existence did violence to the Puritan Ethic. No one could have a "calling"—in Weber's sense of the term—to be a slave. Since slaves were denied the fruits of their labor, they were deprived of the basic motive for industry and frugality. Circumstance made laziness the virtue and frugality the vice of slaves. Work was a necessary evil to be avoided as ingeniously as possible. Such work as was required of slaves—as well as of those who did work slaves typically performed—was rather difficult to associate with the glory of God or many of the finer aspirations of man. Could such work have been endowed with the mystique of a "calling" or a conviction of divine purpose, it might have

[40] Henry Nash Smith, *Virgin Land: The American West as Symbol and Myth* (New York, 1957), 138–150.

rested more lightly on the shoulders of those of whom it was required and on the conscience of those who required it. That seems to have been the way it worked with onerous non-slave work elsewhere. There appears, however, to have been less stomach for such theological exercises—indeed more need for stomach—in the South than in some other parts. Few sermons to slaves indulged in them. Work therefore lacked the sort of sanctification it might have derived from this source. The attitude of the slave toward work, like many of his attitudes and ways, found secure lodgement in the Southern Ethic.

Turning from the slave to the slave holder and the plantation system for a look at their influence on the evolution of the Southern Ethic, we move into more troubled waters. Genuine and important differences of opinion about the fundamental nature of the slave economy exist among experts in the field. Members of one school, the most distinguished of whom was Lewis C. Gray, think of the slave holder as a "planter-capitalist." According to Gray, the plantation system was a "capitalist type of agricultural organization in which a considerable number of unfree laborers were employed under a unified direction and control in the production of a staple crop."[41] The crop was produced for a remote market in response to standard laws of supply and demand by the use of capital sometimes obtained from banks or factors that was invested in land and in slaves. The whole operation was "rational," in the peculiar way economists use that remarkable word—that is, it operated single-mindedly to maximize profits on investment. A contrasting view was that of Ulrich B. Phillips, who believed that the plantation system was not nearly that simple, that it was a complicated "way of life," a social as well as an economic system. It contained numerous "irrational" elements, goals unrelated or antithetical to the profit motive. It was something of an anachronism, a pre-capitalist economy existing in a capitalist world.[42]

It makes a great deal of difference for the implications of the plantation system in accounting for the distinctiveness of the Southern Ethic as to which of these schools is "sound on the goose." For if Gray and his school are right, then there is relatively little to be learned from the political economy of slavery about the distinctiveness of the South from the rest of a uniformly capitalist America. If Phillips is on the right track, however, there might be a great deal to learn. It may be a long time before a consensus on the slave economy is reached among scholars, and certainly no attempt is made to settle the dispute here.

It is instructive to note, however, a convergence between the old-school

[41] Lewis C. Gray, *History of Agriculture in the Southern United States to 1860,* I (Washington, 1933), 302.

[42] Ulrich B. Phillips, *American Negro Slavery: A Survey of the Supply, Employment and Control of Negro Labor as Determined by the Plantation Régime* (Baton Rouge, 1966), *passim.*

views of Phillips and a new-school view developed by the investigations of Eugene D. Genovese.[43] In the findings of the latter, the plantation economy was shot through with "irrationality" (in the market-place sense) and given to wild deviations from the capitalistic norm. "The planters were not mere capitalists," he writes. "They were pre-capitalist, quasi-aristocratic landowners who had to adjust their economy and ways of thinking to a capitalist world market. Their society, in its spirit and fundamental direction, represented the antithesis of capitalism, however many compromises it had to make." He elaborates on the antithesis as follows:

The planters commanded Southern politics and set the tone of social life. Theirs was an aristocratic, antibourgeois spirit with values and mores emphasizing family and status, a strong code of honor, and aspirations to luxury, ease, and accomplishment. In the planters' community, paternalism provided the standard of human relationships, and politics and statecraft were the duties and responsibilities of gentlemen. The gentleman lived for politics, not, like the bourgeois politician, off politics.

The planter typically recoiled at the notions that profit should be the goal of life; that the approach to production and exchange should be internally rational and uncomplicated by social values; that thrift and hard work should be the great virtues; and that the test of the wholesomeness of a community should be the vigor with which its citizens expand the economy. The planter was no less acquisitive than the bourgeois, but an acquisitive spirit is compatible with values antithetical to capitalism. The aristocratic spirit of the planters absorbed acquisitiveness and directed it into channels that were socially desirable to a slave society: the accumulation of slaves and land and the achievement of military and political honors. Whereas in the North people followed the lure of business and money for their own sake, in the South specific forms of property carried the badges of honor, prestige, and power.[44]

He goes on to observe that "at their best, Southern ideals constituted a rejection of the crass, vulgar, inhumane elements of capitalist society. The slaveholders simply could not accept the idea that the cash nexus offered a permissible basis for human relations." The planters reinforced their paternalism toward their slaves by a semipaternalism toward their neighbors and "grew into the closest thing to feudal lords imaginable in a nineteenth-century bourgeois republic."[45]

[43] See for example Genovese's "Foreword" to the 1966 edition of Phillips, *American Negro Slavery* cited above.

[44] Eugene D. Genovese, *The Political Economy of Slavery: Studies in the Economy and Society of the Slave South* (New York, 1965), 23, 28.

[45] *Ibid.*, 30, 31.

Mr. Genovese has greatly complicated and enhanced the fascination of the game of ethic identification. One shrinks at the prospect of encouraging studies of "feudal" and "aristocratic" themes in Southern history, and even more at anticipated glances from colleagues in European history. It would be well to emphasize the prefix *quasi* that Mr. Genovese judiciously attaches to these terms. With these precautions (and misgivings) and with no disposition to prejudge the outcome of the revived and flourishing controversy over the political economy of American slavery, one might at least say that this interpretation of the slave South contains a number of suggestive hypotheses relating to the distinctiveness of the Southern Ethic.

On the themes of pre-capitalist economies the work of Max Weber again becomes relevant. He strongly emphasized the "irrational" characteristics of slave economies, particularly in master-slave relationships, consumer behavior, and politics. At the risk of reviving the Waverly-novel approach, the following characterization of the aristocratic ethic by Weber is offered as summarized by his biographer:

> In feudal ideology the most important relations in life are pervaded by personalized ties, in contrast to all factual and impersonal relationships. . . . From this standpoint luxury is not a superfluous frill but a means of self-assertion and a weapon in the struggle for power. This antiutilitarian attitude toward consumption was of a piece with the equally antiutilitarian orientation toward one's life. Aristocratic strata specifically rejected any idea of a 'mission in life,' any suggestion that a man should have a purpose or seek to realize an ideal; the value of aristocratic existence was self-contained. . . . Aristocrats deliberately cultivated a nonchalance that stemmed from the conventions of chivalry, pride of status, and a sense of honor.[46]

Social role-playing is a broad mark for satire, but all societies engage in it consciously or unconsciously. The sharpest ridicule is reserved for the unfortunate society that is caught at the height of collective posturing, brought low with humiliating exposure of its pretenses, and forced to acknowledge them—or live with them. The Old South has had its share of exposure along this particular line, and more at this juncture has rather low priority among the pressing tasks of historiography. More needful are analytical appraisals of the social content of the patriarchal, paternalistic, and aristocratic values and the remarkable qualities of leadership they developed. A comparative approach could be helpful, but the traditional moralistic comparison with the contemporary society to the north might profitably be ex-

[46] Reinhard Bendix, *Max Weber: An Intellectual Portrait* (New York, 1962), 364–365.

changed for comparisons with English and Latin slave societies to the south that shared more of the South's traditions, institutions, and values.

An abhorrence of slavery and an identification with abolitionists on the part of both liberal and radical historians have skewed and clouded their interpretation of the Old South. In a critique of Marxian and liberal historiography of slavery, Mr. Genovese holds that the main problem "arises from the duality inherent in a class approach to morality" and contends that both liberals and Marxists have made the mistake of judging the ruling class of Southern planters "by the standards of bourgeois society or by the standards of a projected socialist society." With reference to rulers of the Old Regime, he continues:

> These men were class conscious, socially responsible, and personally honorable; they selflessly fulfilled their duties and did what their class and society required of them. It is rather hard to assert that class responsibility is the highest test of morality and then to condemn as immoral those who behave responsibly toward their class instead of someone else's. There is no reason, unless we count as reason the indignation flowing from a passionate hatred for oppression, to withhold from such people full respect and even admiration; nor is there any reason to permit such respect and admiration to prevent their being treated harshly if the liberation of oppressed peoples demands it. The issue transcends considerations of abstract justice or a desire to be fair to one's enemies; it involves political judgment. If we blind ourselves to everything noble, virtuous, honorable, decent, and selfless in a ruling class, how do we account for its hegemony? . . . Such hegemony could never be maintained without some leaders whose individual qualities are intrinsically admirable.[47]

Also needed are discerning assessments of the skill, conviction, and zest which other players brought to the colorful variety of roles assigned them by the Old Regime. That of "Sambo" has been subjected to appreciative analysis of late, with commendable efforts to illuminate the personality and values of his descendants. The roles of his master and mistress, Lord and Lady Bountiful, as well as those of the lesser gentry, the squirearchy, the yeomanry, and the poor whites deserve comparable study. It is possible that a majority of the players identified completely with their roles as "real life" —as completely perhaps as the saints, prophets, and come-outers in other quarters found identity in their roles. At least the cast for the Old South

[47] Eugene D. Genovese, "Marxian Interpretations of the Slave South," in Barton J. Bernstein, ed., *Toward a New Past: Dissenting Essays in American History* (New York, 1968), 114.

drama, slaves included, often acted as if they did, and sometimes they put on rather magnificent performances. Study of the institutional setting in which they performed—the patriarchal tradition, the caste system, the martial spirit, the racial etiquette, the familial charisma—all deserve attention from the historian of the Southern Ethic.

V

After the curtain fell on the Old South in 1865, the same cast of characters had to be taught strange roles and learn new lines. For a people who had been schooled so long in the traditional roles, and especially for those who played them for "real life," this was not an easy assignment. The social dislocations and traumas of Reconstruction and the period that followed can be seen as drastic experiments from two sides: the conservative side trying to preserve the Southern Ethic, and the radical side trying to destroy it. As we shall see, neither of these experiments was destined wholly to succeed.

To convert the ex-slaves miraculously into "slaves of work for work's sake" in the classic model of Weber's "spirit of capitalism" was clearly beyond the reasonable expectations of either side. Given the freedman's age-long indoctrination in a work ethic appropriate to his enslavement, and given the necessity of his now doing the same kinds of work without the old compulsions, the question was whether he could be induced to do any work beyond what would provide him a bare subsistence, if that. Planter conservatives were convinced that the only answer was force in some guise, and in lieu of bondage they put forward schemes of apprenticeship and vagrancy laws embodied in "Black Codes." In effect they offered the old allegiance of paternalistic responsibility for abject dependents while tacitly retaining the sanction of the whip.

Ruling these schemes illegal and a travesty on freedom, Northern agencies, including the Freedmen's Bureau, missionaries, and private speculators, confidently maintained that "normal" economic incentives were the solution: wages, profits, and assurance of the fruits of one's labor. Northern agencies and employers launched their program with a campaign of indoctrination laced with the rhetoric of diligence, frugality, and the sanctity of contracts—staples of the Puritan Ethic. Needless to say, the Puritan Ethic had acquired its own Janus face over the centuries, and it was the face of Yankee acquisitiveness that was presented to the South. Along with this went the promise of free land held out to the freedmen by Congress and the Freedmen's Bureau. But that promise ran afoul of two conflicting principles of their own: the sanctity of property and the doctrine of equal rewards for equal labor. The first blocked the confiscation of planters' property to provide the free land, and the second inhibited the granting of special privilege unearned by honest labor. The North reneged on the promise of free land,

and the freedmen sulked. The "normal" incentives were not operating. Northern business joined Southern planters in demanding that the Freedmen's Bureau get the Negro back to the cotton fields. When General O. O. Howard, head of the bureau, received "authentic complaints of idleness for which no remedy seemed to exist," he ordered enforcement and extension of state vagrancy laws. His assistants withheld relief, compelled freedmen to accept labor contracts, and enforced their harsh terms with penalties of forfeited wages and withheld rations. Gradually the North withdrew and left the freedmen to make what terms they could with planters.[48]

In the meantime the campaign to convert Southern white men went forward briskly and at first hopefully. "It is intended," declared Thaddeus Stevens, "to revolutionize their principles and feelings," to "work a radical reorganization in Southern institutions, habits, and manners."[49] The difficulties of the undertaking were acknowledged. "The conversion of the Southern whites to the ways and ideas of what is called the industrial stage in social progress," wrote Edwin L. Godkin, was a "formidable task." He believed that "the South, in the structure of its society, in its manners and social traditions, differs nearly as much from the North as Ireland does, or Hungary, or Turkey."[50] But the revolutionizing process would go forward, promised Horatio Seymour, "until their ideas of business, industry, money making, spindles and looms were in accord with those of Massachusetts."[51] The Southern whites, like the Negroes, were subjected to indoctrination in diligence, austerity, frugality, and the gospel of work. They were advised to put behind them the "irrationality" of the Old Order, outmoded notions of honor, chivalry, paternalism, pride of status, and noblesse oblige, together with all associated habits of indolence, extravagance, idle sports, and postures of leisure and enjoyment. In the name of "rationality" they were adjured to get in there like proper Americans and maximize profits.

The verbal response from the South, after a refractory interlude and apart from a continued undertone of muttered dissent, must have been gratifying. The antebellum business community, long inhibited by ties to the Old Order, burst into effusions of assent and hosannas of delivery. "We have sowed towns and cities in the place of theories and put business above politics," announced Henry W. Grady to the cheering members of the New

[48] Willie Lee Rose, *Rehearsal for Reconstruction: The Port Royal Experiment* (Indianapolis, 1964), 212–216, 308–310; George R. Bentley, *A History of the Freedmen's Bureau* (Philadelphia, 1955), 79–86; for a revisionary estimate of the bureau see a forthcoming work of William McFeely, *Yankee Stepfather: General O. O. Howard and the Freedmen's Bureau* (New Haven, 1968).

[49] Quoted in Howard K. Beale, *The Critical Year: A Study of Andrew Johnson and Reconstruction* (New York, 1930), 149.

[50] *Nation*, XXXI (1880), 126.

[51] *Herald* (New York), Oct. 31, 1866.

England Society of New York. "We have fallen in love with work."[52] And Richard H. Edmunds of the *Manufacturers' Record,* invoking the spirit of Franklin, announced, "The South has learned that 'time is money.' "[53] A Richmond editor rejoiced that "the almighty dollar is fast becoming a power here, and he who commands the most money holds the strongest hand. We no longer condemn the filthy lucre."[54] The range of New South rhetoric left unsounded no maxim of the self-made man, no crassness of the booster, no vulgarity of the shopkeeper, no philistinism of the profit maximizer. For egregious accommodation and willing compliance the capitulation was to all appearances complete.

But appearances were deceptive, and the North was in some measure taken in by them. The New South orators and businessmen-politicians who took over the old planter states gained consent to speak for the region only on their promise that Southerners could have their cake and eat it too. That was one of the meanings of the Compromise of 1877. The South could retain its old ways, the semblance or outer shell at any rate, and at the same time have an "industrial revolution"—of a sort, and at a price. White supremacy was assured anyway, but home rule and states' rights meant further that the South was left to make its own arrangements regarding the plantation system, the accommodation of the freedman and his work ethic, and his status as well as that of white labor in the new economy and polity. The price of the "industrial revolution" and the reason for the distorted and truncated shape it took was an agreement that the North furnish the bulk of investment capital and entrepreneurship, while the New South managers smoothed the way by a "cooperative spirit" that assured generous tax exemptions, franchises, land grants, and most important of all an abundant supply of cheap, docile, and unorganized labor.

The South got its railroads and mines, its Birmingham heavy industry and its Piedmont factories. That is, they were located in the South. But they were largely owned elsewhere and they were operated in the interest of their owners. They were of one general type: low-wage, low value-creating industries that processed roughly the region's agricultural and mineral products but left the more profitable functions of finishing, transporting, distributing, and financing to the imperial Northeast. The South remained essentially a raw-material economy organized and run as a colonial dependency. On the agricultural side a sort of plantation system survived along with the one-crop staple culture, but the absentee owners dropped the wage contracts, substituted debt slavery for chattel slavery, and organized the

[52] Raymond B. Nixon, *Henry W. Grady: Spokesman of the New South* (New York, 1943), 345.

[53] *Manufacturers' Record* (Baltimore), Nov. 3, 1888.

[54] *Whig and Advertiser* (Richmond), Apr. 4, 1876.

labor force, now more white than black, as share croppers or tenants bound by an iron crop lien into virtual peonage. The cropper-tenants rarely handled any money, subsisted on fatback, cornbread, and molasses, and constituted a mass market for Southern manufacturers of chewing tobacco, moonshine whiskey, and very little else. They were in fact a non-market.

The New South neither preserved the Southern Ethic intact nor abandoned the allegiance entirely. It substituted a compromise that retained a semblance at the expense of the essence. The substitute was more defiantly proclaimed, articulately defended, and punctiliously observed than the genuine article had been. The cult of the Lost Cause covered the compromise with a mantle of romantic dignity and heroism. Surviving heroes in gray became Tennysonian knights. The Plantation Legend took on a splendor that shamed antebellum efforts. There was a place in the new cast —with important exceptions to be noted—for all players of the old roles as well as for newcomers with only imaginary identification with them, and there was a gratuitous upgrading of status all around. Great energy went into the performance. Spectators were impressed with the graciousness and hospitality, the leisurely elegance and quaint courtliness at upper levels, and with a pervasive kindliness, a familial warmth, and a deferential courtesy that prevailed generally.

There were even those who affected the patriarchal and paternalistic roles. Right here, however, came the sad falling off, the point at which the sacrificed essence—aristocratic obligations of noblesse oblige, responsibilities of leadership, solicitude for dependents and subordinates, and an anti-bourgeois disdain for the main chance and the fast buck—gave way to the bourgeois surrogate. For the children of the new patriarchs and the dependents of the new paternalists were the mass of forlorn croppers and tenants, black and white, in their miserable rural slums, undefended victims of ruinous interest rates, mined-out soil, outmoded techniques, debt slavery, and peonage—these and the first-generation industrial proletariat, white and black, in their urban or company-town slums, victims of the lowest wages, longest hours, and deadliest working conditions in the country.

The oppressed were not so docile as to submit without show of resistance. As the nineties came on, Negroes and white labor under the leadership of desperate farmers combined in the Populist Revolt to mount the most serious indigenous political rebellion an established order ever faced in the South. In their panic over the rebellion, the New South leaders relinquished their last claim to responsibility derived from the Old Order. Abandoning their commitment to moderation in racial policy, they turned politics over to racists. In the name of white solidarity and one-party loyalty, they disfranchised the Negro and many lower-class whites and unleashed the fanatics and lynchers. In their banks and businesses, in their clubs and social life, as well as in their inner political councils, they moved over to make room for increasing delegations of Snopeses. In place of the old sense of community based on an ordered if flexible hierarchy, they substituted a mystique of kinship, or clanship, that extended the familial ambit spuriously to all whites—and to such Negroes as had mastered and sedulously practiced the Sambo role to perfection.

There have been lamentations for the passing of the Southern Ethic all down the years and periodic jeremiads for its demise. Referring to the Puritan Ethic, Edmund Morgan writes that "it has continued to be in the process of expiring," that it has "always been known by its epitaphs," and that "perhaps it is not quite dead yet."[55] The future of either of these two historic relics in an affluent, consumer-oriented society of the short work week, early retirement, and talk of a guaranteed income looks rather dubious, though in a giant supermarket world the ethic of the grasshopper would seem to have somewhat more relevance than that of the ant. And puritanical condemnations of leisure already seem a bit quaint. Whether the Southern Ethic is dead or not, the lamentations and jeremiads show no sign of languishing. In fact, the works of William Faulkner constitute the most impressive contribution to that branch of literature yet. If epitaphs are indeed a sign of life in this paradoxical field of ethical history, then the lamentations here, too, may be premature.

[55] Morgan, "The Puritan Ethic," 42–43.

4

The First South

John Richard Alden

A definite consensus persists among students of the southern past that the distinct regional identification, so long a hallmark of southernism, was first articulated and defined via the sectional controversies of the pre–Civil War decades. Such consensus has concluded that The South did not function as a consistent regional entity, nor did it have a particularly graphic perception of itself as distinct from the North, at least not until the decade of the 1820s. John Richard Alden, Professor of History at Duke University, Durham, North Carolina, challenges this standard interpretation, taking notable exception to these "classic" explanations of southern regional consciousness. Lying beyond the historical horizon of the familiar Old South, Alden contends, lies an earlier South—a First South if you will. Though geographically distinct from its later counterpart, the First South was of kindred spirit in terms of climate, people, economy, and social order. In short, the land to the south of the Susquehanna "behaved as a section before 1789." Focusing on the Revolutionary War period, Professor Alden notes that perceptions of a constitutional, economic, and racial nature were already surfacing which foreshadowed an eventual southern Confederacy. It would be for later generations to reinforce and firmly establish these sectional feelings.

We Americans who are not too familiar with our history harbor a haunting memory of an Old South—an Old South of broad plantations; of their gracious masters and charming mistresses; of humble, cheerful, and loyal

From John R. Alden, *The First South*. Baton Rouge, Louisiana State University Press, 1961. Reprinted by permission of the publisher.

slaves who rose occasionally in ferocious revolt; of poor whites fearing naught but the wrath of Heaven; of cotton, magnolias, and Spanish moss— an Old South menaced and at last overwhelmed and demolished by Northern masses and machinery. We see through a glass doubtfully, and it is surely true that every general idea we have of that Old South is subject to exception and fuller description. The thousands of earnest historians who have delved into its remains must and do tell us that it was not as we are accustomed to think it was. Herein it is not intended to try to correct and clarify your vision, erroneous as it may be, of that familiar Old South, but to limn as truthfully as talents and energies will permit an even older South, which shall be named for convenience the First South.

This First South existed during the years 1775–1789. It appeared with the American nation; it was christened as early as 1778; and it clashed ever more sharply with a First North during and immediately after the War of Independence. This First South did not hasten under the Federal Roof with swift and certain steps, but haltingly and uncertainly. Many of her people feared that the Federal cover would offer greater protection north of the Susquehanna than it would south of that river. It should not be said that their alarm was without cause, that they saw troubles which the future did not bring. They feared lest they become a minority in an American union dominated by a Northern majority, lest they suffer in consequence. Whatever may be the merits of measures since imposed upon the South by the North—and the West—it will not be denied that the South has felt the power of external American forces, especially since the middle of the nineteenth century.

Now this First South, the Revolutionary South, the South of Patrick Henry, Light-Horse Harry Lee, and John Rutledge, was not the Old South of John C. Calhoun nor that of Jefferson Davis. In essence, nevertheless, they were the same, for they were alike in land, climate, people, economy, and social order. Even with respect to political structure and relations with the North, they were not so different as historians have commonly conceived. The Old South sought to leave the Union and to form a new nation; the First South—and for similar reasons—was not at all sure in the years 1787–1789 that it was wise to become part of that Union. Indeed, surprising as it may be, there were those in South Carolina, especially William Henry Drayton, who feared that South Carolina might suffer from the tyranny of Congress by giving consent to the Articles of Confederation. To be sure, the doubts of the First South were set aside, and it ultimately endorsed the Constitution of 1787, while the doubts of the Old South regarding the Union became so great that it denounced and sought to leave the Union. Here we have, however, an important difference in degree, not opposites absolutely.

There may be captious scholars—are not scholars by definition captious?

—who will go so far as to deny that there was a South in the Revolutionary time.[1] One may be tempted to find importance in the fact that the First South and the Old South were geographically not the same. Obviously enough, the First South was definitely limited by the Mississippi, while the Old South stretched westward into the empire of Texas; the First South was principally on the Atlantic seaboard, while the Old South contained both that seaboard and the lower half of the valley of the Mississippi. No matter, for the limits of a section, unless they be remarkably narrow, do not determine whether or not it exists.

More seriously, it may be asserted that the First South cannot have been because it lacked unity. It has been well said by Carl Bridenbaugh that there were actually three or four societies in the states from Maryland to Georgia at the beginning of the Revolution: an aristocratic order on the shores of the Chesapeake; another in the Carolina Low Country; a frontier society in the Old West; and possibly a fourth society not easily described in central North Carolina. But if there were three, or even four, societies below the Mason-Dixon line, it must be remembered that these were not three or four permanent societies completely distinct from each other. Those of the Chesapeake and the Low Country actually had much in common, including well-established American aristocracies and very large bodies of Negro slaves; and that of the Old West was actually only a passing phenomenon, since it would vanish with the frontier. Nor did central North Carolina possess one which could easily and positively be distinguished from those of the Chesapeake and the Low Country. The social differences to be discerned in the First South were hardly more impressive than were those in the Old South, the existence of which is not frequently or forcefully denied. The First South was not monolithic; neither was the Old South. Again, during the period 1775–1789, as afterward, heat, geography, racial and national composition, economic pursuits, social order, and even political structure, were ties of unity rather than sources of discord below the Susquehanna. That such was so is proven by events, for the First South frequently behaved as a section before 1789. It may be added that it was increasingly taken for granted by political men of the Revolutionary generation that the South was a distinct area with special and common interests that could not be ignored in the affairs of the nation.

All of which is not to say that there was such a region generally or even frequently referred to in 1775 or 1789 as the South. That name was used on a few interesting occasions, but the region was usually described between those years as the "Southern states." It follows, then, that there was

[1] The writer indicated briefly in his *The South in the Revolution, 1763–1789* (Baton Rouge, 1957) that there was such a South. So far as he is aware, none of the reviewers of that volume expressed dissent.

a South even before the name came into common use, a fact which hardly surprises, since the infant should precede the christening. Before the War of Independence the colonies were often divided by observers into "Eastern" and "Southern," the term "Eastern" covering New England, the word "Southern" including all the colonies from New York to Georgia. Sometimes "Northern" was used as a synonym for "Eastern." Thus in 1767, when advising General Thomas Gage to establish a military base at or near Manhattan, General Guy Carleton pointed out that such a fortified place would not only provide security for military stores but would also "separate the Northern from the Southern colonies." The division between "Eastern" and "Southern" endured through the early years of the war, a usage which has confused some historians, who have occasionally and forgivably assumed that no one could think of Pennsylvania or New Jersey as Southern. It is nevertheless true that a quarrel between men of the Delaware valley and New England troops in 1776 was referred to as one between Southerners and Easterners. Even at that time, however, the word Southern was acquiring a more restrictive meaning, the phrase "Middle states" being used more and more to describe New York, New Jersey, Pennsylvania, and Delaware. These "Middle states" with the "Eastern states" were increasingly put together as the "Northern states," another usage which long endured.

Quickly shorn of the Middle states, the Southern states became a South and a section. The limits of that section were, of course, only gradually established in the minds of men; indeed, they cannot now be firmly laid down between it and the Middle states. There was disagreement about its northern boundaries at the time, although no one doubted that the Carolinas and Georgia were part of it.

Strange to say, none other than George Washington, until the adoption of the Constitution, was reluctant to include Virginia within the First South. In 1787 and again in 1788 he refers in his correspondence to the Carolinas and Georgia as the "Southern states." In 1786 he invited Don Diego de Gardoqui, the official emissary of Spain to the United States, to pay a visit to Mount Vernon "if you should ever feel an inclination to make an excursion into the middle states." It is apparent that Washington, a stout nationalist even before the close of the War of Independence, wished to minimize the South and its special interests. But he was forced to recognize that they existed, and he too began to refer to the region between Pennsylvania and the Floridas as the "Southern states." Not until his first term as president did he fully realize the vitality of a Southern section that included Virginia. Becoming genuinely and even gravely alarmed, he urged his countrymen, in his Farewell Address, to soften their sectional antagonisms.

Except for Washington, I have found no Revolutionary worthy who would have drawn a line between Virginia and the South. And I have discovered only one other Founding Father who did not include Maryland in the "Southern states." That person was William Henry Drayton of South Carolina, who declared most emphatically in the winter of 1777–1778 that Virginia, the Carolinas, and Georgia formed "the body of the southern interest." Almost invariably, men in public life perplexed by North-South contests said or assumed that Maryland belonged to the Southern connection. Frequently politicians referred to difficulties between the eight Northern states and the five Southern ones. Others indicated that the North and the South were set apart by the Susquehanna River. The prevailing view was put flatly in 1787 by Charles Pinckney of South Carolina, who declared, "When I say Southern, I mean Maryland, and the states to the southward of her."

However Maryland may be classified—Southern, border, or Northern—in the nineteenth and twentieth centuries, it is appropriate to place her with the South in the Revolutionary time. It is true that central Maryland and western Maryland, even then, were countries of farms rather than plantations; of corn, wheat, and livestock instead of tobacco; of yeoman farmers rather than white masters and black slaves. But it should be remembered that only eastern Maryland, a plantation region, was then fully settled. It is also true that Maryland was slightly more commercial and a trifle more urban than Virginia. Nevertheless, in the days of the Revolution, the two states above and below the Potomac were fundamentally identical both economically and socially. Maryland at that time belonged with Virginia, and both with the South.

It was assumed soon after the close of the War of Independence that the northern limits of the South were on the Ohio as well as the Mason-Dixon line. Before the end of that conflict Virginia abandoned her claim to the Old Northwest; and Southerners generally sanctioned the Northwest Ordinance, which effectively placed the region between the Ohio, the Mississippi, and the Great Lakes outside the South. There was, however, agreement among politicians Northern and Southern, that the new settlements of Kentucky and Tennessee were Southern. As parts of Virginia and North Carolina until after the adoption of the Constitution, it could hardly be doubted at the time that they were parts of the South. Nor should we doubt it, even though we may not share the alarm then felt by leaders of New England because they saw the occupation of Kentucky and Tennessee as evidence that the South was expanding at the cost of the North. The Revolutionary South included the settlements of Boonesborough and Nashville as well as Annapolis and Savannah.

Proportionally to the remainder of the Union, the Revolutionary South was the largest South, both in size and in people. In fact, the Southern population in the first Federal census of 1790 was only a trifle smaller than that of the rest of the nation, there being then counted about 1,900,000 persons below the Mason-Dixon line, slightly more than 2,000,000 above it. At that time Virginia was by far the most populous state, and North Carolina ranked fourth, behind Massachusetts and Pennsylvania. Had not Maine been a part of Massachusetts, North Carolina would have been the third state in numbers. Moreover, there were Southerners who believed that population was increasing more rapidly in the South than elsewhere. These facts had influence upon the decision of the Southern states to ratify the Constitution, for it could be asserted with some show of reason that the South would soon surpass the remainder of the Union in numbers. It was not fully realized, perhaps, that the three-fifths provision of the Constitution respecting the slaves would place the South in a minority position in the national House of Representatives, even in the composition of the first Congress based on the census. Besides, as it turned out, the appearance of more rapid growth in the Southern population was illusory—the gap between North and South soon widened rather than diminished, as the census of 1800 indicated.

Hitherto it has been asserted rather than shown that there was a Revolutionary South. Nor will all the proof that such was the case be marshalled in detail at this point. Much of the best sort of proof, consisting of sectional quarrels, will be offered later. Nevertheless, it may be well to bring forth at this point certain fundamental reasons why the First South was crudely a unit with interests and views opposed to those of the rest of the Union.

Nature herself certainly set apart the South, giving to the South tropical summers, long growing seasons, and mild winters. Nature also gave soils and waters suitable for growing vast quantities of tobacco and rice, products which could be consumed only in small part in the South, which were much desired by foreign peoples, especially Europeans. In the Chesapeake region tobacco growing long seemed to be the best road to wealth, although it obviously was a road marred by ruts and mudholes; in the Carolina Low Country after the middle of the eighteenth century rice growing, together with the production of indigo, offered a surer and smoother highway to affluence. In consequence, the South had become before the Revolution a country of general farming and also of highly specialized farming that sent forth exports in great quantity and value. Meanwhile, the people of the Northern colony-states, with their colder climates, continued to engage in general farming, fishing, and lumbering, but turned increasingly toward internal trade, shipbuilding, sea-borne commerce, and manufacturing. Thus the economic pursuits of South and North became not only different, but often seemingly opposed. Instances enough of clashes over economic issues in the Revolutionary time will be offered later.

The special farming of the South was also the chief cause for a profound racial divergence between the sections, since the raising of tobacco and rice led to the importation into the South of large numbers of Negroes. In the Northern states, except for Delaware, at the time of the Revolution, the Negroes formed only small minorities. Below the Mason-Dixon line it was otherwise, for in the South 35 of every 100 persons were Negroes. They made up a full 30 per cent of the populations of Maryland and North Carolina, 40 per cent of that of Virginia, and more than half of that of South Carolina. The Negroes, burgeoning in numbers because of the special farming of the South, in turn helped to perpetuate such farming. The Southerners could think of few occupations for them beyond toil in tobacco rows, care of rice plants, weeding of corn, and other field tasks. Moreover, the presence of the Negro, together with the Southern economy and climate, tended to discourage white immigration, a fact which was noted by and which alarmed some astute Southern observers even before 1775, a fact which census returns afterward made evident to all who would bother to read such reports.

Economic and racial divergences between South and North brought with them serious social variation. Negro slavery was quite fixed upon the South, while it had few and weak roots above the Susquehanna. Slavery and special farming widened social cleavage among the Southern whites, giving added strength to the principle of aristocracy below the Mason-Dixon line. At the day of the Revolution there were admittedly socially superior persons in the Northern colony-states, chiefly country magnates and wealthy merchants. They were fewer and less powerful in New England than they were in the Middle states; and they were more conspicuous and more influential on the Chesapeake and in the Carolina Low Country than they were on the Hudson or the Delaware. Even North Carolina had its Tidewater aristocracy. The tobacco and rice lords often could not see eye-to-eye with the dominant middle-class men of the North. John Adams did not feel unmixed respect and liking for the "nabobs" of South Carolina whom he met in Congress after 1774; nor did the aristocratic-minded Southern delegates feel unadulterated admiration for the Yankees with whom they considered men and measures in New York and Philadelphia.

There were indeed important differences between the Northerners and the Southern whites as a whole in the Revolutionary time, as Thomas Jefferson pointed out in a letter to the Marquis de Chastellux in 1785. He said:

In the North they are cool, sober, laborious, independent, jealous of their own liberties, and just to those of others, interested, chicaning, superstitious and hypocritical in their religion. In the South they are fiery, voluptuary, indolent, unsteady, zealous for their own liberties, but trampling on those of others, generous, candid, without attachment or pretentions to any religion but that of the heart.

"These characteristics," asserted the thoughtful Virginian, became "weaker and weaker by gradation from North to South and South to North, insomuch that an observing traveller, without the aid of the quadrant may always know his latitude by the character of the people among whom he finds himself. It is in Pennsylvania that the two characters seem to meet and blend and to form a people free from the extremes both of vice and virtue." We need not accept precisely the opinion of Jefferson regarding either Northerners or Southerners, and we may also doubt that the Golden Mean existed in Pennsylvania, but there is obvious merit in his analysis. Assuredly, it is significant that he saw contrasts, even mistakenly, and that he thought them important enough to relate to his French friend.

Since colonial federation, though occasionally talked about and even planned, never was undertaken, serious clash between North and South did not appear before 1775. There were many contests between colony and colony, but none in which the one region was challenged by the other. It is true that jealousies of a sectional nature arose because some Southern colonists fancied that their Northern brethren were too hasty and too forward in asserting American rights against Britain during the decade before Lexington and Concord. Conversely, Northern defenders of American rights sometimes felt that the Southerners moved too slowly and too uncertainly. When the program of general nonimportation of British goods was rather hastily abandoned in the Northern ports after the repeal of most of the Townshend duties in 1770, just as nonimportation was being effectively put into force in South Carolina, there was genuine resentment in Charleston.[2] But here we have passing irritations rather than enduring troubles. Actually the struggles of the Americans against Britain before 1775, and the War of Independence especially, served to bring the Americans together by supplying them with a common, dangerous, and detested enemy.

Indeed, let us not forget that there were many and powerful forces pushing the Americans together in both the colonial and Revolutionary epochs. Too much may be made of economic and social antagonisms between North and South; too little heed may be given to unifying vigors. It should be recalled that almost all the Americans, save the Negroes, had a common background in the British Isles and that part of the European continent west of the Elbe River; that nearly all of them spoke English—English with perhaps fewer differences between North and South than afterward; and that they shared the benefits and evils of an English cultural and political heritage. Moreover, the Americans had felt alike the influence of similar elements in their New World environment. At the opening of the Revolutionary time they were aware of their oneness, a fact indicated by their ever-increasing use of the term American as descriptive of all the inhabitants of the Thirteen Colonies—a usage which also became dominant in

---

[2] Yankee Josiah Quincy, Jr., found in Charleston in 1773, "a general doubt of the firmness and integrity of the Northern colonies."

Britain after 1763. The beginning of the Revolutionary contest with Britain near the end of the French and Indian War added, as has been suggested, a new dynamic toward unity, Britain the foe of America as a whole. Northerners and Southerners had a common political enemy before 1775; even more important, they were faced by a common military antagonist between 1775 and 1783; after the close of the War of Independence, they continued to share fears of British and European aggressions. Those who fear the same menaces, those who fight the same foes, tend to feel that they are one.

Above all, the War of Independence aroused an American emotion. Virginians served at Boston and Quebec, Carolinians at Brandywine and Germantown, Yankees at Trenton and Yorktown. The "hard core" of the Revolutionary forces was the Continental army; and "Continental" was, or rather soon became, a synonym for "American." Few of the men who served in it could afterward be easily convinced that they fought only for their home state, or for a South, or for a North.[3] For the Continental veteran, officer and man, and doubtless almost to a man, America was his country. None were more devoted to the nation than were Virginia soldiers George Washington, Light-Horse Harry Lee, Daniel Morgan, and John Marshall. If one had suggested to a Southern veteran that he had not found Connecticut or New Jersey troops remarkably congenial, he would almost surely have responded that such was sometimes the case, but that they had been, when all was said and done, true and worthy comrades in a great cause.[4] And that cause could hardly be the creation of a string of small independent countries along the Atlantic coast; or of two or three nations; or even of one confederacy so feeble at its heart that it would be absurd to describe it as an American union.

American nationalism during the Revolutionary era should not be considered minor, nor were the forces creating and supporting it meager or temporary. The same should be said for the divisive tendencies of sectionalism. In that era nationalism was to triumph.

The contest between South and North began even before the Declaration of Independence. In the first general American assembly—in the First Continental Congress in 1774—came the first quarrel. It was, as were most of such struggles before 1789, economic in nature. When that body con-

---

[3] A Virginia newspaper reported in June, 1780 that "Captain Lieutenant Richard Coleman of Spotsylvania county, fell in the defense of his country on the 29th day of May . . . in South Carolina."

[4] In early acquaintance Southerners often disliked New Englanders, whose worst qualities were only too evident, whose finer ones required time to discover. Even in the long run the Yankees were more likely to inspire respect rather than fondness in the Southerner. James Fallon of South Carolina offered an early impression of them in 1779: "The inhabitants hereabouts [Fishkill, N.Y.] are all Yankees. I mean not to reflect *nationally;* but their manners are, to me, abhorrent. I long to leave and get clear of their oddities. They are, for the most part, a *damned* generation."

sidered measures to compel Parliament and Crown to change their course to American wishes, it decided to use a weapon which had become familiar, a boycott of British goods. There was no sectional disagreement regarding the use of this boycott, even though the importation of Negro slaves was also forbidden. Nor was there any difficulty between North and South because the Congress decreed nonconsumption of British goods, this measure being calculated to prevent merchants from pulling profits out of scarcities. It was otherwise when the delegates decided to use the club of nonexportation to Britain and the British West Indies, in case of need, the date for cessation being set at September 10, 1775. The delegates from South Carolina, except for Christopher Gadsden, asked that rice and indigo be excepted from the embargo, and so raised a controversy.

In this clash varying economic interests were basic. On the surface, the South Carolina men in the Congress were asking a special favor for the Low Country; from their point of view they were merely requesting equal sacrifice from all sections. Because of British law and other circumstances rice and indigo markets in England and the British West Indies were very important to South Carolina. Were exportation of those products to those markets forbidden, the Low Country planters, almost utterly dependent upon sales of rice and dye stuffs, must suffer grievously. The Northern colonies would be able to sell outside Britain and the islands, as they had in the past; and even the Chesapeake colonies, their tobacco going largely to London, Bristol, and Liverpool because of Parliamentary law, could escape the worst effects of the self-inflicted punishment of embargo by turning to wheat-growing. Even so, the attitude of the South Carolina delegation was not generous, especially with respect to their fellow planters of the Chesapeake; and Gadsden was prepared to offer a total sacrifice. When Northerners in Congress cried favoritism, the dominant Carolinians withdrew their request for excepting indigo; and for the sake of creating a solid front against Britain, the free sending of South Carolina's rice to sea was permitted. Thus the quarrel was resolved by concession on the part of the others to the Low Country planters. It has been suggested that Gadsden's colleagues should not be judged too harshly; it is worthy of mention that the news of the arrangement did not create great joy in Charleston. Early in 1775 the South Carolina Provincial Congress, considering the situation, and perhaps feeling some pangs of conscience, defeated a motion to ban rice exportation by the narrow margin of 87 to 75.

Early in the Second Continental Congress another issue threatened sectional trouble, and was settled in such fashion that nationalism won a victory of vast consequences. When that body decided to form a Continental army, it was immediately faced by a momentous question: who should be its commander in chief? It is now well known that George Washington had many merits and that these were not entirely unfamiliar in Philadelphia.

However, New Englanders were inclined to favor the appointment of a Yankee, Israel Putnam or some other hero of the lands east of the Hudson. Aware that unity would be secured by choosing a Southerner and that Washington was otherwise suitable, John and Samuel Adams consented to the appointment of the Virginia colonel. The decision did allay sectional feeling at the time.[5] Far more important, the personal fortunes of Washington became entwined with those of a national army. He felt the adverse effects of particularism and sectionalism in the war effort as could no other person. It may even be said that Washington's fame came to depend in part upon the creation of a permanent American union. Were his military achievements to lead to the making of a number of small American nations, he could hardly be the mighty figure he became. Whether the commander in chief was fully conscious that his glory was inextricably linked with that of the United States is a question of no importance. Such was the fact; and there was no more sturdy, no more steady nationalist in the South than the great Virginian at the end of the war. As he said farewell to his army, he begged that his comrades give their support to a solid union; and he was to be more responsible than any other man for putting the Constitution into force. We are all accustomed to praising the man of Mount Vernon for his military merits, and there have been those who have contended—I think, without full cause—that his services as president were even more remarkable than those he offered in his campaigns and battles. Let it not be forgotten that he was also the man above all others responsible for the general adoption of the Constitution. Many a great American of his time and later ones was to be first a nationalist and later a regionalist, or a sectionalist and then a nationalist—the names of John C. Calhoun and Daniel Webster come to mind. Not so with Washington, who stoutly and firmly fought against sectional prejudice in the Continental army, in the struggle over the Constitution, and in the presidency. Even now we perhaps do not value

[5] Long afterward, the Reverend Jonathan Boucher, whose acquaintance with Washington was hardly intimate, said the Southern colonists feared in 1775 that they would be dominated by a Northern army after independence had been achieved and that Washington's acceptance of the supreme command was dictated, "more than anything else," by a desire to prevent such a horrid outcome. At the time, Governor Jonathan Trumbull of Connecticut expressed a hope that the selection of Washington would "cement the union between the Northern & Southern colonies—& remove any jealousies of a N England army (if they should prove successfull) being formidable to the other provinces." In the summer of 1776 General Persifor Frazer of Pennsylvania also commented from Fort Ticonderoga upon fear of New England. "No man was ever more disappointed in his expectations respecting New Englanders than I have been. They are a set of low, dirty, griping, cowardly, lying rascals. There are some few exceptions and very few.... You may inform all your acquaintance not to be afraid that they will ever conquer the other provinces (which you know was much talked of), 10,000 Pennsylvanians would I think be sufficient for ten times that number out of their own country. All the Southern troops live in great harmony."

fully his devotion to the nation. First in war, first in peace, first in the hearts of his countrymen, he was also first in his allegiance and contribution to American unity.

Although the appointment of Washington as commander in chief was a triumph for nationalism, sectionalism also had its victories during that part of the Revolutionary War which preceded the Declaration of Independence. It will be recalled that the movement toward complete separation from Britain during the first fifteen months of the Revolutionary War was accompanied by a movement toward an American union. Thus when Richard Henry Lee of Virginia introduced in Congress on June 7, 1776, his famous resolution declaring that "These United Colonies are and of right ought to be free and independent states," he also called for the making of an American federation. By most public men in Congress and out, independence and political union were considered as virtually inseparable. Indeed, there were Patriot leaders in the spring of 1776, including Patrick Henry, who asserted that the Americans should marry each other before they declared themselves divorced from the British. These claimed that independence would be easier to achieve if union were secured before issuing a formal announcement that America had left the empire. As early as the fall of 1775 the Revolutionary legislature of North Carolina indicated its disapproval of the famous plan of confederation submitted by Benjamin Franklin because it gave New England larger representation in the federal legislature than the North Carolina men were willing to concede to it. This was much to the satisfaction of Josiah Martin, the last royal governor of North Carolina, who claimed that Franklin's arrangements would enable the North "to give law" to the South and who gleefully asserted that the North would use its power, since there was in New England a "lust of domination."

Any argument which might serve to sow dissension among the Patriots was welcomed by Josiah Martin, and also by James Anderson, another supporter of the Crown, who sought to frighten the South to the advantage of Britain. In a pamphlet published at Edinburgh in 1776 Anderson predicted that an independent American union would be disastrous for the Southerners. They would form a minority in an American legislature, and their economic interests would be injured to the benefit of those of the Northerners. Time would bring so great exasperation at the South that the Southerners would seek to form a new nation. They would not be permitted to leave the union peacefully; and, fewer in numbers and enervated by heat, they would be defeated in war. Thereafter they would live in a state of inferiority and subjection to the North. It turned out that there was basic truth coupled with error in Anderson's calculations and predictions. And his reputation as a prophet must also suffer because he foresaw what he wished to foresee, that parting from England would not bring such sweet tomorrows to the Americans.

Josiah Martin and James Anderson, not friends to American freedom, told the Southerners they should not join an American union. Other men not hostile to independence said such a union could not be formed because of the contrarieties which existed in the Thirteen. In the middle of the 1780's it was frequently suggested by Americans not seeking to return to the British empire that two or even three confederacies would rise along the Atlantic coast. One of these would be Southern, including Maryland and the states to her southward. There might be two confederations north of the Mason-Dixon line, one in New England and another composed of the Middle states; or New England and the Middle states might form one union. As late as 1788 Patrick Henry was accused, and not entirely without reason, of seeking to create a Southern confederacy. There were even Southern public men of the Revolutionary period who believed, because of the power of local loyalties, that the Thirteen States must go their separate ways. So Thomas Burke of North Carolina asserted in 1778 that an American union was a "chimerical project." So William Blount of the same state in July, 1787, declared, "I still think we shall ultimately and not many years . . . be separated and distinct governments perfectly independent of each other." To be sure, both Burke and Blount afterward changed their minds.

Because of the difficulty of assessing the conflicting forces which supported state loyalties, regional confederacies, and general union, no one could assuredly predict during the twelve years after the Declaration of Independence what political form or forms the Americans would adopt. It may be guessed that personalities, and even chance, affected the outcome, despite the conviction of George Bancroft that the course of events was personally and intimately directed by the Deity.

It could be safely predicted, however, that troubles must arise between South and North in a union with a central government possessing substantial powers. Sectional conflicts continued throughout the war. When Washington's army was undergoing its ordeal at Valley Forge in the winter of 1777–1778, Virginians and South Carolinians were voicing alarm lest Congress under the Articles of Confederation possess too great authority, to the detriment of Southern interests. That body during the years 1781–1787 was often riven by strife between South and North. Southern fears of Northern domination appeared in the Philadelphia Convention of 1787, and were frequently and forcefully asserted in the contests over ratification of the Constitution which took place below the Mason-Dixon line. Those fears were often based in part upon acute reasoning; indeed, in view of later occurrences, few will say they were without some solid foundation.

5

The Mind of the South:
Of Time and Frontiers

Wilbur J. Cash

Of those myths peculiar to the pre–Civil War South, none has
proved more enduring than the belief in a historically continuous
southern aristocracy. According to the romantic myth of the Old
South, country gentlemen of courtliness and stately hospitality presided over southern society during the antebellum period. The late
Wilbur Cash, freelance writer and former Associate Editor of the
Charlotte (North Carolina) *News,* seeks to counter this image by
forwarding arguments against such a legendary sociology. In pursuing the social reality of the antebellum South, Mr. Cash notes
that two critical factors were perpetually at odds with the idea of
an all-pervasive cavalier society—the element of time and the ever
present frontier environment. In addition, the proven incidence of
social mobility among earlier southerners scarcely suggests the existence of a full-blown, closed aristocracy in the making. To the
degree that subtle notions of class did begin to manifest themselves
in the Old South, such social distinctions were linked, as is invariably the case in most Western societies, not to lineage but rather to
property ownership. The southern "aristocracy" of the Old Regime
was at best one of rank rather than caste—a creation of the mind
of the South.

Though . . . nobody any longer holds to the Cavalier thesis in its overt
form, it remains true that the popular mind still clings to it in essence. Explicit or implicit in most considerations of the land, and despite a gathering

From *The Mind of the South,* by W. J. Cash. Copyright © 1941 by Alfred A. Knopf,
Inc., and renewed 1969 by Mary R. Maury. Reprinted by permission of Alfred A.
Knopf, Inc.

tendency on the part of the more advanced among the professional historians, and lately even on the part of popular writers, to cast doubt on it, the assumption persists that the great South of the first half of the nineteenth century—the South which fought the Civil War—was the home of a genuine and fully realized aristocracy, coextensive and identical with the ruling class, the planters; and sharply set apart from the common people, still pretty often lumped indiscriminately together as the poor whites, not only by economic condition but also by the far vaster gulf of a different blood and a different (and long and solidly established) heritage.

To suppose this, however, is to ignore the frontier and that *sine qua non* of aristocracy everywhere—the dimension of time. And to ignore the frontier and time in setting up a conception of the social state of the Old South is to abandon reality. For the history of this South throughout a very great part of the period from the opening of the nineteenth century to the Civil War (in the South beyond the Mississippi until long after that war) is mainly the history of the roll of frontier upon frontier—and on to the frontier beyond.

Prior to the close of the Revolutionary period the great South, as such, has little history. Two hundred years had run since John Smith had saved Jamestown, but the land which was to become the cotton kingdom was still more wilderness than not. In Virginia—in the Northern Neck, all along the tidewater, spreading inland along the banks of the James, the York, the Rappahannock, flinging thinly across the redlands to the valley of the Shenandoah, echoing remotely about the dangerous water of Albemarle—in South Carolina and Georgia—along a sliver of swamp country running from Charleston to Georgetown and Savannah—and in and around Hispano-Gallic New Orleans, there was something which could be called effective settlement and societal organization.

Here, indeed, there was a genuine, if small, aristocracy. Here was all that in aftertime was to give color to the legend of the Old South. Here were silver and carriages and courtliness and manner. Here were great houses—not as great as we are sometimes told, but still great houses: the Shirleys, the Westovers, the Stratfords. Here were the names that were some time to flash with swords and grow tall in thunder—the Lees, the Stuarts, and the Beauregards. Charleston, called the most brilliant of American cities by Crèvecoeur, played a miniature London, with overtones of La Rochelle, to a small squirarchy of the rice plantations. In Virginia great earls played at Lord Bountiful, dispensing stately hospitality to every passer-by—to the barge captain on his way down the river, to the slaver who had this morning put into the inlet with a cargo of likely Fulah boys, to the wandering Yankee peddling his platitudinous wooden nutmeg, and to other great earls, who came, with their ladies, in canopied boats or in coach and six with liveried outriders. New Orleans was a pageant of dandies and coxcombs, and all the swamplands could show a social life of a considerable pretension.

It is well, however, to remember a thing or two about even these Virginians. (For brevity's sake, I shall treat only of the typical case of the Virginians, and shall hereafter generally apply the term as embracing all these little clumps of colonial aristocracy in the lowlands.) It is well to remember not only that they were not generally Cavaliers in their origin but also that they did not spring up to be aristocrats in a day. The two hundred years since Jamestown must not be forgotten. It is necessary to conceive Virginia as beginning very much as New England began—as emerging by slow stages from a primitive backwoods community, made up primarily of farmers and laborers. Undoubtedly there was a sprinkling of gentlemen of a sort—minor squires, younger sons of minor squires, or adventurers who had got themselves a crest, a fine coat, and title to huge slices of the country. And probably some considerable part of the aristocrats at the end of the Revolution are to be explained as stemming from these bright-plumed birds. It is certain that the great body of them cannot be so explained.

The odds were heavy against such gentlemen—against any gentlemen at all, for that matter. The land had to be wrested from the forest and the intractable red man. It was a harsh and bloody task, wholly unsuited to the talents which won applause in the neighborhood of Rotten Row and Covent Garden, or even in Hants or the West Riding. Leadership, for the great part, passed inevitably to rough and ready hands. While milord tarried at dice or languidly directed his even more languid workmen, his horny-palmed neighbors increasingly wrung profits from the earth, got themselves into position to extend their holdings, to send to England for redemptioners and convict servants in order to extend them still further, rose steadily toward equality with him, attained it, passed him, were presently buying up his bankrupt remains.

The very redemptioners and convict servants were apt to fare better than the gentleman. These are the people, of course, who are commonly said to explain the poor whites of the Old South, and so of our own time. It is generally held of them that they were uniformly shiftless or criminal, and that these characters, being inherent in the germ plasm, were handed on to their progeny, with the result that the whole body of them continually sank lower and lower in the social scale. The notion has the support of practically all the standard histories of the United States, as for example those of John Bach McMaster and James Ford Rhodes. But, as Professor G. W. Dyer, of Vanderbilt University, has pointed out in his monograph, *Democracy in the South before the Civil War,* it has little support in the known facts.

In the first place, there is no convincing evidence that, as a body, they came of congenitally inferior stock. If some of the convicts were thieves or cutthroats or prostitutes, then some of them were also mere political prisoners, and so, ironically, may very well have represented as good blood as there was in Virginia. Perhaps the majority were simply debtors. As for the redemptioners, the greater number of them seem to have been mere children or adolescents, lured from home by professional crimps or outright kidnapped. It is likely enough, to be sure, that most of them were still to be classed as laborers or the children of laborers; but it is an open question whether this involves any actual inferiority, and certainly it involved no practical inferiority in this frontier society.

On the contrary. Most of them were freed while still in their twenties. Every freeman was entitled to a headright of fifty acres. Unclaimed lands remained plentiful in even the earliest-settled areas until long after the importation of bound servants had died out before slavery. And to cap it all, tobacco prices rose steadily. Thus, given precisely those qualities of physical energy and dogged application which, in the absence of degeneracy, are pre-eminently the heritage of the laborer, the former redemptioner (or convict, for that matter) was very likely to do what so many other men of his same general stamp were doing all about him: steadily to build up his capital and become a man of substance and respect. There is abundant evidence that the thing did so happen. Adam Thoroughgood, who got to be the greatest planter in Norfolk, entered the colony as an indentured servant. Dozens of others who began in the same status are known to have become justices of the peace, vestrymen, and officers of the militia—positions reserved, of course, for gentlemen. And more than one established instance bears out *Moll Flanders*.

In sum, it is clear that distinctions were immensely supple, and that the test of a gentleman in seventeenth-century Virginia was what the test of a gentleman is likely to be in any rough young society—the possession of a sufficient property.

Aristocracy in any real sense did not develop until after the passage of a hundred years—until after 1700. From the foundations carefully built up by his father and grandfather, a Carter, a Page, a Shirley began to tower decisively above the ruck of farmers, pyramided his holdings in land and slaves, squeezed out his smaller neighbors and relegated them to the remote Shenandoah, abandoned his story-and-a-half house for his new "hall," sent his sons to William and Mary and afterward to the English universities or the law schools in London. These sons brought back the manners of the Georges and more developed and subtle notions of class. And the sons of these in turn began to think of themselves as true aristocrats and to be accepted as such by those about them—to set themselves consciously to the elaboration and propagation of a tradition.

But even here the matter must not be conceived too rigidly, or as having taken place very extensively. The number of those who had moved the whole way into aristocracy even by the time of the Revolution was small.

Most of the Virginians who counted themselves gentlemen were still, in reality, hardly more than superior farmers. Many great property-holders were still almost, if not quite, illiterate. Life in the greater part of the country was still more crude than not. The frontier still lent its tang to the manners of even the most advanced, all the young men who were presently to rule the Republic having been more or less shaped by it. And, as the emergence of Jeffersonian democracy from exactly this milieu testifies, rank had not generally hardened into caste.

But this Virginia was not the great South. By paradox, it was not even all of Virginia. It was a narrow world, confined to the areas where tobacco, rice, and indigo could profitably be grown on a large scale—to a relatively negligible fraction, that is, of the Southern country. All the rest, at the close of the Revolution, was still in the frontier or semi-frontier stage. Here were no baronies, no plantations, and no manors. And here was no aristocracy nor any fully established distinction save that eternal one between man and man.

In the vast backcountry of the seaboard states, there lived unchanged the pioneer breed—the unsuccessful and the restless from the older regions; the homespun Scotch-Irish, dogged out of Pennsylvania and Maryland by poverty and the love of freedom; pious Moravian brothers, as poor as they were pious; stolid Lutheran peasants from northern Germany; ragged, throat-slitting Highlanders, lusting for elbow-room and still singing hotly of Bonnie Prince Charlie; all that generally unpretentious and often hard-bitten crew which, from about 1740, had been slowly filling up the region. Houses, almost without exception, were cabins of logs. Farms were clearings, on which was grown enough corn to meet the grower's needs, and perhaps a little tobacco which once a year was "rolled" down to a landing on a navigable stream. Roads and trade hardly yet existed. Life had but ceased to be a business of Indian fighting. It was still largely a matter of coon-hunting, of "painter" tales and hard drinking.

Westward, Boone had barely yesterday blazed his trail. Kentucky and Tennessee were just opening up. And southward of the Nashville basin, the great Mississippi Valley, all that country which was to be Alabama, Mississippi, western Georgia, and northern Louisiana, was still mainly a wasteland, given over to the noble savage and peripatetic traders with an itch for adventure and a taste for squaw seraglios.

Then the Yankee, Eli Whitney, interested himself in the problem of extracting the seed from a recalcitrant fiber, and cotton was on its way to be king. The despised backcountry was coming into its own—but slowly at first. Cotton would release the plantation from the narrow confines of the coastlands and the tobacco belt, and stamp it as the reigning pattern on all the country. Cotton would end stagnation, beat back the wilderness, mow the forest, pour black men and plows and mules along the Yazoo and the

Arkansas, spin out the railroad, freight the yellow waters of the Mississippi with panting stern-wheelers—in brief, create the great South. But not in a day. It was necessary to wait until the gin could be proved a success, until experience had shown that the uplands of Carolina and Georgia were pregnant with wealth, until the rumor was abroad in the world that the blacklands of the valley constituted a new El Dorado.

It was 1800 before the advance of the plantation was really under way, and even then the pace was not too swift. The physical difficulties to be overcome were enormous. And beyond the mountains the first American was still a dismaying problem. It was necessary to wait until Andrew Jackson and the men of Tennessee could finally crush him. 1810 came and went, the battle of New Orleans was fought and won, and it was actually 1820 before the plantation was fully on the march, striding over the hills of Carolina to Mississippi—1820 before the tide of immigration was in full sweep about the base of the Appalachians.

From 1820 to 1860 is but forty years—a little more than the span of a single generation. The whole period from the invention of the cotton gin to the outbreak of the Civil War is less than seventy years—the lifetime of a single man. Yet it was wholly within the longer of these periods, and mainly within the shorter, that the development and growth of the great South took place. Men who, as children, had heard the war-whoop of the Cherokee in the Carolina backwoods lived to hear the guns at Vicksburg. And thousands of other men who had looked upon Alabama when it was still a wilderness and upon Mississippi when it was still a stubborn jungle, lived to fight—and to fight well, too—in the ranks of the Confederate armies.

The inference is plain. It is impossible to conceive the great South as being, on the whole, more than a few steps removed from the frontier stage at the beginning of the Civil War. It is imperative, indeed, to conceive it as having remained more or less fully in the frontier stage for a great part—maybe the greater part—of its antebellum history. However rapidly the plantation might advance, however much the slave might smooth the way, it is obvious that the mere physical process of subduing the vast territory which was involved, the essential frontier process of wresting a stable foothold from a hostile environment, must have consumed most of the years down to 1840.

6

Democracy in the Old South

Fletcher M. Green

The view is held by many that the Old South was different. The Mason-Dixon Line is purported to have separated a northern from a southern "way of life," and as a corollary the South is supposed to have achieved a model social order. In the words of the native southerner Thomas Nelson Page, the antebellum South was a magic blend, "the joint product of chivalry and Christianity." Thus a pervasive and prevailing myth concerning the Old South is its alleged aristocratic and even semi-feudal character. This image of antebellum southern society has been strategically reinforced by such disparate groups as abolitionists, southern apologists, Hollywood (*Gone With the Wind*), and historians themselves. Fletcher M. Green, one of the elder statesmen among historians of the South and Kenan Professor of History at the University of North Carolina, here challenges this encrusted stereotype. According to Green, the South before the Civil War was not in any full sense an economic and social democracy; in this respect it scarcely differed from the North. He finds that the South of the Old Regime did, however, manifest important inclinations toward *political democracy*. In the end, the South was not simply the land of aristocratic privilege and *noblesse oblige*. A conspiratorial cadre of "planter aristocrats" did not control southern politics. Rather, the South was as much committed to democratic principles and practice as the country at large.

Fletcher M. Green, "Democracy in the Old South," *Journal of Southern History,* 12 (February 1946), 3–23. Copyright 1946 by the Southern Historical Association. Reprinted by permission of the Managing Editor.

The American dream of democracy and equality, based upon the philosophy of natural rights and popular sovereignty, found full, free, and adequate expression in such Revolutionary documents as the Declaration of Independence and the bills of rights of the state constitutions.[1] "We hold these truths to be self-evident, that all men are created equal, that they are endowed by their Creator with certain unalienable Rights, that among these are Life, Liberty and the pursuit of Happiness." "All power is vested in, and consequently derived from, the people; . . . magistrates are their trustees and servants, and at all times amenable to them." "No man, or set of men, are entitled to exclusive or separate emoluments or privileges from the community but in consideration of publick services." These and similar expressions of democratic equalitarianism were familiar to the people in all the states of the American Union.

The mere declaration of these ideals did not insure their acceptance and enforcement; a vigorous and continuous defense of liberty is essential if it is to be preserved. Thomas Jefferson, spokesman for democracy, early observed that men were by their constitutions naturally divided into two classes: (1) those who fear and distrust the people and seek to draw all power into their own hands; and (2) those who have confidence in the people and consider the people the safest depository of public happiness and general well being. These two classes he called aristocrats and democrats. From the very beginning of American independence these two groups began a contest for control of the governments. This contest between the forces of aristocracy and democracy was one of the most important issues in the political development of the American nation during the first half century of its existence. In the northern states it was fought between the commercial-financial aristocracy and the working men, in the southern states between the aristocratic slaveholding planters and the yeoman farmers.

The first state constitutions were framed in an atmosphere of equality and the recognition of human rights, without hint of race or class distinctions, but they established property and freehold qualifications for voting and office holding, and a system of representation, that gave control of the state governments to the wealthy, conservative, aristocratic classes. The power and influence of the aristocracy were further enhanced by the victory of the conservative group that established the Federal Constitution. The Jeffersonian democrats, accepting, in theory at least, the doctrines of natural rights, popular sovereignty, government by compact and contract, and the perfectability of mankind, began a militant assault upon the strongholds of aristocracy. They demanded and obtained a bill of rights to the Federal Constitution, and an extended suffrage and a greater equality of representa-

[1] [Omitted.]

tion in the state governments. Under their attacks the powers of aristocracy were gradually whittled away. Finally, with the accession of Andrew Jackson to the presidency in 1829, it seemed that democracy would certainly triumph. Most American people agreed with Alexis de Tocqueville that the democratic revolution was an irresistible one, and that to attempt to check it "would be to resist the will of God."[2]

As democratic reform moved into high gear under Jackson its forces were divided by the emergence of the bitter sectional controversy over slavery. The northern abolitionists saw in the institution of slavery the absolute negation of liberty and equality and they began to weigh and to find wanting almost every feature of southern society. In particular they condemned the southern state governments, declaring that in them political democracy was being overthrown by a slaveholding aristocracy. This change, said they, was the result not of caprice or political accident but of deliberate design on the part of the aristocracy; and it was succeeding because *"the non-slave-holding people of the South lacked the enterprise, intelligence and daring to demand and extract their democratic rights."*[3] In other words, they held that the masses of free whites were incapable of understanding or maintaining their rights, and that the planter aristocracy was bitterly hostile to free institutions and the democratic theory of government universally.

By the time the sectional controversy reached the breaking point, the abolitionists had decided that the slaveholders had become a *"Dominant class,* having positive control of the . . . political power of those States. . . . the system of slavery concentrating, as it does all political influence in a few men who are virtually absolute in their respective States."[4] Contrasting the two sections, Richard Hildreth, the historian, declared: "The Northern States of the Union are unquestionable Democracies, and every day they are verging nearer and nearer towards the simple idea and theoretic perfection of that form of government. The Southern States of the Union, though certain democratic principles are to be found in their constitutions and their laws, are in no modern sense of the word entitled to the appellation of Democracies: They are Aristocracies; and aristocracies of the sternest and most odious kind."[5]

This interpretation of southern society and government was based upon

[2] Alexis de Tocqueville, *Democracy in America,* Translated by Henry Reeve, 2 vols. (Fourth edition, New York, 1845), I, 1–2, 5.

[3] Thomas S. Goodwin, *The Natural History of Secession; or, Despotism and Democracy at Necessary, Eternal, Exterminating War* (New York, 1865), 40–41.

[4] Elhanon W. Reynolds, *The True Story of the Barons of the South; or, The Rationale of the American Conflict* (Boston, 1862), 34–35.

[5] Richard Hildreth, *Despotism in America: An Inquiry into the Nature, Results, and Legal Basis of the Slave-Holding System of the United States* (Boston, 1854), 8.

moral hatred of Negro slavery, rather than a true knowledge of southern state governments or a philosophical or realistic understanding of democracy. Its appeal to the excited and hostile North was so powerful that most people accepted it as unquestionably accurate; and the general historians of the United States incorporated it into their writings. For instance, James Ford Rhodes says in his *History of the United States from the Compromise of 1850* that the "slaveholders, and the members of that society which clustered round them, took the offices. . . . The political system of the South was an oligarchy under the republican form." And Lord Acton, the British historian and publicist, wrote that "Secession was an aristocratic rebellion against a democratic government."[6]

The abolitionist promoters of the theory of the aristocratic nature of southern governments never attempted to define just what they meant by either aristocracy or democracy. Indeed democracy has always been difficult of definition. It is a relative term, and has had various meanings among different peoples and for the same people at different stages of their political development. In this paper it will be used in its general sense as a form of government in which the sovereign power is held by the people and exercised through a system of representation in which the representatives are chosen by a fairly large electorate. The electorate has not been a fixed one in the United States. In the early days of the American republic the suffrage was bestowed upon adult male property owners; in the second quarter of the nineteenth century it was extended to all adult white males; during Reconstruction the Negro was given the ballot; and in 1920 women were permitted to vote in all elections. Recently, Georgia has given the ballot to youths eighteen years of age. No one would say that the state governments were undemocratic in 1850 simply because women did not vote; but they were *more* democratic in 1920 because women did vote. The same may be said in regard to Negro suffrage. Furthermore, up to the Civil War the emphasis on democracy was placed on *political* equality; since that time greater emphasis has been placed on social and economic equality. Modern thought presupposes that institutions, in order to be understood, must be seen in relation to the conditions of time, place, and thought in which they appear. It is difficult to look at democracy in this way, for one is prone to judge democracy of the past by the criteria of today. Yet the degree of democracy prevailing under the constitutions and governments of the Old South must be judged by the democracy of that era, not of the present. George Sidney Camp was but speaking for his generation when he wrote in 1840 that democracy "is not of an agrarian character or spirit. Its immediate object is an equal division of political rights, not of property. . . . But

---

[6] See also, Hermann E. von Holst, *The Constitutional and Political History of the United States,* 8 vols. (Chicago, 1876–1892), I, 348–49.

republicanism does aim a death blow at all those laws and usages the object of which is . . . to give it a particular and exclusive direction as a means of political power."[7]

As noted above, the Revolutionary state constitutions utilized to a large degree the framework of colonial governments and constitutional practices of the colonial period which had recognized and established a governing class of the wealthy aristocracy. Only eight of the thirteen states made any change in suffrage requirements; and these changes did not abolish the principle that only property holders should vote, they merely reduced the amount of property required. Property and freehold qualifications for voting and office holding meant that the governing class in the southern states was in large measure a planter aristocracy. The system of representation also favored the planter group of the eastern section. Though democratic in form, these constitutions were certainly not democratic in fact. They did, however, lay the basis for the expansion of popular control, the chief element in a political democracy, to the majority of the people.

Hardly had the landed aristocracy established themselves in power when demands for revision and readjustment were heard in each of the states. Among the specific reforms called for were the disestablishment of the church and the abolition of religious qualifications for office holding; the abolition of the laws of entail and primogeniture; the broadening of the suffrage; the equalization of representation; and the reduction of property qualifications for office holding. All looked toward the curbing of the powers of the landed aristocracy. Piecemeal amendment and revision of the constitutions partially satisfied these demands.

In South Carolina the dissenting Presbyterians and Congregationalists, led by William Tennent, a Presbyterian minister, and Christopher Gadsden, prepared a memorial which was signed by thousands of people and presented a petition to the legislature in 1777 asking "free and equal privileges, both religious and civil" for all Protestants. Another group of reformers joined forces with the dissenters and demanded an elective upper house of the legislature rather than the appointive council. These changes were too democratic for the conservative and aristocratic element; but when the next elections showed a majority of the people favorable to the reform, and after the popular party had blocked an appropriation bill, the conservatives yielded. Even then Edward Rutledge and Arthur Middleton resigned the governorship rather than approve the changes. Maryland, too, modified her constitution in favor of Quakers, Mennonists, and other minor religious groups. Jefferson, Madison, and Richard Henry Lee succeeded in securing

---

[7] George Sidney Camp, *Democracy* (New York, 1841), 155. Harper and Brothers were so anxious to spread the influence of this first general analysis of the principles of democracy by a native American that they brought it out in their Family Library.

the disestablishment of the Episcopal Church in Virginia by legislative enactment.

South Carolina amended her constitution and joined Georgia and North Carolina in prohibiting entails and primogeniture. While no change was made in the Virginia constitution, the democratic element led by Jefferson forced measures through the legislature in 1786 abolishing entails and primogeniture. Jefferson believed that this legislation formed part of a system by which "every fibre would be eradicated of ancient or future aristocracy and a foundation laid for a government truly republican." The Virginia aristocracy never forgave him for this action.

The aristocracy made some slight concessions to the democrats in regard to suffrage and representation. South Carolina reduced the property requirements for voting from one hundred to fifty acres of land, and Georgia reduced it from ten pounds to the payment of all taxes levied by the state. Both states reduced considerably the property qualifications for office holding. And the up-country counties, inhabited largely by small farmers, were given a more nearly equal share of representation in the state legislatures. All efforts at change in these particulars failed in Maryland, Virginia, and North Carolina. In spite of the concessions granted, the conservative aristocracy was still in control of all five of the original southern states at the close of the eighteenth century.

The constitutions of the two new southern states added to the Union during this period of readjustment, Kentucky and Tennessee, show some influence of the frontier ideals of democracy. Kentucky gave the suffrage in 1792 to all free adult male citizens, but limited it to free white males in 1799. Representation was apportioned to free adult male inhabitants in 1792, and to qualified electors in 1799. No property or religious qualifications for office were prescribed, and the governor, after 1799, was to be elected by popular vote rather than indirectly by an electoral college as in 1792. Tennessee showed somewhat more aristocratic leanings in her constitution of 1796. Suffrage was limited to freemen possessed of a freehold; legislators and the governor were required to possess freeholds of two hundred and five hundred acres of land, respectively; representation was apportioned to the counties according to taxable inhabitants; and no person who denied the existence of God was eligible for any civil office. Though somewhat more democratic than the seaboard states, Tennessee nevertheless belongs with the group of older states controlled by the landed aristocracy. It should be pointed out, however, that in all these states there was much cheap land to be had; hence, it was no great burden to qualify for voting in any of these states.

The political revolution of 1800 which brought Jefferson and his party to power in most of the southern states, as well as in the federal government, led to the demand that the principles of the bills of rights be translated into realistic democracy rather than to stand as mere glittering generalities. In every state, democratic leaders condemned the discrimination made between those who had property and those who had none. They declared that where property had representation the people could not be free; and they were able to show that under the existing system of representation a minority of wealthy men of the east had absolute control of the state governments. They appealed to the philosophy of natural rights and demanded equality of political rights and privileges. This movement came largely from the small farmer or yeoman class concentrated in the newer counties of the up-country or the western parts of the states; hence it took on something of the nature of an intrastate sectional fight. It naturally involved social and economic issues as well as political rights.

The rapid settlement of the piedmont and mountain region of these states in the first quarter of the nineteenth century gave to the up-country a majority of the white population. These small farmers had somewhat different interests from the low-country planters. They desired internal improvements—roads, canals, and railroads—at state expense, in order that they might have an economic outlet for their farm produce, cattle, and domestic manufactures. A supporter of reform predicted that if the westerners were given their way roads and canals would be built, domestic manufactures would increase, wealth would multiply, and that the "Old Families . . . imbecile and incorrigible," would be replaced by a "happy, bold and intelligent middle class."[8] But the legislatures were controlled by the planter aristocracy of the east, who feared heavier taxation if the western farmers were given equal representation and resisted all change.

The yeoman farmers were joined by a small class of industrial laborers of the eastern cities. These people were smarting under the provisions of the constitutions that required a freehold for voting just as the yeoman farmers were smarting under the unequal system of representation. The laborers demanded manhood suffrage. The aristocratic planters feared to grant their demands lest the laborers join the small farmers in taxing the wealth of the east.

The democratic reformers demanded conventions fresh from the people with power to rewrite completely the constitutions. But since most of the constitutions left it to the legislature or made no provision for calling a constituent assembly, and since the aristocracy with their control over the legislatures could prevent a call through that body, the democrats were blocked at the very threshold of reform. The aristocratic minority fought doggedly to maintain its favored position, contesting every move of the democrats, and yielding only in the face of an open revolt. In Maryland they permitted a series of amendments between 1805 and 1810 that brought reorganiza-

---

[8] *Niles' Register* (Baltimore, 1811–1849), XXXVII (1829), 145.

tion of the judicial system so as to bring justice closer to the people and make the courts more expeditious and less expensive. Property qualifications for officers were swept away; the suffrage was extended to adult white males, the written ballot was required, and the plural vote was abolished; and some minor officials were made elective. In South Carolina representation was reapportioned in the house on the basis of white inhabitants and taxes combined. By this method the large slaveholding districts and parishes lost some of their representatives as allotted under the earlier constitutions. Suffrage was extended to include all white adult males who had resided in the state two years and were possessed of a freehold of fifty acres or a town lot, or who, if possessed of neither, had lived six months in the election district. This in reality meant white manhood suffrage. A series of amendments in Georgia between 1808 and 1824 made all officers from constable to governor, including judges of all the courts, elective by popular vote. These changes looked toward a greater participation in governmental affairs by the people and made the governments more responsive to the public will but, except in South Carolina, they did not appease the democratic reform spirit. The conservatives had prevented any change in North Carolina and Virginia.

Four new southern states, Louisiana, Mississippi, Alabama, and Missouri, were admitted to the Union during these years. Louisiana, admitted in 1812, fell to the control of the landed aristocracy. Only free white males were permitted to vote, and they were required to pay a state tax before qualifying. Members of the legislature and the governor were required to possess freeholds ranging in value from five hundred to five thousand dollars. Representation was apportioned according to qualified voters, or property holders. The governor and other officers were chosen by popular vote. Mississippi, too, was controlled by property holders. All officers were elected by popular vote; voting was limited to free white males who were enrolled in the militia or paid a tax; representation was based on white population; but members of the legislature and the governor were required to possess land ranging from fifty to six hundred acres, or real estate ranging in value from five hundred to two thousand dollars. Alabama greatly broadened the base of political power. Suffrage was granted to all adult white male citizens; no property qualifications were required for state officials who were elected by popular vote; and representation was according to white inhabitants. Both Mississippi and Alabama declared that freemen only were possessed of equal rights. Missouri required no property qualifications for voting or office holding, though members of the legislature must pay taxes. Only whites could vote, and representation was based on free white male inhabitants.

Thwarted by the aristocratic minority in calling legitimate conventions, the democratic majority in the old states now threatened to take the matter in their own hands and call extra-legal conventions. Mass meetings were held in Georgia, North Carolina, Virginia, and Maryland; polls were conducted in various counties, all of which voted overwhelmingly for calling conventions; grand jury presentments called attention to the need for reform and recommended direct action if the legislatures failed to act; the voters in many counties instructed their representatives in the legislature to support a bill calling a constitutional convention; and hundreds of petitions went to the legislatures demanding relief. Typical of the sentiment for calling extra-legal conventions is the statement of a North Carolinian that if the legislature failed "to comply with the wishes of a great majority of the State," then "A convention will be assembled in the west, and the constitution amended without the concurrence of the east; and this being the act of a majority, and the legal act, will consequently be obligatory on the whole State. The constitution *will be amended.*"[9]

A statewide reform convention assembled at Milledgeville, Georgia, on May 10, 1832, and issued a call for an election of delegates to a convention to meet at the capital in February, 1833, to alter, revise, or amend the constitution, or write a new one. It issued an address to the people in which it declared "that the people have an undoubted right, in their sovereign capacity, to alter or change their form of government, whenever in their opinion it becomes too obnoxious or oppressive to be borne. That crisis . . . has arrived, when the people should assert their rights, and boldly and fearlessly maintain them."[10] The legislature now capitulated and called a convention to meet at the same time and place as that called extra-legally. Comparable action took place in Maryland in 1836, but the legislature passed a series of amendments similar to those proposed by the reform convention and forestalled extra-legal action. In like manner the legislatures of Virginia and North Carolina capitulated to the reform party, and submitted the question of a "Convention or No Convention" to the voters. In both states the call was adopted by large majorities. Mississippi and Tennessee, too, at the demand of the people, called conventions to revise their constitutions. This was one of the most signal victories for majority or popular rule in American history. In these states the people without political voice had, by threat of appeal to numerical majority action, forced the landed aristocracy who possessed the legitimate and constitutional political power to submit the fundamental law to the scrutiny and revision of delegates elected from the people for that purpose alone.

Democracy had won a victory over aristocracy. The people had compelled the wealthy planter class in control of the legislatures to call conventions to revise the fundamental law of the states. Majority rule had

[9] Salisbury *Western Carolinian,* July 17, 1821.
[10] Milledgeville *Southern Recorder,* May 31, 1832.

exerted its power and justified its right. One democratic spokesman declared that the freemen had united their forces "to break to pieces the trammels of aristocracy, and show to the enemies of republican equality that the sons of freemen will still be free."[11]

John C. Calhoun, Abel P. Upshur,[12] and other aristocratic leaders of the South openly denied the Jeffersonian ideal of equality of all men and bitterly condemned majority rule as the tyranny of king numbers; and they had their supporters in the North among such men as James Kent, Joseph Story, and Orestes A. Brownson.[13] The less famous and little known leaders of democracy just as boldly proclaimed the doctrine of political equality. The views of the former have been given much attention by the historian; those of the latter have been generally ignored. The significant thing about the controversy, however, is that the views of the latter prevailed. The bills of rights remained unchanged and the majority forced the aristocracy to grant all white men an equal voice in the state governments. Charles James Faulkner, spokesman for the Virginia democracy in 1850, said that nothing short of a radical and fundamental change in the structure of the state constitution "could satisfy the progressive aspirations of a people who felt that their energies were held in subjugation by artificial restraints of republican freedom and equality." And, after the Virginia convention of 1850 had adjourned, he declared: "Its results was one of the proudest triumphs of popular government which the records of history attest. A revolution as decided in its results as any of those which for the last century have deluged the monarchies of Europe with blood, passed off under the influence of the acknowledged principles of popular supremacy as quietly and tranquilly as the most ordinary county election."[14]

The reform movement begun about 1800 now bore fruit in numerous constitutional conventions,[15] and these conventions rewrote the state constitutions in line with the ideals of Jacksonian democracy. Many writers have attributed the democratic reforms of the 1830's to the influence of the

[11] Salisbury *Western Carolinian*, October 22, 1822.

[12] *Proceedings and Debates of the Convention of Virginia* (Richmond, 1830), 68–71, and *passim*.

[13] For Brownson's opposition to majority rule, see his "Democracy and Liberty," in *United States Magazine and Democratic Review* (Washington, 1837–1859), XII (1843), 374–87, and his "Unpopular Government," *ibid.*, XII, 529–37.

[14] *United States Magazine and Democratic Review*, XLI (1858), 227–28.

[15] Conventions were held in Virginia in 1829–1830, Mississippi in 1832, Georgia in 1833 and 1839, Tennessee in 1834, North Carolina in 1835, and an abortive or revolutionary one in Maryland in 1836. There is a close parallel in the action of the northern states. Beginning with Connecticut in 1818, Massachusetts, New York, Delaware, Vermont, and Pennsylvania, all held general constitutional conventions by the end of the 1830's; and in Rhode Island there was an unconstitutional convention in 1842 that went beyond the extra-legal action in the southern states.

western frontier. A study of the movement in the southern states gives an emphatic denial to this assumption. The people of the southern states were cognizant of what was going on in the West, but the demands for reform grew out of local conditions and would have arisen had there been no "New West" beyond the Appalachians. In fact, it would be more nearly accurate to say that many of the ideas and motives of Jacksonian democracy were southern in origin.

To what extent was aristocracy weakened and democracy strengthened by the work of the conventions of the 1830's? In the first place, property qualifications for voting were abolished in all southern states except Virginia and North Carolina, and with Louisiana still requiring the payment of taxes.[16] The last of the religious restrictions were also abolished. In a similar manner property qualifications for office holding were wiped out except for South Carolina and Louisiana, and age and residence requirements were reduced. A large number of officers heretofore selected by the legislature or appointed by the governor were now elected by popular vote. These include civil and militia officers, justices of the peace, superior court judges, and governors in all the states except Virginia and South Carolina. Rotation in office was generally applied through short terms and restricted re-eligibility. Progress was also made in the equalization of representation. There was no uniformity in the states, however. Some used white population, some qualified voters, some federal population returns, and some a combination of population and taxation. Those states that had heretofore granted special borough representation abolished it.

In still another way these changes broadened the base of democracy. For the first time the people had been consulted as to the revision and amendment of their constitutions. The conventions were called directly or indirectly by action of the people. The revised constitutions were in turn submitted back to them for ratification or rejection. In at least one state the people twice rejected the changes, and forced the desired reforms through by legislative amendments. And the new constitutions provided for future amendment and revision.

In one matter there was a definite reactionary movement. This was the issue of free Negro suffrage. Virginia and North Carolina joined Maryland and Kentucky in taking from the free Negro the ballot he had heretofore possessed. In like manner all new states of the period, North as well as South, denied suffrage to free Negroes. The action of the old southern states was paralleled by that of the northern states. Delaware, Connecticut, New Jersey, and Pennsylvania took the ballot from the Negro. And New York

---

[16] Among northern states, New Jersey and Rhode Island retained property qualifications, and Connecticut, Massachusetts, Pennsylvania, and Ohio retained the tax paying requirement.

in 1821 limited Negro suffrage by requiring that he possess a freehold valued at two hundred fifty dollars over and above all indebtedness. Hence only five of the northern states granted equal suffrage to Negroes. Whether or not Jefferson, Mason, and other Revolutionary proponents of natural rights philosophy intended to include Negroes in the statement that "all men are created equal and endowed with certain unalienable rights" is a debatable question;[17] but in actual practice the American people had decided by their constitutional provisions that Negroes were not included in the *political people.* From the very day of the Declaration of Independence the race problem had caused the American people to make an exception to the doctrine that "all men are created equal." But the partial exclusion of the Negro from the promises of democracy did not impair the faith of the whites in those promises.

The influence of the democratic reforms of the Jacksonian period were far-reaching. Evidence of this is to be seen in many phases of southern life —social, intellectual, economic, and political. But the people were not satisfied with their partial victory, and the signs of progress only made them more determined to complete the democratization of their state governments. Their increased political power made the task of securing additional amendments and revision of their constitutions easier than had been that of calling the conventions of the 1830's. In the first case, they had threatened extra-legal action; in the second, they simply used the powers already possessed to put through additional reforms. This time they determined to take from the aristocratic class its last remnants of special political privileges. Important amendments in Georgia, Missouri, and North Carolina, and revision by convention in Louisiana, Kentucky, Maryland, and Virginia,[18] brought those states in line with the most democratic ones. Virginia in 1851 was the last state to provide for popular election of governor; and North Carolina in 1856 abolished the fifty-acre freehold required to vote for members of the state senate. The three new states, Arkansas, Florida, and Texas, all established complete equality of the whites in political affairs, and made all officials elective by popular vote. *The United States Magazine and Democratic Review,* analyzing the progress of constitutional reform in the nation, declared that the constitution of Louisiana showed "more political insight, and a more absolute reliance upon the principle upon which popular governments are based, than appears in the fundamental law of any other state in the Union." But the Missouri constitution "affords more

---

[17] Samuel E. Morison and Henry S. Commager, *The Growth of the American Republic,* 2 vols. (New York, 1937), I, 82, state that "Jefferson did not mean to include slaves as men."

[18] Louisiana in 1844 and 1852, Kentucky in 1849, and Maryland and Virginia in 1850.

efficient guarantees to individual rights, and leaves fewer opportunities for political corruption and for intercepting the fair expression of the wishes of the people" than that of any other state.

These changes left South Carolina the one remaining stronghold of the landed aristocracy in the South. While she had granted manhood suffrage in 1810, she continued to require her governor to possess a freehold until after the Civil War; the governor and presidential electors were chosen by the legislature; and representation was apportioned on a combination of white population and taxation. But among the northern states, Massachusetts continued to apportion representation in her senate on property until 1853; and Rhode Island continued to require voters and office holders to possess real estate valued at one hundred thirty-four dollars over and above all incumbrances, or with a rental value of seven dollars, until 1888.

The establishment of white manhood suffrage, the abolition of property qualifications for office holders, the election of all officers by popular vote, and the apportionment of representation on population rather than wealth, with periodic reapportionment, dealt a death blow to the political power of the landed, slaveholding aristocracy of the Old South. No longer could the members of that class dictate to the great majority of free white men. The aristocracy still had influence, as the wealthy merchant and industrialist of the northern states had influence, and as men of property in all times and places have influence, but they did not possess that influence because of special political privileges. Some southern planters possessed baronial wealth but this wealth no longer gave them political control. They constituted a social not a political aristocracy. "Such an aristocracy, although it may confer personal independence, cannot create political authority."[19]

If the landed aristocrat wished to sit in the seat of power and administer the affairs of state he must seek the support of the voter, his master. He must recognize every voter, however poor, as his political equal. And in the political hustings landlord and squatter, wealthy planter and poor white, did mingle as equals.[20]

The political revolution also meant that large numbers of the small farmer and yeoman classes began to enter politics, and win seats in legislature, Congress, and the governor's office. The first governor chosen by popular vote in Virginia, in 1851, was Joseph Johnson, whose childhood had been spent in abject poverty without the opportunity for formal schooling.

[19] Frederick Grimke, *Considerations upon the Nature and Tendency of Free Institutions* (Cincinnati, 1848), 311, 314; Camp, *Democracy,* 220–21.

[20] For descriptions of the equality of all classes at the polls, see Hamilton W. Pierson, *In the Bush; or, Old-Time Social, Political, and Religious Life in the Southwest* (New York, 1881), 131–46, and Lester B. Shippee (ed.), *Bishop Whipple's Southern Diary, 1843–1844* (Minneapolis, 1937), 22–23, 52.

Despite these handicaps he had served in the legislature and Congress, beating some of the most wealthy men of his district.[21] Indeed six of the eight men who served Virginia as governor in the years just prior to the Civil War came from the plain people; two began life as farm hands, one as a tailor, one as a mill hand, and another as a mail contractor. Henry County, Virginia, had the second highest percentage of large slaveholders in the state, yet only two justices of the peace, chosen between 1853 and 1858, possessed as many as ten slaves, while seven owned none and five owned only two each.[22]

Few studies of southern leadership have been made, but preliminary investigations suggest that a majority of the political leaders of the Old South between 1830 and 1860 came from the plain people rather than from the large planter class. Many such men received aid from wealthy planters to secure their education, as did George McDuffie and Alexander H. Stephens. The literary societies at the University of North Carolina paid all expenses of one "penniless student" each year. Several of these students rose to high rank in the state, one becoming a United States senator.[23] Dozens of the men who rank at the very top in political leadership began as poor boys, and became planters and men of wealth by their own efforts. Let one of these men tell his own story. "When I was a boy—a very little boy—an honest but poor man settled (squatted is a better word) in a country where I yet reside. . . . Day by day he might have been seen following his plough, while his two sons plied the hoe. . . . The younger [of the sons] studies law and . . . was drawn into politics. He was elected to the State Legislature, to Congress, Judge of the Circuit Court, Governor of his State, to Congress again and again, but he never forgot that he was a squatter's son. He stands before you today."[24] Like Albert Gallatin Brown, many of the leaders of the Old South grew up on the frontier where free men could not and did not recognize any political superior. In fact much of the South was only one generation removed from frontier society in 1860. Aristocracy takes more time to establish itself than one generation.

One test of the effectiveness of democracy is the exercise of the suffrage by those qualified to vote. The southern states met this test to about the same degree that the northern states did. There was considerable variation from state to state in both the North and the South, but the percentage of votes cast, according to the voting population, in the southern states ex-

[21] "Joseph Johnson," in *Southern Historical Magazine* (Charleston, W. Va., 1892), I (1892), 185–87.

[22] Gustavus W. Dyer, *Democracy in the South before the Civil War* (Nashville, 1905), 80–82.

[23] Kemp P. Battle, *Memories of an Old Time Tar Heel* (Chapel Hill, 1945), 93.

[24] Albert Gallatin Brown, *Speech of . . . in the House of Representatives* (Washington, 1852).

ceeded that of the North as often, and to about the same degree, as it failed to reach it. For instance, in the presidential election of 1828, Georgia with a white population of 296,806 cast 18,790 votes and Connecticut with a white population of 289,603 cast 18,277 votes; Alabama, however, with a white population of 190,406 cast 19,076 votes. Thus the vote of Georgia and Connecticut was 6.3 per cent of the voting people, but that of Alabama was 10.1 per cent. In the same election, Massachusetts with 603,351 free people cast 35,855 votes; Virginia with 694,300 whites cast 38,853 votes; but Tennessee with only 535,746 whites cast 46,330 votes. The percentages of these states were 5.9, 5.5, and 8.2, respectively. In the presidential election of 1860, Georgia with a white population of 595,088 cast 106,365 votes; Connecticut with 406,147 white people cast 77,146 votes; and Alabama with 529,121 whites cast 90,307 votes. The percentages for the three states were 18.0, 16.7, and 17.0, respectively. In this election, Massachusetts had 1,231,066 free people and cast 169,175 votes; Virginia had 1,105,453 whites and cast 167,223 votes; and Tennessee with 834,082 whites cast 145,333 votes. The percentages were 13.7, 15.1, and 17.4, respectively. A comparison of all the southern with all the northern states shows a white population of 7,614,018 casting 1,260,509 votes and 18,-736,849 people casting 3,369,134 votes, or a percentage of 16.6 for the South and 17.9 for the North. The western states gave the North the advantage in the over-all comparison. But if one uses adult white male population, which is more accurate for voting percentages, then the South had a percentage of 69.5 and the North of 69.7.[25]

The vote of the southern states was almost equally divided between the Whig and the Democratic parties in the presidential elections from 1836 to 1852 inclusive. In the five elections the total popular vote of the Whig candidates was 1,745,884, that of the Democratic candidates was 1,760,452, or a majority for the Democrats of only 14,568. The Whigs had a majority in three elections, but in 1836 it was only 1,862 votes and its biggest majority was in 1840 with 52,851. The Democratic majority in 1844 was only 23,766, and in 1852, when the Whigs were weakened by the Compromise issue, it was 79,690. There was a total of twenty-seven states in the Whig column and thirty-seven in the Democratic column for the five elections, but except for the election of 1852 there was no overwhelming majority for either party; and in 1848 the parties divided the states equally. Such an equal division of party strength prevented any one group from dominating

[25] White population is used as a basis for all these calculations except that free population is used for the six states that permitted Negroes to vote. South Carolina is excluded, since the presidential electors of that state were chosen by the legislature. Population figures are taken from the United States Census reports; the votes from Thomas H. McKee. *The National Conventions and Platforms of All Political Parties, 1789–1900; Convention, Popular, and Electoral Vote* (Baltimore, 1900).

the political situation in the South. The states were shifting back and forth between the two parties so rapidly that no one could hope to retain power long enough to consolidate party, much less planter class, control. This situation also enabled the southern states to exert popular control over the United States senators who were elected by the state legislatures. With party changes in the states the senators were often instructed by the legislature how to vote on major issues in Congress. While the purpose of instruction was partisan it nevertheless resulted in the senators being made responsible to the majority will as expressed in state elections for many senators voted according to instructions and others resigned rather than do so.

With the coming of manhood suffrage came the demand for popular education so that the voter might cast a more intelligent ballot. It was recognized that democracy and republicanism could work effectively only with an educated electorate. Since "The chief object of constitutions and laws" is "to render its citizens secure in their lives, liberty and prosperity," the importance of "a good education to each individual, to every community, and to the State, cannot be too highly valued," declared a report of the Louisiana constitutional convention of 1844.[26] Popular education, wrote James M. Garnett of Virginia, "is of most importance in all governments. But it is indispensable in ours where all political power emanates immediately from the people, who must be themselves both intelligent and virtuous, or it will rarely happen that their public functionaries will be any better than themselves."[27] Even the aristocratic element recognized the principle that they must now educate their masters, although many did not wish to support education by taxation. One of them declared "that in adopting universal suffrage, we took necessarily the consequences that would flow from it were any portion of the people ignorant and debased. . . . Without you enlighten the sources of political power, we shall have no government. . . . You have adopted the principle of universal suffrage, but the basis is public education."[28]

Recognizing the need every southern state, with the exception of South Carolina where a system of poor schools existed, provided for the establishment of a public school system of education before 1860. North Carolina led off in 1839; the question had first been submitted to popular vote and carried by a large majority. In some states, Louisiana for instance, the constitution required the legislature to provide a state system and to support it

---

[26] *Proceedings and Debates of the Convention of Louisiana, Which Assembled at the City of New Orleans, January 14, 1844* (New Orleans, 1845), 316–19.

[27] James M. Garnett, "Popular Education," in *Southern Literary Messenger* (Richmond, 1834–1864), VII (1842), 115.

[28] *Proceedings and Debates of the Convention of Louisiana* (1844), 909.

by taxation. All the states except Virginia and South Carolina provided for a state superintendent of public instruction; in most states the superintendent was elected by popular vote. The systems of public education in the southern states, in provisions for administration, support, and general results, compare favorably with those in the northern states in 1860.[29]

In like manner, popular control of southern state governments brought measures designed to minister to the economic wants of the people. In fact some leaders of democratic reform boldly proclaimed that this was one of the major purposes of government.[30] Boards of public works, popularly elected, were created to supervise internal improvements and to further the economic progress of the states. They were interested also in the public utilization of the natural resources of the states. Imprisonment for debt was prohibited; banks were brought under state control; provision was made for chartering corporations; monopolies were prohibited; and provisions were made for uniform and equal taxation of property according to value. All these measures were included in the state constitutions. The states, too, safeguarded the rights and interests of the unfortunate classes. State asylums for the insane and schools for the deaf, the dumb, and the blind were established at state expense.

The history of the southern state constitutions and governments from 1776 to 1860 reveals a progressive expansion in the application of the doctrine of political equality. By 1860 the aristocratic planter class had been shorn of its special privileges and political power. It still gave tone and color to political life but it no longer dominated and controlled the political order. On the other hand, the great mass of the whites had been given more and more authority, and majority rule had been definitely established. The interpretation of the southern states as "political aristocracies of the sternest and most odious kind" had no basis in fact. With the exceptions already noted the southern state governments were as democratic in 1860 as their northern sister states. They had not attained the ideal goal of absolute equality, but in spirit and administration as well as in form they had progressively become more and more concerned with the rights and interest of the people.

[29] Edgar W. Knight, *The Influence of Reconstruction on Education in the South* (New York, 1913), 94, 98.

[30] See, for instance, Charles J. Faulkner, "Speech," in *United States Magazine and Democratic Review*, XLI (1858), 218.

7

Who Were the Southern Whigs?

Charles G. Sellers, Jr.

The political reality of the Old South has proven as difficult to assess as the nature of its myth-bound social structure. The tendency has been to project the concept of a "solid South" back into the shadows of an antebellum Eden, and to argue that by 1830 the South found itself politically unified and indomitably resolved in opposition to the nationalistic, anti-slavery, capitalistic North. In the view of Charles G. Sellers, Jr., of the University of California, Berkeley, such a historical portrait has catered to what he aptly describes as "the myth of a monolithic South." Also to be corrected, says Professor Sellers, are the related assumptions of John C. Calhoun's pervasive political leadership after 1830, and the notion that the southern wing of the Whig party consistently aligned itself in support of the state rights position of the great planters. In attempting to redress these well-worn antebellum stereotypes, Mr. Sellers notes the vigorous two-party system which prevailed in the pre–Civil War South, and fashions an array of evidence clearly demonstrating that a correlation between the Whigs and the state rights position never in fact existed. Rather, the unifying strength of the Whig party, South as well as North, lay in the area of banking and financial policy. The major clientele of the Whig party comprised merchants, bankers, and lawyers. Planters, when members, were so for economic reasons, since the Whig party at no time either represented or articulated a blind devotion to state rights. It took more than the leadership of a John C. Calhoun for most southern Whigs to abandon their stance as economic capitalists.

From Charles G. Sellers, Jr., "Who Were the Southern Whigs?," *American Historical Review* (1954). Reprinted by permission of the author.

Students of the Old South have spent much of their time in recent years dispelling myths about the fabled land of moonlight and magnolias. Our understanding of the social, intellectual, and economic life of the ante-bellum South has been considerably revised and immeasurably widened by the work of a large number of able scholars.

Political history, however, has been unfashionable, and one of the results has been the survival of a series of myths about the political life of the South in the 1830's and 1840's. The key myth may be called the myth of a monolithic South: a section unified as early as the 1820's in its devotion to state rights doctrines and its hostility to the nationalistic, antislavery, capitalistic North. The result of approaching ante-bellum history by way of Fort Sumter and Appomattox, this point of view found its classic statements in the apologias of Jefferson Davis[1] and Alexander H. Stephens,[2] but it was made respectable in the first generation of professional scholarship by such historians as Herman Von Holst[3] and John W. Burgess.[4] It colored such early monographs as U. B. Phillips' "Georgia and State Rights"[5] and H. M. Wagstaff's *States Rights and Political Parties in North Carolina, 1776–1861,*[6] and is to be seen in most of the more recent works on the pre–Civil War South.[7] It has also given rise to the corollary myths that Cal-

---

[1] *The Rise and Fall of the Confederate Government,* 2 vols. (New York, 1881).

[2] *A Constitutional View of the Late War between the States,* 2 vols. (Philadelphia, 1868–70).

[3] *The Constitutional and Political History of the United States,* 8 vols. (Chicago, 1876–92).

[4] *The Middle Period, 1817–1858* (New York, 1905).

[5] *Annual Report of the American Historical Association,* 1901, II, 1–224.

[6] Johns Hopkins University Studies in Historical and Political Science, Series XXIV (1906), Nos. 7–8.

[7] See particularly Jesse T. Carpenter, *The South as a Conscious Minority, 1784–1861* (New York, 1930); Robert S. Cotterill, *The Old South* (Glendale, Calif., 1939); and Charles M. Wiltse, *John C. Calhoun,* 3 vols. (Indianapolis, 1944–51). Charles S. Sydnor, in what is, in many respects, the finest work on the ante-bellum South, presents a persuasive restatement of the traditional sectional–state rights interpretation. His chapter headings on politics from the Panic of 1819 to nullification describe a developing sectionalism: "From Economic Nationalism to Political Sectionalism," "End of the Virginia Dynasty," "The Lower South Adopts State Rights," and "Bold Acts and Bolder Thoughts." The 1830's and 1840's, however, present a paradox. Professor Sydnor finds a growing "Regionalism in Mind and Spirit," but a "decline of sectionalism in politics." This he explains as a result of the fact that "major Southern hopes and fears found no champion in either party," so that "party conflict south of the Potomac . . . had the hollow sound of a stage duel with tin swords." "The agrarian South felt little interest," writes Professor Sydnor, in that conflict between the "wealthier and more conservative segments of society" and the liberal, democratic elements "which formed a major issue between the Democratic and Whig parties" in the nation as a whole. *The Development of Southern Sectionalism, 1819–1848* (Baton Rouge, 1948), especially p. 316. Notable for their freedom from overemphasis on sectionalism are Thomas P. Abernethy, *From Frontier to Plantation in Tennessee: A Study in Frontier Democracy* (Chapel Hill, 1932); and Roger W. Shugg, *Origins of Class Struggle in Louisiana* (University, La., 1939).

houn was the representative spokesman and political leader of the South after about 1830, and that the Whig party in the South mainly reflected the state rights proclivities of the great planters.

These myths have been strengthened by Frederick Jackson Turner's sectional analysis of our early national history. Turner's approach has been extremely fruitful, but its sweeping application has tended to exaggerate differing sectional tendencies into absolute sectional differences. The application of geographic sectionalism to individual states, moreover, has fostered the further myth that political strife within the Old South was confined largely to struggles over intrastate sectional issues between upcountry and low country, hill country and "black belt."[8]

All of these myths have some basis in fact. They are, however, the product of a misplaced emphasis which has permeated nearly all the studies of pre–Civil War southern politics. Sectionalism and state rights have been made the central themes of southern political history for almost the entire ante-bellum period. Southern opposition to nationalistic legislation by Congress has been overemphasized. And the social, economic, and ideological lines of political cleavage within the slave states have been obscured. The early history of the Whig party below Mason and Dixon's line shows the character of these distortions.

It is too often forgotten that in the ante-bellum period the South had a vigorous two-party system, an asset it has never since enjoyed. Until at least the later 1840's, the voting southerner was much more interested in the success of his own party and its policies than in banding together with southerners of the opposite party to defend the Constitution and southern rights against invasion by the North. The parties were evenly matched, and elections were bitterly contested. It was rare for any southern state to be regarded as absolutely safe for either party. Of the 425,629 votes cast in the slave states at the election of 1836, the Whigs had a majority of only 243 popular votes. In this and the three succeeding presidential elections, a total of 2,745,171 votes were cast, but the over-all margin, again in favor of the Whigs, was only 66,295, or 2.4 per cent of the total votes. In these four elections the Whigs carried a total of twenty-seven southern states and the Democrats twenty-six.[9]

An equally close rivalry is evident in congressional representation. In the five congressional elections between 1832 and 1842, southern Democrats won an aggregate total of 234 seats, while their opponents captured 263. Whigs predominated among southern representatives in three of these five

[8] See especially William A. Schaper, "Sectionalism and Representation in South Carolina," *Annual Report of the American Historical Association,* 1900, I, 237–463; and Charles H. Ambler, *Sectionalism in Virginia from 1776 to 1861* (Chicago, 1910).

[9] Edward Stanwood, *A History of the Presidency* (Boston, 1898), pp. 185–88, 203–204, 223, 243. *Cf.* Fletcher M. Green, "Democracy in the Old South," *Journal of Southern History,* XII (1946), 20–21.

Congresses, and Democrats in two. In three of them the margin between the southern wings of the parties was five or less.[10] We have then a picture of keen political competition, with a vigorous Whig party maintaining a slight ascendancy.

What did this Whig party stand for? The pioneer account of the southern Whigs was the essay by U. B. Phillips which, significantly, appeared in the *Festschrift* to Frederick Jackson Turner.[11] This study shows Phillips' characteristic tendency to generalize about the entire South on the basis of conditions in his native Georgia. "The great central body of southern Whigs," he declares, "were the cotton producers, who were first state-rights men pure and simple and joined the Whigs from a sense of outrage at Jackson's threat of coercing South Carolina."[12]

Two years after Phillips' essay appeared, Arthur C. Cole published his exhaustive monograph on *The Whig Party in the South*.[13] Less than a third of the Cole volume is concerned with the period before 1844, when Whiggery was of greatest importance in the South, and he generally follows the Phillips interpretation of its origins. His account of the birth of the party devotes three pages to early National Republicanism in the South, twenty to the anti-Jackson sentiment aroused during the nullification crisis, and only four and a half to the fight over the national bank and financial policy.[14] "Various interests," he says, "linked in political alliance with the few

[10] Party affiliations of members of Congress have been determined largely from election returns in *Niles' Register* up to 1837, and from the *Whig Almanac* for the subsequent years. These sources have been supplemented by information from: *A Biographical Congressional Directory* (Washington, 1913); Charles H. Ambler, "Virginia and the Presidential Succession, 1840–1844," in *Essays in American History Dedicated to Frederick Jackson Turner* (New York, 1910), pp. 165–202; Ambler, *Sectionalism in Virginia;* Henry H. Simms, *The Rise of the Whigs in Virginia, 1824–1840* (Richmond, 1929); J. G. de Roulhac Hamilton, *Party Politics in North Carolina, 1835–1860,* James Sprunt Historical Publications, XV (1916); Clifford C. Norton, *The Democratic Party in Ante-Bellum North Carolina, 1835–1861,* James Sprunt Historical Studies, XXI (1930); Phillips, "Georgia and State Rights," *loc. cit.;* Paul Murray, *The Whig Party in Georgia, 1825–1853,* James Sprunt Studies in History and Political Science, XXIX (1948); Theodore H. Jack, *Sectionalism and Party Politics in Alabama, 1819–1842* (Menasha, Wis., 1919); Cleo Hearon, "Nullification in Mississippi," *Mississippi Historical Society Publications,* XII (1912), 37–71; James E. Winston, "The Mississippi Whigs and the Tariff, 1834–1844," *Mississippi Valley Historical Review,* XXII (1937), 505–24; James B. Ranck, *Alfred Gallatin Brown: Radical Southern Nationalist* (New York, 1937); Joseph G. Tregle Jr., "Louisiana and the Tariff, 1816–1846," *Louisiana Historical Quarterly,* XXV (1942), 24–148; and Wendell H. Stephenson, *Alexander Porter: Whig Planter of Old Louisiana* (Baton Rouge, 1934).

[11] "The Southern Whigs, 1834–1854," *Essays in American History Dedicated to Frederick Jackson Turner,* pp. 203–29.

[12] *Ibid.,* p. 209.

[13] Washington, 1913.

[14] Cole, pp. 2–30.

southerners whose interests and inclinations led to the support of latitud-
inarian principles, a still larger faction made up of those who supported
constitutional doctrines on the opposite extreme and whose logical interests
seemed to point against such an affiliation."[15]

An analysis, however, of the record of the Twenty-second Congress
(1831–1833) leads to somewhat different conclusions. It was this Congress
which dealt with the tariff, nullification, and national bank questions, and it
was during this Congress that the groundwork for the Whig party was laid.
Of the ninety southerners in the House of Representatives, sixty-nine had
been elected as supporters of Andrew Jackson, while twenty-one, nearly a
fourth, were National Republicans. Of the sixty-nine Democrats, twenty-
five were subsequently active in the Whig party. Eighteen of the latter were
state rights Whigs, while seven were not identified with the state rights wing
of the opposition. These twenty-five men then, together with the twenty-one
National Republicans, may be regarded as representative of the groups
which formed the Whig party in the South.[16]

These incipient Whigs voted twenty-four to twenty-one in favor of the
tariff of 1832, a measure denounced by state rights men and nullified by
South Carolina.[17] They also voted twenty-four to nineteen for the Force
Bill, which was designed to throttle the nullifiers.[18] This backing of administration measures was hardly a portent of an opposition state rights party.
The real harbinger of Whiggery was the vote on the national bank bill,
which this group supported twenty-seven to seventeen.[19]

The Whig party actually took shape during the Twenty-third Congress
(1833–1835), in which it gained the allegiance of fifty-two of the ninety-
nine southern members of the House. They voted twenty-nine to sixteen in
favor of rechartering the national bank[20] and unanimously in favor of restoring the government deposits to Biddle's institution.[21] By a closer vote of
twenty-two to twenty they supported repairing and extending the Cumber-
land Road.[22] In the Twenty-fourth Congress (1835–1837) the forty-eight
Whig Representatives from the South divided thirty-eight to three in favor

---

[15] *Ibid.,* p. 2. E. Malcolm Carroll, in his scholarly *Origins of the Whig Party* (Durham, N. C., 1925), pays almost no attention to the southern states and follows Cole
where southern developments have to be mentioned. In his one general statement
about the southern Whigs, he takes the position that they were men of property,
who turned instinctively to an association with northerners of similarly conservative
interests. *Ibid.,* pp. 190–91.

[16] See note 10 above.

[17] *House Journal,* 22 Congress, 1 session, pp. 1023–24.

[18] *House Journal,* 22 Cong., 2 sess., pp. 453–54.

[19] *Register of Debates,* 22 Cong., 1 sess., p. 3852.

[20] *House Journal,* 23 Cong., 1 sess., pp. 483–85.

[21] *Ibid.,* pp. 485–86.

[22] *Ibid.,* pp. 758–59.

of Clay's bill to distribute the proceeds from sales of public lands to the states.[23] Other votes showing similar tendencies might be cited, but enough has been said to suggest that, even in the beginning, a majority of southern anti-Jackson men were far from being state rights doctrinaires.

In the light of this record it is not so surprising that only a handful of southern Whigs followed Calhoun when he marched his supporters back into the Democratic household during Van Buren's administration.[24] The record also prepares one for the increasing manifestations of nationalism among southern Whigs which Phillips and Cole found so difficult to explain.[25] The southern wing of the party backed Clay almost unanimously for the Presidential nomination in 1840.[26] Tyler's nomination for Vice President was more a sop to the disappointed Clay men, of whom Tyler was one, than a concession to the state rights proclivities of southern Whiggery, the reason usually given for his choice.[27]

[23] *House Journal,* 24 Cong., 1 sess., pp. 1023–24.

[24] Senator William C. Preston and Representative Waddy Thompson of South Carolina refused to leave the Whig party with Calhoun, and three other Representatives from the state took the Conservative, or anti-Subtreasury, position. Outside his own state Calhoun carried with him only seven members of Congress: Dixon H. Lewis of Alabama; Edward J. Black, Walter T. Colquitt, and Mark A. Cooper, of Georgia (in 1839–40); Samuel T. Sawyer and Charles Shepard of North Carolina; and Robert M. T. Hunter of Virginia (in 1839–41). The Georgia apostates were defeated for the next Congress by the regular Whigs, who made a clean sweep of the congressional elections under the general ticket system. In North Carolina Sawyer was displaced by a loyal Whig at the next election, and Shepard met the same fate two years later. In the Presidential election of 1840 the southern Whigs, far from being weakened, had a majority of 58,675, as compared with 243 four years earlier. See Murray, *Whig Party in Georgia,* pp. 90–95; Hamilton, *Party Politics in North Carolina,* pp. 55, 79; Stanwood, *History of the Presidency,* pp. 165–203.

[25] Phillips, "The Southern Whigs," *loc. cit.,* pp. 216–17; Cole, *Whig Party in the South,* pp. 65–89.

[26] Cole, pp. 53–54.

[27] George R. Poage, *Henry Clay and the Whig Party* (Chapel Hill, 1936), pp. 13, 34–35. Tyler's most recent biographer, Oliver P. Chitwood, maintains that "Tyler was given the second place on the ticket mainly because he was from the South and had been a strong advocate of States' rights," or, in another passage, that "he was put up partly to placate the Clay faction but mainly to satisfy the States' right element of the Whig party." Chitwood bases his position on the ground that it "is the explanation usually given." *John Tyler, Champion of the Old South* (New York, 1939), pp. 172, 194. In taking this position, Chitwood has to discount completely Henry A. Wise's story of an arrangement with Clay leaders in 1839, whereby Tyler was to withdraw as a competitor with W. C. Rives for the Senate but was to receive the Vice Presidential nomination. Chitwood is probably correct in denying that Tyler himself had any part in such an understanding, but he fails to explain why Tyler was expected to be Clay's running mate before the convention met and why the Clay men were so confident of their ability to control Tyler just after he succeeded Harrison. *Ibid.,* pp. 172–73, 210, 215. Chitwood also finds it necessary to try to disprove persistent reports that Tyler intimated during the campaign that he was friendly to a national bank. It cannot be denied that his campaign statements were highly equivocal. *Ibid.,*

The nature of southern Whiggery had its real test when Tyler challenged Clay for leadership of the party. Of the fifty-five southern Whigs in the lower house of the Twenty-seventh Congress (1841–1843), only three stuck by the Virginia President and his state rights principles, whereas Mangum of North Carolina presided over the caucus which read Tyler out of the party, and southern Whig editors joined in castigating him unmercifully.[28] Southern Whigs supported Clay's legislative program—repeal of the Subtreasury, a national bank, distribution, and tariff—by large majorities.[29] Even the Georgians, Berrien, Toombs, and Stephens, defended the protective features of the tariff of 1842.[30]

Having said so much to the point that the Whig party in the South did not begin as and did not become a state rights party, it is necessary to add that neither was it consciously nationalistic. State rights versus nationalism simply was not the main issue in southern politics in this period. It is readily apparent from the newspapers and correspondence of the time that, except for Calhoun and his single-minded little band, politicians in the South were fighting over the same questions that were agitating the North —mainly questions of banking and financial policy.

It is hard to exaggerate the importance of the banking question. State and federal governments, by their policy in this sphere, could cause inflation or deflation, make capital easy or difficult to obtain, and facilitate or hinder the marketing of staple crops and commercial activity generally. And by chartering or refusing to charter banks, they could afford or deny to the capitalists of the day the most profitable field of activity the economy offered.

The banking issue is the key to an understanding of southern as well as northern Whiggery. Merchants and bankers were most directly concerned in financial policy, but their community of interest generally included the other business and professional men of the towns, especially the lawyers, who got most of their fees from merchants, and the newspaper editors, who were dependent on the merchants for advertising revenues. The crucial

---

pp. 188–94, 171–77. On one occasion Tyler endorsed Harrison's contention that "There is not in the Constitution any express grant of power for such purpose [a national bank], and it could never be constitutional to exercise the power, save in the event the power granted to Congress could not be carried into effect without resorting to such an institution." *Ibid.*, p. 190.

[28] Cole, pp. 92–93.

[29] Southern Whigs in the House voted forty-four to four in favor of Clay's original bank bill. *House Journal*, 27 Cong., 1 sess., pp. 409–10. They supported the tariff of 1842 by a vote of twenty-nine to eleven. *House Journal*, 27 Cong., 2 sess., pp. 1440–41.

[30] Murray, *Whig Party in Georgia*, p. 109; Rudolph Von Abele, *Alexander H. Stephens* (New York, 1946), pp. 86–87.

point for southern politics, however, is that the large staple producers were also closely identified economically with the urban commercial groups.[31] These were the principal elements which went into the Whig party.

The Whigs generally defended the national bank until its doom was sealed, then advocated a liberal chartering of commercial banks by the states, and finally, after the Panic of 1837, demanded a new national bank. The Democrats fought Biddle's institution and either favored state-operated banks to provide small loans for farmers, as distinguished from commercial banks, or tried to regulate banking strictly or abolish it altogether.[32]

Much of the misunderstanding about the Whig party in the South may be traced to the technique of plotting election returns on maps. Such maps tell us much, but they may also mislead. They show, for example, that the "black belts" of the lower South were the great centers of Whig strength. This has led scholars to reason: (1) that the Whig party was a planters' party *par excellence,* (2) that planters were necessarily rigid state rights men, and (3) that the Whig party was, therefore, a state rights party. *Q. E. D.!*

What the maps do not illustrate, however, is the dynamics of the political situation—the elements of leadership, impetus, financing, and propaganda, which are the real sinews of a political organization. In the case of the Whig party, these elements were furnished mainly by the commercial groups of the cities and towns, with their allied lawyers and editors. Lawyers were the practicing politicians for both parties, but the greater incidence of lawyers among the Whigs is an indication of the commercial affiliations of the party. Seventy-four percent of the southern Whigs who sat in Congress from 1833 to 1843 are identified as practicing attorneys, as compared with fifty-five percent of the Democrats.[33] In the lower house of the Ten-

[31] Ralph C. H. Catterall, *The Second Bank of the United States* (Chicago, 1903), pp. 140–44; Thomas P. Abernethy, "The Early Development of Commerce and Banking in Tennessee," *Mississippi Valley Historical Review,* XIV (1927), 316–19; Thomas P. Govan, "Banking and the Credit System in Georgia, 1810–1860," *Journal of Southern History,* IV (1938), 164, 178–84.

[32] Charles H. Ambler, *Thomas Ritchie: A Study in Virginia Politics* (Richmond, 1913), pp. 176–78; Ambler, *Sectionalism in Virginia,* pp. 237–39; George T. Starnes, *Sixty Years of Branch Banking in Virginia* (New York, 1931), pp. 71–103; William K. Boyd, *The Federal Period, 1783–1860,* Vol. II of *History of North Carolina* (Chicago, 1919), pp. 274–75; Norton, *Democratic Party in North Carolina,* pp. 54–59, 188–92; Hamilton, *Party Politics in North Carolina,* pp. 80, 88; Govan, "Banking in Georgia," *loc. cit.,* pp. 164–84; Jack, *Sectionalism in Alabama,* pp. 61–63; William O. Scroggs, "Pioneer Banking in Alabama," in *Facts and Factors in Economic History: Articles by Former Students of Edwin Francis Gay* (Cambridge, Mass., 1932), pp. 421–23; Abernethy, "Banking in Tennessee," *loc. cit.,* 321–24; Eugene I. McCormac, *James K. Polk: A Political Biography* (Berkeley, 1922), pp. 88, 169–70, 190; Shugg, *Class Struggle in Louisiana,* pp. 134–38.

[33] Based on vocational identification in *Biographical Congressional Directory.*

nessee legislature of 1839, farmers predominated, but a fourth of the Whigs were lawyers, as compared with only a tenth of the Democratic membership.[34]

The size and importance of the urban middle class in the Old South has yet to be fully appreciated. As early as 1831, Nashville, for example, contained twenty-two wholesale houses and seventy-seven retail stores, not to mention numerous other businesses, such as the sixty taverns and tippling houses.[35] Even the little county seat town of Gallatin, Tennessee, boasted in 1840 ten mercantile firms, a grocer, a merchant tailor, three hotels, five lawyers, five doctors, a paper and grist mill, and eighteen artisans' establishments of one kind or another.[36]

Businessmen dominated the towns socially, economically, and politically, and the towns dominated the countryside.[37] This was particularly true of the "black belts" of the lower South, since the great cotton capitalists of this region were especially dependent on commercial and credit facilities for financing and carrying on their extensive planting operations.[38] In recognition of the urban influence on politics, congressional districts were commonly known by the names of the principal towns in each—as, for example, the Huntsville, Florence, Tuscaloosa, Montgomery, and Mobile districts in Alabama.

Other evidence points in the same direction. A large majority of the stockholders in Virginia banks in 1837 lived in the areas of heaviest Whig voting. The principal commercial towns of the state—Richmond, Petersburg, and Norfolk—gave unbroken Whig majorities throughout the period 1834–1840.[39] In North Carolina twenty of the twenty-one directors of the

[34] Vocational identification from "List of Members of the House of Representatives of the Tennessee Legislature," broadside (Nashville, 1839). Party affiliations from a memorandum by James K. Polk in the Polk Papers (Library of Congress), First Series, placed at end of November, 1839.

[35] Nashville *Republican and State Gazette,* Oct. 20, 1831.

[36] Gallatin *Republican Sentinel,* Jan. 28, 1840.

[37] Lewis E. Atherton, *The Southern Country Store, 1800–1860* (Baton Rouge, 1949), especially pp. 191–92. This study is of great significance in indicating the importance of commercial interests and of even the smaller interior merchant in the life of the ante-bellum South. Atherton does not deal with the political activities of merchants in this volume, but in a similar study for Illinois, Missouri, and Iowa, he found the merchants active in politics. Seventy per cent of a sample for whom political affiliation could be determined were Whigs. *The Pioneer Merchant in Middle America,* University of Missouri Studies, XIV (1939), No. 2, pp. 23–26.

[38] Clanton W. Williams, "Early Ante-Bellum Montgomery: A Black-Belt Constituency," *Journal of Southern History,* VII (1941), 510–11, 515; Shugg, *Class Struggle in Louisiana,* p. 138; Stephenson, *Alexander Porter,* pp. 33–35; J. Carlyle Sitterson, "Financing and Marketing the Sugar Crop of the Old South," *Journal of Southern History,* X (1944), 188–99.

[39] Simms, *Whigs in Virginia,* pp. 13, 167–92.

two principal banks in 1840 were Whigs.[40] The first Whig governor of North Carolina was a railroad president; the second was a lawyer, cotton manufacturer, and railroad president; and the third was one of the wealthiest lawyers in the state.[41]

Similar party leadership obtained elsewhere. In Virginia, younger men of the type of John Minor Botts of Richmond and Alexander H. H. Stuart of Staunton actually directed the party of which Tyler and Tazewell were nominal leaders. Senators George A. Waggaman and Judah P. Benjamin were typical of the New Orleans lawyers who guided Louisiana Whiggery. Poindexter and Prentiss in Mississippi were intimately associated both personally and financially with the bankers and businessmen of Natchez. The Tennessee Whigs were led by John Bell, Nashville lawyer and iron manufacturer, who had married into the state's leading mercantile and banking house; Ephraim H. Foster, bank director and Nashville's most prominent commercial lawyer; and Hugh Lawson White, Knoxville lawyer, judge, and bank president.[42]

This commercial bias of the Whig party did much to pave the way for the industrial development of the South after the Civil War. It was no accident that former Whigs provided a large part of the leadership for the business-minded Conservative-Democratic parties which "redeemed" the South from Republican rule and then proceeded to make the conquered section over in the image of the victorious North, often in the interest of northern capital.[43]

Commercial considerations and the banking question did not, of course, determine political alignments in the Old South by themselves. Pro-tariff sentiment made for Whiggery among the sugar planters of Louisana, the

[40] Boyd, *Federal Period,* p. 274.

[41] Hamilton, *Party Politics in North Carolina,* pp. 36, 57, 92–94.

[42] Lawyers provided much of the leadership for the Democratic party also, but they tended to be from the smaller towns rather than the big commercial centers—as, for example, James K. Polk, Cave Johnson, and Aaron V. Brown, in Tennessee. There were also a goodly number of "Democrats by trade"—men like James K. Polk's merchant-banker-mail contractor brother-in-law, James Walker—who were active in Democratic politics for personal profit. The top Whig leadership, however, contained few men of the decidedly noncommercial backgrounds of such Democrats as Andrew Johnson, the Greenville tailor; Bedford Brown, the upcountry small planter who inherited Nathaniel Macon's mantle in North Carolina; Richard M. Johnson, the ebullient Tecumseh-slayer, who continued to wait on customers in his Great Crossings inn while Vice President of the United States; David Hubbard, the self-educated carpenter who championed the poor whites of northern Alabama; Franklin E. Plummer, the picturesque loco-foco from the piney woods of eastern Mississippi; and General Solomon W. Downs, who led the "Red River Democracy" of northern Louisiana in the fights for suffrage extension and bank reform. Davy Crockett was, of course, the exception among the Whigs that proved the rule.

[43] C. Vann Woodward, *Origins of the New South, 1877–1913* (Baton Rouge, 1951), pp. 1–50.

hemp growers of Kentucky, and the salt and iron manufacturers of western Virginia and Maryland. The more liberal policy of the Whigs toward internal improvements by both the state and federal governments won them support in landlocked interior sections and along the routes of projected transportation projects. And the fact that the Democrats generally championed a broadened suffrage, apportionment of congressional and legislative seats on the basis of white population, and other measures for extending political democracy, inclined propertied and conservative men to rally to the Whig party as a bulwark against mobocracy.

These factors, however, merely reinforced the commercial nature of southern Whiggery. The business orientation of the Whigs and the relative unimportance of their state rights wing become quite apparent if the party is described as it actually developed in the various states, rather than on the basis of general assumptions about southern politics.

A state by state analysis would indicate that, in the four border slave states and Louisiana, Whiggery was simply National Republicanism continued under a new name. The National Republicans were also strong in Virginia, but here they were joined in opposition to the Democrats by a body of state rights men alienated from Jackson by his attitude toward nullification. The National Republican and commercial wing of the party, however, was the dominant one, especially after the business-minded Conservative Democrats joined the Whigs on the Subtreasury question.[44] In North Carolina and Tennessee, the Whig party was formed by the secession of pro-Bank men from the Democratic party, aided in Tennessee by the local popularity of Hugh Lawson White as a Presidential candidate in 1835–1836.[45]

[44] Ambler, *Sectionalism in Virginia,* pp. 219–50, especially p. 222; Simms, *Whigs in Virginia, passim.*

[45] Boyd, *Federal Period,* pp. 181–84; Burton A. Konkle, *John Motley Morehead* (Philadelphia, 1922), p. 127; Lawrence F. London, "George Edmund Badger in the United States Senate, 1846–1849," *North Carolina Historical Review,* XV (1938), 2–3; Powell Moore, "The Political Background of the Revolt against Jackson in Tennessee," *East Tennessee Historical Society's Publications,* No. 4 (1932), 45–66; Thomas P. Abernethy, "The Origin of the Whig Party in Tennessee," *Mississippi Valley Historical Review,* XII (1927), 504–22; Joseph H. Parks, *John Bell* (Baton Rouge, 1950), pp. 58–133. The difficulty historians have had understanding why the North Carolina planters perversely remained in the Democratic party arises from the initial error of regarding the Whig party as primarily a planter group. The basic explanation is that the Old Republican planters of North Carolina, unlike the agricultural capitalists of the lower South, were antagonistic toward the commercial-financial group, rather than identified with it. With a smaller investment in land and slaves than his Mississippi counterpart, with little chance to make large profits by further investment, and relying less on a single cash crop, the average North Carolina planter was much less dependent on the town merchant and banker. For some years before the Jackson era, the planters had been resisting demands for banks and internal improvements, while simultaneously trying to stem the tide of democratic discontent with planter rule. It was the union of these two anti-planter forces, commer-

The state rights element was more conspicuous in the four remaining states of the lower South. But it was by no means the majority wing of the Whig party in all of them. Both Alabama and Mississippi had an original nucleus of pro-Clay, anti-Jackson men, and in both states the nullification episode caused a substantial defection from the Jackson ranks. In Mississippi, however, a greater defection followed the removal of government deposits from the national bank. The state rights men were clearly a minority of the opposition party, which elected an outspoken foe of nullification to the governorship in 1835 and sent the ardent Clay partisan, Seargent S. Prentiss, to Congress two years later.[46]

The state rights defection seems to have been more important in Alabama, where it was led by the able Dixon H. Lewis. The Lewis faction, however, maintained only a tenuous connection with the regular Whigs, and in 1837 Lewis and his supporters followed Calhoun back into the Democratic party. The significant fact is that in neither Alabama nor Mississippi were the Whigs greatly weakened by the departure of Calhoun's admirers.[47]

Only in South Carolina and Georgia did avowed state rights men make up the bulk of the anti-Jackson party. When the real nature of the new party alignments became apparent, the politicians of Calhoun's state gave proof of their sincerity (and of the Presidential aspirations of their chief) by moving back to the Democratic ranks at the first decent opportunity.

The principal Whig leader in Georgia was John M. Berrien, a Savannah lawyer and attorney for the United States Bank who had been forced out of Jackson's cabinet by the Peggy Eaton affair. At the time of the election of 1832, Jackson's Indian policy was so popular in Georgia that Berrien did not dare oppose the President openly. Instead, he went about stirring

---

cial and democratic, which produced the Whig party in 1833–1835. Businessmen controlled the new party, but they retained popular support by championing constitutional reform and by progressive legislation in the fields of internal improvements and public education. There is no adequate account of the North Carolina Whigs in print. The situation in Virginia was somewhat similar, in that a majority of the planters, Phillips and Cole to the contrary notwithstanding, remained Democrats. In the period 1833–1843, the twelve congressional districts of plantation Virginia, lying east of the Blue Ridge and south of the Rappahannock, were represented thirty-eight times by Democrats and twenty-two times by Whigs or Conservatives, with nine of the Whig elections being won in the commercial Norfolk, Richmond, and Fredericksburg districts. The Democratic party of Virginia differed from that of North Carolina, however, in having a much larger popular element.

[46] Hearon, "Nullification in Mississippi," *loc. cit.,* pp. 37–77; Winston, "Mississippi Whigs and the Tariff," *loc. cit.,* pp. 505–24; James E. Winston, "The Mississippi Whigs and the Annexation of Texas," *Southwestern Historical Quarterly,* XXIX (1926), pp. 161–80; Ranck, *Alfred G. Brown,* pp. 4–15; Dallas C. Dickey, *Seargent S. Prentiss: Whig Orator of the Old South* (Baton Rouge, 1945), pp. 45–266.

[47] Jack, *Sectionalism in Alabama,* pp. 21–85.

up anti-tariff and state rights sentiment, while secretly trying to prevent anti-Bank resolutions by the legislature. Immediately after Jackson's re-election, however, Berrien and his allies managed to reorganize the old Troup political faction as an openly anti-Jackson state rights party. In view of Berrien's pro-Bank attitude and his subsequent staunch support of Clay's policies, it seems probable that he was merely capitalizing on state rights sentiment to defeat Democratic measures which he opposed on other grounds. At any rate, the Georgia Whigs were soon arrayed against the Jackson financial program, and they held their lines nearly intact in the face of the desertion of state rights Whigs to the Democrats on the Sub-treasury issue. By 1840 Berrien had brought his Georgia followers into close harmony with the national party.[48]

This summary sketch of southern Whiggery raises, of course, more questions than it could possibly answer definitively. It has attempted to suggest, however, that preoccupation with the origins and development of southern sectionalism has led to distortions of southern political history in the 1830's and 1840's. Specifically, it is suggested:

That only John C. Calhoun and a small group of allied southern leaders regarded state rights as the most important issue in politics in this period.

That the southern people divided politically in these years over much the same questions as northern voters, particularly questions of banking and financial policy.

That the Whig party in the South was built around a nucleus of National Republicans and state rights men, but received its greatest accession of strength from business-minded Democrats who deserted Jackson on the Bank issue.

That the Whig party in the South was controlled by urban commercial and banking interests, supported by a majority of the planters, who were economically dependent on banking and commercial facilities. And finally,

That this alliance of the propertied, far from being inherently particu-laristic, rapidly shook off its state rights adherents and by 1841 was almost solidly in support of the nationalistic policies of Henry Clay.

There is a great need for intensive restudy of southern politics in the 1830's and 1840's, and particularly for critical correlation of local and national developments. The story as it comes from the contemporary sources is full of the resounding clash of solid interests and opposing ideol-

---

[48] Thomas P. Govan, "John M. Berrien and the Administration of Andrew Jackson," *Journal of Southern History*, V (1939), pp. 447–67; Phillips, "Georgia and State Rights," *loc. cit.*, pp. 113–50; Murray, *Whig Party in Georgia, passim*. Despite the defection of three congressmen to the Democrats on the Subtreasury issue, the Georgia Whigs won the subsequent congressional election and carried the Presidential election of 1840 by three times their majority in 1836.

ogies, hardly having "the hollow sound of a stage duel with tin swords" which one historian seems to detect.[49] And recent events should make the student wary of state rights banners, especially when raised by conservative men against national administrations not conspicuously devoted to the interests of the propertied.

[49] Sydnor, *Development of Southern Sectionalism*, p. 316.

8

Romance and Realism
in Southern Politics

T. Harry Williams

ignored the real causes (and issues)

A sense of history, soil, climate, and race have all, at various times,
served as a basis for explaining the distinctiveness of the southern
past. But assuming that a successful formula for the uniqueness of
the southern experience has yet to be proven sufficiently persuasive,
T. Harry Williams, Boyd Professor of History at Louisiana State
University, offers the "romance" of southern politics as a possible
alternative. Anticipating later emphasis on the mythological content of southern history, Professor Williams deciphers the codes of
southern political conduct during the pre–Civil War decades in
terms of its affinities for image-building. The interchange of issues
with the North, he argues, forced the South to react defensively,
signaling a retreat into the less hostile confines of the southern
mind. Southern political behavior was clearly tinged by its penchant
for failing to grasp the essence and reality of key political issues.
As such, the South unknowingly came to compromise the possibility
of eventual victory in the intersectional struggles by virtue of this
rather basic flaw in its political character. As the crisis of civil war
approached, the South exhibited an inability to sustain natural political affiliations with the West, and proved unwilling to shape critical
issues in accordance with anything other than the defense of slavery. In lieu of coming to terms with political realities—construed
as "the puny inadequateness of fact"—the South became a cultural
prisoner of its psychological impulse for the romantic. Indeed,
given this proclivity toward romanticism perhaps the "lost cause"
was predestined.

From "The Distinctive South" in *Romance and Realism in Southern Politics,* by
T. Harry Williams. Athens, Georgia: The University of Georgia Press, 1961. Reprinted by permission of the publisher.

We are accustomed to saying that there is a place called the South and that it is inhabited by an identifiable people known as Southerners. We know that this is so, but many of those who most often tell us about it, including natives of the section, would have trouble defining their phrases if pressed for a formula. Even the specialists, the scholars who study the structure of Southern society—historians, sociologists, political scientists—have had trouble in deciding what made the South distinctive or what elements determined the pattern of Southernism. Ironically enough, in attempting to ascribe reasons for coherence, they have come up with diverse analyses. They have pointed to the South's agrarian economy and its staple crops, its rural society and English gentry ideals, its plantation system and institution of slavery, its conservative way of thought and stable way of life, and its consciousness of race and fixation on race relations. And these are not all the formulas advanced to explain the South. The literary artists, sometimes more perceptive in social analysis than the social scientists, have had their go at the problem. As we might perhaps expect, they have seen the land itself as a powerful factor. The physical environment was such that it sustained life without too much expenditure of energy. Not having to conquer his environment, the Southerner was free to exploit its pleasures. "Soil, scenery, all the color and animation of the external world tempted a convivial race to an endless festival of the seasons," wrote Ellen Glasgow. "In the midst of a changing world all immaterial aspects were condensed for the Southern planter into an incomparable heartiness and relish for life. What distinguished the Southerner . . . from his severer neighbors to the north was his ineradicable belief that pleasure is worth more than toil, that it is even worth more than profit."

The most recent attempts by historians to explain what is distinctive about the South have got away from the older formulas of race, economics, or ruralism. Now the purpose is to show in what ways the South has not shared in or has stood apart from the common American tradition. Thus Professor Vann Woodward, who has done so much to illumine our understanding of the region, points out that the South has not participated in three of the great national legends and that its experience in these areas is quite un-American. In a land of plenty the South was from the Civil War and until recent times a region of poverty. In a nation whose history has been an unbroken success story the South has known "frustration, failure, and defeat." Their heritage affords Southerners no basis for the American conviction that there is nothing beyond the power of humans to accomplish. In a society bemused with innocence and optimism the South has lived with evils—slavery and the aftermath of emancipation—and it does not believe that every evil has an easy cure. "In that most optimistic of centuries in the most optimistic part of the world, the South remained basically pessimistic in its social outlook and its moral philosophy," Woodward concludes. "The experience of evil and the experience of tragedy are parts of the Southern heritage that are as difficult to reconcile with the American legend of innocence and social felicity as the experience of poverty and defeat are to reconcile with the legends of abundance and success."

Professor Woodward is also responsible for another current notion— that more than any other Americans Southerners have a sense of history. This is not to be taken in a literal sense as meaning that the people below the Potomac have an unusual devotion to a full and objective record of their past or that, happily, they read a large number of history books or honor history professors above other savants. Rather, it is, to borrow a phrase that Woodward borrowed from Toynbee, that Southerners know history has happened. They know this because Southern history has been compounded of tragedy and many of the elements of that tragedy are still apparent today. More poignantly than other Americans, they realize that the past impinges on the present, and more often than their fellows in other sections they relate the present to something in the past. Indeed, one commentator, Henry Savage, has suggested that this sense of history is the thing that has made the South an entity. "With the exception of what their history did to them, Southerners are much like Americans anywhere in the country," Savage writes. He adds that outsiders would understand the South better if they realized that Southern differences are solely the products of history.

Although most observers admit the existence of this attachment to the past, not all view it with affection or even amusement. Some have found it irritating and have easily proceeded to the conclusion that it is dangerous. Thus Marshall Fishwick explodes: "How can people who know and intuit so much not know that a constant posture of looking backward is the hallmark of stagnation? Very few of us who purport to be historians know much about history. But everything we do know indicates that history is incapable of running backward."

It may be that the critics on both sides are exaggerating the Southerner's consciousness of history. All of this alleged identification with the past may be only another demonstration of his undoubted great ability to deceive himself as well as to spoof the outsider. And this may be the quality that makes him unique among Americans. Far beyond any native competitors, he is marvelously adept at creating mind-pictures of his world or of the larger world around him—images that he wants to believe, that are real to him, and that he will insist others accept. This is another way of saying that the Southerner is likely to be a romantic and that in many situations he almost certainly will refuse to recognize reality. It is an attitude that has fascinated and frustrated beholders. Harry Ashmore, who admits to both reactions, speaks of the Southerner's "remarkable capacity for unreality, which still enables him to hold out against the logic of arguments and of events." W. J. Cash, in *The Mind of the South,* that brilliant book which has been so praised and so damned but which is always quoted by critics from both sides, dealt caustically with the Southerner's capacity for self-deception: "To say that he is simple is to say in effect that he necessarily lacks the complexity of mind, the knowledge, and above all, the habit of skepticism essential to any generally realistic attitude. It is to say that he is inevitably driven back upon imagination, that his world-construction is bound to be mainly a product of fantasy, and that his credulity is limited only by his capacity for conjuring up the unbelievable."

If we admit here at the beginning that the Southerner is, more than other Americans, a romantic, it is pertinent to ask at this point of departure: What are the factors or forces that have made him what he is? The question is by nature a slippery one, and the answers perforce must be elusive. Nor will the vast apparatus of scholarship be of much help to us. The historian with all his documents and the social scientist with all his data cannot throw appreciable light on this problem. But we may with some, but not complete, confidence turn for possible clues to the literary artists who have depicted the Southern scene. There fortunate folk have not been inhibited by the scholar's proper caution in dealing with the inner nature of man. On the contrary, as is proper with them, they have felt impelled to explain man in terms of their art. It would seem significant that in interpreting man, or any other manifestation of the Southern scene, they give great weight to the physical environment. Some have believed that the very nature of the Southern world—the climate, the colors, the odors, the foliage—militates against reality. That "subtle, murky, slumberous clime . . . swart hot land of pine and palm . . . the sweet and sensuous South," wrote James Maurice Thompson. Cash, in one of his most impressionistic passages, contended that the environment constituted "a sort of cosmic conspiracy against reality in favor of romance." Describing the land as a pattern of blurred softness, Cash spoke of the mood it induced: "It is a mood, in sum, in which directed thinking is all but impossible, a mood in which the mind yields almost perforce to drift and in which the imagination holds unchecked sway, a mood in which nothing any more seems improbable save the puny inadequateness of fact, nothing incredible save the bareness of truth."

More quotations from the literary community could be introduced, but if the more mundane-minded suspect the validity of observations from this source we may summon a colder witness, a New England Adams. Henry Adams attested the effect the South first had on him in words that might have come from a Southern poet: "The May sunshine and shadow had something to do with it; the thickness of foliage and the heavy smells had more; the sense of atmosphere, almost new, had perhaps as much again; and the brooding indolence of a warm climate and a negro population hung in the atmosphere heavier than the catalpas. The impression was not simple, but the boy liked it: distinctly it remained on his mind as an attraction, almost obscuring Quincy itself." If the Southern scene could almost obscure the stark reality of Quincy in the mind of an Adams, it must have been powerful indeed. With this, let us be content and assume that something in the Southern background produced a tendency toward romanticism in thought and politics.

Of all the mind-pictures created by the romantic Southerner, the greatest, the most appealing, and the most enduring is the legend of the Old South. The minute investigations of the historians, the political scientists, and even the sociologists have not succeeded in destroying it or even seriously modifying it. Even those Southern writers who have believed that the legend was bad for the South, when they have come to write about it, expended their most eloquent passages, so in a perverse way testifying to its attraction.

Cash seems carried away despite himself in describing the image of the South that was, "shimmering there forever behind the guns of Sumter. . . . Perpetually suspended in the great haze of memory, it hung, as it were, poised, somewhere between earth and sky, colossal, shining, and imcomparably lovely. . . ." Depicting the growth of the legend after 1865, Henry Savage, who thinks it has held the South in a bondage of prejudice, nevertheless can write: "But in the past, the sky was yet still bright with a shining glory. Although it was but afterglow of the glorious sunset of a magnificent day which was done, it was still something with which Southerners could identify themselves to relieve the terrible gloom of their contemporary lot."

This cherishing of an ideal dream-world in the past was both a reflection of the Southerner's capacity for unreality and a cause of his continuing reluctance to face the realities of the modern world; for obviously the myth of a perfect society was a powerful argument against change, against even considering whether there was any need for change. And here we may observe that if the Southerner were as aware of history as some of the writers suppose, he would have pursued a different course in some of the social conflicts of modern times. Presumably a people that have experienced evil, defeat, and repression would realize the advantage of adjustment and accommodation in political relations, techniques not noticeably present in the recent South.

But the legend of the Old South is only one demonstration of the Southern talent for fantasy. We see it in many areas of Southern life and in almost every segment of Southern history. It is in the writings of intellectuals like Donald Davidson, who could declare that the cause of the fantasy

South in the 1920's was "the cause of civilized society against the new barbarism of science and technology controlled and directed by the modern power state." It was in the speeches of politicians in the depression-ridden 1930's, speeches that ignored the harsh economic realities while harking back to old glories that had been destroyed by alien persecutors. It first appeared when the South emerged as a section, when Southern leaders chose to stake the destiny of a whole people on one issue to be fought for with one strategy.

Historians differ as to the exact date when the South became an entity, recognized by itself and other areas as a distinct section. Although some scholars claim that the states below the Potomac realized they had separate interests as early as the Constitutional Convention, most put the time much later. There is pretty general agreement that the phenomenon we know as the South was at least taking shape by the 1830's. Certainly Southerners were then becoming aware, and often bitterly so, that they were in some way different from people in the rest of the country. These years witnessed the beginning of the abolitionist attack on slavery, the nullification crisis, and the first burgeoning of the Northern industrial order. Suddenly the Southern states were thrown on the defensive—morally, politically, economically. And it was at this moment, exclaims Henry Savage, that the South was born, "the old South of book and song, romance and tragedy, of adulation and castigation." Essentially the same conclusion was reached by the most thoughtful historian of the region in the 1830's, Charles S. Sydnor. By the close of the decade, Sydnor decided, Southerners had come to have a feeling of "oppression, of defeat, and even of desperation." 1830's on "From this time onward," he wrote, "it is not always possible to explain Southern actions and attitudes by a rational analysis of the facts in each new episode." To Sydnor the salient development was that for the first time Southerners realized they were different. Although they had possessed a distinctive social system, they had not known it until outsiders told them so. Now and rather abruptly "the Southern mind was turned inward to a consideration of its own society."

Unquestionably the South was under attack in the 1830's. But a people whose institutions are being criticized may react in a number of ways. They may, if they are sure of themselves and their security, disdain the criticisms. They may concoct defenses of various kinds, political and polemical, and of varying intensity. Or they may, if they are adept at accommodating themselves to power, which no Americans are, prepare to accept adjustments in their system that will involve a minimum of dislocation. But the Southern response was none of these. Instead, Southerners assumed the position that their society, lying under the disapproval of not just the North but of the whole Western world, was the highest example of civilization to be found on the planet. Other peoples have

looked forward or backward to a golden age, but those of the antebellum
South proclaimed that they lived in one. "Surely, Southerners had come
a long way from Jefferson and a long way out of reality," Sydnor concluded
with apparent sadness. "Fighting to defend their way of life, they had taken
refuge in a dream world, and they insisted that others accept their castle
in the sky as an accurate description of conditions in the South."

Whatever the precise movement when the South passed from a geographic region to a political section, it is evident that the transition was
an ominous one, both for the South and the nation. We cannot say with
certainty that the change was inevitable. Given all the factors in the situation—the nature of Northern and Southern opinion, the convulsing currents
working in the political system, the transforming upheavals occurring in
the economic sphere—it probably was. But one of these factors was particularly important in driving the South into a mood of insecurity and
isolation. Then, as in later crises, external attacks would have the effect
of solidifying internal divisions in a region that naturally was one of great
contrasts. And then, as later, the North would show little understanding
of or sympathy for the problems of the South.

Many of the condemnations flung against the South went far beyond
the bounds of legitimate social criticism, and were, whether or not mis-
chievously conceived, calculated to inflame Southerners to extreme reaction rather than to calm examination of their society. Witness these
examples. From the New York *Tribune:* "The Southern plantations are
little less than Negro harems. . . . Of all the Southern presidents hardly
one has failed to leave his mulatto children. . . . The South is a perfect
puddle of amalgamation." From the New York *Times:* "The Southern
character is infinitely boastful, vainglorious, full of dash, without endurance, treacherous, cunning, timid, and revengeful." From a Northern
minister: "A foaming fountain of insecurity and alarm, of violence and
crime and blood, the institution of slavery is." From *Harper's Weekly:*
"Their civilization is a mermaid—lovely and languid above, but ending in
bestial deformity."

Under almost constant assault after the 1830's, in its response the South
committed almost every political error in the book. First, it permitted the
opposition to define the issue, slavery, thus putting itself at an immediate disadvantage. Second, it identified every other issue and, indeed,
its whole way of life with the defense of slavery. Finally, as Woodward
writes: "Because it identified the internal security of the whole society
with the security of its labor system, it refused to permit criticism of that
system. To guarantee conformity of thought it abandoned its tradition
of tolerance and resorted to the repression of dissent within its borders
and the forcible exclusion of criticism from outside."

There had been a time when some of the most intelligent social criticism in vogue emanated from Southerners. Indeed, the South had furnished the most informed critics of the institution of slavery itself. But by 1850 this atmosphere of free inquiry and free expression was gone. No longer could Southerners, as in the days of Jefferson and Mason, disapprove of aspects of life in their sections or agree with the strictures of outsiders and remain honored at home. Now most Southerners refused even to view slavery as a discussable question or to consider its relation to their or man's future. A taboo on the subject, unofficial but the more stringent and repressive because it represented the feeling of the community, a kind of folk-enforcement, enveloped all of Dixie. The taboo extended to subjects related to slavery even indirectly—to, in fact, anything that could be considered un-Southern. Nor was it enough for men merely to observe the taboo, to remain silent. They must, if they were not to be suspect, speak out in glorification of slavery, and align themselves actively with its defenders. If this was not enforced conformity of thought, it was close to it. Certainly that freedom of the spirit that Jefferson had said was necessary to the good society did not exist in the South before the Civil War. There is a grim irony in the situation. Inevitably one wonders what would have happened to the Sage of Monticello if he had returned to his native section in the 1850's.

It may be objected that in this presentation of the South there is an apparent glaring paradox. Strait-jacket conformity does not seem to fit in with the tradition of Southern individualism. And we know that Southerners, particularly those of the ruling class, were as individualistic a set of men as America has produced. Mrs. Chesnut has left us an unforgettable picture of a representative of the aristocratic order, her father-in-law: "Partly patriarch, partly *grand seigneur,* this old man is a species that we will see no more; the last of the lordly planters who ruled this Southern World. His manners are unequalled still, but underneath this smooth exterior lies the grip of a tyrant, whose will has never been crossed. . . . If a lady's name is given, he uncovers and stands hat in hand until she passes. He has still the Old World art of bowing low and gracefully. He came of a race that would brook no interference with their own sweet will by man, woman, or devil; but then such manners would clear any man's character, if it needed it." Mrs. Chesnut, ordinarily so perceptive in her judgment, was in this case perhaps misled by mere exterior attractiveness. She was writing at the end of the Civil War when the whole Southern world was about to crash after military defeat, a defeat that in part had been brought about by the very traits in the Southern character that she depicted in her father-in-law. Too many Southerners, and often those in high places, had simply refused to impose on themselves the discipline that modern war demands.

And here we have the resolution of the paradox. Southern individualism

Southern
extention

was of a particular type. It expressed itself in matters of speech and conduct, in self-assertion, sometimes for its own sake, and in self-will, sometimes just to prove somebody had a will. It could not express itself in other areas because dissent in thought was not generally permitted. Could it be that the conformity of the slave system bred an individualism that helped to destroy the Confederacy? If this be true, we have another irony to add to a long list in Southern history.

Perhaps the greatest error committed by the South in the political battles of the antebellum years was in alienating its natural ally, the West. On a number of issues, primarily economic in nature, the two sections had worked together, often to the South's advantage. There was a strong probability that the alliance might have continued. It did not, and largely because again the South insisted on identifying everything with the one issue of slavery. The South demanded that the West accept its position on the status of slavery in the territories. Now people in the West might have varying feelings about the morality of slavery, some being much agitated on the question and others very little, but they were united on one conviction: they did not want to meet the competition of slave labor in the national domain. And so the South lost the West to the Northeast—by insisting on the acceptance of a system utterly unadapted to the needs of the West.

If this seems like unrealistic strategy, we may point to other examples. To the student of politics it is a matter of marvel that Southerners would let their stand on many issues be determined not by political requirements or realities but by the stand of "the enemy," the Northern antislavery elements. Thus at the time of the debate on the Kansas-Nebraska Bill it was freely admitted all over the South that the measure would be of no practical value to the section and might even injure it. Yet Southerners supported it. The Charleston *Mercury* explained why: "Can the South stand listlessly by and see the bill repealed, when this is made the direst issue against her...? There is no alternative for the South. When the North presents a sectional issue, and tenders battle upon it, she must meet it, or abide all the consequences of a victory easily won, by a remorseless and eager foe."

The final and tragic climax to the one-issue strategy came at the Democratic national convention at Charleston in 1860, when Southerners demanded that the party adopt a platform on slavery in the territories that they admitted would bring defeat in November. The Western Democrats refused, the party split into two wings, Lincoln won the election, and the South was left standing alone.

When the Southerners could not get what they wanted at Charleston, they walked out. They departed, says Avery Craven, "under the impression that they were upholding a principle," but in reality most of them did not know what to do and only followed an aggressive few who pretended to know the answer. Hitherto in this review of developments since the 1830's we have stressed that the South had a certain latitude of choices as to the course it would take and that because of certain factors in the Southern situation and psychology it took the wrong course, wrong in the sense that the strategy decided on defeated its purpose. We can believe this to be true, and at the same time agree with Craven that in the successive crises before 1860, or in the one of that year, most Southerners simply acted out of a feeling of apprehension or frustration. That is, although they may have had the possibility of choice they were also, to an extent, controlled by circumstance.

Humans do not always have the freedom of decision that later scholars may think. There is an element of inevitability in many episodes of history, and the one present in antebellum America may have been particularly puissant. Much of what happened was not planned or plotted by anybody. Great changes occurred, but they were the result of impersonal rather than personal forces. The North moved ahead into the modern world, while the South remained static, its economy and society not greatly different from the colonial period. The South fell to the status of a minority and blamed the North or, more accurately, men in the North for its reduction. But no men had done it, Craven points out. "The Industrial Revolution was the real culprit."

What the Industrial Revolution did was epitomized in the career of the ablest man to come out of the South since Jefferson. Nobody has described the tragedy of John C. Calhoun more eloquently than Craven. By circumstance *and* choice, Craven emphasizes, Calhoun was forced into a position "from which he had to defend slavery when all the rest of the Christian world was leaving it behind; he had to defend the political rights of the locality when all the forces of modern technology and business were producing interdependence and the need for centralized efficiency; he had to uphold strict construction of the Constitution when the forward sweep of the whole modern social-economic order demanded a broader view; he had to speak for an agricultural interest and way of life just as industry and the city were about to take over; he was forced to be a voice out of the past while he yet lived. . . ."

Whether it was choice or circumstance or both that impelled the South along the course to secession and the Civil War, we cannot with certainty say. We do know that the course was taken and we know what the results were for the South. The war did many things to the section. Among other things, it ensured that the South would remain a section for a long time to come. History provides a number of examples of civil conflicts between classes or factions diffused throughout a country but few in which the contestants faced each other over some kind of geographical line. In the

Civil War it was not just a people that had been defeated but also a distinct region. Even if the South had wanted to forget that it was a section, the North hardly would have permitted it to do so. The South, of course, did not want to forget. Rather, it wanted to remember, perhaps had to remember. "Defeated on the actual ramparts of Virginia," wrote Clarence E. Cason, "the Southerners retired to the ramparts of the mind. Here the glories of the old South became an impregnable castle over which was flown the invincible banner of 'the Lost Cause.' Since reality was unbearable, mythology became supreme." It was now that the legends of the Old South of the golden age before Sumter and of the Lost Cause destroyed in the guns after Sumter came to fullest fruition. Perhaps the legend-making was necessary in the conditions prevailing immediately after Appomattox. We are accustomed to saying that the war set the South back economically, but we forget that it also did something perhaps more serious—it threw the South back culturally and socially a century. This being so, Southerners could hardly be expected to respond to all situations in contemporary terms. But we shall have occasion to note that they would cling to the legends long after the circumstances existing in the postwar years had changed if not disappeared.

We have stressed that in the politics of the Old South there was a theme —others, of course, could be developed—and in treating it we have used words like romance and unreality. That is, we have tried to say that in large part politics did not operate in its normal or proper sense to resolve and compromise class and group differences while at the same time maintaining that plurality of opinion ordinarily found in democratic societies. There was a singular oneness about Southern politics—by the 1850's, for all practical purposes, only one party existed; the defense of the section against outside attack was identified with one issue; and the defense was pitched to one strategy.

It has been argued that all of this indicates a tendency to lose reality, to live in a Never-Never land. But after 1865 the South would emerge into a new world. Many of the forces that had molded it had gone with the war. Would the politics of this new South be different from that of the old? Would Southerners learn something from the tragic past that would change their future?

9

The South and the Myth of the Garden

Henry Nash Smith

Basic affiliations and political relationships between South and West
date at least from the time of early colonial western land claims.
Such associations were reinforced by the fact that, with "the roll
of frontier upon frontier—and on to the frontier beyond," settlement of the great interior of virgin land was invariably in flux.
Settlement patterns of West and South became, over time, almost
inextricably intertwined. Observing that this kinship between South
and West has often been reflected in the mirror of national politics,
Henry Nash Smith, Professor of English, University of California,
Berkeley, seeks to isolate the factors responsible for the sections'
gradual disaffection. Despite southern efforts to the contrary, the
potent South-West political coalition fell victim to developing
technological and economic realities. The Erie Canal, steamship
traffic on the Great Lakes, and the implementation of an east-west
railway line worked together to overcome the "natural" alliance
of geography and political sentiment which southerners had sought
to cultivate with the developing West. In addition, the process of
political disenchantment was abetted by psychological and philosophical contentions based on contrasting and conflicting images of
their shared frontier experience. As the West became increasingly
enamored with the ideal of the yeoman farmer and the "myth of
the garden," the South was undergoing the psychological process
of enshrining the plantation legend. As the one celebrated the industrious and free yeoman farmer as a cultural model, the other
mentally applied an aristocratic veneer to the slave system. In the
end, it was conflicting visions of Eden which prompted and reinforced the prewar isolation of the South.

Reprinted by permission of the publishers from Henry Nash Smith, *Virgin Land: The
American West as Symbol and Myth,* Cambridge, Mass.: Harvard University Press.
Copyright 1950, by the President and Fellows of Harvard College.

By the 1850's the South had become actively hostile to the yeoman ideal which had been developed as a rationale of agricultural settlement in the Mississippi Valley. But this break with the Northwest came only after a long struggle on the part of the Southern leaders to maintain economic and political ties with all the interior basin.

The first advance beyond the Alleghenies, in the last quarter of the eighteenth century, had been decidedly Southern in coloring. Virginia and North Carolina had been the bases for the settlement of Kentucky and Tennessee. Even the earliest Anglo-American penetration north of the Ohio, in the wake of George Rogers Clark's expedition during the Revolution, was largely a Southern venture. The history of Western exploration is filled with Southern names, from Boone and Lewis and Clark to James Clyman of Virginia and John Charles Frémont of South Carolina. Through Jefferson, Virginia had provided the geographical insight and the strategic planning for the first half-century of westward advance. So marked was the Southern dominance of this process that as late as 1846 the Pennsylvanian William Gilpin could, to be sure with an element of exaggeration, ascribe the entire impulse to the South. "The progeny of Jamestown," he declared, "has given to the Union twelve great agricultural States; has created that mighty production and generating capacity on which are based the grand power and prosperity of the Nation." Among Southern accomplishments he listed not only the settlement of Kentucky, Tennessee, Missouri, and the Southwest, but also that of Ohio, Indiana, Illinois, and Iowa.[1] Even after the Civil War Whitman declared in his poem "Virginia —The West" that Virginia had given to the nation the stalwart giant of the West whose plenteous offspring had put on uniforms of blue and preserved the Union against the rebellious Confederacy.[2]

The association between South and West had been reflected in national politics. Many representatives of the Middle States and New England had feared from the beginning that the development of the trans-Allegheny would unduly strengthen the South. In August, 1786, James Monroe wrote to Patrick Henry from New York, where Congress was sitting, that the Northerners meant to break up the settlements on the western waters in order to "keep the States southward as they now are."[3] In the Constitutional Convention of 1787 Gouverneur Morris of Pennsylvania proposed inserting into the Constitution a provision "That the number of representatives in ye first branch from the States hereafter to be established

---

[1] 29 Cong., 1 Sess. Senate Report No. 306. Committee on the Post Office and Post Roads (April 20, 1846), pp. 28–29.

[2] *Leaves of Grass,* inclusive edition, ed. Emory Holloway (Garden City, New York, 1931), pp. 248–249.

[3] *The Writings of James Monroe,* ed. Stanislaus M. Hamilton, 7 vols. (New York, 1898–1903), I, 150.

shall not exceed the representatives from the States already confederated."[4] Delegates to the Convention regarded this proposal as a clear test of strength between North and South. It was rejected by the close vote of four states to five, with Pennsylvania divided. The states favoring the measure were Massachusetts, Connecticut, Delaware, and Maryland (which, having no claim to Western territory, was jealous of Virginia). Those opposing it were New Jersey, Virginia, North Carolina, South Carolina, and Georgia.[5]

During the next twenty years the alignment of South and West against North and East persisted through a series of crises, of which the most spectacular arose from Federalist opposition to the Louisiana Purchase in 1803 and to the War of 1812, especially in its Western phase. As Benton picturesquely summarized the attitude of New England Federalists, the cry was, "The Potomac the boundary; the negro States by themselves! The Alleghanies the boundary, the western savages by themselves! The Mississippi the boundary, let Missouri be governed by a Prefect, or given up as a haunt for wild beasts!"[6] The alliance of West and South continued into the 1850's as a political force to be reckoned with. It was the basis of the careers of Jackson, Benton, Douglas, and other Democratic leaders; and even after the Northwest had been won for the Republican Party in the election of 1860, Western sympathy with the South found expression in the powerful Copperhead movement of disaffection during the Civil War. But the changes in the structure of American society recorded in the Republican victory of 1860 had begun soon after the War of 1812. Although the introduction of steamboats on the western waters for a time strengthened the sway of New Orleans throughout the Mississippi Valley, the Erie Canal, steam transportation through the Great Lakes, and the east-west trunk line railways eventually tied the Northwest to New York rather than to the Gulf of Mexico.

The changes which had begun to take place in the relations among the sections were fully explored in the famous Webster-Hayne debate of 1829–1830, noted in the history books for its bearing on constitutional theory, but originating in a Southern bid for Western support. The doctrine of nullification which Hayne, acting as the mouthpiece for Calhoun, announced in the course of this debate, and which South Carolina put into effect two years later in its declaration that the tariff of 1832 would not be enforced in ports of the state, expressed the Southern fear that a coalition

---

[4] Max Farrand, ed., *The Records of the Federal Convention of 1787*, 4 vols. (New Haven, 1911–1937), I, 533.

[5] *Ibid.*, II, 2.

[6] *Speech of Mr. Benton, of Missouri, in Reply to Mr. Webster: The Resolution Offered by Mr. Foot, Relative to the Public Lands, Being under Consideration. Delivered in the Senate, Session 1829–1830* (Washington, 1830), pp. 53–54.

of North and West would soon outweigh the strength of the South within the Union. From this time on the South wavered between two strategies. One was to surrender its long-standing but now weakening dominance of the West and fall back on constitutional minority rights. The other was to try to regain control of the West through development of trade routes from the south Atlantic coast to the Ohio Valley. Southern spokesmen in Congress resisted federal aid in the construction of canals and other means of bringing the Northwest and New England closer together, and tried to protect the position of New Orleans as queen of the trade on the western waters.

Benton stated the doctrine underlying such efforts: ". . . every canal, and every road, tending to draw the commerce of the Western States across the Alleghany mountains, is an injury to the people of the West." His desire for a continued economic alliance of South and West clouded his vision of the impending revolution in transport. Here, as in his discussion of a transcontinental trade route, he insisted that the steamboat would always outweigh the railway in importance. The bulky products of Western farms and packing houses would continue to make their way to market downstream through New Orleans. "As to the idea of sending the products of the West across the Alleghanies, it is the conception of insanity itself! No rail roads or canals will ever carry them, not even if they do it gratis!" Commercial routes from East to West could be useful only for carrying manufactured goods of relatively small bulk. If Westerners bought these goods they endangered their own market at New Orleans; for New Orleans could not buy if she were not allowed to sell. Besides, decline of the trade with New Orleans threatened to destroy the immensely important steamboat system of the West, which already, in 1829, had grown to three hundred thousand tons.[7]

The desire to strengthen economic ties with the West accounts for one of the strangest moments in the career of Calhoun, archchampion of the strict construction of the Constitution which most Southerners believed forbade federal aid for internal improvements. Having reluctantly accepted an invitation to attend the Memphis Commercial Convention of November, 1845,[8] Calhoun was elected president of the meeting and delivered the

---

[7] *Ibid.*, p. 65.

[8] James Gadsden, urging Calhoun to accept the invitation, wrote: "Now is the time to meet our Western friends at Memphis—to set the ball in motion which must bring the Valley to the South: and make them feel as allies of the Great Commercial and Agricultural interests—instead of the Tax gathering and Monopolizing interests of the North" (J. Franklin Jameson, ed., *Correspondence of John C. Calhoun* [Washington, 1900], p. 1062). Calhoun's attitude is discussed in Herbert Wender, *Southern Commercial Conventions 1837–1859,* Johns Hopkins University Studies in Historical and Political Science, Series XLVIII, No. 4 (Baltimore, 1930), p. 54.

opening address. This discourse shows what a strong attraction was being exerted by the West on Southern constitutional theory. Calhoun begins with the assumption that the Western and the Southern states occupy a single physiographic region, consisting of the Mississippi Valley and the Gulf Plains from the Atlantic to the Rio Grande—a patent translation of political desire into geographical terms. He dwells on the need for free and ready transit for persons and merchandise among the various portions of this vast region of the world. Integration of the South with the West obviously depended upon the utmost possible development of the river systems, especially of the Mississippi, whose current drew the produce of every part of the valley to the Southern metropolis of New Orleans.[9]

The crucial importance to the South of maintaining this commercial connection along the channels of the inland waterways demanded every effort to foster navigation, including federal appropriations to remove snags, dredge channels, install lighthouses, and so on. Calhoun Democrats had opposed such appropriations for twenty years as unconstitutional. But before an astonished and delighted audience Calhoun himself now proceeded to perform the mental gymnastics necessary to reach the conclusion "that the invention of Fulton has in reality, for all practical purposes, converted the Mississippi, with all its great tributaries, into an inland sea. Regarding it as such," he continued, "I am prepared to place it on the same footing with the Gulf and Atlantic coasts, the Chesapeake and Delaware Bays, and the Lakes, in reference to the superintendence of the General Government over its navigation."[10] Indeed, under the influence of this new exaltation, Calhoun even found himself celebrating the passage to India. In words that might almost have come from the lips of William Gilpin he announced in conclusion:

you occupy a region possessing advantages above all others on the globe, of the same extent, not only for its fertility, its diversity of climate and production, but in its geographical position; lying midway between the Pacific and Atlantic Oceans, in less than one generation, should the Union continue, and I hope it may be perpetual, you will be engaged in deliberations to extend your connection with the Pacific, as you are now with the Atlantic; and will ultimately be almost as intimately connected with the one as the other. In the end, you will command

[9] *Reports and Public Papers of John C. Calhoun,* being Volume VI of *Works,* ed. Richard K. Crallé (New York, 1856), pp. 273–274.

[10] *Ibid.,* p. 280. Benton had called the Mississippi and its tributaries *"mare nostrum"* in his speech during the Webster-Hayne debate fifteen years before (*Speech of Mr. Benton . . . in Reply to Mr. Webster,* p. 66). An anonymous contributor to the *Southern Quarterly Review* of Charleston, more orthodox than the Pope, greeted Calhoun's "inland sea" doctrine with the cry, *"Et tu, quoque, Brute?"* (IX, 267, January, 1846).

the commerce . . . of the world, as well as that of our greater Union, if we preserve our liberty and free popular institutions.[11]

But Calhoun's effort was in vain. The South failed in the end to maintain its hold on the developing Northwest, and the failure was a turning point in American history. When the break between North and South came in 1860, the Northwest went along with the Union. The weakening of the South's hold on the area north of the Ohio can be traced in the history of the now familiar symbols which expressed the ultimate purposes of the two sections. The richest vein of Southern materials bearing on this subject is the file of *DeBow's Review*, established in New Orleans in 1846 and devoted to the promotion of commercial relations between the South and the West along the lines endorsed by the Memphis Convention. DeBow and his contributors constantly urged the development of trade routes connecting New Orleans with the upper Mississippi Valley. They warned the South of the ominous increase in trade from the Great Lakes through the Erie Canal.[12] They urged New Orleans to waken from her complacent reliance on the Mississippi and build railways.[13] In accordance with the geographical conception advanced by Calhoun, which regarded the South and the Mississippi Valley as forming one region, DeBow celebrated the progress of the Great West as enthusiastically as Benton himself.[14] This policy led him to publish contributions from Western spokesmen developing the theme of the garden of the world. As late as 1858 DeBow included in his *Review* two characteristic essays by William Gilpin.[15] He also published articles by Jessup W. Scott of Ohio, who had long been a contributor to *Hunt's Merchants' Magazine* of New York on the development of the West. Scott, who will come up for fuller discussion in another connection, elaborated for DeBow's readers the familiar ideas of manifest destiny, predicting that the Star of Empire would "shine for ages and ages from the zenith on our central plain."[16]

DeBow's commitment to the theme of Western progress, which implied national unity if it was to benefit the South, early came into conflict with

---

[11] *Works*, VI, 284.

[12] Buckner H. Payne, "New Orleans—Her Commerce and Her Duties," *DeBow's Review*, III, 39–48 (January, 1847).

[13] Thomas B. Hewson, "Thoughts on a Rail-Road System for New Orleans," *ibid.*, X, 175–188 (February, 1851).

[14] "Progress of the Great West in Population, Agriculture, Arts and Commerce," *ibid.*, IV, 31–85 (September, 1847).

[15] "Hemp-Growing Region of the United States," *ibid.*, XXIV, 56–58 (January, 1858); "The Great Basin of the Mississippi," *ibid.*, XXIV, 159–165 (February, 1858).

[16] "The North American Plain," *ibid.*, XXVI, 564 (May, 1859). Scott also contributed "Westward the Star of Empire," *ibid.*, XXVII, [125]–136 (August, 1859).

his enthusiastic support of slavery. As early as 1851 he was speaking of secession as a step the South might have to take if Northern attacks continued.[17] Southern leaders were eventually forced to recognize that the notions of the course of empire and of the coming dominance of the West were implicitly free-soil. By 1860 Senator Louis T. Wigfall of Texas could put this awareness into words in an attack on Andrew Johnson's expansionism:

> The Senator from Tennessee [declared Wigfall] supposes that we have a sort of blatherskiting Americanism that is going to spread over the whole continent, and cross the Pacific, and take in the Sandwich Islands; and that, in the area of freedom, we are going to take in the whole world, and everybody is going to benefit us. The whole of that is false doctrine. I think it is a doctrine that no Democrat should ever entertain.

There was no manifest destiny, Wigfall insisted, in the Kentucky and Virginia Resolutions. "We ought to begin and repudiate and trample on this national idea," he exclaimed. The notion of colonizing and extending the area of freedom was nothing but "Red Republicanism; it is Federalism; it is nationalism; it is an ignoring of history."[18] Wigfall's instinct was sound. The very men to whom DeBow turned in the late 1850's for celebration of the imperial destinies of the Mississippi Valley were free-soilers, soon to enter the Republican party. The hero of their expansionism was Gilpin's soldier of the pioneer army, the axe man, the industrious farmer, the independent yeoman of the Western agrarian tradition. And this man was free.

Nothing could stand in greater contrast to the symbols which had meanwhile been created to express the ideal ends of the slave system. These symbols were grouped in the powerful and persuasive myth of the Southern plantation. Originating within the nostalgic and sentimental mode of Washington Irving, and first applied to the South in John P. Kennedy's *Swallow Barn* (which was published in 1832 at the turning point of Southern history), the picture of aristocratic masters, brilliant and charming heroines, and devoted slaves reached full development in the historical fiction of the Virginian John Esten Cooke in the middle 1850's. So compelling to the imagination was this group of symbols, bathed as they were in the charm of pastoral tradition and feudal romance, that they long survived the destruction of the plantation system itself. In the hands of such Southern

[17] "The Cause of the South," *ibid.*, X, 107 (Janaury, 1851).

[18] 36 Cong., 1 Sess., *Congressional Globe*. Senate (March 22, 1860), pp. 1303–1304.

writers as Thomas Nelson Page after the Civil War the idealized image of the plantation proved to have a strong appeal to Northern as well as to Southern audiences, and indeed to this day forms an apparently indestructible part of the national store of literary themes.[19]

But the briefest glance at the plantation in literature shows why it could not compete with the myth of the garden of the world as a projection of American experience in the West, and therefore why men like DeBow had no imaginative weapons to supplement their geographical and economic arguments for maintaining the Mississippi Valley under the hegemony of the South. The fiction dealing with the plantation emphasizes the beauty of harmonious social relations in an orderly feudal society. It presupposes generations of settled existence and is inimical to change. Literary plantations are almost always in the older South, and when they are situated in the new, developing Southwest, they are unhistorically depicted as duplicates of the Virginia and Carolina estates on which the convention was first based. Such symbols could not be adapted to the expression of a society like that of the West, either South or North, where rapidity of change, crudity, bustle, heterogeneity were fundamental traits.

It is true that during this same period the Southwest produced its own striking symbols, embodied in the newspaper sketches and oral tales which were called, collectively, Southwestern humor. These symbols were also destined to survive the Civil War and to have important consequences for American literature. They formed the tradition out of which developed Mark Twain. But Southwestern humor was of little or no use politically because while it depicted a society containing slaves, it dealt with slavery only incidentally and had no case to make for the institution. The boisterous mood of this writing veers toward satire rather than toward apologetics; it makes no appeal to sentiment, which proved to be the most powerful weapon of both defenders and attackers of slavery.

During the 1830's and early 1840's the case for westward expansion of the plantation system was the case for the annexation of Texas. The fertility of this enormous region beyond the Sabine, the mildness of its climate, its unexampled resources of every kind were presented so enthusiastically by travelers and settlers that an epidemic of "Texas fever" raged in the South.[20] Despite Mexican laws, slavery had been established in Texas from the earliest days of Anglo-American settlement, and it was generally recognized that the region offered a vast area suitable for the

[19] Francis P. Gaines, *The Southern Plantation. A Study in the Development and Accuracy of a Tradition* (New York, 1925).

[20] Lewis C. Gray, *A History of Agriculture in the Southern United States to 1860*, 2 vols. (Washington, 1933), II, 906–907.

cultivation of cotton and other plantation crops. Yet pro-slavery advocates of annexation failed entirely to create symbols comparable to the free-soil symbol of the yeoman. They were prepared to defend slavery as such with the standard doctrines, and to state the familiar propositions of manifest destiny, but they were not able to endow the westward expansion of the slave system with imaginative color. One of the most celebrated statements of the case for annexation is a letter written by Robert J. Walker of Mississippi for circulation as campaign literature in 1844. Asserting that the reannexation of Texas is "the greatest question, since the adoption of the constitution, ever presented for the decision of the American people,"[21] Walker makes the standard appeal to the need for restoring the integrity of the Mississippi Valley. The Creator, he declares,

> has planed down the whole valley, including Texas, and united every atom of the soil and every drop of the waters of the mighty whole. He has linked their rivers with the great Mississippi, and marked and united the whole for the dominion of one government and the residence of one people; and it is impious in man to attempt to dissolve this great and glorious Union.[22]

The oratory moves with assurance toward the images that had become a part of the folk heritage:

> Who will desire to check the young eagle of America, now refixing her gaze upon our former limits, and repluming her pinions for her returning flight? . . . Who will oppose the re-establishment of our glorious constitution, over the whole of the mighty valley which once was shielded by its benignant sway? Who will wish again to curtail the limits of this great republican empire, and again to dismember the glorious valley of the West? . . . Who will refuse to heal the bleeding wounds of the mutilated West, and reunite the veins and arteries, dissevered by the dismembering cession of Texas to Spain?[23]

[21] *Letter of Mr. Walker, of Mississippi, Relative to the Annexation of Texas: In Reply to the Call of the People of Carroll County, Kentucky, to Communicate his Views on That Subject* (Washington, 1844), p. 5.

[22] *Ibid.*, pp. 8–9. The prevalence of this argument is indicated by Albert K. Weinberg, *Manifest Destiny. A Study of Nationalist Expansionism in American History* (Baltimore, 1935), pp. 52–56. It should be pointed out that many proslavery Southerners were opposed to the annexation of Texas (Chauncey S. Boucher, "In Re That Aggressive Slaveocracy," *Mississippi Valley Historical Review*, VIII, 27, June–September, 1921).

[23] *Letter of Mr. Walker*, p. 9.

But in his treatment of the problem of slavery Walker falls back upon the defensive, picturing the economic ruin of the North and the social chaos of the South that would follow emancipation.[24] The annexation of Texas, he argued, would drain Negro population away from the older Southern states. A large and increasing number of Negroes, attracted by a congenial climate, would cross the Rio Grande and mingle with the population of the Latin-American republics to the South on a basis of social equality. Indeed, this process would eventually bring about universal emancipation. Slavery, announced the prophet with the emphasis of italics, "will certainly disappear if Texas is reannexed to the Union. . . ."[25] Providence would open Texas "as a safety valve, into which and through which slavery will slowly and gradually recede, and finally disappear into the boundless regions of Mexico, and Central and Southern America."[26]

Although this is ingenious, it is not an ideology of slavery expansion. The only Southern expansionist dream which had imaginative depth led in a different direction. This was the notion of a Caribbean slave empire, which found its most spectacular expression in the Ostend Manifesto of 1854. The Southern diplomats who in this remarkable document threatened forcible conquest of Cuba if Spain refused to sell the island to the United States, were trying to put into effect a geopolitical conception developed in part from the general notion of manifest destiny and in part from the idea of the passage to India. The oceanographer Mathew F. Maury, leading Southern scientist of his day, had called the Gulf of Mexico the American Mediterranean. Into this sea emptied the Mississippi, and the archaic Southern tendency to emphasize the primacy of natural waterways allowed Southern thinkers to conceive of the Gulf as dominating the whole interior valley. On the east the Gulf merged into the Caribbean, which touched the Isthmus of Panama, gateway to the Pacific; control of the Gulf was said to mean mastery of the dominant commercial route to the Indies. Southward the Caribbean led to South America, where the slave empire of Brazil in the fabulous basin of the Amazon offered the world's most promising theater for expansion of the plantation system.[27] The key to all this potential empire was Cuba: ". . . if we hold Cuba," wrote an editorialist in the Richmond *Enquirer,* "in the next fifty years we will hold the destiny of the richest and most increased commerce that ever dazzled the cupidity of man. And with that

[24] *Ibid.,* p. 11.
[25] *Ibid.,* p. 14.
[26] *Ibid.,* p. 15.
[27] Mathew F. Maury, "Gulf of Mexico," in James D. B. DeBow, ed., *The Industrial Resources, Etc., of the Southern and Western States,* 3 vols., (New Orleans, 1852), I, 365–373.

commerce we can control the power of the world. Give us this, and we can make the public opinion of the world."[28]

Well might a Southerner point out that the South had a manifest destiny different from that of the North.[29] The conception of a tropical empire occupying the basins of the Amazon and the Mississippi and controlling the trade of the Pacific, populated by Negroes brought from Africa through a reopened slave trade—"the purple dream," as Stephen Vincent Benét calls it,

> Of the America we have not been,
> The tropic empire, seeking the warm sea,
> The last foray of aristocracy,—*[30]

offers a glaring contrast with the myth of the garden of the world which expressed the goals of free-soil expansion into the Mississippi Valley. But the dream was powerful enough to inflame a young printer and newspaperman in Keokuk, Iowa, Sam Clemens by name, who set out down the Mississippi in 1856 on his way to found a coca plantation on the Amazon.[31]

[28] Reprinted in *DeBow's Review*, XVII, 280–281 (September, 1854). The Democratic platform in 1856 demanded that the United States maintain its ascendency in the Gulf of Mexico to protect the mouth of the Mississippi, and that American "preponderance" in the Interoceanic Isthmus be guaranteed also.

[29] "J. C.," "The Destinies of the South," *Southern Quarterly Review*, N. S. XXIII, 201 (January, 1853).

* Copyright, 1927, 1938, by Stephen Vincent Benét.

[30] *John Brown's Body* (Garden City, New York, 1928), p. 374.

[31] Albert Bigelow Paine, ed., *Mark Twain's Letters*, 2 vols. (New York, 1917), I, 34–35. Mark Twain mentions the report by Lieutenants William L. Herndon and Lardner Gibbon (*Exploration of the Valley of the Amazon, Made under Direction of the Navy Department*, 2 vols. and volume of maps, [Washington, 1853–1854], 32 Cong., 2 Sess. Senate Executive Document No. 36). Herndon was a Virginian and the brother-in-law of Maury, whose views about the development of the Amazon valley as a slave empire he shared (I, 193, 281). The expedition was ordered by John Pendleton Kennedy, Secretary of the Navy, and bore an obvious relation to Southern policy. Coca, in which Mark Twain was interested, is mentioned at I, 88–89, 249; II, 46–47.

10

Cavalier and Yankee: Synthetic Stereotypes

William R. Taylor

By 1859 the plantation legend and its complement the southern cavalier had become the dominant images shaping southern social psychology. Though critical to the development of incipient southern nationalism, the South's psychological construction of the "cavalier image" was to be but one of a cluster of images which were eventually to emerge supporting the view that southerners were a distinct people. The important void yet to be filled on the historical landscape was a counter-image—the "yankee" stereotype. William R. Taylor, Professor of History at the University of New York, Stony Brook, delineates the political and psychological forces responsible for the emergence of Cavalier *and* Yankee as contending symbols of alien cultures North and South. Following a coalition of historical circumstances—particularly John Brown's raid at Harper's Ferry in October of 1859 and the election of Abraham Lincoln as President in November of 1860—the "incompatability of temper" evident in political matters now began to manifest itself psychologically. John Brown's "private war" served to reinforce the predatory Yankee image, thus maximizing psychological and political tensions. Lincoln's election, given the South's erroneous image of him as a tool of the abolitionists, worked to the same end. The quest for an independent and uncontaminated South was now largely completed. A whole new set of assumptions had emerged and taken hold, so forcefully in fact that even after the war images of Cavalier and Yankee would continue to engage the imaginations of southerners and northerners alike.

By the summer of 1861 the subdued, candid and reasonable exchange of
views which had taken place between Jefferson and John Adams some
45 years before seemed to belong to another, faraway age.[1] Early that
year, as every schoolboy knows, a separate Southern government had been
organized in Montgomery, Alabama. Fort Sumter had fallen in April, a
peace conference in Washington had collapsed and by July the United
States were at war with themselves. Historians agree that the vast majority
of people in the North and South had not wanted secession, to say nothing
of war, but events swept them up in a whirlwind of excitement and pre-
cipitant action over which no one, finally, could exercise control.

In the South the move to separate had at first received massive support.
Of those who hung back, some, perhaps most, were genuinely undecided,
others confused or indifferent, and still others afraid to acknowledge their
secret convictions. Little recourse was left open for moderation. The
choice, to use the language of the time, lay between "secession" and "submission." The insurgents, capitalizing on the fears inspired by Lincoln's
election and emboldened by their confidence in the invincibility of the
united South, had moved ahead, heedless of dissenting views.

One by one the "erring sisters" had departed "in peace"—South Carolina on December 20; Mississippi, Alabama, Georgia, and Louisiana during the month of January, and Texas on February 1. Not until late spring
or early summer did Tennessee, North Carolina, and Arkansas finally
secede. Only on April 17, and after Lincoln had called upon her for her
militia, did Virginia, the historical leader of Southern opinion, pass an
ordinance of secession. Missouri, Maryland, and Kentucky, although
tragically divided, chose to remain with the Union.

Along this middle tier of states, which separated New England and the
Northwest from the lower South, a resolution of conflicting loyalties was
arrived at only after agonizing and prolonged reflection and debate. Lincoln
correctly gauged the mood which existed in these still uncommitted parts
of the South when he inserted into his Inaugural Address, delivered in
March of that year, a pointed reference to Hamlet's Third Act soliloquy.
Was the South, he asked, contemplating suicide?

Will you hazard so desperate a step while there is any possibility that
any portion of the ills you fly from have no real existence? Will you,
while the certain ills you fly to are greater than all the real ones you
fly from, will you risk the commission of so fearful a mistake?[2]

[1] [For an interesting letter on secession] See Representative David Clopton of
Alabama to Senator Clement C. Clay, Dec. 13, 1860, in Clement Eaton, *A History of
the Southern Confederacy* (New York, 1954), p. 12.

[2] Richard Hofstadter (ed.), *Great Issues in American History: A Documentary
Record* (New York, 1958), p. 392.

In the state capitals, county seats, in village assemblies and in individual families, anguishing, seldom unanimous, decisions were made, and by midsummer the peoples of the North and South, sometimes with reluctance and sometimes in a fever of excitement, were beginning to array themselves on opposite sides of the battle lines. In a poem written that year, one of the Union's warmest advocates caught the sense of the moment in a few lines of verse.

> Beat! beat! drums!—blow! bugles! blow!
> Make no parley—stop for no expostulation,
> Mind not the timid—mind not the weeper or prayer. . . .[3]

The most memorable war in American history was about to begin.

Historians have long debated the causes which precipitated this rapid series of events, and doubtless they always will. Much has been learned about the subtle shifts of opinion which occurred within various Southern states between John Brown's raid on Harper's Ferry in October, 1859, and Lincoln's fateful decision in April, 1861, to send supplies to the beleaguered garrison at Fort Sumter. Careful studies have been made of the parochial political circumstances which heightened the sensitivity of parts of the South to sectional issues and made the election of Abraham Lincoln, as the Northern President backed by a Northern party, a nightmarish prospect. The list of Southern grievances against the federal government, it has been made clear, had been growing since the debates over Missouri in 1819–20; and the constitutional arguments employed at the time of secession have a history almost as long as the Union itself. The growth of the Southern movement for independence has been traced back to the statements of its earliest proponents in the thirties. It is the importance of this idea of Southern nationality, the popular supposition that Southerners and Northerners were distinct and different peoples, which has prompted the present study. If this idea had not been firmly embedded in the consciousness of extremists on both sides and vaguely present in the thinking of countless others, it seems doubtful that secession and Civil War would have taken place at the time and in the way that they did.

No one, of course, will ever be able to recapture in their totality the elusive feelings of individual Southerners in the face of these bewildering events, but it is clear that a significant shift in attitude took place after 1859. For a time during the early fifties the threat of open rebellion seemed to have disappeared. Problems there were, and some of them very grave, but concessions had been made. The South was enjoying flush times with

---

[3] Walt Whitman, "Beat! Beat! Drums!" *Complete Poetry and Selected Prose and Letters* (ed.), Emory Holloway (London, n.d.), p. 260.

cotton and slave prices at an all-time high, and Democrats responsive to Southern opinions were in control of the government in Washington. Then came the brief rehearsal for civil war, between Northerners and Southerners fighting over the corpse of "bleeding Kansas," the appearance on the scene of a sectional party with growing strength, a sudden and disastrous economic depression and Lincoln's highly publicized "House Divided" speech, made during his senatorial campaign in 1858. Lincoln himself conceded that some kind of crisis lay ahead, and a great many people who saw eye to eye with him on little else were inclined to agree. Then, in quick succession, came two events which shattered what little complacency remained in the South. Miscalculation of the significance of these dramatic moments was in the spirit of the times, rumors consciously launched grew rapidly out of control and genuinely conciliatory gestures on the part of the North slipped by unnoticed.

The first shock was provided by John Brown's Private War, as C. Vann Woodward has called it. This brief but highly publicized skirmish began near Harper's Ferry on the night of October 16, 1859, when Brown and 18 cohorts captured a federal arsenal. The struggle was of short duration, and it collapsed in a matter of hours. It left in its wake some 15 dead, a great mass of documents compromising Brown's supporters in the North and one of the most controversial prisoners ever to be arrested and executed by an American state. For many Southerners who took the documents at face value and let their imaginations play over the potential consequences of a massive conspiracy of this kind, John Brown personified Northern predatory intentions which they all along had suspected lurked behind the reasonable and accommodating gestures of Northern statesmen. His name evoked almost everything hateful about the Yankee character: destructiveness, conspiracy, and hypocrisy. Upon this one man for a time were focused the emotions which for close to 30 years had been gathering around the figure of the Yankee. Brown's defense by a few New Englanders such as Emerson and Thoreau, who looked upon him as a saint and a martyr, only quickened Southern response. The possibility that he may have been mad was dismissed by his attackers and supporters alike. The fact that certain of his defenders, like the Reverend Theodore Parker of Boston, were actively implicated in his conspiracy led to gross exaggerations of his real support in New England and the magnitude of his enterprise generally. Although not a single slave rose in rebellion and Brown's action was deplored in Washington by all but a few extremists in the North, the South in a matter of weeks was thrown into a state of panic and one of the worst witch-hunts in American history occurred as eccentrics and "suspicious characters" of all kinds, many of them innocent strangers passing through, were mobbed, beaten, and tarred and feathered in a vigilante effort to root out Yankees and potential Southern subversives.

No relaxation of tension followed. Rumors of slave insurrections swept the South during the next year. Finally, the election of Lincoln, who was popularly believed to be the pawn of abolitionists, and the anticipated prominence in his coming administration of William Seward, of "Irrepressible Conflict" fame provided the finishing touches to the picture of a Northern conspiracy about to be launched against the South.[4]

The state of feeling that existed in the South during these fateful months can be suggested in a series of brief tableaux. In Washington Southern congressmen, and in the South, federal judges, began to resign their offices; some like Senator James H. Hammond with hesitation, some with feelings of vindictiveness and triumph. Northerners who happened to be stranded in the South were threatened, mistreated, and even mobbed, and most of them rapidly headed for home. Daniel Hundley, a Southerner living in Chicago, fled the city under cover of night out of fear for his life. There was in fact a general exodus of Southerners from Northern cities. On December 22, 1859, a trainload of students from Philadelphia arrived in Richmond, marched past the stately capitol designed by Jefferson, and assembled before the governor's mansion to hear a speech from Governor John A. Wise on Southern self-sufficiency. "Let Virginia call home her children!" the governor told them, and he went on to advocate self-sacrifice and austerity. "Let us," he said, "dress in the wool raised on our own pastures. Let us eat the flour from our own mills, and if we can't get that, why let us go back to our old accustomed corn bread."[5] Troops of "Minute Men" wearing the blue cockade drilled before admiring Negroes who caught only the holiday spirit of color and display. Everywhere the hated Yankee became a figure of ridicule and contempt. He was a conspirator and a hypocrite, but he was also a coward. He would never fight, and he could certainly never win.

The move to dissociate the South from every contaminating northern influence had reached almost hysterical proportions by the time of Lincoln's inauguration. The capital was almost empty of its former official occupants. Southern politicians and their ladies, including many of the city's most prominent hostesses, had departed for home, leaving the incoming Northern administration to run the country and—such as it was—Washington society. It was all a little mad, Senator Hammond, himself once an ardent secessionist, frankly conceded—and suicidal too. "It is an epidemic and very foolish," he wrote in December, 1860. "It reminds me of the Japanese who when insulted rip open their own bowels."[6]

---

[4] C. Vann Woodward, "John Brown's Private War," *The Burden of Southern History* (Baton Rouge, 1960), pp. 41–68.

[5] Eaton, *Confederacy*, p. 1.

[6] *Ibid.*, pp. 9–10.

By the following summer, then, communications between North and South had broken down—even the mail had stopped moving across the Potomac—and many leading spokesmen of both sections now regarded one another suspiciously and hostilely as symbols of alien cultures. To Mrs. Chesnut, who was inclined to see things somewhat melodramatically and—like Lincoln—in familial terms, it was also a question of a divided household and a marriage gone bad. "We separated," she wrote in her diary, "because of incompatibility of temper; we are divorced, North from South, because we have hated each other so."[7] "And for so long a time," she might have added without greater exaggeration than she had already employed, since the hatred to which she referred had been slowly intensifying for over 30 years, and along with it the awakening sense of a divided culture.

Two English astronomers, Charles Mason and Jeremiah Dixon, in an effort to settle a boundary dispute, had run a line between Pennsylvania and Maryland in the 1760s, but no one had then conceived of such a boundary as dividing a North from a South. Jefferson had seen the danger of such a distinction at the time of the Missouri Compromise, but a popular belief in a precise demarcation between North and South was a development of the decades which followed, and the frontier was still indistinct even after secession. Maryland, immediately south of the line, remained loyal and other so-called slave states like Missouri and Kentucky, both of them in some measure Southern in their traditions and style of life, remained officially in the North. If there was a line, and increasingly Americans agreed that there was, it possessed no geographical definition. It was a psychological, not a physical division, which often cut like a cleaver through the mentality of individual men and women everywhere in the country.

The shift in attitude which occurred during the fifties and the alignment which rapidly appeared during the tense months following Lincoln's election in 1860, much as they owe to particular contemporary events, are deeply rooted in an equally significant but much less easily defined reorientation of American mentality which had been taking place at least since the thirties. If separation as a political and social fact was the immediate result of the political pressures, miscalculations and excited activism of these tumultuous months, the idea of a coherent South, of a distinct and different Southern civilization was not new in 1850, to say nothing of 1859; yet it was an idea which would have startled both Jefferson and Adams in 1816, and did in fact alarm Jefferson when he caught the first intimation of it in 1820.

---

[7] Mary Boykin Chesnut, *A Diary from Dixie* (Boston, 1949), p. 20; cited by Eaton, *Confederacy*, p. 17.

PARVENU — one who has recently acquired wealth, + has not yet secured the social position appropriate to it. *Arrivenate*

Cavalier and Yankee: Synthetic Stereotypes 139

Neither Jefferson nor Adams, furthermore, had thought of the natural aristocrat—their choice for the republican leader—as possessing any particular regional traits. Neither, certainly, would have localized either lower-class villainy or aristocratic honor and virtue in any North or South which they knew. Adams, with his alertness to the danger of a false aristocracy in New England and with his keen sense of fallibility, saw evil and ambition lurking in every man's heart. He probably would have found the fully developed idea of the Yankee laughable and yet a little appealing, but he scarcely would have looked for better human materials south of the Potomac. Jefferson would have looked upon the full-blown Cavalier ideal with something like loathing and seen in its currency the undoing of much that he had worked to accomplish. Yet some three decades were sufficient to bring about these changes and to usher in a whole new set of assumptions concerning the history, cultural background, and racial composition of the two regions from which these two men had sprung— and for which they had made themselves the spokesmen. The nature of these changes is implicit in the preceding chapters, but the pattern of change is a somewhat complicated one and perhaps deserves brief reiteration.

The Southern Cavalier Redivivus

The first quarter of the nineteenth century had not passed before a significant number of Americans in both the North and the South had begun to express decided reservations about the direction progress was taking and about the kind of aggressive, mercenary, self-made man who was rapidly making his way in their society. In everyone's eyes this type of parvenu came to express a worrisome facet of the national character, to symbolize, in fact, both the restless mobility and the strident materialism of new world society. In the face of the threat which seemed to be posed by this new man, Americans—genteel and would-be genteel—began to develop pronounced longings for some form of aristocracy. They longed for a class of men immune to acquisitiveness, indifferent to social ambition and hostile to commercial life, cities, and secular progress. They sought, they would frankly have conceded, for something a little old-fashioned.

Writers like Cooper, Sarah Hale, and Paulding, themselves representative spokesmen of a much larger group, were particularly attracted by the idea of a conservative country gentry such as England possessed—or, at least, had possessed—only purer and better. The equalitarian character of life in the North provided an unsuitable terrain in which to locate, even in fantasy, an aristocracy of this kind. By the 1830s the legendary Southern planter, despite reservations of one kind or another, began to seem almost perfectly suited to fill the need. His ample estates, his spacious style of life, his Cavalier ancestry and his reputed obliviousness to money matters gained him favor in the eyes of those in search of a native American aristocracy. More and more, he came to be looked upon *the* characteristic expression of life in the South. Meanwhile, the acquisitive man, the man on the make, became inseparably associated with the North and especially with New England. In the end, the Yankee—for so he became known— was thought to be as much the product of the North as the planter-Cavalier of the South. By 1850 these two types—the Cavalier and the Yankee— expressed in the popular imagination the basic cultural conflict which people felt had grown up between a decorous, agrarian South and the rootless, shifting, money-minded North.

No such absolute division, of course, ever really existed between the North and the South. Southerners engaged in business, speculated on real estate, sought profits, lived in towns and cities, voted for the same national parties and subscribed to many of the same ideals and values as other Americans. What differences they developed, as over the issue of Negro slavery, did not lead many of them to formulate a totally different set of social objectives; these differences simply complicated their response to objectives which they already in large measure had accepted. Thus, in crying out against the Yankee North, Southerners who did so were, in a sense, striking out at part of themselves. By 1860 they had become self-divided, frustrated in their hopes and wishes, increasingly unrealistic in their social aspirations and ripe for some kind of bloody showdown.

The problem for the self-conscious South finally lay in the need which it felt to isolate—to quarantine—itself from the contaminating influence of the Yankee North, which it both feared and envied—and which, finally, was so much a part of itself. The result was the creation of an exclusively Southern historical, and even racial, heritage. Outvoted or overruled in national affairs, outgrown in population, outproduced and, as many Southerners at least secretly felt, outraged on the justice of slavery, the South in 1860 sought some kind of redemption in separateness, only to set up a Confederate government which was not essentially different, even in its constitutional details, from the federal republic from which it had just seceded.

The "Southern" problem was, then, for these men a condition of paralysis brought on by conflicting loyalties—they finally could not believe in either their own regional ideals or those of the country as a whole. Belief in the one conflicted with belief in the other; the result was confusion, indecision, and a kind of gnawing dispiritedness. By the 1850s, certainly, they no longer believed wholeheartedly in the effectiveness of the Cavalier gentleman, since they, too, came to measure achievement by financial success and the gentleman planter was, almost by definition, born to fail. But neither could they worship success, since it was measured in dollars and cents rather than in honor and cultural elevation. The improvident, generous-hearted gentleman planter for them became increasingly a symbol of a Lost Cause—an insurgent, a dueler, a fighter against overwhelming odds—in short, a figment of a utopian social world which was doomed to be submerged under a tide of middle-class materialism.

Without quite acknowledging it, many Southerners during these years had been waging a kind of war with themselves. Increasingly their ideal of a stable social order came into conflict with the social and political realities with which they were confronted. The lowly, whether white or black, gave clear evidence that they did not wish to remain lowly and feudally dependent upon the planter's goodwill. Even women were beginning to speak out in their own names, and some of the things they said represented a distinct challenge to the patriarchal role which the planter had assumed for himself and to many of the values which he thought of himself as embodying. Meanwhile, in the larger sphere of political events, the planter class in the Southern states, divested of the support of the West and challenged at home by its own yeomanry, found its power threatened both in Washington and in state legislatures. And what was an aristocrat who did not possess the power to order his own home, to say nothing of ruling over the national councils, especially when he was beginning to question some of the sanctions upon which his power had been based?

The Alabaman, Daniel Hundley,[8] for example, expressed his ambivalent attitude toward the force of the Cavalier ideal in his *Social Relations in our Southern States,* the book which he published on the eve of the war. In it he drew an ominous picture of the aristocrat in the South surrounded by predatory, or at least more forceful, social types, who seemed destined to overthrow his cultural and political domination. His book contained chapters devoted to the Southern Yankee, the southern bully, the poor white, and the enterprising and forward-looking representative of the new middle class. While he argued for the aristocratic ethos of the Southern gentleman, his confidence in his effectiveness clearly wavered before the vision of a rising Southern bourgeoisie.

Few figures in Southern history exemplify better than Edmund Ruffin the tensions and frustrations felt by those who had long battled for the Lost Cause. Ruffin, for years one of the South's leading agricultural scientists and an advocate of a diversified farm economy, was never reconciled to the defeat of the Cavalier ideal. Toward the end of his life, weary and partly deaf, he became obsessed by the idea of an independent, uncontaminated South and fought every inroad of what he regarded as Yankeeism. Dressed—rather conspicuously—in coarse Southern homespun; or,

---

[8] Hundley is discussed at greater length in another section.

in 1859, at the age of 63, attending John Brown's hanging clad in the uniform of a VMI cadet; or, as a volunteer in the Palmetto Guards, pulling the lanyard that sent one of the first shells toward Fort Sumter, he became a kind of Lanny Budd of the Old South, his every act a symbolic representation of Southern intransigeance before the Yankee North.

Few men more keenly sensed or more deeply resented the obstacles with which true Southernism was confronted within the South itself; no one, certainly, lashed out at the Yankee with greater bitterness or, finally expressed his feelings of frustration and self-defeat more melodramatically. As an agitator he repeatedly faced indifferent Southern audiences and, poor speaker that he was, he constantly reproached himself for his failure to bring the South to a boil. Virginia he early abandoned as reprobate; he was appalled to find the large planters in Kentucky holding strong Unionist views; and even South Carolina constantly disappointed him by her unwillingness, as in 1850, to take deliberate action. On a visit to White Sulphur Springs in August, 1859, he was astonished to find himself virtually alone among some 1600 Southern guests in calling for secession. For a time after John Brown's raid he hoped "the sluggish blood of the South" would be stirred,[9] and he personally sent pikes with which Brown had intended to arm the slaves to the governors of all the Southern states; but once again he was disappointed in his expectations. Even when confronted with the virtual certainty of Lincoln's election, no state except South Carolina expressed a willingness to take the initiative in seceding. The election of 1860, in which the more moderate Bell triumphed over Breckinridge within the South by a majority of 136,875, only confirmed his fear that the South would never act.

Then, as Southern states began to pass ordinances of secession, his hopes soared one final time. After a lifetime of ceaseless struggle, his dream of an independent South seemed about to become a reality. Once the exciting days of Fort Sumter were over, even these hopes were dashed as Jefferson Davis neglected former secessionists and formed a government dominated by moderates and men Ruffin regarded as would-be reunionists. Davis himself, furthermore, seemed slow to move and indecisive, and left Southern extremists generally dissatisfied with his leadership. But for Ruffin—as for most Southerners—the most crushing blow, one which destroyed for all time the myth of Southern invincibility, was the military defeat of the South by the Northern armies that swarmed across his beloved Virginia, destroying his plantation "Beechwood" and leaving obscene graffiti scrawled on the walls of his house. His plantation a shambles, deserted

[9] Avery Craven, *Edmund Ruffin Southerner: A Study in Secession* (New York, 1932), p. 171.

by his slaves, his hearing gone, and the alien North on his very doorstep, he had little left to him that he valued save his sense of honor, his bitterness, and his pride, to which he regularly gave expression in a diary kept through these trying years.

On June 17, 1865, after he had digested the news from Appomattox, he made this entry in the diary:

> I here declare my unmitigated hatred to Yankee rule—to all political, social and business connections with the Yankees and to the Yankee race. Would that I could impress these sentiments, in their full force, on every living Southerner and bequeath them to every one yet to be born! May such sentiments be held universally in the outraged and downtrodden South, though in silence and stillness, until the now far-distant day shall arrive for just retribution for Yankee usurpation, oppression and atrocious outrages, and for deliverance and vengeance for the now ruined, subjugated and enslaved Southern States! . . . And now with my latest writing and utterance, and with what will be near my latest breath, I here repeat and would willingly proclaim my unmitigated hatred to Yankee rule—to all political, social and business connections with Yankees, and the perfidious, malignant and vile Yankee race.[10]

Almost before the ink of this entry had dried the old man performed his most symbolic act. Seating himself erectly in his chair, he propped the butt of his silver-mounted gun against a trunk at his feet, placed the muzzle in his mouth and, as his son reported in a letter to members of the family, "pulled the trigger with a forked stick."[11]

Coda

With Edmund Ruffin's suicide and the collapse of the Confederacy which it symbolized, the Old South as a concrete entity passed beyond history and into legend. One prolonged attempt to establish and sustain an aristocratic ideal in the face of obstacles of the kind invariably thrown up by American circumstances had ended. It was not the first such attempt, as colonial historians have shown,[12] nor was it to be the last, as those

---

[10] *Ibid.*, p. 259. The information about Ruffin, except for the details of his death, derives entirely from Professor Craven's biography.

[11] Edmund Ruffin, Jr., to his sons, June 20, 1865, in "Death of Edmund Ruffin," *Tyler's Quarterly Historical and Genealogical Magazine,* V (January, 1924), 193.

[12] Bernard Bailyn, "Politics and Social Structure in Virginia," *Seventeenth-Century America: Essays in Colonial History* (ed.), James Morton Smith (Chapel Hill, 1959), pp. 90–115.

familiar with elitist groups at the end of the century can testify;[13] but perhaps, because of its bearing on the course of American history before 1861 and because of its more general consequences for the development of our cultural self-awareness, it has been the most important.

The Cavalier ideal was predestined to fail, as some of its earliest proponents secretly knew. The men who originated it were not aristocrats in any sense which Europeans would have recognized. Often they themselves were self-made men, provincial in their outlook and historically naïve, who possessed no sure sense of any cultural tradition. I have spoken, principally as a matter of convenience, of "the South" and "the planter class" in assigning a specific locus to the kind of thinking which I have been describing; but at no time, I suspect, was the Cavalier ideal as it was defined by Beverley Tucker, for example, widely understood or embraced by Southern planters in general, to say nothing of other people living within the South. Such an ideal was significant because it exemplified an important American cultural problem and because it defined a tendency in Southern thought which ultimately affected political events.

As it moved toward implementation, of course, the ideal was repeatedly and necessarily compromised. The constitution of no Southern state, not even that of South Carolina, provided for anything more than a kind of modified planter oligarchy; most of the older states within the South yielded to democratic pressures before the war; and the newer states of the Southwest were no more exclusive in their political arrangements than comparable states in the North. The Confederate constitution, finally, despite its explicit recognition of slavery, was in no sense meant to set up an aristocracy, and in certain ways it provided more assurance of popular government than the federal Constitution.

The legacy left behind by the Cavalier ideal is a little difficult to define; a careful consideration of it would require a study in itself. The close of the war did not mean, certainly, that some kind of aristocratic ideal ceased to form a part of Southern thinking, nor did it mean, once Reconstruction was over, that some kind of planter class ceased to dominate Southern politics. Quite the contrary. The century had virtually ended before the old dominant groups in the South and their new business allies received any substantial challenge from the majority of Southerners, whose affairs they had historically directed. After the war, as everyone knows, the legend, far from dying away, was given a new lease on life and, in the North, probably enjoyed greater popularity and evoked more interest than at any other time. Its vitality, it seems apparent enough, has not yet

---

[13] Barbara Miller Solomon, *Ancestors and Immigrants: A Changing New England Tradition* (Cambridge, Mass.; 1956); Arthur Mann, *Yankee Reformers in The Urban Age* (Cambridge, Mass., 1954).

exhausted itself today after more than a century of discussion and dramatic reembodiment. The nostalgia felt by Americans for the antebellum South and for the drama of the Civil War is a phenomenon which continues to startle those unfamiliar with our culture, with our collective anxieties about the kind of civilization we have created, and with our reservations concerning the kind of social conformity which, it appears, it has been our destiny to exemplify before the world. Some of our greatest writers—Henry Adams and Henry James within the nineteenth century—have employed the Cavalier legend as a means of defining and measuring the failures and limitations of our culture at large. It seems scarcely necessary to add that this same concern has characteristically engaged the imagination of William Faulkner. But for the great mass of Americans, even those who take their impression exclusively from popular novels, television plays, and Civil War centennials, the Old South has also become an enduring part of our sense of the past. At odd moments probably even the most skeptical of us allow our thoughts to play over this lingering social image, and to concede with mingled pride and wonderment: "Once it was *different* down there."

idolaters — a worshiper of idols

11

The Confederate Myth

Frank E. Vandiver

To the minds of most, the War Between the States represents the greatest watershed and psychodrama of the national experience. It represents as well the most acute trauma in southern historical consciousness. The southern mind and its mystique are clearly wedded in the Civil War. To Frank E. Vandiver, Professor of History and Provost at Rice University, Houston, the impact of the war and the consequent emergence of the Confederate States of America had been debilitating as regards the social imagination of the South. It was the war experience that reinforced the "pseudo-past" of the Old South. It was by virtue of "the crusade of the planters" that a related, but nonetheless new, mythical edifice began to emerge from the ashes of Shiloh, Vicksburg, and Chattanooga. Ironically, however, it was not the mythologized Confederate leadership which functioned as principle architects of the "Confederate Myth," but rather future idolaters with an appetite for historical romance. In the wake of civil war, Confederate political and military leaders continued at the cutting edge of historical change. They stood in the vanguard of a New South, a redeemed South based on economic progress. It would be subsequent generations who would function as the mythmakers and falsifiers of history—seeing the revolutionary generation as strict state righters, blind patriots to a "lost cause," and preservers of southern racial integrity. As has often been the case in other political circumstances, it was "enterprising conservatives" who led a historical pilgrimage to the shrine of dead radicals.

From Frank E. Vandiver, "The Confederate Myth," *Southwest Review,* 46 (Summer 1961), 199–204. Reprinted with permission of the publisher and author.

In the states of the old Confederacy the Centennial celebration of the Civil War is to be largely a refurbishing of the Confederate myth. The Confederate myth is a vital part of life in the South. According to this legend, sanctified southern ancestors fought valiantly against virtually hopeless odds to sustain a "way of life" peculiar to the section of long, hot summers, and Negro field hands. This "way of life" never seemed to be wholly understood, but it found description in various paeans of nostalgia and in the self-image of all southerners. Key elements in the southern mode of living were tradition, dedication to the protocols of lineage, land, cotton, sun, and vast hordes of blacks. Tending southern life were a special breed represented by the planters. Not everybody by any means was a planter, but the myth holds that everybody wanted to be and that all had the same chance to rise to that pinnacle of grace—all save the noncitizens with dark skin. The planters came to hoard their status with a certain grim zeal. Under increasing pressure throughout the 1830's, 40's, and 50's, they turned to all types of protection—censorship, intimidation, propaganda, open hostility to fellow-Americans.

But their tactics were glossed by myth into a creditable struggle for self-determination against a tide of urban nationalism which threatened extinction of the "way of life" so happy and so alien to the time.

The crusade of the planters spread to a campaign for Southern Rights, and hence the small farmer, the town merchant, the southern clergy found themselves sharing the planter's war. What was good for the planter was good for the South.

War, according to the myth, may not have been the only way to save the social and economic order, but it showed how deeply dedicated were the southerners to their inarticulated "rights." Against forces most formidable the southerner pitted himself, his small fortune, his Lilliputian industry, his life, and his girded honor. He lost, but lost magnificently. He lost wholly, utterly, but out of the ashes of his homes, his cities, his broken generation, he salvaged his sacred honor. And with this scrap of victory he could build the myth that has sustained him, has shackled him to a false image, and has convinced him of a lasting difference between himself and the rest of the United States.

Marshall Fishwick, in a brave and controversial essay, "Robert E. Lee: The Guardian Angel Myth" (*Saturday Review,* March 4, 1961), points out that Lee's noble virtues, peerless leadership, and heroic acceptance of defeat fixed in the southern mind the meaning of the Lost Cause. That cause represented the true acme of southern achievement: for it died the flower of the South, and those who yielded up their blood were such southerners as all those who came since would like to be. They were the shining model, the marble image, the men above men who lived a brief moment as destiny's chosen. They were the South.

They still are the South, for they stand above, around, and beyond what the South now is, and loom as silent prophets to lesser men in troubled times. And so they are God and curse, inspiration and death. Their stone faces look from countless shafts to the past, and their sons, grandsons, and great-grandsons look with them. They are different from the present; they were alien to their time. So, too, the modern southerner who points to difference, to his ageless "white man's burden" and his genteel poverty. His ancestors lurking from musty picture frames stood against the leviathan state and its leveling tendencies. He, too, stands with his own perception of past obligations and future duties. If the rest of the nation has lost its agrarian innocence, the southerner remembers. He, at least, is faithful to a dim Jeffersonian image and to a Greek democracy ideal which came, was fleetingly touched by life and sustained by blood, and faded to the pantheon of lost glories. But the brief blood bath lent a strange endurance and gave hope to generations held tight in inertia, fear, poverty, and the horror of a lost dream and a shattered mirror. The broken image had to be conjured again, and when it came it was twisted into a grotesque sort of plaster beauty which satisfied its designers and doomed the past it seemed to limn to a hundred years of distortion.

Distorting Civil War southerners was not easy. They lived larger than most, fought, raged, cowed, bled, spoke, and died with the nobility of desperation. They were, like their northern brethren, touched with timeless animation. They were unique and so should have been immune to the myth-makers and falsifiers of history. But myth-makers are determined and their works often approved by necessity. So the Confederate changed from a human, striving, erring being to something much different. All Confederates automatically became virtuous, all were defenders of the rights of states and individuals, all were segregationists, all steadfast, all patriotic.

Like all lasting myths, this one had enough validity to sound good. The Lost Cause came on to the present as the last American resistance against the Organization State, against racial indistinction, against mass and motor.

And while post-Civil War southerners were pushing as fast as they could into the New South, were grasping Yankee dollars with enthusiasm, they purified their motives in the well of Lost Causism. Politicians found it a bottomless source of bombast and ballots, preachers found it balm and solace to somewhat reluctant middle-class morals, writers found it a noble and salable theme. What the South had been could be the touchstone for the future, could be the fundament of a section going into the industrial age with part of its heart and holding firm to the past with the other.

Lost Causism came to fulfil a role similar to that of the pro-slavery argument in ante-bellum times. It offered justification for resistance to the leveling tendencies continued by harsh Reconstruction measures. It cloaked the lawless Klansman and lent license to the segregating Christian. It was, finally, the cornerstone of the New South.

The tragedy is that the Confederate myth is so wrong. That the Confederacy could come to represent in the present things it never represented in its lifetime is an irony of the present southern dilemma.

What, then, are some of the axioms of the Confederate myth?

First: The Confederate States represented the unified nationalistic yearning of all the state rights advocates in the South.

Wrong. State righters were not unified and there is considerable doubt that they were in the majority when the Confederacy took form in February, 1861. Certain it is that they failed to gain control of the government under Jefferson Davis, and although they did much to impede the Confederate war effort, they did not dominate the high councils.

Second: The Confederacy was defended to the last by gaunt gray heroes who went with Lee and Johnston and others to the bitterest end.

Wrong again. There was probably more per capita desertion from Confederate ranks than from the ranks of the Union. Far more Rebel troops were absent from roll call at the end of the war than were with the colors. Much bravery, even shining, incredible heroism the southern men did display, but that they were all blind patriots is demonstrably untrue.

Third: Any Confederate could lick ten Yankees.

Possibly, but in the end the Rebels were "overwhelmed."

Fourth: Everyone behind the Confederate lines showed the same dauntless dedication to oblivion as the soldiery. Men, women, and children all served the cause to the last shred of cloth, the last window weight, the last crust of bread.

Not so. While there were many magnificent examples of fate-defying loyalty by southern civilians, there were also many examples of petty speculation, wanton brigandage, Unionism, criminal selfishness, and treason. Defection behind the lines, open resistance to Confederate laws, became a matter of national scandal before the conflict ended.

Fifth: All Confederate leaders were unswervingly dedicated to the cause and would have preferred to perish rather than survive under a despised and crushing victor.

Still wrong. Many Confederate leaders, including Davis, Stephens, Lee, and Stonewall Jackson, looked on secession with a jaundiced eye. Legal they thought it to be, but they doubted its practicality. And when the war ended only a few of the leaders who survived buried themselves in the past. Davis did, and so did lasting disservice to the section he strove to defend. Lee, on the other hand, put the war behind him and worked unsparingly for a prosperous New South sharing fully the destiny of a re-United States. His example set the tone for most veterans. Numbers of former generals, to be sure, used their combat records to gain some personal advantage, but most wanted that advantage to further a career in business or politics and hence partook of the new industrial age.

Sixth: The Confederacy fought not only for state rights, but also and especially to preserve racial integrity. The government and the people of the embattled southern states were solidly against letting down racial barriers and understood that a northern victory would mean abolition. The Negro was kept in his place in the Confederacy, was used only for agricultural and menial tasks, and what was good enough for the Confederates is good enough for us.

False, and this is false on two levels. During the war the South did attempt for a time to shore up the bonds of servitude, but when the pressure of defeat grew grim, various southern leaders, including Lee and Davis, came to advocate the use of slaves in the army; some even suggested freedom in return for service. And after the war, on the level of special pleading, the South engaged in a long paper conflict with northern historians about the causes of the fighting. A point which the southerners strove staunchly to sustain was that the war had not been fought to preserve slavery, but to preserve the "Southern Way of Life," of which slavery was only an aspect. Finally some argued that the war had been fought solely to gain independence, and cited the offer to England in March, 1865, of total freedom in exchange for recognition as proof.

Seventh: The Confederate government was a supreme, unsullied example of a state rights organization that remained loyal to the principles of Calhoun, even in the face of defeat.

This is the wrongest of all assumptions. Davis and his administration tried for a while to do what seemed constitutional under the narrow southern view of law, but war and a curiously unnoticed strain of mind in the South changed the course of governmental conduct.

Union sentiment, long-standing in many parts of the South, united with conservative Democratic sentiment and with latent Whiggery to introduce a new element in southern politics. Men who looked on violent change with repugnance banded together to prevent the secessionists from carrying the Confederacy to revolutionary excesses. These men, including Davis himslf, kept the Montgomery Convention in hand, saw to it that the trend toward vast, ruinous upheaval was halted by moderate counsel. The result of moderate control at Montgomery was a Confederate constitution much like that of the Union, a government based on established and familiar federal principles, and a president who had not camped with the fire-eaters. Many with these cautious views were elected to the various Confederate congresses and so held some authority through the war.

Caution and the natural conservatism of some Democrats and Whigs did not mean that these members of the Confederate Congress were unwilling to fight a hard war. Most of these southern moderates were men dedicated to strong central government as the main bulwark of law and order. They hated disturbance and resisted disruption of the Union. But when it came, they "went with their state," they stayed with family and land. They stayed, too, with principles of steady government, strong law, and established order. Consequently they stood for power in the hands of the executive, power in the federal government, and a stern war effort. It was these Whiggish moderates who came to represent the Confederate "left" and to urge big government to fight a big war. They knew something of the corporate state, saw that it had virtues for organization, and urged Davis and his cabinet to centralize and command. These neo-organization men supported the growth of a large army, strict taxation (in keeping with sound Whig monetary views), conscription, impressment of private property, and finally the use of Negro slaves in the ranks—even to the point of manumission in return for service. When the war ended, these same "leftists" of the Confederacy moved into the New South.

Many became leaders in new southern industries, some went into politics and supported the coming of northern capital, most stood for sound finances, restoration of order, and the onward march of business. These moderates, these quiet men who abhorred revolution but used it when they had to, were the ones who brought about the greatest revolution of the South. They changed the Confederacy right under the eyes of the rabid secessionists from a localistic community into a small industrial power run along centralized lines. They aroused resistance from the Confederate "right"—state righters and fire-eaters—but kept control and forced their opponents to adopt modern centralist measures to resist them. When their attempt to remake the wartime South ended in defeat, they continued their efforts with the aid of Radical Republicans and ultimately achieved their goal. The Old South disappeared in the smoke of Chattanooga's and Birmingham's iron furnaces, in the dust of Alabama's coal pits, in the busy marts of Atlanta, Houston, Memphis, and New Orleans. These quiet, soft action men were the ones who set the base for the rise of a new industrial giant south of Mason and Dixon's Line, a giant whose future, according to Professor Walter Prescott Webb, is limitless because of its natural resources.

But in one salient respect these Whiggish gentlemen failed to remold their native section: this boundless potential painted by Webb and many chambers of commerce is sharply restricted by the Confederate myth. Although the moderate businessmen of the Confederate and New South were willing and partially able to set the black man free, and did break the bonds of southern agriculture, they could not unshackle the mind of the South—the Negro became a symbol of all troubles, and the Confederacy lingered as the herald of the South's greatness. The myth holds that the South was so great when it fought with piteous ardor for a twisted past and for principles aged and vestigial, that there was no future left for it. Its future lay buried with its gray dead.

This stultifying acceptance of decline is the wages of the Confederate myth. What was, was pure and better than what is, and in what was lies a sort of self-realization. While the South was transformed by Confederates into a moderately modern, progressive nation, the myth twists the achievement of the rebellious generation and dooms descendants to cheating themselves. Acceptance of the illusion of rabid Confederate racism, for instance, leads the modern Confederate to waste a vast source of manpower—a source which could be of inestimable value if the South is to move into the rosy future that some have predicted for it.

The Centennial years could best be devoted to revising the Confederate myth and bringing it up to date. Instead of standing for a pseudo-past, for false traditions and sham virtues, it should be repaired by the reality of perspective into what it has always been. Lee, Davis, members of the Confederate Congress, many soldiers who fell gallantly on scores of fields, were alert, forward-looking southerners. They were willing, for the sake of their cause, to abandon old shibboleths, to change the very nature of their body politic and body social. Instead of looking back and making war with weapons withered by age, they looked at the new ones their enemies used and copied, improved, progressed. The Confederate States of America did not have America in the name for nothing. Confederates were Americans, too, and so had no fear of challenge. The Rebels accepted challenge and almost met it. Most of them surely would regard with scorn their descendants who look backward in frustration.

12

Dawn without Noon:
The Myths of Reconstruction

Carl N. Degler

With the afterglow of the sectional conflict still firing their imaginations, southerners and northerners collectively began the arduous process of reshaping the social and political configuration of the Southland. The desire to "bind up the nation's wounds," to redirect the frenetic energy of the Civil War into reconstructive channels, was a major compulsion of post–Civil War America. Indeed, the war for the Union had settled many issues, but had left as many outstanding. Unfortunately for "posterity," the historical record of the dozen years of Reconstruction—in fact, that of the total postwar experience from 1865 to 1900—has been extremely difficult to assess. An important challenge to the resultant legends of the Reconstruction era has been sounded by Carl Degler, Professor of History at Stanford University. Since the so-called "tragic era," Americans North and South have become addicted to a view of the postwar era depicting corruption and graft, military despotism, black political control, and white disfranchisement—all, of course, arranged by a vengeful and vindictive Congress. After examining the major deficiencies of such a view, Professor Degler concludes that black disfranchisement and *de jure* segregation did not ensue upon the withdrawal of federal troops in 1877. Rather, the southern attempt to keep the freedman "in his place" is a late nineteenth, indeed a turn of the century, phenomenon. In important ways, then, the southerner's image of the Negro as forged by the legacy of slavery continued in a reconstructed but largely undiluted biracial form into the twentieth century.

From pp. 217–232 in rev. ed., *Out of Our Past* by Carl N. Degler. Copyright © 1970 by Carl N. Degler. By permission of Harper & Row, Publishers, Inc. (Footnotes have been renumbered.)

There is a myth of Reconstruction history to which most Americans, Northerners and Southerners alike, give credence. In brief outline it goes something like this. In 1867, a vengeful Congress placed the southern states under a military despotism which supported by its bayonets an alien regime in each of the states, composed of white adventurers—the carpet-baggers and scalawags—and their ignorant Negro allies. For a decade thereafter, the story continues, these regimes looted the treasuries of the southern states, impoverished the region with high taxes, denied the southern white people any say in their own governance, and spread terror throughout the Southland. Not until the withdrawal of federal troops in 1877, it is said, did this nightmare end and decency in government return to the South. As in most myths, there is some truth in this one; but a balanced picture of Reconstruction is quite different.

For one thing, though it is common to think of Reconstruction as lasting the ten years from 1867 to 1877, the actual duration of the military and Radical regimes varied considerably from state to state. Democratic or conservative governments came to power in Virginia and North Carolina as early as 1870 (in fact, Virginia never experienced a true Radical civilian government at all); in Georgia in 1871; in Texas, Arkansas, and Alabama in 1874; in Mississippi in 1876. Only South Carolina, Florida, and Louisiana depended upon the withdrawal of federal troops in 1877 for the overthrow of their Radical government. In brief, Radical Reconstruction, including the military phases as well as the civilian, lasted as short a time as three years in two states and as long as ten years in only three.

Because it is so often assumed that Radical Reconstruction was synonymous with military rule, the role of the Army in the South during this period must be precisely understood. Under the congressional plan of Reconstruction as set forth in the acts of 1867, the South was divided into five military districts, each under a major general. It was the responsibility of these generals to oversee the establishment of registration lists for voters for the constitutional conventions and the election of new governments in the states of their districts. Once this was accomplished, civil governments based on the new constitutions would assume power. Generally, the ending of military rule roughly coincided with the date at which Congress admitted the state to the Union. Thus military rule ended in 1868 in all of the southern states except Virginia, Texas, and Mississippi, and in those states it was over in 1869 or 1870. (Only in Georgia was military rule ever imposed again.) Often, it must be admitted, the Radical civil governments required or utilized the aid of militia and sometimes the federal troops to support their regimes, but this does not mean that an extraconstitutional government was in power. For the greater part of Radical Reconstruction, then, the southern states were under civil, not military, government, and, in most cases, these were governments which conservative white Southerners could influence with their votes. Indeed, it was by losing elections that many of the Radical governments fell into conservative hands before 1877.

But even when the southern states were under the military, it should not be assumed that the government was corrupt, oppressive, or unfair toward the whites. Contrary to the usual conception of the military occupation of the South, the number of troops actually stationed in the whole region was very small. No more than 20,000 men were involved in the whole "occupation," of whom fully 7,000 were concentrated in the two states of Louisiana and Texas. No garrison, except those in Richmond and New Orleans, which contained 1,000 each, numbered more than 500 men. The relative weakness of the military force, of course, is a measure of the southern acceptance of northern control.

Though weak in manpower, the military was supreme in law. In fact, the whole machinery of government and law was at the disposal of the Army; its authority was final. But the acquiescence in this on the part of the Southerners—for there was no organized opposition—is weighty testimony to the relative fairness of the administration. "It would be hard to deny that, so far as the ordinary civil administration was concerned," William A. Dunning, the authority on Reconstruction and no friend of the Radicals, has written, "the rule of the generals was as just and efficient as it was far-reaching. Criticism and denunciation of their acts were bitter and continuous; but no very profound research is necessary in order to discover that the animus of these attacks was chiefly political. . . ." There is good reason for believing, he continued, "that military government, pure and simple, unaccompanied by the measures for the institution of Negro suffrage, might have proved for a time a useful aid to social readjustment in the South, as preliminary to the final solution of political problems."

Even later, when the federal troops intervened in the South, it was with care and with a concern for fairness to the whites. President Grant in 1871, much disturbed by the attacks of the Ku Klux Klan upon Negroes, prevailed upon Congress to pass an act to aid in the suppression of the violence. Only once, however, did the President invoke the broad powers which Congress granted; this was in the famous incident of the nine counties of South Carolina in 1871. But even in this instance, Grant was careful enough to have the Attorney General investigate the situation in the area before he acted, and the President withdrew his order for one county when he found he was mistaken as to the disorders and conditions there.

In the prosecution of Southerners for infractions of the so-called enforcement acts, passed in 1870–71 to assist in the suppression of opposition to Negro suffrage, the federal courts tried hard to be fair. Out of the hundreds of cases against whites for infringements of these laws, there were relatively few convictions. One authority, William W. Davis, a Southerner, has estimated that only about 20 percent of the cases under the acts resulted in conviction; and about 70 percent of them were dismissed or nolle-prossed. "The Federal courts," Davis has written, "insisted on reasonable testimony, and the judges, with some notorious exceptions, were generally fair in their rulings." Moreover, he added, "White judges were inclined toward leniency in judging the white man prosecuted under the force acts on the testimony of black men." In summary, then, it would seem that justice was obtainable for the white man even during the grimmest days of so-called Black Reconstruction.[1]

Perhaps the explanation most commonly offered for the ascendancy of the Radicals and the Negroes in southern state governments is that the conservative whites were disfranchised at the same time the Negroes were enfranchised. As a literal and nonquantitative statement, this is true, but as an explanation it will not hold water. At no time were sufficient whites deprived of the ballot to permit the Negroes and Northerners to take over the governments of the southern states by default.

Before the numbers involved can be discussed, the two different kinds or phases of disfranchisement must be understood. The first was during military rule, when Congress stipulated that those who had deserted federal office for the Confederacy or had voluntarily given aid to that cause were to be denied the suffrage and officeholding. Though it is impossible to obtain a completely accurate record of the number disfranchised under this rule (thousands of whites, for example, refused to register as a form of protest, but they are sometimes counted as disfranchised), the figure usually accepted is 150,000 for the whole South. This is to be compared with a total registration for whites in 1868 of about 630,000. Regardless of the size of the figure, under this disfranchisement only two elections were held, one for the choosing of the delegates to the state constitution conventions and the other for the selection of the officers of the new governments created under the constitutions. After that, the qualifications for voting would be those decided upon in the conventions and written into the new constitutions. And that was the second phase of disfranchisement.

Again, contrary to the usual opinion, the states, on the whole, in their Radical-dominated conventions were not as ruthless in disfranchisement as one might expect. And those which were, found that their disabling

[1] Even a work as critical and penetrating as W. J. Cash, *The Mind of the South*, published as recently as 1941, contains exaggerated presentations of what happened during Reconstruction. "For ten years the courts of the South were in such hands that no loyal white man could hope to find justice in them as against any Negro or any white creature of the Yankee policy; for twenty years and longer they continued, in many quarters, to be in such hands that such justice was at least doubtful."

clauses were removed before ratification. In the end, only Louisiana, Alabama, and Arkansas actually enforced suffrage and officeholding restrictions against whites; the other seven states placed no legal obstacle in the way of white voting. Finally, it should be noted that the number of southern leaders upon whom the disabilities of the Fourteenth Amendment were visited was greatly reduced as early as 1872. At that date no more than 750 Southerners, those who had occupied high office under the United States in 1860–61 and had deserted to the southern cause, were still barred from officeholding. The disabilities against these men were not removed until the time of the Spanish-American War.

In view of the foregoing, it is illusory to look to white disfranchisement for an explanation of the electoral successes of the Radicals in the southern states. Rather it has to be sought in the fact that many whites did not vote, either in protest or because of indifference, while many Negroes did, either from understanding of the issues or from compulsion from their white and Negro leaders. It should not be forgotten, in this regard, that the proportion of Negroes in the southern states was uniformly greater at that time than it is now. Three states, for example—Louisiana, South Carolina, and Mississippi—contained a majority of Negroes, and one would expect, everything being equal, to encounter a Negro-Radical majority in those states. Moreover, a comparison of the number of Negroes registered in 1868 in each of the southern states with the number of Negro males over twenty-one as listed in the Census of 1870 discloses that only in Alabama was the actual number of Negro registrants out of line with the potential number as counted in the census. In all the other states the registration figures are plausible and not the result of obvious padding or fraud.

This is not to suggest that fraud did not occur in Reconstruction elections any more than it is meant to convey the impression that New York City elections at this time were innocent of fraud; undoubtedly there was much in both places and on both sides of the political fence. The purpose here, rather, is to show that there is solid justification for the strong showing which the Radicals made at the polls and that it is not to be casually attributed to the "counting out" of the whites. As a matter of fact, even under military-run registration in 1868, white voters outnumbered Negro voters in Georgia, Virginia, Texas, and North Carolina, a fact which rather effectively demolishes the argument that military reconstruction disfranchised the white majorities. Yet, of the two phases of disfranchisement, this was the stricter.

Looming over all discussions of Reconstruction, whether by Southerners or Northerners, is always the question of Negro domination. Surely, in the fear-ridden mind of the South, the unforgettable evil of Reconstruction was the participation of the Negro in government. Actually, though, aside from the exercise of the suffrage, which will be left until later, the Negro played a relatively minor political role in the Reconstruction of the southern states. Indeed, so limited were the number of offices available to Negroes that some of the Negro leaders, one southern authority has written, complained to their white mentors that their race was getting too few plums of office. Often northern whites who came to the South did not look with favor upon Negroes in office, and Southerners who collaborated with the Radicals, retaining, at least in part, their southern-born attitudes on race, were chary of permitting too many Negroes to hold office.

Negroes, of course, did hold some offices under Reconstruction; in fact, outside the position of Governor, which no Negro held in any state, black men filled each executive office at one time or another. In only one state, however, was a Negro a member of the Supreme Court; that was in South Carolina. The vast majority of Negro officeholders, however, were local officials like county superintendents of education and justices of the peace.

Contrary to the legend, Negroes did not dominate the legislatures of the southern states. The popularity of James S. Pike's sensational and partisan book, *The Prostrate State,* a contemporary description of the South Carolina legislature, has fostered the erroneous conclusion that such a body was typical of Radical regimes. In truth, Negroes were a majority in the legislatures of South Carolina and Louisiana only, and even there not for all the sessions of the period. Negroes were also a minority in all of the constitutional conventions called under the military, except, again, in the instance of South Carolina, and in Louisiana, where the whites and Negroes were equally divided. (South Carolina and Louisiana stand out in this regard because each contained a large and old city in which lived numbers of free Negroes who had some education and experience outside of slavery.)

Perhaps if there had been Negro domination, Reconstruction in the southern states would have been milder, for in both the conventions and the legislatures of the states the Negro members were the opposite of vindictive toward the whites. "I have no desire to take away any rights of the white man," said Tom Lee, delegate to the Alabama Constitutional Convention in 1867, "all I want is equal rights in the court house and equal rights when I go to vote." Even in the Negro-dominated legislature of South Carolina, there was no disfranchisement of whites beyond that prescribed for officeholding in the Fourteenth Amendment. Whenever the question of amnesty for Confederates came up in the United States Congress, where several Negroes sat during Reconstruction, the Negroes were usually found on the side of leniency toward the white man.

The South Carolina convention was extreme and unrepresentative of its sister conventions when it sought to ban terms of opprobrium like "Nigger" and "Yankee." South Carolina was also out of line with the other states insouciant - lighthearted, unconcerned.

when it provided for racially integrated schools; only two other states
followed that example. For the overwhelming majority of Southerners,
Reconstruction did not involve the mixing of races in the public schools.
Nor did it mean the legalization of intermarriage between the races; the
ante-bellum statutes prohibiting such unions were retained by the Radical
regimes. The Negroes, in the main, wanted equality, not dominance.

Among the advantages which Radical Reconstruction brought to the
southern states were the new constitutions which the Negroes and Radical
whites wrote in each of the states. These organic laws stand up well upon
comparison with earlier and subsequent ones in the South. As E. M.
Coulter of the University of Georgia, and no friend of Reconstruction
Radicals, has written, "The Constitutions finally turned out were much
better than the Southerners had ever hoped for: in fact, some of them were
kept for many years after the whites again got control of the governments."
Generally they were "more democratic than the documents they supplanted,
made so by increasing the electorate through Negro suffrage, requiring the
total population as the basis for representation, reducing the terms of
office, and by adding such principles as homestead exemptions and non-
imprisonment for debt." The constitutions also provided for "free education for all and favored the economic development of the South," Coulter
concludes.

Unquestionably, the evil most often charged against Reconstruction was
the extension of the suffrage to a people the overwhelming majority of
whom had only recently emerged from the dependent status of slavery. It
is true that Negro suffrage in the South, aside from the intense fears
it stirred up in the whites, was conducive to fraud, deception, and, at the
very least, thoughtless voting. But viewed through the glasses of hindsight
and with the recognition that universal suffrage is fundamental to a democratic society, the enfranchisement of the Negro appears considerably less
"radical" today. The insouciant manner in which the suffrage was proffered
to former slaves and the universality of the extension are certainly open
to question, but the elementary justice of some form of Negro suffrage
cannot be denied by any sincere advocate of democratic government.[2]

[2] It should not be thought that illiteracy was one of the legitimate arguments
against Negro suffrage. Thousands of southern whites enjoyed the franchise even
though they could neither read nor write. In 1880, for example, white illiterates
averaged over a quarter of the population in Georgia, Alabama, and North Carolina.
J. T. Trowbridge, the journalist, who made a tour of the South in 1865–66, concluded that the Negroes should be granted the suffrage. "They are," he wrote, "by
all moral and intellectual qualifications, as well prepared for it as the mass of poor
whites in the South." In a good number of states of the Union at this time, even
immigrants were granted the vote prior to their acquisition of citizenship. The only
valid argument against universal Negro suffrage, it would seem, was the lack of independent experience which was inherent in the Negro's former slave status.

Unfortunately, on the matter of suffrage, neither white Southerners nor northern Radicals were prepared to adjust their conception of the Negro to reality. Though some free Negroes were obviously capable of voting intelligently in 1865, as Lincoln, for example, recognized, and most Negroes would be after the mentally crippling effects of slavery had had a chance to be outgrown, few Southerners could shed their blanket view of the Negro as an incompetent. "The fact is patent to all," a South Carolina convention of whites asserted in 1867, "that the Negro is utterly unfitted to exercise the highest functions of the citizen." The South would not change. "Left to itself," southern historian Francis Simkins has concluded, "the region would not have accorded the Negro the vote or other manifestations of equality. . . ."

On the other hand, the northern Radicals, fearful that the South, once back in the Union, would deny the vote to all Negroes, and especially desirous of creating a large number of new Republicans, went to the other extreme and decreed universal Negro suffrage. This solution, however, overlooked the obvious disabilities which slavery had temporarily stamped upon a majority of the Negroes and seriously underestimated the tenacity of the historically ingrained racial feeling of the whites. Today the only comfort which can be drawn from the thoughtless and opportunistic policy of the Radicals is that it did provide a means for the inclusion of the Negro in the electorate, even if the means almost smothered the ideal with disrepute.

Radical Reconstruction in the South left a more permanent monument than the Negro's transient experience in public office and a nobler one than the southern white's nightmares of racial amalgamation. This was the laying of the foundation of southern free public education. Almost all of the Reconstruction conventions and legislatures erected or revived systems of free public education—a not insignificant manifestation, it might be noted parenthetically, of the Radical propensity for making over Dixie in the image of the North. In most of the southern states, these Reconstruction efforts in behalf of public education remained after 1877 to become the bases upon which post-Radical governments built their school systems. Though the South had always had some free schools and even some local public-school systems, free education as it was known in the North by the 1850's began in the South only after the War for Southern Independence.

The other educational achievement of Radical Reconstruction in the South was the conversion of the whites to the view that Negro education was not only desirable but a necessity. This was largely the work of the Freedmen's Bureau. Prior to Radical Reconstruction in Georgia, for example, as Mildred Thompson has pointed out, the postwar government provided public education only for whites. Education for the Negroes was viewed as a waste of effort and perhaps even dangerous. All over the

South in 1865–67, northern whites who attempted to instruct Negroes were subject to attack and violence. The blazing Negro schoolhouse of this period was the predecessor of the later burning cross.

Despite such opposition, the Freedmen's Bureau succeeded in establishing Negro schools before 1867. At its height, the Bureau operated over 4,000 primary schools, 74 normal schools, and 61 industrial schools for Negroes. George Bentley, a recent historian of the Bureau, concludes that by 1867 Negro and white alike in the South had come to accept the necessity for public education of the former slave. "Certainly in this respect," Bentley observes, "the Bureau had performed a commendable service for the Negroes, for the South and for the nation."

By the time the reader has gotten this far in the "other side" of Reconstruction, he is probably somewhat annoyed at the absence of references to the well-known corruption and fraud so much a part of the conventional picture of the period. He is convinced that this noisome aspect will be conveniently forgotten. There is no denying the disreputable character of all too many of the Radical state governments. Certainly the histories of Louisiana, South Carolina, Florida, and Alabama during this period provide rather painful examples of what corruption can be and what government should not be.

But again it is necessary to emphasize that the total picture is not all dark. Mississippi, for example, under Radical Republican rule enjoyed a government as administratively honest as most Democratic ones, and in some ways decidedly more honest. "The only large case of embezzlement among the state officers during the post-bellum period," writes James Garner, the historian of Mississippi Reconstruction, "was that of the Democratic state Treasurer in 1866." Mildred Thompson, writing about her native state, says that in comparison with states like Alabama and South Carolina, Georgia under Radical Reconstruction "shows a marked moderation in her government, a lesser degree of reconstruction evils, less wanton corruption and extravagance in public office, less social disorder and upheaval. In Georgia," she concludes, "Negroes and carpet-baggers were not so conspicious, and conservative white citizens were better represented."

Though Virginia escaped entirely the period of Radical Reconstruction which other southern states endured after the cessation of military rule, she did not escape extravagance. In 1869, the first and last election under military rule brought the defeat of the Radicals in a free polling. But under the conservatives who then took office, Virginia contracted as staggering a public debt as those run up in the Radical-dominated states. Even the usual stories of the high taxes imposed by the Radical governments in the various states are susceptible of a different interpretation when put into some perspective. In 1870, for instance, when the average tax rate for the southern states was 15 mills, that of Illinois was 45.

The fraudulent dealings of the Radical regimes appear less exceptional and noteworthy if they are placed within the context of the times. For instance, it is instructive to realize that after the end of Reconstruction, each of the conservative Democratic governments in Georgia, Alabama, Virginia, Mississippi, Louisiana, and Tennessee had treasurers or other officials who absconded with or embezzled state funds, the individual defalcations often running to half a million dollars. Then, of course, the years of Reconstruction also included the Tweed swindles in New York City, in which perhaps over $100 million was robbed from the public treasury. And on the national level, the frauds and stealings carried out under the unseeing eye of President Grant serve to round out the picture.

Though not at all excusing the Radical frauds, the corrupt climate of the times does make it clear that the Radical pilferings were little more than particular instances of a general postwar phenomenon. And once this fact is grasped, it becomes apparent that it is not corruption which has fastened disrepute upon these short-lived regimes, but the fact that Negroes participated in them. "Corruption and extravagance increased the intolerance with which the Negro regimes were regarded," southern historian Francis Simkins has written, "yet even if these regimes had shown exemplary statesmanship they would have been unacceptable to white Southerners as long as Negroes comprising any part of them were regarded as political equals."

The tragedy of Reconstruction is that it failed. Rather than liberating the South from its fear of the Negro, Reconstruction exacerbated it; instead of re-establishing a two-party political system, it further fastened a benumbing single party upon a region which once had led the nation in political creativity. Yet neither that section nor the North was alone responsible for the failure; both have to bear the national burden—the South for its intransigent conservatism, the North for its bungling idealism.

As is apparent today, it was imperative in those first years after Appomattox that a way be found whereby the nation and the Negro might confidently look forward to the former slave's full and equal participation in American life. But the unique opportunity of those first years was squandered. Neither Southerners nor Northerners were capable of disenthralling themselves, as Lincoln had counseled; both continued to act within their historically determined attitudinal patterns. Lincoln himself, for that matter, failed to grasp the crucial nature of the postwar era, so far as the Negro was concerned. His plan for the rapid restoration of the southern states indicated that he was quite prepared to throw away the single opportunity for realizing the equalitarian precepts of the Declaration of Independence to which he so often referred. And though the Radicals succeeded in enshrining in the Constitution their vision of equality for all, thereby illuminating the path the nation was ultimately to follow, they were woefully unequal to the complicated and delicate task of implementing their vision. Having failed to meet the problem of the black man at its inception, white Americans have been compelled to grapple with it in each succeeding generation down to our own day.

The inability of the Radicals to translate their equalitarian ideals into reality through the use of force[3] brought an end to the first phase of the search for a place for the Negro in America. During the years which followed, the South was left free to work out for itself what it considered the Negro's proper niche. Contrary to popular conceptions of Reconstruction and its aftermath, the South was neither united nor decided on what that position should be. The evolution of the region's place for the Negro would take another generation.

The southern leaders and people in 1867 had been extremely doubtful about the wisdom of Negro suffrage; but when Reconstruction came to a close, they did not move to eliminate the Negro from southern politics. Instead there was a substantial period during which the South freely experimented with Negro voting. In states like Mississippi and South Carolina, where the Negroes were a majority, a policy of bringing them into the Democratic party was tried. During the 1880's in South Carolina, for instance, several Negro Democrats sat in the legislature. A Negro was nominated by the Mississippi State Democratic Convention of 1877 for the office of secretary of state, and it was not unusual in that state for fusion tickets to be set up in black counties with Negro candidates. Such moves, however, were scattered instances, rather than general conditions; most Negroes remained in the Republican party.

As Republicans the Negroes in the South after 1877 continued to vote and to hold office, though when they threatened the supremacy of the whites, fraud, violence, and intimidation were used to right the balance.

---

[3] At the risk of seeming to condone the often cynical methods employed by the Radicals in the South, the principle behind Reconstruction deserves some attempt at a defense. It is a common argument that force cannot change ideas or dissolve prejudices, and that, therefore, from the outset Reconstruction flew in the face of experience. It is true that ideas are best changed by sincere, inner conversion, but this is not always possible; and weak as enforced conversion may be as a foundation on which to build sympathy and understanding, it is sometimes the only alternative. In both Japan and Germany after 1945, the western powers, notably the United States, undertook to impose certain concepts and forms of democratic life upon the defeated peoples. The only essential difference between these efforts to change people's minds by compulsion and that of Reconstruction was in method; the modern effort was, all things considered, intelligently and efficiently handled. The principle, however, was precisely the same as that which animated Radical Reconstruction in the South. It would seem that only those who oppose the principle of forcible democratization of Germany and Japan can consistently condemn the leaders of Radical Reconstruction for trying to solve by force, albeit ineptly, the problem of the black man in a white America.

Negroes served in the South Carolina legislature right down to 1900, usually elected, of course, from predominantly Negro districts; during the 1880's and 1890's black representatives sat in the legislatures of North Carolina, Mississippi, and Tennessee. Negroes also represented the South in Washington after Reconstruction. Between 1877 and 1900, Negro representatives and senators from the South appeared in every Congress of the United States except the Fiftieth (1887–89). The Fifty-first Congress (1889–91), for example, counted three Negroes, one each from North Carolina, South Carolina, and Virginia.[4] All this came to an end, however, at the turn of the century, a pivotal date in the nation's search for a place for the Negro.

The first permanent law for segregating Negroes from whites in railroad cars was passed as early as 1881 in Tennessee, but it is erroneous to assume, as many have done, that the so-called Jim Crow laws went onto the statute books contemporaneously with the withdrawal of federal troops. Aside from bans on intermarriage and the initiation of legal segregation on trains, the large body of discriminatory legislation that characterized race relations in the South until very recently was unknown before 1898.

Before that date the mingling of whites and Negroes in public places was often quite unrestricted. In 1878, Thomas Wentworth Higginson, scion of a prominent Boston family, abolitionist, and former officer in a Negro regiment in the war, toured South Carolina to see the results of the resurgence of white conservative rule. He found the Negroes traveling on first-class cars, serving on the police force, and generally mingling with the whites in public places. Almost twenty years later in 1897, when a move was afoot to enforce segregation on railroad cars, a Charleston editor, by implication, indicated how little segregation there was in South Carolina. "Our opinion is that we have no more need for a Jim Crow system this year than we had last year, and a great deal less than we had twenty and thirty years ago." Such a system, he said, "would be a needless affront to our respectable and well behaved colored people." One anonymous Northerner, writing in the *Atlantic Monthly* in 1882, was told by the head of a racially mixed school in the South that "mixed schools" would come to the South. The author himself became convinced "that there will soon be mixed schools, for white and colored children, in many parts of the South. There are already a few such schools." Southern leaders acknowledged this possibility, he went on, and "they are not disturbed by the prospect."

Writing in *Harper's Monthly* three years later, Charles Dudley Warner,

[4] All during these same years, the North sent no Negro representatives at all, though it is only fair to add that the number of Negroes in that section was then very small. Not until 1929 did the first northern Negro sit in the Congress of the United States.

on a visit to the South, noted that "In New Orleans the street cars are free to all colors; at the Exposition white and colored people mingled freely. . . . " A Negro clergyman, he reported assisted at the services of the major white Episcopal church in that city. He was told by one Negro woman that in Mobile the Negroes had their votes courted by white politicians, and served in minor municipal offices and on the police force. Even the whites' Opera House, this woman told him, was turned over to the Negroes for an exhibition which the whites also attended.

To many visitors from the North, the South in the mid-eighties seemed to be making great strides in the direction of relaxation of racial discrimination. Part of this impression was merely a reflection of increasing northern sympathy for the southern point of view now that the emotion-packed years before 1865 were receding. But a substantial part was obviously a mirroring of the true situation. The end of the Reconstruction and the restoration of white rule had not resulted in the erection of a wall between Negroes and whites in the South.

But those who thought they detected a trend toward equality were destined for disappointment. Instead of expanding the realms of equality for the Negro, the South ultimately developed a pattern of race relations which clearly marked the Negro as a second-class citizen. The 1880's was a period when the legal racial pattern was still in flux, but already there were several signs pointing in the direction the South would go. For example, though there were very few laws requiring segregation, discrimination certainly existed, particularly in hotels, theaters, and on trains. And already in the 1880's, the ugly practice of lynching was spreading ominously. Between 1882 and 1903, almost 2,000 Negroes were lynched in the southern states, as against 567 white persons.

It was the Farmers' Revolt, coming to a head in the early 1890's, which finally brought the balance down on the side of increased restrictions on the Negro. The first form this took was the legal elimination of the Negro from southern politics. Aside from the small farmer's ever-present fear and hatred of the Negro, the aroused agrarian movement had new and compelling reasons for wanting to see the Negro deprived of the vote once and for all. The farmers believed, and sometimes rightly so, that the Negro vote was often mobilized against them, corruptly or otherwise, by the conservatives and the business interests against which they were fighting. Nor were these conservative leaders reluctant, if it served their purpose, to accuse the newly formed farmers' party of splitting the white vote and thereby endangering white supremacy. The complete removal of the Negro from politics, the farmers reasoned, would permit the whites to fight out their differences untroubled by the explosive and confusing issue of white supremacy. A further impetus to the elimination of the Negro from politics was given by politicians like "Pitchfork Ben" Tillman of South Carolina and James Vardaman of Mississippi, who were eager to use the poor man's Negrophobia as a handy vehicle to power.

The movement to eliminate the Negro voter permanently and constitutionally was led by the Mississippi Constitutional Convention of 1890, and the pattern arrived at there became the model for the rest of the southern states. During the nineties and the opening years of the new century, a veritable parade of southern constitutional conventions literally wrote an end to Negro participation in southern politics. To circumvent the prohibitions of the Fifteenth Amendment and yet eliminate effectively the bulk of the Negro voters, the conventions resorted to ingenious subterfuges. Poll taxes, complicated balloting procedures, and literacy tests were among the devices employed to strike Negroes from the registers.

Because the mass of poor white farmers had always harbored deep fears of the black man, these new constitutional provisions were only a translation into law of their own emotions and attitudes. But such legal narcissism exacted a price. The procedures adopted to exclude the Negro from the suffrage also operated to disfranchise thousands of poor, untutored white men who could not surmount any of the hurdles. White registration under the new Louisiana constitution, for instance, dropped 39,000 from what it had been only three years before under the old constitution; Negro registration fell over 125,000. But even this contraction in the white electorate—the reversal of a century of uninterrupted suffrage expansion—seemed worth the candle if it meant the elimination of a threat to white supremacy.

Under the momentum of these political changes, the southern states at the turn of the century began to issue a flood of legislation narrowing the Negro's sphere of activity and carefully defining his place in southern life. Segregation of the races was decreed on street-cars (only Georgia had such a law in the nineteenth century), in waiting rooms, in hospitals, in cemeteries, in housing, in prisons, at drinking fountains, and even in telephone booths (Oklahoma, 1915). Actually, the races were already segregated in practice in many of these areas without laws as sanctions, but in some instances the new laws, in logically extending the principle of separation of the races pressed the application even into minor aspects of life, such as drinking fountains and telephone booths. Certainly no such rigid and petty segregation of the races had existed in the South before; to that extent, at least, the law was creating "custom" rather than only reflecting it.

The segregation proposals of the late 1890's came as a shock to some white Southerners. One editor in Charleston, S.C., for example, where segregation was probably the least advanced in the South, voiced his opposition to legally enforced segregation on trains. He attempted to ridicule into oblivion the principle by carrying it out to what he thought was an obvious absurdity. "If there must be Jim Crow cars on the railroads, there should be Jim Crow cars on the street railways," he wrote. "Also on passenger boats . . . if there are to be Jim Crow cars, morever, there should be Jim Crow waiting saloons at all stations, and Jim Crow eating houses. . . . There should be Jim Crow sections of the jury box, and a separate Jim Crow dock and witness stand in every court—and a Jim Crow Bible for colored witnesses to kiss. It would be advisable also to have a Jim Crow section in county auditors' and treasurers' offices for the accommodation of colored taxpayers." But, as C. Vann Woodward has dryly observed, "What he intended as a *reductio ad absurdum* and obviously regarded as an absurdity became in a very short time a reality. . . . All the improbable applications of the principle suggested by the editor in derision had been put into practice—down to and including the Jim Crow Bible."

The southern solution to the problem of the races was to be a caste system for the black man in a society "dedicated to the proposition that all men are created equal."

13

The Old South to the New

Robert S. Cotterill

It is indeed fashionable to demarcate southern history into two
segments—the Old South and the New. Fundamental to the acceptance of such a division is the belief that the Civil War represented the epitaph of the Old Order and the herald of the New.
But even though the discriminating historian uses such period
pieces and watershed events with distinct mental reservation, Robert
S. Cotterill, former President of the Southern Historical Association, argues that their acceptance has gone beyond intellectual
convenience to become hardened stereotypes. Indeed, standard
interpretations resurrect historical replicas of an Old South—an
agrarian Cotton Kingdom—replete with bluebloods, rednecks, and
blacks. In turn, the rising New Order after The War for Southern Independence is held to represent its economic antithesis—
a "new" South bent on achieving economic salvation in terms of
an entente with northern industrialism. In opposition to such views
Professor Cotterill argues that the postwar decades witnessed a re-
newal of longstanding economic energies in the South. Perhaps it
was in the New South era that the region first developed an industrial awareness; but with the possible exception of furniture production, most significant forms of southern manufacturing were rather
clearly in evidence before the war. In sum, the New South was
clearly not "barren of ancestry, destitute of inheritance." Southern
economic life in the years after civil conflict drew its vitality and
direction from a potential already present, though as yet largely unrealized. The "New South" was anything but a historical aberration.
It was instead a continuation of The South as it had always been.

Robert S. Cotterill, "The Old South to the New," *Journal of Southern History*, 15
(February 1949), 3–8. Copyright 1949 by the Southern Historical Association. Reprinted by permission of the Managing Editor.

The term "New South," if not coined by Henry W. Grady, at least first put into circulation by him, had reference originally only to the cotton manufacturing development of the 1880's.[1] To contemporary observers the name was justified since it seemed evident to them that the South was at that time altering the pattern of its economic life, turning its back on its own history, and entering upon new roads to economic salvation. In the course of years the meaning of the term was broadened to include all phases of southern life since 1865. But the very name "New" South implies an "Old" South, and this latter term now became attached to the period prior to that conflict which southern people, stubbornly and ungrammatically, insist on calling the War Between the States. Inherent in the two terms is the concept not merely of a difference in time but of a change in civilization.

This concept of discontinuity between the Old South and the New has been strengthened in two ways. One of these is the glorification of the War Between the States and the emphasizing of the ruin and devastation it brought to the South. Denied the pride of victory, the southern people developed a pride of suffering. And the thought was an inevitable one that in a tragedy so terrible and a ruin so complete no previous pattern of life could possibly have survived. Therefore, the Old South must have died. The other way in which the idea of discontinuity has been increased is by the growth of a legend of the Old South as a land of plantations, slaveowners, aristocracy, and agricultural philosophy. White people, according to the legend, disdained manual labor and refrained from any debilitating practice of it. All work was done by Negro slaves, apparently in intervals between singing the praises of the Old Kentucky Home and making metrical demands to be carried back to Old Virginny. What few common people there were in the Old South were serfs subsisting on the economic crumbs which fell from the gentry's table. Such was the Old South of legend, and since the people of the New, looking around them, saw nothing even remotely resembling it, they reasoned, quite logically, that it must have died—as the genealogists so deftly put it, O. S. P.

These, then, are the three concepts inherent in the terms "Old South" and "New South"—a legendary "Old South" that has no present counterpart, a "New South" with a pattern of life unrelated to the Old, and between them a war so devastating that it destroyed the old order making it necessary to start all things anew.

The first of these ideas may be dismissed without argument. If the Old South of legend be no longer present, it is not because it died but because it never existed. It is a figment of imagination, originating in the ignorance, or malice, of northern abolitionists and adopted by southerners suffering

---

[1] [Omitted.]

from nostalgia. It was at once a distortion and an idealization, and in neither capacity could it transmit any part of itself to later times.

But the cotton manufacturing development of the 1880's which first gave rise to the name "New South" was no hallucination. The only question about it is not whether it existed but whether it was *new*. Certainly the people of that time called it "new," and its coming was accompanied by such a rash of publicity as had not broken out on the southern body politic since the railroad building of the 1840's. Editors, orators, ministers, poets, novelists, and businessmen hymned its praises, and canny politicians hastened to cast their political bread on its waters. They proclaimed that a New South was being born. There were some people then (and there have been more since) who viewed the development of manufacturing as a surrender of southern ideals and the adoption of a low, Yankee culture. But most commentators have considered it as a beneficent dispensation which had been denied to the Old South because of the enervating effects of slavery. The most noted of these has declared in one of his books: "In the face of a freed negro population, the idea of work first seriously presented itself to the Southern white mind."[2] But since the fifteen years that had elapsed between the adoption of the Thirteenth Amendment and the supposed beginning of the manufacturing movement seemed a bit longer than should have been necessary for such a powerful regenerative force as emancipation to get into mass production, supplementary explanations had to be given. These ranged all the way from the resumption of specie payment to the psychological shock of James A. Garfield's election. They ascribed the beginning of the manufacturing movement to the poverty of the 1870's and to the prosperity of the 1880's, to jubilation over the collapse of carpetbaggery and to despair caused by war and reconstruction, to exultation over the preservation of southern ideals and to repentance for ever having had any. But although the writers differed on the origin of the phenomenon, they all agreed on the nature of it. They all agreed that it was new: it was a revolution, unrelated to the past, barren of ancestry, destitute of inheritance.

But the student of history is insistent on sequence and consequence, he demands continuity and cause. He is uncontent to find an explanation of mundane affairs in the doctrine of virgin birth. Every historical event, he considers, must have a family tree as an accessory before the fact.

The difficulty writers have experienced in explaining the origin of the "Industrial Revolution" in the South may be primarily owing to the fact that there was no Industrial Revolution to explain. The so-called Revo-

---

[2] Broadus Mitchell, *The Rise of Cotton Mills in the South,* in Johns Hopkins University *Studies in Historical and Political Science,* Ser. XXXIX, No. 2 (Baltimore, 1921), 57.

lution was, in fact, not a Revolution but an *evolution* from the Old South to the New. If in the Old South manufacturing was only a handmaiden to agriculture, it was not because of agricultural philosophy but of agricultural profits. By 1860 the South had 188 cotton mills, the yearly output of which was valued at $14,000,000. If it be true that it was in the face of a freed Negro population that "the idea of work first seriously presented itself to the Southern white mind," it is pleasant to reflect that all this was done without effort. The recipe seems to have been lost. Certainly the growth of manufacturing in the Old South was sufficient to excite the apprehension of northern mill-owners, apparently unaware of the fact that manufacturing was impossible in a slavery regime. And if it were not uncharitable, one might suspect that the patriotic fervor of General William T. Sherman in destroying southern cotton mills was not unadulterated by a desire to eliminate competition. But Sherman, unlike Kilroy, was here only once and some two-thirds of the southern mills escaped his evangelical efforts. It is only reasonable to suppose that the war stimulated southern interest in manufacturing. But when southern people after the war engaged in manufacturing it was neither because of prosperity during the war nor of poverty after it. It was because cotton manufacturing was one of the recognized and accepted ways of making a living. They did not *begin* manufacturing after the war: they *resumed* it; they were actuated not by novelty, but by tradition. By 1870 the losses of war were almost fully recovered: then came the seven lean years of the early 1870's, the recovery late in the decade, and then the well-trumpeted development of the 1880's. But the South in the 1880's did not become suddenly *industrial;* it only became suddenly *articulate.* The beginning was not in *manufacturing,* but in *publicity.*

The industrial inheritance of the New South from the Old was not confined to cotton manufacturing. The derivation of the Durham cigarette from Russia and of the Tampa cigar from Cuba cannot alter the fact that the paternity of southern tobacco manufacturing lies in the Old South. In the ante-bellum period it was the output of plug tobacco from southern factories that lifted expectoration in the United States to a position among the fine arts along with music and painting, and made the cuspidor standard equipment in the American home. As for iron manufacturing, even in colonial days it was important enough to be prohibited and too important to be prevented. Of the other manufactures of the New South, the only important one lacking an Old South pedigree is furniture. Even the manufacture of cottonseed oil had its beginning in the Old South, although quite a bit of it in the process of labeling seems to have undergone a metamorphosis into olive oil. The Old South discovered the coal mines of Maryland, Kentucky, Tennessee, and Alabama and exploited them so far as transportation facilities permitted. And if the petroleum industry be considered a species of mining, we may remember that Louisiana discovered oil before she discovered secession.

The only important change made by the New South in its agricultural inheritance was the substitution on its plantations and larger farms of share-cropping for slave labor and of the country store for the factorage system. Both share-cropping and the country store were Old South institutions now expanded into wider uses. Share-cropping, of course, did not originate in the Old South, but is as old as agriculture itself. The first record of it is found in Genesis 29-31 where it is told how Jacob tended on shares the flocks of his uncle Laban in the land of Pandan-aram. It may be noted, incidentally, that Jacob broke his contract, moved away secretly, and took a considerable portion of his landlord's property with him—thereby establishing a precedent that has been followed extensively to this day.

In no place of its economic life was the New South new. It was not a Phoenix rising from the ashes of the Old; not a revival; not even a reincarnation: it was merely a continuation of the Old South. And not only in its economic life: the New South inherited, also, the *spirit* of the Old. It inherited its racial pride, and if anyone wants to call it racial prejudice, there can be no objection, because pride and prejudice were inseparable companions long before Jane Austen proclaimed their union. The student of history cannot turn moralist either to exalt or to condemn this racial pride, but he must take note of its continuing existence. The New South inherited, also, a laissez-faire philosophy of living which manifested itself subjectively in an indifference to progress and objectivity in a distaste for reforming its neighbors or to confessing other people's sins. It inherited the Old South conviction that certain questions could not be surrendered to the jurisdiction of public law. The one quality of the Old South apparently uninherited by the New was self-confidence and consequent self-assertion. Says a Confederate arithmetic: If one southerner can whip twelve Yankees, how many Yankees can six southerners whip? Although the premise of this problem seems to have been somewhat unstable, it evidences a spirit of confidence that for a long time seemed lost to the New South. It may be, however, that the aggressiveness and boastfulness so characteristic of the Old South instead of dying out after the war simply followed the trail of cotton and migrated to Texas. From the time they annexed the United States in 1845 until their recent singlehanded and unaided conquest of Germany and Japan, Texans have been noted for their aversion to understatement. But it is possible that when Texans talk "big" they are speaking not as Texans but as southerners. Certainly, that Texan was speaking the language of the Old South when he rose at a banquet and gave this toast to his state: "Here's to Texas. Bounded on the north by the Aurora Borealis, bounded on the east by the rising sun, bounded on the south by the precession of the equinoxes, and on the west by the Day of Judgment."

As to the final factor in our concept, the War Between the States cannot be considered as a mighty cataclysm engulfing the Old South or as a chasm dividing the Old South from the New. The pondering of might-have-beens is normally an exercise taken in vain, but it seems clear that in no essential way did the war alter or deflect the course of southern development. It was an interruption but not a cleavage. It was, in long perspective, only an episode in a continuous southern history: a tragic episode, but even its tragedy was transient. No southerner can be tempted to belittle the war or deplore the remembrance of it. Surely it was worthy of all remembrance —a war of heroism unrewarded, of suffering uncompensated, of hopes unrealized, and of dreams that have no waking. But for the South it marked no end and no beginning: it neither buried the Old South nor brought the New to birth. There is, in very fact, no Old South and no New. There is only The South. Fundamentally, as it was in the beginning it is now, and, if God please, it shall be evermore.

14

The Enigma of the South

David M. Potter

To a considerable degree the idea of a South segregated from national cultural and political patterns, and the cluster of images supporting that proposition, produced civil war in 1861. But despite the cathartic nature of the war experience, notions of southern distinctiveness continued to find sanction in the postbellum decades. Fascination with the South's legacy of agrarianism, for example, remained a southern predisposition long after the war itself had passed into historical memory. Countering the opinions of some historians and important segments of the southern literary establishment, David M. Potter, late of Stanford University, attests that the tempting equation of southernism and agrarianism is a myth. Though apparently stemming from the tradition of the southern sage Thomas Jefferson, and crystalized in the image of the antebellum cavalier, agrarianism has proven an arid formula for explaining the essence and nature of southernism. The "true South," Professor Potter concludes, is an enigma—both elusive and deeply paradoxical. The "concrete realities of the land" seem rather to yield a South predicated upon a distinct folk culture. What such a historical dissection suggests, of course, is yet additional irony in the southern past. The agrarian-industrial dichotomy, which Mr. Potter identifies as the core of the southern enigma, was to prove itself the major tension and dialectic of the New South era. Truly, the New South's "abandonment" of agrarianism could hardly have existed, since the South as an agrarian society had never been more than "an illusion, nourished by a wish."

From "The Enigma of the South," by David M. Potter, in *The Yale Review*. Copyright © 1961 by Yale University Press. Reprinted by permission of the publisher.

Among the many flourishing branches of American historical study during the last half-century, one of the most robust has been the history of the South. Fifty years ago, there was already one large body of literature on the Southern Confederacy, especially in its military aspects, and another on the local history of various Southern states, but the history of the South as a region—of the whole vast area below the Potomac, viewed as a single entity for the whole time from the settlement of Jamestown to the present —is largely a product of the last five decades. Today, a multivolume history, a number of college textbooks, a quarterly journal, and a substantial library of monographic studies all serve as measures of the extent of the development in this field.

Anyone who seeks an explanation for this interest in Southern history must take account of several factors. To begin with, the study of American regions is a general phenomenon, embracing not only the South but also New England, the Middle West, and the great physiographic provinces beyond the Mississippi. In a nation as vast and as diverse as ours, there is really no level higher than the regional level at which one can come to grips with the concrete realities of the land. But apart from this regional aspect, the Southern theme has held an unusual appeal for the people of the South because of their peculiarly strong and sentimental loyalty to Dixie as their native land, and for Americans outside the South because of the exotic quality of the place and because it bears the aura of a Lost Cause. Union generals, for some reason, have never held the romantic interest that attached to Stonewall Jackson, Jeb Stuart, George Pickett, Bedford Forrest, and, of course, Robert E. Lee. Today, the predilection of Yankee children for caps, flags, and toys displaying the Rebel insignia bears further witness to the enduring truth that lost causes have a fascination even for those who did not lose them.

But it seems unlikely that either the South as an American region, or the South as Dixieland, or the South as a Lost Cause could hold so much scholarly and popular attention in focus if the South were not also an enigma. To writers for more than half a century the South has been a kind of sphinx on the American land.

To some who viewed it, this sphinx has seemed a great insensate monolith, a vast artifact of the past with no meaning behind its inscrutable expression. Its domain has been just what H. L. Mencken said it was—a cultural desert, a Sahara of the Bozart. But to others this sphinx' has seemed to hold a secret, an answer to the riddle of American life.

To many people today, who think of the South in terms of Freedom Riders and lunch-counter sit-ins, of Tobacco Road and Central High School in Little Rock, of robed Klansmen and burning crosses, and perhaps of a Monkey Trial at Dayton, Tennessee, it may seem hard to believe that not long ago the South was regarded by many thoughtful and liberal-minded people as a kind of sanctuary of the American democratic tradition. What is now deplored as the "benighted South," or the "sick South," was, until recently, regarded by many liberals as the birthplace and the natural bulwark of the Jeffersonian ideal—a region where agrarian democracy still struggled to survive, fighting a gallant rearguard action against the commercialism and the industrial capitalism of the Northeast.

It would be a major undertaking to trace the evolution of this concept. The general idea that American democracy is essentially frontier democracy—which closely resembles agrarian democracy—is forever linked with Frederick Jackson Turner, but Turner gave it a Western rather than a Southern orientation. Certainly one of the earliest writers to apply it to the South was William E. Dodd. In 1911, when Dodd had been but recently appointed to the University of Chicago, and twenty-two years before Franklin Roosevelt sent him as our unswervingly democratic ambassador to Hitler's Berlin, he wrote a sketchy little book, now largely forgotten, entitled *Statesmen of the Old South,* with the significant subtitle, *From Radicalism to Conservative Revolt.* The statesmen whom he treated were Jefferson, Calhoun, and Jefferson Davis, and the theme which he developed was that the democratic or radical South of Thomas Jefferson—an equalitarian South of small subsistence farmers—had been subverted by the increasingly aristocratic and hierarchical South of the great slaveholders whose property interests found embodiment in Calhoun and Davis.

In three brief and seemingly artless chapters, Dodd achieved two very subtle effects. First, he defined to suit himself what may be called a normative South—the South of Thomas Jefferson—and thus established an arbitrary basis for identifying all future developments of a Jeffersonian tenor as truly or intrinsically Southern, and for rejecting all conservative or hierarchical developments as aberrations of Southernism. Using this device, he then proceeded to dispose of the whole conservative, slaveholding South of antebellum fame as a kind of deviation or detour in the true course of Southern history. Thus he finessed the basic question whether the true and realistic image of the South might not be a dualism, with as much of Calhoun as of Jefferson in it, or even whether the true South, historically, is not hierarchical and conservative rather than radical and equalitarian.

In justice to Dodd, one must recognize that his version of Southernism was by no means without foundations. Jeffersonianism, as well as Jefferson, did have distinctively Southern origins, and at almost every decisive turning point in the advancement of American democracy—whether at the time of Jackson, or Bryan, or Wilson, or Franklin Roosevelt—the South has thrown crucial weight on the democratic side. Still, there was something of a tour de force about the way in which Dodd reconciled his love for his native South and his commitment to democracy, and, with very little disclosure of the wishful thinking which was involved, identified the land he loved with the values he cherished.

Whether later writers were directly influenced by Dodd or not, the theme of agrarianism has persisted ever since in the literature of the South, sometimes with the most startling implications. Thus when Charles and Mary Beard came to write about the Civil War in their *The Rise of American Civilization* (1927), they pictured it as a conflict between Southern agrarianism and Northern industrialism; in this way, the defenders of slavery were transmuted into democrats, more or less, since agrarianism was, in the Beards' lexicon, by definition democratic, and industrialism was antidemocratic. Again, at the hands of the Beards and of the late Howard K. Beale, in his *The Critical Years,* published in 1930, Reconstruction was not primarily a contest over the rights of Negro freedmen, but rather a series of coups by industrial capitalism to consolidate its ascendancy and to retain its wartime gains, consisting of tariffs, subsidies, and a monetary system favorable to creditors. The Fourteenth Amendment was not a Magna Carta of freedmen's rights, but rather a bulwark for property interests, disguised as a Negro rights measure in order to catch votes. Again, the implications were ironic: for instance, under this formula Andrew Johnson, a onetime slave-owner and an obdurate foe of Negro rights, appeared as a champion of democracy against the predatory capitalists. Thus Johnson received ecstatic praise in a biography (1929) by that archliberal attorney Lloyd Paul Stryker, who later became a crusading spokesman for Negro rights.

Through all of these treatments there runs a persistent implied affirmation of Dodd's cleverly articulated premise: that which is agrarian in the South is truly Southern; anything not in the agrarian tradition is somehow extraneous—a cowbird's egg in the Southern nest. Almost automatically, this formula reduced the factor of biracialism and caste to secondary importance, or even kept it out of sight altogether. Again, some interesting results follow in the literature. For instance, when Howard W. Odum and his associates at Chapel Hill prepared their great compendium *Southern Regions of the United States* (1936), they deployed no less than six hundred maps and charts to show that the agricultural South, despite its rich natural resources, was worse off in almost every measurable respect than the rest of the country. That is, they mapped, measured, and charted the plight of the agricultural South. But not one graph, map, or chart showed the relatively worse plight of the Negroes within the South. In other words, the most careful reader of this encyclopedic survey of Southern economic and social conditions could almost have overlooked the fact that a biracial system prevailed in the South and that under this system the Negroes experienced adverse differentials in almost every respect. No doubt Odum and his associates chose this presentation deliberately, and certainly not because of any blind agrarianism, for they advocated economic diversification for the South. Their purpose may even have been to avoid dulling the concern of white Southerners about differentials by admitting that these differentials fell more heavily upon the Negro than upon the white component in the Southern population. Or, they may have wished to treat Negroes and whites indiscriminately alike as being handicapped by regional differentials. But in any case, their survey of Southern problems left out the greatest problem of all. Like the doctrinal agrarians with whom they disagreed, they presented an image of the South which emphasized the plight of farmers rather than the plight of Negroes.

In quite a different way, the agrarian premise shows itself also in many of the writings of C. Vann Woodward, the foremost historian of the modern South. In Woodward's biography of Tom Watson (1938), for instance, the protagonist of the drama is Watson the agrarian, and the antagonists are the Bourbon Democrats who have betrayed the interests of the South to the forces of industrial capitalism. Or alternatively, one could say, the protagonist is the earlier Watson, who championed Populism and defended Negro rights, while the antagonist is the later Watson, a reactionary racist who betrayed the ideals of his youth. Though Woodward's treatment is deeply subtle and sensitive to complexities, while Dodd's was superficial and grossly oversimplified, both are alike in regarding the agrarian South as, almost a priori, the true South, and any force within the South which runs counter to it as an aberration. This is, of course, quite a different thing from merely favoring the agrarian cause.

Although a whole generation of writers have made this tempting equation between Southernism and agrarianism, it requires only a limited analysis to see that in many respects the Southern economy and the Southern society have not been agrarian at all—in fact, have embodied almost the antithesis of agrarianism. Agrarianism implies an escape from the commercialism of the money economy, but Southern cotton and tobacco and sugar cultivators have consistently been agricultural businessmen producing for market and for cash income. Agrarianism implies production for use rather than production for sale, and therefore diversification rather than specialization, but the Southern agriculturist stuck to his one-crop system in the past as tenaciously as he clings to segregation at the present. It implies the independence of a husbandman who looks to no one else either for his access to the land or for the necessities of his living, but the Southern cultivator has been historically either a slave or a sharecropper, without land and often without opportunity even to grow his own turnip greens in a garden patch. Meanwhile the Southern landowner, whether an absentee planter or a mortgage-holding bank, frequently failed to follow the ennobling agrarian practice of laboring in the earth. To one who is impressed by these aspects, it may seem realistic to regard Calhoun rather than Jefferson as the typical leader of the South; the plantation producing raw materials for the textile industry, rather than the subsistence farm producing for use, as the typical economic unit; hierarchy rather than equality as the typical social condition; and conservatism rather than radicalism as the typical mode of thought.

One man who was long the leading historian of the South saw the region to some extent in these terms. This was Ulrich B. Phillips, who began his career around the turn of the century with studies of Southern political history and the history of Southern transportation. But wherever his investigations began, they always led him, as he himself said, back to one feature of life in the South which was constant both before emancipation and after, namely the presence of Negroes and whites whose destinies were inextricably intertwined but whose paths in life were separated by a biracial system. Accordingly, Phillips gave only slight attention to the agrarian theme. Instead he concentrated on the staple-crop economy with its plantation units and its slave labor. With supreme thoroughness in research, he made what remains the basic study of slavery as a system of labor (*American Negro Slavery*, 1918). Later he developed an artistry in writing which matched his soundness in research, and he achieved a felicitous conjunction of both talents in a study of the society and economy of the antebellum period (*Life and Labor in the Old South*, 1929).

When Phillips looked at the Southern economy, the image which seemed visible to him was not an independent husbandman laboring in the soil, but a Negro field hand picking cotton. The persistence of this figure, either as a slave or as a sharecropper, and the persistence of the system which kept him in his subordinate role led Phillips, five years before his death in 1934, to write an essay, "The Central Theme of Southern History," in which he stated what he had found at the core of distinctive Southernism. This was not some agrarian ideal, but rather a fixed purpose on the part of the Southern whites to preserve biracialism, or, as he said, in unvarnished terms, to assure that the South "shall be and remain a white man's country."

Although Phillips' stature is still recognized even by his critics, liberal historians have been reluctant to accept his views. Kenneth Stampp has written a new account of slavery (*The Peculiar Institution*, 1956) which emphasizes, as Phillips never did, the harsh and exploitative aspects of the system; Richard Hofstadter has criticized Phillips for giving too much attention to the plantation, and not enough to the slaves held in small holdings; and at least two writers have questioned the "Central Theme."

It is in some ways ironical for liberals, concerned as they are with the "sick South," to reject a formula which explains so cogently the chronic nature of the illness. But what they found fault with was not in fact the accuracy of Phillips' conclusion; it was rather the lack of moral indignation in his statement of it. By asserting that the policy of biracialism is and will continue to be a central aspect of Southernism, without personally repudiating this policy, he made it difficult for liberals to identify with him. When Harry Ashmore, more recently, said in *An Epitaph for Dixie* (1958) that the South will cease to be the South when it ceases to be segregated, the statement was almost identical with that of Phillips, but liberals could accept Ashmore's because he expects the South, in the old sense, to vanish (hence "an epitaph"), whereas they could not accept Phillips', because he seemingly expected the South to survive, with the implied corollary that efforts at integration must fail. Moreover, in the case of liberals who want to love the South, as some do, but who find it psychologically impossible to love an embodiment of biracialism, the only recourse is a resort to Dodd's original formula: dispose of the factor which is troublesome (in this case the biracialism) by treating it as a great aberration. Here even so excellent a book as Vann Woodward's *Strange Career of Jim Crow* (1955) is a case in point, for though it was intended to emphasize a thoroughly valid observation—namely, that the patterns of biracialism have varied and are not immutable—it lends itself to being read as a statement that caste does not have very deep roots in the South. The preface to the paperback edition (1957) showed that Woodward was himself concerned that his work had been taken too much in this way.

When one considers the degree of hardheadedness and realism which went into Phillips' view that biracialism lay at the core of Southernism, and the vulnerability of the doctrine that agrarianism was the heart of the matter, it seems strange that writers have been so abstinent in accepting the former and so addicted to the latter. Clearly, the agrarian interpretation has drawn its strength from something other than the sheer weight of evidence, and it is worth pondering what the real basis of its acceptance is. In the purely historical literature, this basis is hard to detect, for the historian purports merely to be describing the agrarianism which he finds in the past—not to be advocating it. But in 1930 agrarianism enjoyed open advocacy at the hands of a group of writers, all centered at Vanderbilt University, in the famous manifesto entitled *I'll Take My Stand*. The twelve Southerners who joined in this profession of faith categorically rejected the industrial way of life, which they regarded as the prevailing or American way, and with equal conviction they subscribed to an agrarian way, which they identified as a Southern way. They hoped to carry this Southern way to the nation through "a national agrarian movement."

In the extensive and often heated discussion which followed, attention was focused very heavily upon the operative practicability of their proposals. They were accused of medievalism, and of quixotically renouncing all the benefits of modern science and technology. They were also accused, with somewhat more justice, of being in disagreement among themselves as to whether agrarianism was designed to provide a livelihood for dirt farmers or to restore cultural amenities for the landed gentry. Whether they advocated populism or élitism no one could quite make out. While controversy raged between them and their assailants, not much attention was given to the ideological implications of agrarianism, nor to the question why this particular line of thought had appeared at this particular time. Indeed, the historical significance of agrarian thought has still never been adequately analyzed.

But it is clearly evident that agrarianism appealed to many liberals, both before and after the Nashville group, partly because they were looking for an alternative to the prevailing American way of life. Some writers, like Charles A. Beard, used agrarianism so enthusiastically as a stick with which to beat capitalism that it had some of the appearance of a disguised Marxism. But its real significance lay in the fact that it offered an alternative to Marxism. Here, in fact, was a way in which a man could renounce industrial capitalism and all its works without becoming a Marxist. This is perhaps why the agrarian ideal held so much attraction for such a large number of social thinkers. It gave them a chance to express their dissent from the prevailing system without going outside the American tradition in order to do so.

Another significant feature in making agrarianism attractive was its affirmation that the South had something of value in its tradition to offer to the nation. The Nashville group really felt convinced that the Southern sphinx did have an answer to the riddle, if not of the universe, at least of American life. Their affirmation came at a time when it was being asserted by critics like Mencken that the Southern tradition amounted to little more than a sterile, backward-looking form of ancestor worship. Now suddenly men were saying in a fresh and arresting way that the Southern tradition was not merely a pressed flower in the nation's scrapbook of memories, but rather an urgent message which Americans, deafened by the roar of progress, had failed to hear. To Southerners who yearned to believe that there was some element of vitality in the history of their region, this idea seemed immensely appealing.

The continued acceleration of industrial growth and the failure of the Nashville group to rally a popular following soon showed that agrarianism had no future, but it was still widely believed to have a past, and historians continued to apply it to the interpretation of American history. Henry Bamford Parkes made brilliant use of it in his *The American Experience* (1947), and as recently as 1949, Frank L. Owsley, in his *Plain Folk of the Old South,* delineated the structure of antebellum society in terms in which large slaveholders and plain farmers were practically indistinguishable. In these and many other writings, a number of time-honored propositions continued to find acceptance: that American democracy has been nourished primarily from agrarian roots; that agrarian attitudes are inherently democratic; and that the South peculiarly embodies the agrarian tradition.

But of late the first two of these propositions have come under criticism, and the agrarian view has been attacked, for the first time, at its foundations. As long ago as 1945, Arthur Schlesinger, Jr., in his *The Age of Jackson,* offered the then heretical view that Jacksonian democracy owed more to the East and to class-conscious urban workingmen than to the frontier and its coonskin equality. More recently, Richard Hofstadter, in his *Age of Reform* (1955), has gone even further by arguing that Populism had little affinity with liberal democracy, and was in fact a seedbed for such illiberal manifestations as prohibition, nativism, immigration restriction, Red-baiting, and the like. Thus, according to Schlesinger, democracy was not agrarian, and according to Hofstadter, agrarianism was not democratic.

In literal form, the agrarian formula fitted the South remarkably badly. It envisioned a subsistence economy, agricultural diversification, a wide distribution of small landholdings, a large class of independent husbandmen, and an unstratified society. The cold fact is that none of these features has ever been dominant in the South. In the light of these flaws, as well as of recent criticisms, the whole idea of the South as an agrarian society now seems more and more an illusion, nourished by a wish. But once it is discarded, the question reverts to the enigma of the South. All theory aside, is the South, at a purely descriptive level, distinguishable? And if it is, does the distinction lie in anything more than the fact that biracialism takes a form in the South differing from the form it takes elsewhere?

This is a question which the literature of the future will perhaps explore further. Vann Woodward, in *The Burden of Southern History* (1960), has already moved in this direction with incisive and fertile arguments that certain distinctive experiences of the South have put their mark upon the Southern people: the experience of defeat and frustration, in an America of monotonous, taken-for-granted success; the experience of guilt because of the Negro, in an America with a cult of Adamic innocence; the experience of poverty, in an America with abundance which has caused people to confuse life with a standard of living. But though Woodward discusses these factors as experiences impinging upon the Southern culture, we still need a dissection of the culture itself upon which they impinge.

On the face of it, it seems a matter of observation and not of theory to say that the culture of the folk survived in the South long after it succumbed to the onslaught of urban-industrial culture elsewhere. It was an aspect of this culture that the relation between the land and the people remained more direct and more primal in the South than in other parts of the country. (This may be more true for the Negroes than for the whites, but then there is also a question whether the Negroes may not have embodied the distinctive qualities of the Southern character even more than the whites.) Even in the most exploitative economic situations, this culture retained a personalism in the relations of man to man which the industrial culture lacks. Even for those whose lives were narrowest, it offered a relationship of man to nature in which there was a certain fulfillment of personality. Every culture is, among other things, a system of relationships among an aggregate of people, and as cultures differ, the systems of relationship vary. In the folk culture of the South, it may be that the relation of people to one another imparted a distinctive texture as well as a distinctive tempo to their lives.

An explanation of the South in terms of a folk culture would not have the ideological implications which have made the explanation in terms of agrarianism so tempting and at the same time so treacherous. But on the other hand, it would not be inconsistent with some of the realities of Southern society, such as biracialism and hierarchy, whereas agrarianism is inconsistent with these realities. The enigma remains, and the historian must still ask what distinctive quality it was in the life of the South for which Southerners have felt such a persistent, haunting nostalgia and to which even the Yankee has responded with a poignant impulse. We must now doubt that this nostalgia was the yearning of men for an ideal agrarian utopia which never existed in reality. But if it was not that, was it perhaps the yearning of men in a mass culture for the life of a folk culture which did really exist? This folk culture, we know, was far from being ideal or utopian, and was in fact full of inequality and wrong, but if the nostalgia persists was it because even the inequality and wrong were parts of a life that still had a relatedness and meaning which our more bountiful life in the mass culture seems to lack?

15

The New South Creed:
A Study in Southern Mythmaking

Paul M. Gaston

The term "New South" has been variously defined as both a doctrine and a period of time. In either case, it is said to have been
the means by which the South "redeemed" its heritage. It marked
an escape from the backlog of frustration and defeat dating from
the Civil War, and launched the region into new realms of power
and prestige. The New South, in short, is purported to have
brought with it a multiple endowment: economic abundance, an
equitable settlement of the racial issue (to be duly canonized by
the "separate but equal" prescription of *Plessy* v. *Ferguson* in
1896), and political redemption. Indeed, by the late nineteenth
and early twentieth centuries, it is said that the South had at last
sampled the American Dream. But economic fulfillment, racial
justice, and political parity with the North, though critical elements
of a developing New South Creed, scarcely materialized in succeeding decades. As argued by Paul M. Gaston of the University of
Virginia, perpetual dreams of an emerging "new" South, though
sharply etched in the southern imagination, have since fit rather
poorly with the facts of southern experience. Nearly every facet
of the New South Creed has proven to be a mirage—tantalizing
yet elusive. Its major dividend has been mismanagement and decay
for the region's physical and human resources. All too often race
relations, economic opportunity, and political progress have suffered
from benign neglect and served as little more than convenient
slogans. Perhaps as striking, Professor Gaston maintains, was the

compatability which the New South found with the Old; images of an Old South Creed were marshaled to support the New. What The South achieved, in the end, was simply the acquisition of new volumes for its growing library of sacred beliefs.

One of the ironies of Southern history lies in the simultaneous rise during the 1880's of both the New South creed and the mythic image of the Old South. Sweet "syrup of romanticism," to use Professor Woodward's term, flowed over the Old South in the same decade that the New South spokesmen's ideal of a bustling, rich, and reconstructed South captured the American imagination. Joel Chandler Harris introduced Uncle Remus to the general public in 1880 and Thomas Nelson Page's idyllic old Virginia became a national treasure after the publication of "Marse Chan" in 1884.[1] [Henry] Grady's landmark address before the New England Society of New York was only two years later. To compound the irony, most of the New South spokesmen accepted the mythic view of the past, rarely failing to preface a New South pronouncement with warm praise and nostalgic sighs for the golden age that had passed. While Old South idolaters such as Charles Colcock Jones, Jr., shuddered with horror at the mention of the New South, its spokesmen showed no such single-mindedness, and the warm reception they gave the emerging legend further emphasizes the attempt to relate their movement to the values and aspirations of the past.

The legend of an Old South whose character was shaped by a noble plantation regime did not, of course, emerge unheralded in the 1880's. Its origins are in the antebellum period itself. In his illuminating study, *Cavalier and Yankee,* William R. Taylor shows that the mythmaking first appeared shortly after the War of 1812. William Wirt's biography of Patrick Henry, published in 1818, was the most notable precursor of the later tradition. "It was a utopia set in the past," Taylor writes.[2] Wirt "constructed for himself exactly the kind of legendary Southern past into which successive generations of Southerners were to retreat in full flight from the problems of the present."[3] Wirt's preliminary work was overshadowed in importance in the thirty years before the war by polemics and novels, reflecting the increasing alienation of Southern thought from dominant

---

[1] Joel Chandler Harris, *Uncle Remus: His Songs and His Sayings* (New York, 1881 [i.e., 1880]); Thomas Nelson Page, "Marse Chan," *Century Magazine,* XXVII (April 1884), 932–42.

[2] William R. Taylor, *Cavalier and Yankee: The Old South and American National Character* (New York, 1961), p. 82.

[3] *Ibid.,* p. 92.

American values and ideals. From Thomas Roderick Dew in the early 'thirties to George Fitzhugh in the mid-'fifties, Southern pro-slavery theorists lauded a stratified agrarian society in terms which they thought the ancient Greeks might have understood.[4] In fiction, John Pendleton Kennedy inaugurated the plantation tradition in 1832 by idealizing his own times and by presenting much of plantation life at its best.[5] "Doing so," remarks one historian of the plantation in literature, "he gave matter and method for a literary tradition."[6] The tradition was amply exploited by a host of other writers in the next thirty years.

The intensity of the abolition controversy led both defenders and opponents of slavery to enlarge and perpetuate the myth. The defenders, for obvious reasons, exaggerated the grandeur of their civilization, while the abolitionist assault had the ironic outcome of adding credibility to the myth. In drawing pictures of the horror of Southern society, abolitionists invariably had their dramas of exploitation played on enormous estates presided over by wealthy planters who lived life on the grand scale. The contrast between the opulence of the planter and the misery of the slave no doubt served the abolitionist purpose, but it also contributed to one of the rare points of agreement between Southerners and Northerners. As Francis Pendleton Gaines observes, the opponents in the slavery controversy "agreed concerning certain picturesque elements of plantation life and joined hands to set the conception unforgettably in public consciousness."[7] A half-century after Harriet Beecher Stowe outraged the South with *Uncle Tom's Cabin,* Joel Chandler Harris took puckish delight in telling a Northern audience that "all the worthy and beautiful characters in her book . . . are the products" of a slave society, while the "cruelest and most brutal character . . . is a Northerner."[8]

When the war came, both sides entered it with rival myths which succored them during the four years. The North's "Armageddonlike vision," Edmund Wilson writes, directed a "holy crusade which was to liberate the

[4] Thomas Roderick Dew, *Review of the Debate in the Virginia Legislature of 1831 and 1832* (Richmond, 1832); George Fitzhugh, *Sociology for the South; or, the Failure of Free Society* (Richmond, 1854); George Fitzhugh, *Cannibals All! or, Slaves Without Masters* (Richmond, 1857). The standard monograph on the pro-slavery philosophy is William S. Jenkins, *Pro-Slavery Thought in the Old South* (Chapel Hill, 1935).

[5] John Pendleton Kennedy, *Swallow Barn; or, a Sojourn in the Old Dominion* (Philadelphia, 1832).

[6] Francis Pendleton Gaines, *The Southern Plantation: A Study in the Development and the Accuracy of a Tradition* (New York, 1924), p. 23.

[7] *Ibid.,* p. 30.

[8] Julia Collier Harris, ed., *Joel Chandler Harris, Editor and Essayist: Miscellaneous Literary, Political, and Social Writings* (Chapel Hill, 1931), pp. 116–17.

slaves and to punish their unrighteous masters." While Northerners saw themselves as acting out the "Will of God," Wilson continues, Southerners undertook the equally noble cause of "rescuing a hallowed ideal of gallantry, aristocratic freedom, fine manners and luxurious living from the materialism and vulgarity of the mercantile Northern society."[9]

Neither myth, of course, died with the conclusion of the war. During the Reconstruction era, the rhetoric of the Northern press and the "bloody shirt" campaigns of victorious Republican politicians kept the vision of a holy crusade alive, although it became hopelessly tarnished as time passed. Curiously, however, Northern novelists began in 1865 to develop a theme of reconciliation that dominated fictional treatments of the war and paved the way for the later emergence of Southern writers on the national scene. Examining the works of fifty-five novelists who produced sixty-four civil war books between 1865 and 1880, Joyce Appleby writes that "for the Northerner who wrote a novel simply to entertain, forgiveness was the order of the day." The plantation romance, as it would appear in the 'eighties, was undeveloped in these works, but all of the later themes of honest misunderstanding, purity of motive, and the integrity of Southern civilization are present.[10]

The sympathetic mood cultivated by the Northern novelists was expanded by the Southern writers of the late 'seventies and 'eighties into a national love feast for the Old South. Southern authors began appearing regularly in the pages of the national periodicals in the mid-'seventies, in the wake of the enthusiasm created by Scribner's "Great South" series, a detailed and sympathetic description of the region by Edward King.[11] By 1881, the editor of Scribner's was noting that a recent number of the magazine had contained seven contributions by Southerners. Hailing the new contributors, he confidently announced that "a new literary era is dawning upon the South."[12] A decade later the same editor would report

[9] Edmund Wilson, *Patriotic Gore: Studies in the Literature of the American Civil War* (New York, 1962), p. 438.

[10] Joyce Appleby, "Reconciliation and the Northern Novelist, 1865–1880," *Civil War History*, X (June 1964), 117–29. See also Robert A. Lively, *Fiction Fights the Civil War: An Unfinished Chapter in the Literary History of the American People* (Chapel Hill, 1957).

[11] The articles appeared in book form shortly after they were published in the magazine: Edward King, *The Great South: A Record of Journeys* (Hartford, Conn., 1875).

[12] "Southern Literature," *Scribner's Monthly*, XXII (September 1881), 785–6. See also Herbert F. Smith, "Joel Chandler Harris's Contributions to Scribner's Monthly and Century Magazine, 1880–1887," *Georgia Historical Quarterly*, XLVII (June 1963), 169–79; and Charles W. Coleman, Jr., "The Recent Movement in Southern Literature," *Harper's New Monthly Magazine*, LXXIV (May 1887), 837–55.

to Joel Chandler Harris the petulant query of a Northern author, "When are you going to give the North a chance!"[13]

The new development came as no surprise to Albion W. Tourgee, the carpetbag judge of North Carolina whose own fiction had a considerable following in the period. As early as 1865 he had predicted that, within thirty years, "popular sympathy will be with those who upheld the Confederate cause . . . our popular heroes will be Confederate leaders; our fiction will be Southern in its prevailing types and distinctively Southern in its character." Writing in 1888, Tourgee felt that his prediction had been more than borne out, seven years in advance of the deadline. "Our literature has become not only Southern in type," he declared, "but distinctly Confederate in sympathy." Poring over all the popular monthlies of recent issue, Tourgee could not find a single one without a "Southern story" as one of its most "prominent features."[14]

Thus it was that the romantic view of the Southern past achieved what Gaines calls a "complete conquest" in the 'eighties. An enormous number of authors, the most prominent of whom were Harris and Page, "fed to the public fancy some variety of the plantation material."[15] At the same time, the mythic view of the past was achieving the status of an inviolable shibboleth through other means as well. Schoolbooks and educational curricula carefully guarded the old memories. Religious imagery and political rhetoric were built on appeals to former glory. And numerous organizations devoted their full time to perpetuating the correct view of the past. To Jones' Confederate Survivors' Association there were soon added the United Daughters of the Confederacy, for women, and the United Confederate Veterans for men. All basked in the admiration shown them by *The Confederate Veteran,* a reverent journal established in Nashville in 1893 to represent the various memorial groups. One contributor to the *Veteran* stated simply what had now become the orthodox Southern view of the past:

In the eyes of Southern people all Confederate veterans are heroes. It is you [the Confederate veterans] who preserve the traditions and memories of the old-time South—the sunny South, with its beautiful lands and its happy people; the South of chivalrous men and gentle women; the South that will go down in history as the land of plenty and the

[13] R. W. Gilder to Joel Chandler Harris, March 5, 1891, Harris Papers, Emory University.

[14] Albion W. Tourgee, "The South as a Field for Fiction," *The Forum,* VI (December 1888), 404–7.

[15] Gaines, *The Southern Plantation,* p. 82.

home of heroes. This beautiful, plentiful, happy South engendered a spirit of chivalry and gallantry for which its men were noted far and near.[16]

In the mythic image of a chivalric and gallant South there remained no traces of the corrupting influences once imputed by the abolitionists. The descendants of Garrison were ambushed after the war, and by 1880 nothing remained of the abolitionist tradition except the exaggerated accounts of plantation splendor. "Abolitionism was swept from the field," according to Gaines; "it was more than routed, it was tortured, scalped, 'mopped up.' "[17] Remaining was only the enchanting picture of a near-perfect society in which, as Thomas Nelson Page believed, "even the moonlight was richer and mellower . . . than it is now."[18] This rich and mellow moonlight beamed on a country studded with magnolias that offered sweet scents and a becoming background for beautiful maidens. The fathers of the maidens, invariably courtly, noble, and generous, presided over enormous plantations and thousands of lovable, amusing, and devoted slaves. Work was apparently infrequent and leisure was put to constructive and cultivating uses. During the numerous holiday seasons—and especially at Christmastime—the regal splendor of the regime was particularly brilliant, enriching the lives of both white and black. Patriarchal in the extreme—yet underneath wholesomely democratic—the stratified society provided precisely the right niche for each member: each fulfilled his true nature; none was dissatisfied.

The New South prophets had no objection to the beautiful maidens, but their program would amend or replace many other aspects of the civilization cherished in the myth. Whirring cotton mills and crimson blast furnaces were preferred to magnolias and moonlight; the factory with its hired hands was superior to the inefficient plantation; bustle and energy and the ability to "get ahead," rather than a penchant for leisure, should characterize the leadership of the New South. Grady made the difference clear when he told his New York audience: "We have sowed towns and cities in the place of theories, and put business above politics."[19]

Unmindful of paradoxes, the New South spokesmen subscribed with ardor to the mythical conception of the Old South. Grady expressed reverence for the "imperishable knighthood" of the old regime; he admired

---

[16] Ethel Moore, "Reunion of Tennesseans: Address of Welcome by Miss Ethel Moore," *Confederate Veteran*, VI (October 1898), 482.

[17] Gaines, *The Southern Plantation*, pp. 63–6.

[18] Thomas Nelson Page, *Red Rock: A Chronicle of Reconstruction* (New York, 1898), p. viii.

[19] Joel Chandler Harris, ed., *Life of Henry W. Grady, Including His Writings and Speeches* (New York, 1890), p. 88.

the leisure and wealth which gave to the Old South an "exquisite culture";
he praised the civilization that produced gentle women, honest and devout
citizens—all in that dreamlike time when "money counted least in making
the social status." On another occasion, he referred to the sea-island
plantations of Georgia as "royal homes: . . . principalities in area, duke-
doms in revenue." The man who promised an industrial utopia to his own
generation could say of the past that "the civilization of the old slave
regime in the South has not been surpassed, and perhaps will not be
equaled, among men."[20] The reciprocal love between master and slave, a
basic foundation on which the society rested, was a thing of beauty which
came into glorious blossom during the South's great testing time. Speaking
before a group of Boston merchants, Grady related a "vision" of the war:

> The crisis of battle—a soldier struck, staggering, fallen. I see a slave,
> scuffling through the smoke, winding his black arms about the fallen
> form, reckless of the hurtling death—bending his trusty face to catch
> the words that tremble on the stricken lips, so wrestling meantime with
> agony that he would lay down his life in his master's stead.[21]

[Richard Hathaway] Edmonds, among the most versatile of the New South
leaders, crusaded tirelessly for the industrial order of his day, traced a
continuity of development from the Old to the New South, and urged upon
his fellows the romantic view of the old regime. He would never want
Southerners to forget, he wrote, "to hold in tenderest reverence the memory
of this Southern land; never forget to give all honor to the men and women
of ante-bellum days; remember . . . that the Old South produced a race of
men and women whose virtues and whose attainments are worthy to be
enshrined not only in every Southern, but in every American heart."[22]
Moreover, in the midst of the South's industrial development, he warned
Southerners never to let it be said "that in the struggle for industrial advancement the South has lost aught of the virtues, domestic and public,
aught of the manliness and self-reliance, aught of the charms of her women
and the honor of her men which hallow the memory of the Old South."[23]

By the turn of the century, as these examples suggest, it caused no em-
barrassment for New South prophets to espouse the creeds of both the Old
and the New South. A North Carolina bank president was typical of the
New South accommodation of both creeds when he began an address before the American Bankers' Association by paying reverential homage to

[20] Grady, *New South,* ed. Dyer, pp. 148–60, 260.
[21] Harris, ed., *Grady,* p. 195.
[22] Edmonds, *Old South and New,* p. 11.
[23] Edmonds, *Tasks of Young Men of the South,* p. 12.

the Old South before praising the New. "Prior to the civil war," the talk began, "our Southern land . . . was the home of culture and refinement. With thousands of slaves to cultivate their broad acres, our people lived in ease and plenty."[24]

The allegiance given to the myth of the Old South by the propagandists for the New Order is in itself evidence of the extent to which the romantic view prevailed in the South. Further evidence is found in unsuspected places, the most notable of which is in the writings of Booker T. Washington. Normally, one would not expect the most influential champion of Negro freedom of his generation to contribute to a romanticized view of the slave regime into which he had been born. And, of course, there are many aspects of Washington's picture of the Old South which do not harmonize with the Thomas Nelson Page version. Washington's picture differed from the stereotype in his emphasis on the miserable living conditions of the slaves, the torturous flax shirt, the unpalatable rations, and the absence of the kind of "civilized" living that he was later to champion. Important, too, is his contention that the slaves he knew understood and desired freedom, receiving it first with great jubilation and later with a sobering sense of responsibility.[25]

However, much of Washington's picture resembles the stereotyped version. He stresses the loyalty of the slaves to their masters and insists that it was based on a genuine love. When young "Mars' Billy" died there was great sorrow in the quarters and it "was no sham sorrow but real." There is no sense of resentment, and when emancipation brought hard times to a former master the slaves rallied and stood by him in his adversity. Washington explained that "nothing that the coloured people possess is too good for the son of 'old Mars' Tom' "[26] One is reminded of Irwin Russell's famous lines which began by extolling the virtues of "Mahsr John" and conclude:

> Well, times is changed. De war it come an' sot de niggers free,
> An' now ol' Mahsr John ain't hardly wuf as much as me;
> He had to pay his debts, an' so his lan' is mos'ly gone—
> An' I declar' I's sorry for my pore ol' Mahsr John.[27]

Washington's account of Reconstruction is equally congenial to the romantic version. In his autobiography he includes the standard comic view

---

[24] Brown, *The New South,* p. 3.

[25] Booker T. Washington, *Up From Slavery* (Garden City, 1901), pp. 1–12.

[26] *Ibid.,* pp. 12–14.

[27] Irwin Russell, *Christmas Night in the Quarters and Other Poems* (New York, 1917), p. 67.

of the newly freed Negro, stating that the principal crazes were for Greek and Latin and public office. He is critical of the precipitous way in which the Negro was pulled up from the bottom rung of society, and he has harsh words to say about Negro preachers, teachers, and politicians. Most important of all is what is not said: nowhere in *Up from Slavery* does one find an indictment of the native white Southerners' behavior during Reconstruction. The Negro suffered in the end, Washington felt, in large part because "there was an element in the North which wanted to punish the Southern white men by forcing the Negro into positions over the heads of Southern whites."[28]

The commitment of both black and white New South prophets to the romantic view of the past was not made without purpose. To some extent, to be sure, there was no alternative for many of them, for their own emotional requirements as well as the need for public acceptance dictated that they operate within the intellectual framework of the time and place in which they lived. But however compelling the emotional and strategic considerations may have been, they were matched in appeal to the New South spokesmen by several concrete, useful functions which the myth of the Old South could perform in the cause of the New South movement. Washington, as will appear in the next chapter, had special reasons for mythmaking. The white leaders in the movement quickly perceived and ably exploited the benefits that the myth offered them. For one thing, they would not have agreed with those later historians who saw the romantic legend exclusively as a source of fruitless ancestor worship and rancorous sectionalism. On the contrary, a close examination shows that it was nationalism rather than sectionalism, an identification rather than a separation, of interests that emerged as benefactors of the myth.

The triumph of the romantic legend in the North in the 'eighties was essential to this result. Once before, in the antebellum period, the Southern mythmakers had found allies in the North, although the Yankee authors of the Southern myth were a distinct and largely uninfluential minority in their society. Several Northern writers, disturbed by a rapid social mobility and an accelerating materialism which produced, in Taylor's words, "glowing optimism and expectations of a secular millennium," consciously cultivated the plantation theme to bare the disquieting developments in their own region. To them, the culture of the South had "many of the things which they felt the North lacked: the vestiges of an old-world aristocracy, a promise of stability and an assurance that gentility—a high sense of honor, a belief in public service and a maintenance of domestic decorum—could be preserved under republican institutions."[29] In the New South era similar

[28] Washington, *Up From Slavery,* pp. 80–7.
[29] Taylor, *Cavalier and Yankee,* p. 18.

doubts caused some of the North's finest writers to use the Southern romance to damn the excesses of the Gilded Age. Woodward has recently called attention to the fact that Herman Melville, Henry Adams, and Henry James each wrote works which included a Confederate veteran who "serves as the mouthpiece of the severest stricture upon American society or, by his actions or character, exposes the worst faults of that society." These three authors, Woodward writes, detested the "mediocrity, the crassness, and the venality they saw around them," and they found the Southerner "a useful foil for the unlovely present or the symbol of some irreparable loss."[30]

To most Northern writers and readers of the 'eighties and 'nineties, however, the commitment to the romantic legend masked few disturbing social thoughts and stemmed from simple needs. According to Gaines, the Northerner had a romantic, innate "love of feudalism" and a yearning to identify vicariously with aristocratic societies. The plantation, "alone among native institutions," he continues, satisfied "this craving for a system of caste."[31] Both the craving and the myth that satisfied it continued long beyond the years of the New South movement. Gunnar Myrdal, noting the enduring fascination of the American with the romantic legend, wrote in 1944:

> The North has so few vestiges of feudalism and aristocracy of its own that, even though it dislikes them fundamentally and is happy not to have them, Yankees are thrilled by them. Northerners apparently cherish the idea of having had an aristocracy and of still having a real class society—in the South. So it manufactures the myth of the "Old South" or has it manufactured by Southern writers working for the Northern market.[32]

The complex strands that wove together the myth of the Old South— alienation of the Southerner from national values and ideals in the antebellum period; alienation of a few Northerners, both before and after the war, from the strident pace of material progress; innocent love for another, grander civilization on the part of most—did not obscure for the New South spokesmen the incalculably valuable service it could perform in the cause of sectional reconciliation, a basic tenet of the New South creed. If

---

[30] C. Vann Woodward, "A Southern Critique for the Gilded Age," in *The Burden of Southern History* (Baton Rouge, 1960), pp. 109–40. The three works discussed by Woodward are Melville's poem, *Clarel* (1876); Adams's novel, *Democracy* (1880); and James's novel *The Bostonians* (1886).

[31] Gaines, *The Southern Plantation*, pp. 2–3.

[32] Gunnar Myrdal, *An American Dilemma: The Negro and Modern Democracy*, 2 vols. (New York, 1944), II, 1375.

the myth in antebellum days had bespoken alienation on the part of Southerners from national ways, in the postbellum period it worked in precisely the opposite direction, uniting the two sections. To the South it gave a vitally necessary sense of greatness to assuage the bitter wounds of defeat; to the North it offered a way in which to apologize without sacrificing the fruits of victory.

Henry Grady has always been regarded as the chief peacemaker among the New South spokesmen, but Joel Chandler Harris, his friend and colleague on the Atlanta *Constitution,* served the reconciliation cause in a more subtle and perhaps more effective manner. Many of Harris's stories are unmistakable attempts to heal sectional wounds and unite former enemies. While Grady was serving the cause as the ever-available orator, the shy Harris worked quietly in the background through Uncle Remus.

How Harris served the cause of reconciliation—and, in a larger sense, how the plantation literature promoted national identification of interests —is tellingly illustrated in the comparison of two versions of one of Harris's early stories. The original version appeared in the *Constitution* in 1877 under the title "Uncle Remus as a Rebel: How He Saved His Young Master's Life."[33] The second version, entitled "A Story of the War," appeared in the first of Harris's books, *Uncle Remus: His Songs and His Sayings,* published late in 1880.[34] The plot is similar in both stories. Uncle Remus saves his young master from certain death by shooting a Yankee sniper. In both stories Remus thinks only of his love for his master and mistress. He knew the Yankee was there to free him, but when he saw what was going to happen he "des disremembered all 'bout freedom" and pulled the trigger.[35] In the first version, that intended for relatively local consumption, the Yankee is killed. In the second telling, however, Harris is aware of his national audience. Here the sniper loses an arm, but not his life. He is nursed by Remus and Miss Sally, the plantation belle, regains his health, and wins the hand of his lovely nurse. Clearly, the second version reveals Harris consciously courting the North, as John Stafford points out, by demonstrating that "a Yankee is good enough to join the Southern aristocracy." Moreover, "the North and the South are symbolically wed; and the North accepts the paternalistic pattern. Thus is the patron flattered and at the same time the self-respect of the South retained."[36]

[33] The text is available in Robert Lemuel Wiggins, *The Life of Joel Chandler Harris: From Obscurity in Boyhood to Fame in Early Manhood, with Short Stories and Other Early Literary Work not Heretofore Published in Book Form* (Nashville, 1918), pp. 263–8.

[34] Harris, *Uncle Remus: His Songs and His Sayings,* pp. 175–85.

[35] *Ibid.,* p. 184; Wiggins, *Harris,* p. 267.

[36] John Stafford, "Patterns of Meaning in *Nights With Uncle Remus,*" *American Literature,* XVIII (May 1946), 94–5.

The intersectional marriage, symbol of reconciliation, was a standard device used by Southern writers of the period. Harris used it to good effect again in "Aunt Fountain's Prisoner." Aunt Fountain, the plantation mammy, says of the Yankee bridegroom: "He ain' b'long ter we-all folks, no furder dan he my young mistiss ole man, but dee ain' no finer w'ite man dan him. No, suh; dee ain'." Cheered by this judgment, New South readers both North and South must have been pleased also to read that this Yankee revived the sagging fortunes of the old plantation by a stern application of "vim and vigor," New South qualities *par excellence*.[37] Thus, as Harris would have it, the marriage of a Yankee to a Southern belle, lovely flower of the old regime, excited Northern sympathy and admiration for the honorable qualities of Southern life and, at the same time, showed Southerners that their future would be prosperous if new concepts of work and organization were accepted.

The role of the Negro and of race relations was of special importance in the romantic legend and, in persuading the North to view the "quaint darky" through Southern eyes, the mythmakers accomplished at least two important results. First, by convincing Northern readers that relations between the races were kindly and mutually beneficial a principal obstacle in the way of sectional harmony was removed. The North had doubted this point, but on the authority of Harris and others it came to accept the Southern point of view.[38] Second, the acquiescence by the North in the Southern scheme of race relations permitted the South to deal with (or to fail to deal with) its race problems unmolested.

Humor was a standard and effective device used by Southern writers to mollify the Northern conscience, for, as Sterling Brown caustically observes, "if the Negro could be shown as perpetually mirthful, his state could not be so wretched."[39] In a more sophisticated vein, Stafford comments that Harris's use of ironic comedy invariably produced the "understanding laugh" which gave emotional release from doubts and guilt feelings and induced whites to tolerate what otherwise would appear to be an evil situation. The "pure humor" of Uncle Remus, then, won "acceptance for the existing class harmony."[40] To humor there was added the element of the essential difference between white and black, the image of the Negro as an exotic primitive, as

[37] Joel Chandler Harris, *Free Joe and Other Georgian Sketches* (New York, 1887), pp. 72–98.

[38] See Stafford, "Patterns of Meaning," p. 97; Paul H. Buck, *The Road to Reunion, 1865–1900* (Boston, 1937), chap. 8; and John Donald Wade, "Profits and Losses in the Life of Joel Chandler Harris," *American Review*, I (April 1933), 28–9.

[39] Sterling A. Brown, "Negro Character as Seen by White Authors," *Journal of Negro Education*, II (April 1933), 188.

[40] Stafford, "Patterns of Meaning," 98–103, 108.

> Original in act and thought,
> Because unlearned and untaught.[41]

To make the ideal of blissful race relations a convincing one, the humorous and primitive Negro is, in hundreds of contemporary stories, the guardian of the old memories and traditions. Far from resenting his life under slavery he finds freedom uncongenial—"I wants ter git shet er dis heah freedom," exclaims a Negro who was freed by his master before the war[42]—or at least not as satisfactory as the "old days," and to every passerby he recounts the glories of yesteryear. Tourgee designated this stereotype the "poor 'nigger' to whom liberty has brought only misfortune, and who is relieved by the disinterested friendship of some white man whose property he once was."[43] In Page's "Marse Chan" and "Unc' Edinburg's Drowndin'," two of the Virginian's most famous tales, it is the former slave who tells the story, glorifies the past, and laments its passing.[44] In one of Harry Stillwell Edwards's stories the old mammy lives out her years in sight of the grave of her mistress, where she may better preserve the memory of happier days.[45] The longing for the past is everywhere expressed. Old Sam, the faithful body servant in "Marse Chan," declares "Dem was good ole times, marster—de bes' Sam ever see."[46] Chad, the loyal servant in Francis Hopkinson Smith's novel of the Virginia gentleman, feels likewise: "Dem was high times. We ain't neber seed no time like dat since de war."[47] And, in one of the poems of Miss Howard Weeden, the old Negro feels that

> I ought to think 'bout Canaan, but
>   It's Ole Times crowds my mind,
> An' maybe when I gits to Heaben
>   It's Ole Times dat I'll find![48]

Behind the façade of this pleasant fable of Negro happiness and devotion in the regime of slavery there were, of course, harsh realities. Tourgee ad-

---

[41] The lines are from Irwin Russell's "Christmas Night in the Quarters," the text of which may be found in his *Christmas Night in the Quarters*, pp. 3–24.

[42] Virginia Frazer Boyle, "A Kingdom for Micajah," *Harper's New Monthly Magazine*, C (March 1900), 35.

[43] Tourgee, "South as a Field for Fiction," 409.

[44] Thomas Nelson Page, *In Ole Virginia; or, Marse Chan and Other Stories* (New York, 1887), pp. 1–38, 39–77.

[45] Harry Stillwell Edwards, " 'Ole Miss' and Sweetheart," *Harper's New Monthly Magazine*, LXXVII (July 1888), 288–96.

[46] Page, *In Ole Virginia*, p. 10.

[47] Francis Hopkinson Smith, *Colonel Carter of Cartersville* (Boston, 1891), p. 61.

[48] Howard Weeden, *Bandanna Ballads* (New York, 1899), p. 10.

mitted that there were some real examples upon which the stereotype was built, "but they are not so numerous as to destroy the charm of novelty." About the Negro "as a man, with hopes, fears, and aspirations like other men," he wrote, "our literature is very nearly silent."[49] Moreover, as John M. Webb observes, "the fable applies only to the house slaves who had intimate contact with the whites."[50] But, as the legend would have it, the pleasant state of affairs was a general, not a particular or isolated, characteristic of antebellum life.

The generality of the situation, of course, was meant to apply to the postwar years as well as to the slavery regime. In addition to promoting sectional reconciliation and, in further removing the North from agitation of the race question, the image of the happy Negro helped to destroy one of the burdensome obstacles in the way of Northern investments in the South. Northern capitalists constantly complained of the unsettling conditions in the South stemming from racial friction. To the New South spokesmen it semed clear that friction would disappear and capital come rolling in once the race question were left entirely up to Southern determination. This is what Tompkins meant when he wrote that "an excess of zeal in the cause of freedom" on the part of Northerners could serve no useful purpose and was, in the long run, to the disadvantage of the Northern capitalists themselves.[51] The myth of the Old South, with its charming picture of the lovable and loving Negro, served well to jettison the zeal which Tompkins felt was rocking the boat.

Finally, in the South itself the romance of the past was used to underwrite the materialism of the present. The names and signatures of Confederate generals were everywhere in demand by railroad companies and corporations, for the New South prophets were well aware that the blessing of a "colonel" (if there were no generals handy) would do as much to float bonds and raise subscriptions as a dozen columns of optimistic statistics in the *Manufacturers' Record*. In *Colonel Carter of Cartersville,* a successful third-rate novel of the period, one of the characters observes wisely that "in a sagging market the colonel would be better than a war boom."[52] The marriage of the gentle life of the past and the bustling era of the present was perhaps nowhere better symbolized than in the advertising columns of that journal of worship, *The Confederate Veteran*. There one learned that Confederate flags could be purchased from a New York firm and the aspiring capitalist found notices of potentially prosperous factories up for sale.[53]

---

[49] Tourgee, "South as a Field for Fiction," 409.

[50] John M. Webb, "Militant Majorities and Racial Minorities," *Sewanee Review,* LXV (Spring 1957), 335.

[51] Tompkins, *Manufactures,* p. 22.

[52] Smith, *Colonel Carter,* p. 99.

[53] See, for example, *Confederate Veteran,* VI (October 1898), 493–8.

The several specific uses to which the mythic conception of the Old South were put to serve the needs of the New South movement help to make intelligible the paradoxical commitment of the New South prophets to the legendary romance. Professor Woodward, in his skeptical assessment of the movement, feels that the "bitter mixture of recantation and heresy" which infused the New South creed "could never have been swallowed so readily had it not been dissolved in the syrup of romanticism."[54] But the sugar coating of the pill of the New Departure, important though it was, does not fully account for the phenomenon of mythmaking. More profound, more universal and less tangible forces were at work as well. Henry James suggested some of these when he wrote:

The collapse of the old order, the humiliation of defeat, the bereavement and bankruptcy involved, represented, with its obscure miseries and tragedies, the social revolution the most unrecorded and undepicted, in proportion to its magnitude, that ever was; so that this reversion of the starved spirit to the things of the heroic age, the four epic years, is a definite soothing salve.[55]

That there were deep wounds whose treatment required a soothing salve is abundantly clear. The South had so irrevocably committed its soul to the war that when defeat came it was more than a surrender of ambitions for independence; it was a crippling blow to the most basic assumptions upon which life in the region was lived. Pride and hope were destroyed by defeat, and humiliation was added by the Reconstruction. Under the circumstances, the search for self-confidence and a return of pride quite naturally involved more than a program of building on the ashes. Somehow the ashes themselves had to be ennobled. The myth worked powerfully to achieve this purpose: it gave back those very things which the Yankee had tried to take away—the knowledge of a proud past and a noble heritage. Without that knowledge, Grady once remarked, "the New South would be dumb and motionless."[56]

The search for a noble past, like the attempt to discover a heritage of nationalism and industrialism, engaged Southerners in an emotional and intellectual quest common to other people in other times. Nations that have been either victimized or blessed by profound social upheaval have commonly undergone, in one way or another, the experience of replanting the bared roots to the past; of developing the mythmaking process to satisfy collective needs. And for Southerners of the New South era, should they be charged with distortion of the past, their reply might be, with the Vir-

---

[54] Woodward, *Origins of the New South,* p. 158.
[55] Quoted in *ibid.,* p. 157.
[56] Grady, *New South,* ed. Dyer, p. 147.

ginia novelist James Branch Cabell, that "no history is a matter of record; it is a matter of faith."[57]

Allegiance to both the myth of the Old South and the dream of a New South was but one of several contradictions imbedded in the New South creed. There were many others: an institutional explanation of industrial backwardness in the Old South coupled with the faith that natural resources could not help but assure industrialization in the New; an elaborate propaganda campaign to attract immigrants into the region negated by hostility to the immigration pool easiest to tap; a gospel of economic interdependence and reconciliation with the North as part of a campaign for independence and domination; a lauding of freedom for the Negro in a politics of white supremacy; dreams of equal treatment of allegedly unequal races in separate societies devoted to mutual progress—these are among the most obvious.

Rich in paradoxes, the New South creed also had an ironic outcome. Designed to lead the region out of poverty, it made converts by the thousands in all parts of the country of men who looked forward confidently to a South of abundance. Instead, the expectations were unrealized and the South remained the poorest and economically least progressive section of the nation. The plans for regional and personal success, the restoration of self-confidence, and a position of influence and respect in the nation likewise fired the imagination and gained legions of adherents, but they too were largely unfulfilled and at the end of the New South crusade the region found itself in the uncomfortable, if familiar, role of a colonial dependent. Rid of many of the humiliating frustrations of the early postwar years, it was saddled with new ones that had greater staying power. Finally, the dream of a just and practical solution to the race question appealed to former abolitionists and radicals as well as to longtime racists because it promised that justice and practicality could be balanced, that Southerners themselves could do what Yankee reformers had failed to do, and that a harmonious biracial society would emerge and permit Americans to forget about injustice to the black man. Instead, violence increased in the 'eighties, and disfranchisement and rigid segregation followed later as the Negro reached the nadir of his history as a free man.

Unable to bequeath to the next generation of Southerners a legacy of solid achievement, the New South spokesmen gave them instead a solidly propounded and widely spread image of its success, a mythic view of their own times that was as removed from objective reality as the myth of the Old South. In creating the myth of the New South, they compounded all of the contradictions originally built into their creed, added others, and crowned their professions of realism with a flight of fantasy.

[57] Cabell, *Let Me Lie*, p. 74.

16

The Progressive Movement
in the South, 1870–1914

Arthur S. Link

Much has been accomplished in the American historical profession
toward arriving at a more valid assessment of the first "ism" to
dominate the twentieth century—progressivism. In making these
judgments, however, the South has traditionally been excluded from
serious consideration. Even at the time, national Progressive leaders
such as Robert M. LaFollette "wrote off" the region because he
considered democracy basically lacking there; later historians seem
to have found it difficult to fit the area into the urban middle-class
model. In this article America's premier Woodrow Wilson scholar,
Princeton historian Arthur S. Link, directs himself to this im-
balance and carefully redresses it. After defining the terms "conservative" and "progressive," Professor Link briefly traces southern
progressivism as it developed out of late nineteenth-century southern radical agrarianism and notes its subtle shift from a rural-eco-
nomic to an urban-political emphasis. In addition, the positive impact
of Woodrow Wilson (a Virginian by birth) on the Progressive movement in the South was significant, as southerners, particularly educators, clergymen, and editors, took up the cause. The article then
goes on to list southern accomplishments as compared to national
progressive goals in areas such as railroad regulation, reform of
party machinery, and corrupt practices legislation. Professor Link
also notes selective achievements in economic and social fields such
as the sixty-hour work week in the textile mills and child labor legislation. If there were southern progressive deficiencies, comparatively

Arthur S. Link, "The Progressive Movement in the South, 1870–1914," The North
Carolina Historical Review, 23 (1946), 172–195. Reprinted with permission of the
publisher and author.

they were perhaps no more numerous or gross than those on the national level as a whole—especially since it is now somewhat common to see the entire Progressive movement as complex and laden with paradox. If one can accept imperialism, immigration restriction, and prohibition as "progressive," then certain regressive tendencies in the South (e.g., treatment of the Negro) do not necessarily disqualify that region from the century's first "ism."

Before assessing the nature and extent of progressive democracy in the South, a definition of terms, as they are meant to be understood in this discussion, is necessary.[1] Conservatism, as it is generally understood, connotes a tendency to maintain the status quo and a disposition of hostility to innovations in the political, social, and economic order. Oftentimes the classes that possess a conservative point of view are the wealthy classes, but, of course, this is not always the case. In short, conservatism is usually a reasoned or unreasoned resistance to change.[2] Progressivism, on the other hand, implies a philosophy that welcomes innovations and reforms in the political, economic, and social order. Progressives are usually persons who strive for reforms that alleviate the ills of society, that assure to the people a broader control of their governments, and that look toward affording greater economic, political, and social justice to the people. These progressives are the so-called "liberals," not "radicals"; they have been, as a general rule, essentially conservative insofar as basic property rights and the fundamental capitalistic structure are concerned.[3]

The popular notion that such a thing as progressive democracy in the South was non-existent during the period 1870–1914, or practically so, that the Southern states were ruled by tyrannical political machines, that they were almost unbelievably backward, economically, politically, and socially, has become so persistent that it is hard to down. Most writers ignore the progressive movement in the South altogether; those that do recognize its existence characterize it as a result of Western progressivism. The extremist's view that there was no progressive democracy in the South was expressed by the late Senator Robert M. LaFollette, himself a foremost

---

[1] Research on this article was made possible by a grant from the Julius Rosenwald Fund.

[2] See *Encyclopaedia of the Social Sciences*, IV, 230–232, for a discussion of conservatism.

[3] For a discussion of this idea see David J. Saposs's provocative article, "The Role of the Middle Class in Social Development, Fascism, Populism, Communism, Socialism," in *Economic Essays in Honor of Wesley Clair Mitchell*, pp. 395–424, especially p. 399.

progressive, in a speech at Saginaw, Michigan, on New Year's day, 1912. He said:

> I don't know of any progressive sentiment or any progressive legislation in the South. . . . A true American believes in democracy. He believes men and women are equal and entitled to an equal chance. But the Democratic party of the South is not by inheritance that sort of organization. All the strength of the party is the aristocracy. The Southern Democrat despises alike the poor white and the negro and that is not the sentiment that makes for popular government.[4]

Despite Senator La Follette's blanket indictment, only his ignorance prevented him from knowing that there was in 1912, and had been for some decades, a far-reaching progressive movement in the South. Basically and primarily it was, before 1900, agrarian in composition and principle, generated by agricultural unrest that came as a result of social, political, and economic causes. Farmers throughout the nation saw control of the national government pass from their hands into the hands of the industrial class after the Civil War. They saw the formation of large combinations in industry, which enabled the industrialists to eliminate competitors and to maintain a monopolistic price level. They saw themselves economically oppressed by the railroads by means of discriminations between persons and places, unjustly high freight rates, pools, and the granting of rebates. They felt themselves economically injured by the national bank system that furthered the interests of the business groups and prevented a free flow of credit to agricultural communities.

The Granger movement was the first attempt by the farmers to strike back at the industrial and railroad giants oppressing them. The economic platform of the Grange is illustrative of this point. It advised farmers to dispense with middlemen and commission agents, expressed violent opposition to monopolies and trusts, demanded regulation of the railroads by the state and national governments in the interests of the producers, and advocated agricultural and industrial education.[5] The year 1871 saw the introduction of the Grange into South Carolina, Mississippi, and Kentucky, and by the end of 1872 the movement had spread widely throughout the South. By the end of that year, for example, South Carolina ranked next to Iowa in the number of granges.[6] The influence of the movement is clearly discernible in the demand for railroad regulation that made headway in the Southern states in the 1870's. There are numerous instances of Granger agitation for

[4] *San Antonio Express,* January 2, 1912.
[5] Solon J. Buck, *The Granger Movement,* p. 64.
[6] Buck, *Granger Movement,* pp. 52–55.

railroad regulation in the South. The state grange of Arkansas petitioned the legislature in 1877 for a law establishing maximum rates. In Virginia and Tennessee the state granges were interested in efforts to secure reduced rates by negotiation with the railroad companies. The state grange of South Carolina appealed to the legislature in 1877 and again in 1878 for laws to prevent unjust rates, discrimination, and other railroad malpractices.[7] Obviously the movement for railroad regulation was an early manifestation of the Southern progressive movement. Numerous cooperative stores, banks, manufactories, and insurance companies were also begun by the Grange leaders in the South.[8]

Many causes were responsible for the decline and failure of the Granger movement in the South and in the nation.[9] Even after the passing of the organization as a powerful body, its influence lived on and subsequent agrarian movements became its heirs. The Grangers organized to do battle with the new capitalism—the railroads, the middlemen, the trusts, and the bankers—and, having failed to gain all their objectives, retired from the field.

The Greenback-Labor movement was the successor to the Granger movement, but primarily because it was a third party organization it made little headway in the South. In 1880 a state convention of the Alabama Greenback-Labor party adopted a platform which demanded adequate educational facilities, denounced the convict-lease system, and demanded an equalization of the tax burden.[10] Alabama was the only state in which the party made any headway at all, but in that state "Greenbackism . . . was a significant experiment in political discontent, and gave impetus to Populism as its successor in the state."[11]

The most significant and the largest farmers' organization in the nineteenth century South was the Farmers' Alliance. The Southern Farmers'

---

[7] Buck, *Granger Movement*, pp. 252–273. See also Francis B. Simkins, *The Tillman Movement in South Carolina*, p. 17.

[8] For Texas, see Ralph A. Smith, "The Grange in Texas, 1873–1900," *Southwestern Historical Quarterly*, XLII (April, 1939), 297–315.

[9] Among the causes for the decline of the Granger movement may be listed the following: (1) The laxness of organization permitted many persons who were not interested in the farmer and his problems to join. For example, it was not uncommon for politicians to use the Grange for their own political advancement. (2) The huge, unwieldy mass within the organization led to dissension within the ranks. (3) The connection of the Grange with a number of political movements led to its decline. (4) The Grange failed to secure permanent and effective railroad regulation. (5) The main cause was the failure of the Granger cooperative endeavors which went to pieces and left a burden of discredit and indebtedness. Buck, *Granger Movement*, pp. 70–74.

[10] John B. Clark, *Populism in Alabama*, p. 25.

[11] Clark, *Populism in Alabama*, p. 28.

Alliance had its origin in a cattlemen's association in Lampasas County, Texas, in the middle 1870's. Within a decade the Texas Alliance had spread throughout the state and under the guidance of its leader, C. W. Macune, began in the late 1880's to absorb similar farmers' organizations in other Southern states. By 1890 the Southern Alliance boasted a membership of over a million and was the most powerful farmers' organization in the country. It was the spearhead of the last great concerted agrarian effort in this country. It and its political successor, the People's party, marked the culmination of the agrarian progressive movement in the South.

When agrarian efforts to liberalize the Democratic party failed, Southern farmers joined their comrades in the West and launched in 1892 the People's party. The platform of the agrarian Democrats and the Populists, as members of the People's party were called, comprehended a broad program of economic and political reforms in the interest of the agrarian and debtor classes. Since the third party was organized in every Southern state, it is possible to see the objectives for which these progressives were fighting. The populistic group in Alabama adopted a platform in 1892 that included the progressive demands of the Democrats and also called for fair elections and a national graduated income tax, and denounced national banks and trusts. A platform of 1894 demanded the removal of convicts from, and prohibition of child labor in, the mines.[12] The Alliance-controlled Democratic party in Tennessee in 1890 demanded free coinage of silver, extension of the public school system, lien laws to protect laborers and mechanics, good roads, and abolition of the convict-lease system.[13] The Democracy in Georgia in 1890, in the control of the Alliance, came out in favor of an enlargement of the powers of the state railroad commission, abolition of the convict-lease system and other prison reforms, revision of the tax system, extension of the public school system, and laws to ensure fair primaries and elections.[14] The 1892 North Carolina Populist platform called for economy in state government, adequate aid to the state educational institutions, reduction of the legal rate of interest to six percent, adequate taxation of the railroads, and a ten-hour day for laborers in mines, factories, and public works.[15]

All of the Southern state parties endorsed the national Populist platform,

---

[12] Clark, *Populism in Alabama*, pp. 133, 152.

[13] Daniel M. Robison, *Bob Taylor and the Agrarian Revolt in Tennessee*, pp. 144–145.

[14] Alex M. Arnett, *The Populist Movement in Georgia*, pp. 105–106. See also James C. Bonner, "The Alliance Legislature of 1890," in J. C. Bonner and Lucien E. Roberts (eds.), *Studies in Georgia History and Government*, pp. 155–171.

[15] Simeon A. Delap. "The Populist Party in North Carolina," *Historical Papers of the Trinity College Historical Society*, XIV, 52.

but none had so complete a program as did Texas Populism. The 1892 Texas platform reaffirmed the traditional American doctrine of the equality of man and demanded the elimination of certain economic inequalities that weighed heavily upon the farmers. It demanded the recovery of Texas land from railroads and corporations and the prohibition of alien ownership. The Texas Populists advocated, moreover, government construction of railroads, abolition of national banks, free silver, and the issuance by the federal government of legal tender notes to the amount of fifty dollars per capita, while the sub-treasury plan was the means by which the money would be put into circulation. The taxation system and Democratic extravagances in government were criticized. An anti-trust program was endorsed and a labor program which included an eight-hour day, mechanics' lien laws, the establishment of a state board of labor and arbitration, and the abolition of the convict-lease system was adopted. Such political reforms as the direct election of Senators, the President, and the Vice President, proportional representation, and the initiative, referendum, and recall were also endorsed.[16]

The influence of the Alliance and Populist movements in the South was so profound and of such portent to Southern political life that its significance can be understood only when it is realized that it shook the very foundations of Democratic supremacy in the region. Although, with the single exception of North Carolina, the Populists failed to gain control in any Southern state, the agrarians in the Farmers' Alliance seized control of the Democratic party machinery and elected governors and Congressmen in several Southern states. And Populism itself, despite the paucity of its actual gains, had a significant influence on the political life of the South. The movement effected, for the first time since the Civil War, a real cleavage within the Democratic ranks and forced the retirement of many of the old conservative leaders. What is more important, it forced the Southern Democratic party, at least for a time, to become almost as progressive as the Populist party.

An examination of the history of the several Southern states during the 1890's will illustrate this point. In Texas in 1894 the Democrats adopted the Populist program with regard to convict labor. In 1896 they approved the national Populist planks calling for free silver, the issuance of legal tender notes by the federal government, the abolition of national banks as banks of currency issue, the election of United States Senators by the

[16] Roscoe C. Martin, *The People's Party in Texas*, pp. 46–54. This is the best of the state studies on Southern Populism. Again, it should be emphasized that the national Populist platform concerning land, money, and railroad regulation was heartily approved by Southern Populists. It will be remembered, also, that the "sub-treasury" plan was a Southern invention and was one of the chief planks of Southern Populism.

people, and the institution of the income tax. A railroad commission had been established and an alien land law had been passed early in the 1890's by the legislature.[17] The Democrats of Alabama in 1892 adopted a platform demanding free silver, the abolition of the convict-lease system, adequate support for the public school system, primary election laws, and the secret ballot.[18] A farmer-controlled legislature in Tennessee in 1890 and 1891 passed a stringent anti-trust law, drastically raised taxes on corporations, and passed a resolution calling on Tennessee's Congressmen and Senators to support a constitutional amendment for the direct election of United States Senators.[19] By 1896 the Democratic party in that state had become almost completely converted to Populism. Its platform demanded free silver, the abolition of national banks, the repeal of the tax on state bank notes, and a national income tax.[20] In South Carolina Benjamin R. Tillman led the white small farmers to victory in 1890 and subsequently inaugurated a number of reforms, many of which were in the interests of the farmers.[21] In Virginia the conservative Thomas S. Martin organization was forced to take a stand in favor of free silver and the Democratic convention of 1896 was a free-silver carnival.[22]

An Alliance legislature in Georgia in 1890–1891, led by Alliance Governor W. J. Northen, extended the jurisdiction of the state railroad commission, instituted certain reforms in the banking laws of the state, extended the system of state inspection of fertilizers, and established a Negro agricultural and mechanical college.[23] By 1896 the Georgia Democratic convention was demanding free silver, the repeal of the Resumption Act that gave President Cleveland authority to issue United States bonds in order to maintain the gold reserve in the Treasury, the repeal of the federal tax on state bank notes, an income tax amendment, and a revenue tariff.[24] In North Carolina the Farmers' Alliance had captured the legislature by 1890, and in 1891 a state railroad commission was established and en-

[17] Martin, *People's Party in Texas,* pp. 266–267.

[18] Clark, *Populism in Alabama,* p. 132.

[19] Robison, *Bob Taylor,* pp. 152–153.

[20] Robison, *Bob Taylor,* p. 197.

[21] Simkins, *Tillman Movement,* chapters VI, VII, and VIII. Some of the reforms of the Tillman regime were: increased aid to the agricultural college, establishment of a woman's college, reorganization of the insane asylum, raising the valuation of corporation property for taxation purposes, the establishment of a more powerful railroad commission in 1892, a bill limiting the hours of labor in industry, and the dispensary system.

[22] William DuBose Sheldon, *Populism in the Old Dominion,* chapter V.

[23] Bonner, "The Alliance Legislature of 1890," pp. 155–171. See also Arnett, *Populist Movement in Georgia,* p. 121.

[24] Arnett, *Populist Movement in Georgia,* pp. 194–195.

dowed with complete ratemaking authority.[25] In 1895 a fusion Populist-Republican legislature passed an election law aimed a wiping out entirely corruption at the ballot boxes. The election machinery was made completely bipartisan. The people were given the right to elect county commissioners; the legal rate of interest was set at six percent; increased appropriations for public institutions were made, while all corporations which had been exempted from taxation were hereafter to be subject to taxation.[26]

Such were the objectives and achievements of Southern agrarianism and Populism. Of course, the fact that the Populist revolt had forced out the conservative Bourbon leadership within the Democratic party and had necessitated a reorganization and reorientation within the party is not particularly surprising. The movement was nation-wide. It resulted in the expulsion of the Cleveland Democrats of the conservative East from power in party circles in 1896 and the inauguration of the progressive, Bryan-dominated era. Moreover, the return of large numbers of former Populists to the Democratic party upon the fusion of the Populists with the Democrats in 1896 further stimulated the progressive leaven within the Democratic party. The result of a decade of agitation was a much greater emphasis in the South on popular education and social and economic reform. Populistic and agrarian agitation against the railroads and banks resulted in increased regulation of these institutions by the state governments. The activities of state departments of agriculture were expanded and greater emphasis was given to agricultural and vocational education. Significant reforms in the political machinery of the states were effected by the utilization of the party primary instead of the state convention as the method of nominating party candidates, the replacement of the old party ballot with the secret ballot, and the adoption by many Southern cities of the commission form of city government.

Although the Populist revolt caused the downfall of the Bourbon domination, it brought to the fore in Southern political life a new type of leadership, the leadership of the demagogues. Men like Cole L. Blease of South Carolina, Jeff Davis of Arkansas, and Theodore G. Bilbo of Mississippi were typical demagogues who stirred the people to democratic revolt and who rose to power by class agitation and race hatred, but who offered their constituents few measures of progressive legislation.

Throughout the decades of agrarian revolt, class agitation, and conflict, there remained a great number of Democrats who were neither Bourbons nor Populists, but middle-of-the-road progressives. As a general rule, this group found its recruits in the middle classes of the South among the more

[25] John D. Hicks, "The Farmers' Alliance in North Carolina," *North Carolina Historical Review,* II (1925), 174–175.

[26] Delap, "Populist Party in North Carolina," pp. 57–59.

prosperous farmers, small business men, school teachers, editors, and other professional groups. They looked askance alike at the defection of the Populists and the conservatism of the Bourbons. But to a great degree the aims of the Southern progressives—popular education, reforms looking toward greater popular control of the state governments, and the abandonment by the state governments of laissez-faire as a guide for economic and social action—were much the same as those of the Populists. In Virginia the progressives were led by Carter Glass, Andrew J. Montague, and William A. Jones; in North Carolina by Charles B. Aycock, Josephus Daniels, Claude and William Kitchin, and Walter Clark. In Georgia, Hoke Smith and Thomas W. Hardwick; in Florida, Frank L. Mayes; in Alabama, Benjamin B. Comer; in Louisiana, John M. Parker; in Kentucky, Ollie M. James and John C. W. Beckham; in Oklahoma, Robert L. Owen and Thomas P. Gore; and in Texas, James Stephen Hogg, Charles A. Culberson, and Robert L. Henry were representatives of this middle-class progressivism. Indeed, the statement might perhaps be made that no region of the country, in proportion to its population, could boast a greater galaxy of progressive leaders.

After 1900 the Southern progressive movement reveals itself in a somewhat different light from the nineteenth century agrarian radicalism. In the first place, the farmers of the South and of the nation as well entered upon a period of relative prosperity around 1897 which continued with few interruptions until 1920. As money became more plentiful farm prices rose and consequently agrarian demands for extreme financial reforms diminished. In the second place, what was perhaps the farmers' paramount problem—adequate regulation of railroad rates and services—was gradually being taken care of by federal and state action. As a consequence, there was a gradual shift in emphasis in the Southern progressive platform. It ceased to be almost entirely agrarian in outlook, while the leadership of the movement passed from the hands of the farmers to progressive editors, politicians, and other urban groups. The chief issues of the progressive movement in the early part of the twentieth century, from 1900 to 1914, were primarily political. Once again, it should be pointed out that this development within progressive ranks was nation-wide.

The culmination of the Southern progressive movement came as a result of a national development—the Woodrow Wilson presidential campaign both before and after the Baltimore convention of 1912. Even by 1911 Wilson was displacing Bryan as leader of the progressive Democrats and liberal Southerners hastened to join the New Jersey governor's ranks. Wilson's New Freedom philosophy and program had a powerful appeal to certain groups in Southern society. The fact that he had taken the lead in smashing a reactionary political machine in New Jersey won him the support of liberals in every Southern state who were fighting to overthrow conservative political organizations. The most significant fact about the Wilson movement in the South was that these Southern progressives seized upon it as a weapon to use against the conservatives in order to gain control of their own state governments. Wilson's economic philosphy was very much like Bryan's and the New Jersey governor's campaign against the "money trust," big business, and in favor of a revenue tariff naturally won him the support of the old Bryan men. The educational leaders in the South—from the universities and colleges to the country schools—played an important role in the movement. Southern teachers were naturally gratified to see one of their fellows step from college halls to the national political stage and the remarks of anti-Wilson editors which reflected on the candidate because he had been a professor drove thousands of teachers into the Wilson ranks. Wilson was popular, not only with the educators in the South, but also with the college students and the enthusiasm for him which swept through college campuses was phenomenal. As Wilson was supported by Southern educators, so was he likewise supported by many Southern clergymen. Wilson's adherence to and profession of the Christian faith, and his Christian life were reasons enough for thousands of ministers and members of the church to enlist in his cause. The religious press, abandoning its usual hands-off policy in political campaigns, generously supported Wilson in the prenomination campaign of 1912.[27]

If the writer had to single out the group of men that made the greatest contribution to the Wilson movement in the South he would almost inevitably name the Southern editors who heralded the coming of the New Freedom. Their work in presenting the man to the people and in engendering enthusiasm and support for his cause was the foundation stone of Wilson's campaign in the South. It is not strange that many of the strongest Wilson editors—Josephus Daniels, William E. Gonzales, Frank L. Mayes, and Luke Lea—were also devoted followers of William Jennings Bryan. Nor is it strange that most of the anti-Bryan editors were also antagonistic to the New Jersey governor. The powerful leavens of progressivism and conservatism necessitated such an alignment. Many of the Southern editors were also politicians of influence.[28]

[27] See, for example, *Christian Advocate* (Nashville), March 8, 1912; *Birmingham Age-Herald,* August 20, 1912; Raleigh *News and Observer,* April 2, 1912; *Atlanta Constitution,* Febrary 5, 1912; *Atlanta Journal,* April 16 and 26, 1912; *Presbyterian Standard* (Charlotte), March 24, 1911, April 24, and July 17, 1912; *Presbyterian of the South* (Richmond), February 8, 1911.

[28] Daniels and Robert Ewing were national Committeemen, respectively, from North Carolina and Louisiana. Gonzales dominated the progressive faction of the party in South Carolina. Lea and E. B. Stahlman were spokesmen for the progressive Democrats in Tennessee. James R. Gray of the *Atlanta Journal* was allied with the political fortunes of Hoke Smith and the progressive faction of the Georgia Democracy.

The Wilson movement in the South became in effect a struggle for progressive Democracy, and progressive Southern politicians were in the vanguard of the movement. Men who had been Bryan's spokesmen for nearly sixteen years—Daniels, Tillman, Gonzales, Hoke Smith, Frank L. Mayes, Nathan P. Bryan, Braxton B. Comer, Luke Lea, Charles A. Culberson, Robert L. Henry, William H. Murray, and Thomas P. Gore—perhaps realized that the Commoner's day as a presidential candidate had passed and found a new leader in Woodrow Wilson. There were, of course, Bryan men in the South who supported Champ Clark, who was running as a progressive. On the other hand, the consistent opposition of the conservative Southern state organizations came as a result of the liberalism of the Wilson movement.

The Wilson movement was moderately successful in achieving its immediate goal, the winning of the Southern delegations. Wilson won proportionately as much support in the South as in any other section of the country. From the long-range point of view the movement was significant in that it became the spearhead of a great progressive revolt. It brought to the fore important issues which demanded solution; it engendered a tremendous amount of discussion concerning popular government and progressive reform.[29]

So much for the general development of the progressive movement in the South from the Granger movement to the Wilson era. An interrogator might reasonably ask: if the South had such a considerable body of progressives and was so visibly affected by the progressive movement, why did not the region show results by way of progressive reforms? Such a question creates a perplexing problem in the establishment of a yardstick of progressivism. It might be helpful to consider the reform measures that were outstanding during this period and to analyze the accomplishments of the Southern states.

One example of progressive reform in which Southern states were virtual pioneers was the difficult problem of railroad regulation. In the rebuilding of the railroads in the South after the destruction that occurred during the Civil War, Northern capitalists played an influential part. And with the subsequent consolidation of Southern railroads into large systems also came the attendant evils of monopolistic control. The railroads levied fares and freight rates at their pleasure and often to the oppression of the

[29] Spatial limitations have required that the writer merely summarize the general characteristics of the Wilson movement in the South. For a fuller discussion, however, see Arthur Link, "The South and the Democratic Campaign of 1912," unpublished Ph.D. dissertation in the library of the University of North Carolina. "The Wilson Movement in Texas, 1910–1912," *Southwestern Historical Quarterly*, XLVIII (October, 1944), 169–185; "The Democratic Pre-Convention Campaign of 1912 in Georgia," *Georgia Historical Quarterly*, XXIX (September, 1945), 143–158.

people, while stock watering, discrimination in rates, the free pass evil, and under-assessment for taxes were frequently practiced evils. The political corruption attendant upon the railroads' suspicious and frequent sorties into politics, as well as the malpractices mentioned above, led soon after the restoration of home rule to a popular demand that the railroads be subjected to public control.

Virginia took the first step and in 1877 the legislature of that state established a state advisory railroad commission on the order of the Massachusetts type.[30] The powers of the Virginia commission were purely supervisory and recommendatory and it was not until 1901 that popular agitation for a commission with power to set rates finally culminated in the establishment of a powerful Corporation Commission with complete administrative, legislative, and judicial powers over railroads and other corporations.[31] A year following the establishment of the first Virginia commission, South Carolina set up an advisory railroad commission modeled after it.[32] Four years later, however, the legislature amended the law so as to endow the commission with full power to set freight and passenger rates.[33]

Georgia was the first Southern state and, along with California, the first state in the country effectively to regulate railroad rates and operations.[34] The Georgia constitution of 1877 made the establishment of a railroad commission by the legislature mandatory and, in compliance with this emphatic directive, the legislature in 1879 established the state commission. The Georgia commission had extraordinary powers to fix and compel fair and uniform rates, to forbid discrimination among persons and places, and to abolish the discrimination inherent in the long-and-short-haul practice. Schedules of rates established by the commission were to be accepted as just and fair by the state courts, while railroad companies were compelled to submit to the commission their records and business files.[35] The Georgia commission was exceedingly effective in bringing the railroads of the state under its control, and it secured reductions

[30] *Acts of the General Assembly of the State of Virginia,* 1876–1877, chapter 254, pp. 254–257.

[31] See the *Virginia Constitution of 1902,* article XII, sections 155–156, in *Acts of the General Assembly of the State of Virginia,* 1902–1903–1904, pp. 31–37.

[32] *Acts and Joint Resolutions of the General Assembly of the State of South Carolina,* 1878, chapter 662, pp. 789–792.

[33] South Carolina, *Acts,* 1881–1882, chapter 595, pp. 791–841.

[34] The earlier legislative efforts of the Midwestern states of Illinois, Minnesota, Wisconsin, and Iowa during the heyday of the Granger movement were ineffective and short-lived.

[35] *Acts and Resolutions of the General Assembly of the State of Georgia,* 1878–1879, chapter 269, pp. 125–131.

in passenger and freight rates of between fifty and sixty percent.[36] In addition to the fact of its successful career, the Georgia commission is significant in that practically all other Southern states subsequently established commissions modeled after it. In 1907, largely due to the persistent efforts of Hoke Smith, leader of the progressive wing of the Democratic party in Georgia and governor of the state in 1907, the legislature reorganized the railroad commission and greatly extended its jurisdiction. It was in reality transformed into a corporation or public utilities commission. The most interesting feature of the new law was a provision which made it the commission's duty to promulgate such rules regarding the issuance of stocks and bonds as would put an end to over-capitalization and guarantee honest values to purchasers of securities.[37]

Kentucky in 1879 established an advisory railroad commission.[38] The commission was, however, deprived of all authority to supervise railroad rates by a decision of the Kentucky Court of Appeals in 1896, but an act of the legislature in 1900 conferred the authority upon the commission to prescribe "reasonable and just" freight and passenger rates.[39] After a prolonged battle with the Louisville and Nashville Railroad the commission's right to prescribe reasonable maximum intrastate rates was confirmed by the Supreme Court of the United States.[40]

The Alabama legislature in 1881 established a railroad commission, but withheld from it the authority to fix rates and fares. The carriers were required to submit to the commission their tariffs of freight and passenger charges for examination and if the commission should find any charge which it deemed unreasonable, it was directed to notify the railroad in question.[41] The provisions of the Alabama law were a decided improvement upon the law establishing the Virginia commission but were obviously inadequate effectively to deal with the problem of railroad regulation. Consequently, in 1883 the legislature gave the commission authority to determine reasonable rates.[42] The Alabama commission was successful in decreasing tariff charges, but there was considerable popular agitation for an act to increase the commission's powers. The leader of the move-

[36] Jim David Cherry, "The Georgia Railroad Commission, 1879-1888," unpublished M.A. thesis in the library of the University of North Carolina.

[37] Georgia, *Acts,* 1907, chapter 223, pp. 72-81.

[38] *Acts of the General Assembly of the Commonwealth of Kentucky,* 1879, chapter 1019, pp. 92-95.

[39] Kentucky, *Acts,* 1900, chapter 2, pp. 5-7.

[40] Maxwell Ferguson, *State Regulation of Railroads in the South,* pp. 123-124. This is the only general work on the subject.

[41] *Acts of the General Assembly of Alabama,* 1880-1881, chapter 91, pp. 84-95.

[42] Alabama, *Acts,* 1882-1883, chapters 103 and 104, pp. 177-178.

ment for more effective regulation after 1900 was Braxton Bragg Comer, who was elected president of the commission in 1904. In 1906 Comer was elected governor on a railroad-regulation platform and in 1907 called upon the legislature to abolish the "debauching lobby" maintained by the railroads at Montgomery and to pass laws providing for thorough railroad regulation.[43] In compliance, the legislature passed a series of acts which extended the jurisdiction of the commission to include most of the public utility companies of the state, reduced the freight rates on one hundred and ten articles of common production, and reduced passenger rates to two and one-half cents a mile.[44] A bitter fight between Governor Comer and the Louisville and Nashville Railroad resulted. In 1913, however, this railroad gave up its fight against the Alabama commission and accepted its schedules.[45]

Tennessee in 1883 established a railroad commission and authorized it to set just and reasonable rates,[46] but the railroads of the state were able to halt the work of the commission by use of judicial injunctions. As a consequence, the commission law of 1883 was repealed in 1885. However, in 1897 a new commission was established and endowed with full authority to regulate rates and tariffs.[47] It was successful in effecting a drastic reduction in transportation charges.[48] The Mississippi legislature in 1884 established a commission[49] which effectively reduced freight rates during 1886 and 1887. Passenger rates, because of the competitive practices of the Mississippi railroads, were already exceedingly low.[50] Florida in 1887 established a commission modeled almost exactly after the Georgia commission of 1879.[51] The Florida legislature, however, abolished the commission in 1891 because it did not approve of the new chairman appointed by the governor and it was not until 1897 that the commission was reestablished.[52] In 1899 the legislature considerably strengthened the

[43] Albert B. Moore, "Braxton Bragg Comer," *Dictionary of American Biography,* IV, 329–330.

[44] *General Laws of the Legislature of Alabama,* 1907, chapter 17, p. 80; chapter 30, p. 104; chapter 31, pp 105–107; chapter 69, pp. 135–166; chapter 329, pp. 404–405.

[45] Ferguson, *State Regulation,* p. 138. For a discussion of Comer's battle with the Louisville and Nashville Railroad see Rupert B. Vance, "Spell-Binders of the New South," unpublished manuscript in possession of Professor Vance.

[46] *Acts of the State of Tennessee,* 1883, chapter 199, pp. 271–279.

[47] Tennessee, *Acts,* 1897, chapter 10, pp. 113–126.

[48] Ferguson, *State Regulation,* pp. 140–146.

[49] *Laws of the State of Mississippi,* 1884, chapter 23, pp. 31–41.

[50] Ferguson, *State Regulation,* pp. 148–151.

[51] *Acts and Resolutions Adopted by the Legislature of Florida,* 1887, chapter 3746, pp. 118–126.

[52] Florida, *Acts,* 1897, chapter 4549, pp. 82–94.

commission's authority by more clearly defining its powers and giving it judicial authority,[53] and in 1901 it promulgated a comprehensive freight rate schedule.[54]

After many years of agitation, the legislature of North Carolina in 1891, dominated by members of the Farmers' Alliance, established a railroad commission based on the Georgia model.[55] Within less than a year's time freight and passenger schedules were promulgated that brought about numerous reductions.[56] In 1899 the railroad commission was transformed into a corporation commission, one of the first of its kind in the United States. The powers and duties of the old railroad commission were transferred to it, but its jurisdiction was extended to cover all carriers, as well as telephone companies, public and private banks, loan and trust companies, and building and loan associations.[57] The North Carolina commission attempted to bring to an end the discriminatory rates levied by the Virginia railroads to favor Virginia cities and to eliminate the discrimination practiced by the north-south lines running through the state.[58]

The Trans-Mississippi Southern states kept well abreast of the Southeastern states in the perplexing and difficult business of railroad regulation. Texas, under the progressive leadership of Governor James Stephen Hogg, in 1891 established a railroad commission to set reasonable rates,[59] and in 1893 the legislature enacted a stock and bond law designed to prevent the railroads from increasing and collecting fictitious debts by means of increasing the rates.[60] In Arkansas a railroad regulation amendment to the state constitution was adopted in 1897, and in 1899 the legislature established a commission. The railroads were required to furnish rate schedules to the commission, to keep rate schedules posted, and to furnish facilities for the care of persons and property transported. Discriminations of any sort, rebates, pooling, and the long-and-short-haul practice were prohibited. The commission was empowered to determine the valuation of the railroads, to conduct hearings, and to regulate freight, express, and passenger rates.[61] In 1907 the commission's jurisdiction was extended to

[53] Florida, *Acts,* 1899, chapter 4700, pp. 76–93.

[54] Ferguson, *State Regulation,* pp. 154–161.

[55] *Laws and Resolutions of the State of North Carolina,* 1891, chapter 320, pp. 275–288.

[56] Martha Frances Bowditch, "The North Carolina Railroad Commission, 1891–1899," unpublished M.A. thesis in the library of the University of North Carolina.

[57] North Carolina, *Laws,* 1899, chapter 164, pp. 291–307.

[58] Ferguson, *State Regulation,* pp. 174–177.

[59] *Revised Civil Statutes of the State of Texas,* 1895, chapter 13, pp. 909–920.

[60] Texas, *Statutes,* 1895, chapter 14, pp. 920–923.

[61] William F. Kirby (ed.), *A Digest of the Statutes of Arkansas,* sections 6788–6826, pp. 1407–1415.

sleeping car companies.[62] A railroad commission was established in Louisiana by a provision of the constitution of 1898. The commission was directed to set reasonable rates and was given authority over sleeping-car, express, telephone, and telegraph companies, and steamboats and other water craft as well as the railroads.[63] The first endeavor of the commission was to put an end to the disastrous competition between the railroads and steamboats, while numerous reductions in freight rates were effected.[64] Oklahoma's progressive constitution of 1907 restricted railroad and corporate activities in many ways. Considerable space was given to expressing the limitations and regulations of railroads and other public corporations which were regulated by a corporation commission of three members.[65]

In concluding this discussion of state railroad regulation in the South, it may reasonably be said that commissions in every Southern state regulated the transportation companies, for the most part, in the public interest and that the movement was successful in bringing benefits to the people in the form of reductions in rates, uniformity of schedules, and increased taxation of the railroads. It is the conclusion of the only authority in the general field that state regulation in the South effectively ended discrimination and reduced freight and passenger rates to an unjustly low level.[66]

The Southern movement for railroad regulation was manifestly a part of the nation-wide movement, and it is interesting to note that Southerners exercised considerable influence in the national movement for railroad reform. It is a well-known fact that John H. Reagan of Texas was regarded as the father of the Interstate Commerce Act of 1887. Robert M. LaFollette, writing years later, declared that "To Reagan of Texas, more than any other man in the House, belongs the credit for the passage of the act."[67] La Follette also wrote that he and his progressive lieutenants in Wisconsin had profited greatly from Reagan's wise advice when they drew up Wisconsin's railroad regulation law.[68] The advocates of national railroad legislation always had the overwhelming support of Southern representatives and Senators, and Senator Ben Tillman of South Carolina gave conspicuous service to the Roosevelt administration when he piloted the Hepburn rate bill through the Senate in 1906.[69]

[62] Charles W. Fornoff, "The Regulation of Public Service Corporations," in David Y. Thomas, *Arkansas and Its People, a History, 1541–1930,* I, 338–341:

[63] *Constitution of the State of Louisiana, 1898,* articles 283–289.

[64] Ferguson, *State Regulation,* pp. 180–184.

[65] *Constitution of the State of Oklahoma,* 1907, article X, sections 2–35.

[66] Ferguson, *State Regulation,* pp. 207–212.

[67] R. M. La Follette, *La Follette's Autobiography,* p. 119.

[68] La Follette, *Autobiography,* pp. 119–120.

[69] Henry F. Pringle, *Theodore Roosevelt,* pp. 420–425; Claude G. Bowers, *Beveridge and the Progressive Era,* pp. 225–226. Tillman received considerable support from Senator Joseph Weldon Bailey of Texas in the fight for the Hepburn bill.

In any discussion of the program of the progressive movement the measures advocated by progressives directed toward the reform of the party machinery loom large. One of the most important of these measures was the direct primary, by means of which reformers hoped to wrest control over the nominating process from the political bosses and to restore it to the people. Under La Follette's leadership, Wisconsin in 1903 adopted the mandatory state-wide direct party primary. Before 1890, however, every county in South Carolina used the primary system for the nomination of local officers and legislators, and in 1896 the state-wide Democratic party primary was inaugurated.[70] As early as 1897 the legislature of Arkansas had legalized primary elections.[71] The Mississippi legislature in 1902 enacted a law requiring that all nominations for state, district, county, and county district officials be made by primary elections.[72] The primary system was in use in Virginia at least by 1905, and in that year the United States senatorial primary was adopted by the Democratic party.[73] The first state-wide primary in Georgia was held on June 7, 1898, and the primary system was used regularly by the Democrats thereafter.[74] In 1902 Alabama Democrats adopted the primary system for nominating their candidates. Following the primary for state officers in 1902, the friends of the primary system began to agitate for a senatorial primary by means of which the voters could instruct the members of the state legislature upon their preference for United States Senator. The system was adopted in 1906.[75] Governor William S. Jennings, elected in 1900, was the last

[70] David D. Wallace, *History of South Carolina*, III, 336, 356. The South Carolina legislature in 1896 enacted a statute to prevent frauds at the primary elections, but the party primary was not made legally mandatory nor brought within the protection of the general election laws. South Carolina, *Acts and Joint Resolutions*, 1896, chapter 25, p. 56.

[71] Kirby (ed.), *Status of Arkansas*, 1904, chapter 57, sects. 2892–2897, pp. 705–706. In 1917 an act adopted by the initiative required primary elections of the major parties. T. D. Crawford and Hamilton Moses (eds.), *Digest of the Statutes of Arkansas, 1919*, chapter 54, sects. 3757–3782, pp. 1075–1083.

[72] Mississippi, *Laws*, 1902, chapter 66, pp. 105–112. Section 18 of this law also provided for the nomination of United States Senators by the senatorial primary.

[73] Robert C. Glass and Carter Glass, Jr., *History of Virginia Democracy*, I, 292. In 1912 the Virginia legislature passed an act "to establish and regulate the holding of primary elections." Virginia, *Acts*, 1912, chapter 307, pp. 611–619.

[74] Walter G. Cooper, *The Story of Georgia*, III, 370. A Georgia law of 1900 provided that primary elections should be held under the regulations prescribed by the party, but also provided that clerks of the superior courts should receive and count the election returns. Georgia, *Acts*, 1900, chapter 117, pp. 40–41.

[75] Albert B. Moore, *History of Alabama*, I, 909–910. In 1903 the Alabama legislature enacted a law which gave legal sanction and protection to all party primaries that might be held in the state. Alabama, *General Laws*, 1903, chapter 417, pp. 356–365.

In 1911 the legislature made a sweeping revision of the primary act and exempted from its application parties that polled less than 25 per cent of the votes at the general election. Alabama, *General Laws*, 1911, chapter 479, pp. 421–449.

governor of Florida nominated by a political convention. The legislature, early in his administration, enacted the primary system into the body of Florida laws.[76] By 1908, at least, Florida had instituted the senatorial primary.[77] The primary system had been in operation in Tennessee for some time before 1901, for in that year the state legislature enacted a law to legalize and regulate party primaries. All primary elections in the state were to be conducted under the provisions of the general election laws.[78] During the administration of Governor John C. W. Beckham, around 1905, the Kentucky Democratic party adopted the primary system,[79] while Texas[80] and Oklahoma[81] adopted the system in the early years of the twentieth century. Although the primary system had been in use since 1900 in the counties of North Carolina, it was not until 1915 that the legislature made its use mandatory on a state-wide basis.[82] Thus it would appear that the primary election idea was almost indigenous to the South, as far as its use in this country is concerned. It is clearly evident that a good majority of the Southern states were using the system by the time Wisconsin adopted it.

Another measure of reform advocated by progressives in the early part of the twentieth century was corrupt practices legislation, designed to purify the election process. By the end of the Wilson period every Southern state had enacted legislation making it a criminal offense to give bribes to influence a voter, and every Southern state except Florida had enacted severe legislation against the receiving of such bribes. Arkansas, Louisiana, Mississippi, North Carolina, Oklahoma, Tennessee, and Texas prohibited candidates from promising appointments before elections, while Arkansas and Texas had declared it unlawful for candidates to pay for the conveyance of voters to the polls. Alabama, Arkansas, Louisiana, and Mississippi

[76] The Florida law was passed in 1901. It provided for complete state regulation of party primaries. Florida, *Acts,* 1901, chapter 5014, pp. 160–165.

[77] Harry Gardner Cutler, *History of Florida,* I, 179.

[78] Tennessee, *Acts,* 1901, chapter 39, pp. 54–59. The poll tax requirement for voting did not apply in the primary election.

[79] George Lee Willis, *Kentucky Democracy,* I, 391–392. In 1912 the Kentucky legislature instituted the mandatory primary system which included the United States senatorial primary. Kentucky, *Acts,* 1912, chapter 7, pp. 47–77.

[80] A Texas law of 1905 made primary nominations mandatory for all candidates for state, district, and county offices. The law affected at the time, however, only the Democratic party since it applied only to parties polling more than 100,000 votes. Texas, *General Laws,* 1905, chapter 11, pp. 543–565. See also O. Douglas Weeks, "The Texas Primary System," in Frank Carter Adams (ed.), *Texas Democracy,* I, 531–554, especially p. 531.

[81] Oklahoma in 1909 adopted the mandatory primary as the method by which all political parties were to nominate candidates for all state offices. Oklahoma, *Session Laws,* 1909, Senate Bill No. 5, pp. 270–274.

[82] North Carolina, *Public Laws,* 1915, chapter 101, pp. 154–168. See also Robert D. W. Connor, *North Carolina, Rebuilding an Ancient Commonwealth,* II, 481–482.

denied party leaders the right to solicit campaign funds from candidates. By 1919 every Southern state had enacted laws of varying effectiveness and severity prohibiting the intimidation of voters, while Alabama, Texas, Mississippi, Tennessee, Florida, and Kentucky had made it unlawful for employers to intimidate or attempt to influence the voting of their employees. Arkansas, Florida, Kentucky, Oklahoma, Tennessee, and Texas also required employers to give their employees ample time to vote on election day. Tennessee, South Carolina, Oklahoma, Alabama, Georgia, Kentucky, Louisiana, Mississippi, and North Carolina passed legislation prohibiting illegal and unqualified registration, while all of the Southern states endeavored to prevent illegal and fraudulent voting. Kentucky, Louisiana, Mississippi, and Tennessee prohibited distinguishing marks or signs on election ballots, and Louisiana, Tennessee, and Virginia made it unlawful for a person to participate in a primary or convention of a party other than his own. Alabama, Arkansas, Florida, Texas, and Virginia required that political advertisements in newspapers be clearly denoted as such, while North Carolina, Louisiana, Mississippi, Florida, Arkansas, and Alabama required that political posters and advertisements bear the names and addresses of the persons responsible for issuing them. Florida and Virginia made it unlawful for a candidate to purchase editorial support in a political campaign. In the matter of campaign expenditures, Alabama, Arkansas, Florida, Kentucky, Louisiana, North Carolina, Oklahoma, South Carolina, and Virginia limited the amounts a candidate for governor might expend in his campaign for nomination and election. The sums varied from $3,000 in Oklahoma to $10,000 in Alabama. Virginia allowed an expenditure of fifteen cents for every voter who cast his vote for the highest party candidate at the last election. All of the states except Mississippi and Tennessee required candidates to file statements of their campaign expenditures either before or after the primary and election, or both. Alabama, Florida, Georgia, Kentucky, Louisiana, Mississippi, North Carolina, Oklahoma, Tennessee, and Texas attempted either to prohibit or to regulate the contributing by corporations to campaign funds.[83]

Four other political reforms were prominently in vogue in 1912: the presidential preferential primary, the commission form of city government, the direct election of Senators, and the initiative, referendum, and recall. During the presidential prenomination campaign of 1912 the issue of the presidential primary, in which the voters instructed delegates to the national convention to vote for their specified candidate, arose. The system, which supposedly deprived the political bosses of the power to select

[83] This discussion of corrupt-practices legislation in the Southern states is based upon Earl R. Sikes, *State and Federal Corrupt-Practices Legislation,* and is taken directly from the tables in pp. 258–291. It is difficult to determine the effectiveness of the laws. Sikes deals only with the legislation and not with the application of the laws.

presidential candidates, was adopted in the South in 1912 by Florida, Georgia, and Mississippi. In 1913 a preferential primary law was enacted by the Texas legislature.[84]

The commission form of city government originated in Galveston, Texas, in 1900 under extraordinary circumstances.[85] What was begun as an emergency administrative measure proved so effective a method of city government that it was not only retained in Galveston, but spread throughout the country. By 1914 commission government was operative in most of the larger Southern cities—in Galveston, Birmingham, Mobile, Montgomery, Shreveport, New Orleans, Wilmington, Oklahoma City, El Paso, Columbia, Chattanooga, Knoxville, Memphis, Dallas, San Antonio, Fort Worth, Houston, and Austin—and in many of the smaller cities as well.[86] It is interesting to note in this connection that Staunton, Virginia, was the first city in the country to adopt the city manager form of government.[87]

There was, and had been since the days of the agrarian revolt, a widespread demand in the South for the adoption of a constitutional amendment providing for the popular election of United States Senators.[88] As a matter of fact, by the time the amendment went into effect senatorial candidates in every Southern state were first nominated by the people in a party primary. The principles of the initiative, referendum, and recall never found widespread acceptance in the South, although Oklahoma in 1907 and Arkansas in 1909 wrote the reforms into their bodies of law.[89]

[84] Weeks, "The Texas Primary System," p. 532.

[85] In 1900 a great hurricane and flood swept over the city and, in order to facilitate the progress of reconstruction, the citizens of Galveston placed the government and job of rebuilding in the hands of a business commission.

[86] Aside from the cities named above the following places had the commission form of government by 1914: Anthony, Beaumont, Corpus Christi, Denison, Kennedy, Lyford, Marshall, Marble Falls, Palestine, Port Lavaca, Sherman, Waco, and Greenville, Texas; Ardmore, Bartlesville, Duncan, Enid, Miami, McAlester, Muskogee, Sapulpa, Tulsa, and Wagner, Oklahoma; Bristol, Clarkesville, Etowah, and Richmond City, Tennessee.

Commission city government was almost unanimously favored by the press of the South. See, for example, editorials in Raleigh *News and Observer*, March 15, 16, 17, 1911; Wilmington *Morning Star*, December 20, 1910, March 14, 15, 1911; *Charlotte Daily Observer*, November 16, 1911; *Pensacola Evening News*, January 13, 1912; Columbia *State*, April 13, 1911; *San Antonio Express*, January 9, 1911; *Mobile Register*, December 24, 1910; Petersburg (Va.) *Daily Index-Appeal*, February 19, 20, 21, 22, 23, 1911; Oklahoma City *Daily Oklahoman*, March 11, 1911; *Birmingham Age-Herald*, May 2, 1911.

[87] Benjamin P. DeWitt, *The Progressive Movement*, pp. 309–310.

[88] See, for example, editorials in Tulsa *World*, February 25, 1911; New Orleans *Times-Democrat*, December 19, 1910; Nashville *Tennessean and American*, December 20, 1910.

[89] Arkansas adopted only the initiative and referendum. Thomas, *Arkansas and Its People*, I, 320. For Oklahoma, see Grant Foreman, *History of Oklahoma*, p. 314. For editorials favorable to the initiative referendum, and recall, see: New Orleans *Time-Democrat*, December 15, 1910; Nashville *Tennessean and American*, December

Although Southern progressives gave emphasis to the struggle for political reform, they by no means were oblivious of the necessity of reform in the economic and social fields. As early as 1889 the Georgia legislature passed a law limiting work in the textile mills to sixty-six hours a week,[90] and in 1892 South Carolina enacted a similar law.[91] In 1911 both Georgia and North Carolina set the maximum number of hours per week operatives could work in textile factories at sixty.[92] In the matter of child-labor legislation, Southern progressives were likewise active. "There are only a few characteristics of the child labor struggle in the South which differentiate it from the movement in the nation at large, and even in them the difference is largely one of degree rather of kind," writes the authority on this movement.[93] The leader in the struggle of child labor legislation in the South was Edgar Gardner Murphy of Alabama, who was chiefly instrumental in the organization of the National Child Labor Committee.[94] Alexander J. McKelway, a Presbyterian minister of Charlotte, was the executive secretary in the South for the committee and for years carried on a struggle for child labor reform. The advocates of child labor legislation were not successful in accomplishing all of the objectives for which they were striving, but they did secure a number of reform laws in the textile states and presented vividly the child labor problem to the southern people.[95]

It is undoubtedly true that Southern editors led the fight for progressive reforms in the South.[96] Especially was this true in the fight against the notorious convict-lease system and the iniquitous fee system that make crime profitable to sheriffs and constables. The editor of the *Mobile Register,* editors Frank L. Mayes of the *Pensacola Journal,* Fred Seeley of the *Atlanta Georgian,* and Edward W. Barrett of the *Birmingham Age-Herald*

21, 1910; Oklahoma City *Daily Oklahoman,* February 17, 1911; *Mobile Register,* December 30, 1910; Columbia *State,* May 24, 1911; Little Rock *Arkansas Democrat,* December 2, 1910.

[90] Elizabeth H. Davidson, *Child Labor Legislation in the Southern Textile States,* pp. 69–70.

[91] Davidson, *Child Labor Legislation,* p. 90.

[92] Davidson, *Child Labor Legislation,* pp. 163, 206.

[93] Davidson, *Child Labor Legislation,* p. 2.

[94] Davidson, *Child Labor Legislation,* p. 125.

[95] Miss Davidson (*Child Labor Legislation,* pp. 275–278) lists in a table the laws controlling child labor passed by the Southern states.

[96] Among the progressive newspapers in the South during the period after 1900 the following were outstanding: *Mobile Register,* Raleigh *News and Observer,* Petersburg *Daily Index-Appeal,* Columbia *State, Atlanta Georgian, Atlanta Journal, Pensacola Journal, Birmingham Age-Herald, Birmingham News,* Nashville *Tennessean and American,* New Orleans *Times-Democrat,* Little Rock *Arkansas Democrat,* Galveston *Daily News,* Dallas *Morning News, Houston Chronicle, Louisville Post,* Oklahoma City *Daily Oklahoman,* and the Richmond *Times-Dispatch.*

led in the fight against these twin evils.[97] Progressive editors and leaders were also active during this period in an effort to secure adequate public health programs and insurance laws.[98]

Insofar as the foregoing movements for reform were progressive, it can be stated that there was a well organized progressive movement in the South aimed at remedying the ills of the region's social and economic and political order. It, of course, had serious deficiencies. None of the Southern editors, as far as this writer knows, who were agitating for political reforms, gave any consideration to the ominously steady increase in farm tenancy. The perplexing problems of the economic, social, and political development of the Negro likewise escaped serious attention from Southern editors. Although practically all the Southern editors severely condemned lynching, none dared to advocate political rights for the black man. As far as progressive democracy went in the South, it was progressive democracy for the white man.

It is only too apparent to the student of recent Southern history that many Southern institutions and practices were, during this period, antiquated and backward. Bearing this fact in mind, it may none the less be stated with emphasis that there were few sections of the country in which the masses of the people were more powerful than in the South. Certainly many of the dominant Southern political leaders during this period were not representative of the conservative classes. Demagogues like James K. Vardaman of Mississippi, Jeff Davis of Arkansas, or Cole Blease of South Carolina ostensibly represented the lower classes in a very definite class movement against the Bourbon conservatives. Progressives like Hoke Smith of Georgia; Robert L. Owen of Oklahoma; Charles A. Culberson, James S. Hogg, Thomas W. Gregory, and Robert L. Henry of Texas; Andrew J. Montague, William A. Jones, and Carter Glass of Virginia; Ollie M. James and J. C. W. Beckham of Kentucky; Luke Lea of Tennessee; Josephus Daniels, Claude and William W. Kitchin, and Walter Clark of North Carolina; Frank P. Glass and B. B. Comer of Alabama; William E. Gonzales, Ira B. Jones, and Ben R. Tillman of South Carolina; John M. Parker, Arsène Pujo, and Newton Blanchard of Louisiana; or Nathan P. Bryan and Frank L. Mayes of Florida continually fought the reactionaries and conservatives and were in the vanguard of the progressive movement, not only in the South, but in the nation as well.

[97] The following editorial from the *Mobile Register,* October 10, 1911, is characteristic of the anti-convict-lease editorials:

"The Register has constantly fought this leasing system and has shown up its abuses and inhumanity. It is a relic of barbarism which is a stain on Alabama. . . . The leasing system is wrong in principle, unsafe in operation and cruel in effect."

[98] For the early years of the North Carolina public health board, see Hilda Jane Zimmerman, "The Formative Years of the North Carolina Board of Health, 1877–1893," *North Carolina Historical Review,* XXI (1944), 1–34.

17

After Suffrage: Southern Women in the Twenties

Anne Firor Scott

The Southern Lady has always enjoyed a special niche in the inner chambers of the southern mind. Passive, demure, and properly innocent, the fabled southern "belle" assumed the role of indispensable helpmate to the mannered "Southern Gentleman." Indeed, it was together that they fashioned the distinct setting of instinctive ease so long associated with southern life before the Civil War. This mythic profile of Southern Womanhood, this artifact of the South's historic past, survived the war and in fact enjoyed a sustained measure of acceptance in the decades thereafter—even into the twentieth century. Such misty renditions of the Southern Woman, according to Anne Firor Scott, Professor of History at Duke University, cannot withstand the scrutiny of historical scholarship, nor do they meet even minimal standards of reality. This "chivalric nonsense," though long pampered, exquisitely preserved, and although periodically demonstrated false during the late nineteenth century, suffered a strategic setback with the passage of the Nineteenth Amendment. It was at this juncture, and only after earlier abortive attempts at emancipation, that the southern "belle" was at last armed with a legal basis from which she might do battle with her encrusted stereotype. Moving "from pedestal to politics" with greater velocity and vengeance after 1920, southern women staged important forays into general governmental reform. Child welfare, labor conditions, and race relations all served as focal points for southern feminists. As a result, the energies of southern women in the twen-

Anne Firor Scott, "After Suffrage: Southern Women in the Twenties," *Journal of Southern History*, 30 (August 1964), 298–318. Copyright 1964 by the Southern Historical Association. Reprinted by permission of the Managing Editor.

ties, although only selectively successful, did much to question the
cult of Southern Womanhood, and also to damage the associated
notion that southern politics was invariably nonprogressive and
"conservative."

In few parts of the country was the nineteenth amendment awaited with
higher expectations than among an earnest group of Southern women. Not
unlike the present-day Southern liberal who yearns for a federal civil rights
bill because the road to state and local legislation is so long and rocky,
Southern women who had labored for state suffrage and for social reform
against an opposing tide looked to the federal amendment for help. For
them the vote had also become a symbol of something much larger—the
image of the "new woman." Long constrained by Southern tradition about
woman's place in Southern life, they saw the amendment as a grant of
freedom and a new measure of independence.

One of these women remarked in a private letter in 1920 that she was
planning a trip to Europe because "once we *really* get into politics (i.e.,
once the suffrage amendment is ratified) I will never be able to get away."[1]

Another, in North Carolina, thought "the advent of women into political
life" would mean "the loosening of a great moral force which will modify
and soften the relentlessly selfish economic forces of trade and industry in
their relation to government. The ideals of democracy and of social and
human welfare will undoubtedly receive a great impetus."[2] For many years
these earnest women had organized themselves, talked to legislators,
worked for or against congressmen in their home districts, testified at hearings, haunted the polls on election day, cajoled money, written newspaper
articles, watched the progress of more advanced Northern and Western
women—and now, at last, had the federal help that promised to open the
way to substantial achievement.

By 1920 Southern women had come to exert increasing influence in
public affairs, but many of the problems that concerned them were still
unsolved: the dislocations caused by industrialization, the conditions of
work for women and children, the inadequacies of the educational system,
the lack of opportunity for many children, prison conditions, the ravages
of alcohol and disease, injustice to Negro citizens. To all such problems,
and some new ones they would discover along the way, the newly en-

[1] Madeline McDowell Breckinridge to Allie S. Dickson, March 20, 1920, in Breckinridge Family Papers (Manuscript Division, Library of Congress).

[2] Notes for speech in Mary O. Cowper Papers (Mrs. Cowper, Durham, N. C.).

franchised women now addressed themselves with renewed hope. Their successes as well as their failures have tended to vanish—in Vann Woodward's phrase—in that twilight zone between living memory and written history. An examination of what they tried to do, of the goals reached, the obstacles encountered, the failures endured, throws new light on the South in the twenties and upon the springs and motives behind the emancipation of Southern women.

What this record shows will depend upon the questions we ask. If we ask whether woman suffrage led to progress in social reform in the Southern states and to a more active political life for women, the answer is clearly that it did. If we ask in addition whether the broader hope, the dream of a new life for Southern women in which their independence, their right to think for themselves, to work for the things they believed in, to be respected as individuals regardless of sex, was accomplished in the twenties, the answer must be much more qualified.

It may be worth recalling at the outset that early in the nineteenth century the South had adopted a more rigid definition of the role of women than any other part of the country and had elevated that definition to the position of a myth. There were inherent contradictions in the elements of women's role as the culture defined it: women were supposed to be beautiful, gentle, efficient, morally superior, and, at the same time, ready to accept without question the doctrine of male superiority and authority. On matters not domestic they were to be seen and not heard, while in the domestic sphere it was taken for granted that a woman would rule. For those without inherited means, marriage was the only road to economic security (as for inherited wealth, its control passed at marriage into the hands of the husband). For those who did not marry, the only acceptable pattern was to become the pensioner—and often *de facto* servant—of some male relative. Hints that some women felt the contradictory nature of these expectations, and resented them, appeared from time to time before the Civil War. After the war, changes which seemed likely to alter the culture pattern appeared on all sides; but, as part of the comforting glorification of the past with which the South tended to evade present problems, the image of the Southern Lady—whatever the reality—survived relatively unchanged.[3] The force of this culture image was so strong that Southern women had to follow a more devious road to emancipation than those elsewhere. It was only after long apprenticeship in such outwardly safe organizations as church societies and the Woman's Christian Temperance

[3] W. J. Cash goes so far as to argue that woman's role was more rigidly defined after Appomattox and emancipation than before. *The Mind of the South* (New York, 1941), 131. He cites no evidence; and, on the basis of much reading in diaries, letters, newspapers, and church and organization records, I think he overstates his case.

Union that they began to venture into women's clubs and suffrage organizations.[4]

From this process a few women emerged as recognized leaders. These few had in common impressive social standing and family background, intelligence, courage, and a degree of inner security that permitted them to survive criticism. Such were Madeline Breckinridge in Kentucky, Mary Munford in Virginia, Nellie Sommerville in Mississippi, Sallie Cotten in North Carolina, Pattie Jacobs in Alabama—each highly respected in her own state by men as well as women.[5] Now, with the power of the ballot and the new freedom it symbolized, they hoped not only to be more effective in public life but also to modify significantly Southern thought about the proper role of women.[6]

They were well aware that the older image of the Southern Lady, although undergoing modification in a number of ways, was still very much alive in 1920. The image was, of course, made up of a number of components, some external: beauty, gentleness, winning ways. Other components related to appropriate behavior: modesty, domesticity, chastity, and submission to male opinions. It was a lovely image that could be maintained with a minimum of strain whenever the woman in question was lucky enough to be well endowed with the outward qualities (the proportionate number so endowed was doubtless about the same in 1920 as in

[4] Anne Firor Scott, "The 'New Woman' in the New South," *South Atlantic Quarterly*, LXI (Autumn 1962), 473–83.

[5] The obituaries upon Madeline Breckinridge's untimely death in 1920 suggest she was Kentucky's leading citizen as well as its leading woman. Certainly she had a hand in almost every reform movement in that state for twenty years; and, by way of the Lexington, Ky., *Herald*, her voice was widely heard. A close study of her biography reveals all the elements that created the Southern "woman movement." See Sophronisba Preston Breckinridge, *Madeline McDowell Breckinridge, a Leader in the New South* (Chicago, 1921) and Breckinridge Family Papers.

[6] Madeline Breckinridge, for example, regularly advised every woman to read Margaret Fuller, John Stuart Mill, and Olive Shreiner. The private papers of the women upon whom this study is centered reveal their vision of an ideal woman, educated and fully developed and free to undertake the work that interested her most. They were so often criticized for wanting to "be like men" that it is worth pointing out that their ideal human being was not a man but some other woman (Jane Addams, Anna Howard Shaw, Frances Willard, for example) and that they did not think men were doing a very good job with politics and government or in shaping society generally. What they aimed for was not freedom to be like men but freedom to be themselves. Economic independence loomed large in the minds of the pioneers—they had nothing against marriage, and most were married, but they objected to it as an economic necessity. It is interesting to find exactly the same arguments in the most recent comprehensive work on the subject, Simone de Beauvoir, *The Second Sex*, H. M. Parshley, trans. and ed. (New York, 1953). Mary Johnston and Ellen Glasgow were active suffrage women, and their novels are rich in oblique attacks on the existing system. See especially Glasgow, *Virginia* (New York, 1913) and Johnston, *Hagar* (Boston, 1913). Both novels will repay careful reading for anyone interested in the inner springs of the woman movement.

1820). But it was the definition of appropriate behavior that women were most anxious to modify. In earlier years the effective leaders of the movement had had to conform behavior to the image. As a Virginia woman remarked in 1918, "the wise suffrage leaders here have realized . . . that success depends upon showing their cause to be compatible with the essentials of the Virginia tradition of womanliness, and both instinct and judgment have prevented the adoption here of the more aggressive forms of campaigning."[7]

In the twenties, maintaining the ladylike image was still considered to be good politics, but the active women continued to alter behavior remarkably. A few of the more radical wanted to dispense, once and for all, with what they called the "chivalric nonsense" that put woman on a pedestal in order to keep her out of the affairs of the real world. A young North Carolina woman, for example, reflected:

Last year I travelled from one end of our State to another. I saw thousands of women, old and young, mothers and little girls, working in stores and factories ten or eleven or twelve hours a day; or worse, working in the factory all night, and taking care of their homes by day. And I asked, where is this chivalry that so protects women? And I saw working in the fields, hoeing cotton and corn and doing all kinds of hard labor, women and children, white as well as black. And again I asked, whom does chivalry protect? In the last session of the legislature, I heard arguments about a bill which would have raised the amount allowed from the estate to a widow and her children for the first year of widowhood. And many were the jokes made and the slurs slung about mothers who would spend the amount for silk stockings instead of on the care of children. Respect for motherhood, reverence for womanhood, was not the ruling thought when the bill was considered, for it was voted down. It was not the political rights nor any of the deeds of the "new woman" who took the working women from their homes and made them labor as if there was no such thing as chivalry and pedestals. . . . Genesis says that after the Lord had created male and female, he gave them dominion over the earth and then he rested. The two were created to work out welfare for all on earth. Why not go on with the work and stop babbling about chivalry when there is no chivalry except for the small class whose financial conditions prevents their needing it.[8]

[7] Orie Latham Hatcher, "The Virginia Man and the New Era for Women," *Nation,* CVI (June 1, 1918), 651.

[8] Mary O. Cowper, "That Pedestal Again," North Carolina League of Women Voters, *Monthly News,* November 1927. See also the very interesting series of articles by Nell Battle Lewis in Raleigh, N. C., *News and Observer,* May 1926, in which she discusses the question thoroughly and perceptively.

The older ideal of the Southern Lady cropped up in another way when the opponents of reforms for which women worked used it as a weapon. It was hardly politic to argue in public that one believed in child labor or enjoyed the profits that stemmed from women laboring long hours into the night, but—given the Southern frame of reference—it was quite possible to attack the proponents of reform on the ground that they were "unwomanly" and thus to discredit the cause for which they fought. This was done repeatedly, and the cry was often echoed, of course, by other men who feared for their own domestic comforts.

Even before the Nineteenth Amendment was ratified state suffrage organizations began to turn themselves into leagues of women voters with the announced purpose of educating newly enfranchised citizens and working for "needed legislation." Leaders gathered in Chicago for intensive training, organized by a political scientist from the University of Chicago, and went home with instructions to pass along all they had learned. "Citizenship schools" blossomed over the Southern landscape, and courses with reading lists worthy of graduate instruction in political science were found side by side with mundane classes in election law, registration procedures, and How to Mark a Ballot. The troops were receiving basic training.[9]

At the same time every state had its legislative council in which women's groups of the most diverse kinds joined together to work for legislation. The Alabama council was typical; it was made up of sixteen organizations, ranging from the Women's Trade Union League to the Methodist Home Missionary Council. Despite their diverse origins the organized women were in surprising accord on legislative goals.

Whether the goal was a social reform such as the abolition of child labor, or a political one such as the reorganization of the state government, veterans of the suffrage movement were political realists and skilled lobbyists. Their lobbying technique, developed before they had any votes to deliver, was based upon tact and superior information rather than upon threats. Though they were trying to throw off the shackles of chivalry, women voters were not above appealing for chivalric responses in a good cause.

An example of typical methods may be seen in a letter from a Virginia lady of the old school describing her efforts to persuade Congress to adopt a child labor amendment:

I got busy about the child labor amendment and stirred up the Virginia Federation of Labor and the Ministerial Union of Richmond which means all the Protestant clergymen of the city . . . the Federation of

[9] Charles E. Merriam, "The Chicago Citizenship School," *Journal of Social Forces,* I (September 1923), 600.

labor sent official communications to all senators and all congressmen and our papers have given us good notices. . . . I carried your summary of the situation to our leading morning paper and he promised to use it and comment on it editorially.[10]

A favorite device was the publication of complete lists of legislators with their views on various issues presented for the voters' information. Indeed, education of the electorate was a basic technique, and there was always an effort to develop support for their programs among "the people back home." The experience of the suffrage campaign came into play at every turn.

The ideological milieu of the twenties was nowhere conducive to social reform. The Red Scare had affected every part of the country, and programs considered mild in 1912 were now labeled Bolshevik.[11] The reform-minded women in the South were little disturbed at the outset by the fact that many of the causes in which they had long been interested were now termed radical. The president of the Tennessee League of Women Voters remarked mildly,

> Some good souls are pleased to call our ideas socialistic. They are indeed uncomfortable often for some folk. Some timid souls of both sexes are only half converted to the new order . . . [yet] every clear thinking, right feeling and high minded man and woman should consecrate his best talents to the gradual re-organization of society, national and international.[12]

The ink was scarcely dry upon the suffrage amendment before legislatures began to realize that women now expected more respectful attention

[10] Kate Pleasants Minor to Mrs. John J. O'Connor, April 18, 1924, in League of Women Voters of the United States Papers (Manuscript Division, Library of Congress), Virginia file.

[11] Note, for example, the comment of the foremost woman progressive of the day: "Social progress during the decade from 1919 to 1929 was conditioned at every turn by the fact that we were living in the midst of post-war psychology. . . . Any proposed change was suspect, even those efforts that had been considered praiseworthy before the war. To advance new ideas was to be radical, or even a bolshevik. . . . Throughout the decade this fear of change, this tendency to play safe was registered most conspicuously in the fields of politics, but it spread over into other fields as well." Jane Addams, *The Second Twenty Years at Hull House, September 1909 to September 1929, with a Record of a Growing World Consciousness* (New York, 1930), 153. Or this characterization from the center of Southern liberalism: "Besides there is mighty little freedom of opinion anywhere in the old South as you know. . . ." E. C. Branson to R. W. Hogan, Chapel Hill, N. C., December 17, 1922, in Eugene Cunningham Branson Papers (Southern Historical Collection, University of North Carolina Library).

[12] Report of the President, Tennessee League of Women Voters, January 1923, in League of Women Voters Papers, Tennessee file.

than in the past. "The men were scared to death of what the women might do," one North Carolina woman recalled.[13] In that state, as a measure of insurance against reprisal for having rejected the suffrage amendment, the governor and legislature agreed to appoint the president of the Federated Clubs as commissioner of charities and public welfare, one legislator being overheard to remark that she was "pretty, anyway, and won't give us any trouble." The insurance turned out to be inadequate, for in short order North Carolina women, abetted behind the scenes by the same pretty welfare commissioner, were demanding that the Woman's Bureau of the United States Department of Labor be invited to survey the working conditions of women in North Carolina textile mills.

Textile manufacturing was a major economic interest in the state, and working conditions in the mills were frequently bad, wages were low, and many children were employed. The mill-owners reacted strongly. The women were accused of being unwomanly to mix in things about which they knew nothing, of being dangerous radicals or at the very least dupes of Northern manufacturers bent on spoiling the competitive advantage that child labor and cheap female labor gave the South. The YWCA, one of the groups joining in the request for a survey, was threatened with a loss of contributions. The state president of the League of Women Voters was hailed before a self-constituted jury of millmen and lectured severely. The suggestion reached her that her husband's sales of mill machinery would diminish rapidly if she and the league continued their interest in women's working conditions. Families divided as wives argued with husbands about the survey. Textile men brought pressure upon the governor and upon agencies of the state government. In 1926 the governor, while standing firm against allowing "outsiders" to meddle in North Carolina's business, agreed to order his own Child Welfare Department to make the study—but nothing happened. In 1929 when the Gastonia strike became a national issue, the North Carolina League of Women Voters, in publishing an explanation of the strikers' side of the argument, remarked that if the women's request for a survey of working conditions had been granted the problems that had led to a bloody strike might have been ameliorated.[14]

---

[13] Interview with Mrs. Kate Burr Johnson of Raleigh, N. C., November 1, 1963. See also comment of the Georgia women who drew up a bill in 1921 to remove the civil disabilities of women: "These legislators were so courteous and obliging the women could scarcely believe it was the Georgia Legislature. They gave everything asked for and asked 'is there anything more we can do for you?'" Elizabeth Cady Stanton and others (eds.), *The History of Woman Suffrage* (6 vols., New York, 1881–1922), VI, 142.

[14] The story of the long fight between millmen and North Carolina women's groups is covered in detail in Mary O. Cowper Papers. Mrs. Cowper was executive secretary of the North Carolina League of Women Voters. The outlines as given here are confirmed by Mrs. Kate Burr Johnson, who was commissioner of welfare

North Carolina women were more successful in their efforts to bring about stronger state child labor laws.[15] In every Southern state, in fact, women worked strenuously against the use of child labor. Many of them supported the federal child labor amendment that Congress adopted in 1924 and then went on to work for its ratification by their legislatures. In the meantime, an intensive effort to establish broad programs of child welfare took shape. In Virginia, for example, the women urged the legislature to set up a Children's Code Commission and, having secured it, persuaded the governor to appoint five of their number to it. When the commission brought in twenty-four recommendations for new laws, ranging from a statewide juvenile court system to compulsory education, the women turned their attention once more to the legislature, and as a result of their unceasing toil eighteen of the twenty-four recommendations became law in the 1922 session.[16]

That same year a combination of women's groups in Georgia secured the passage of a children's code, a child-placement bill, and a training school bill but failed when they joined forces with the Federation of Labor for a legislative limitation on hours of work for women. The hearing on this last proposal brought out "every cotton mill man in Georgia," and, while the eloquent testimony of Mrs. Elliott Cheatham persuaded the committee to report the bill, the millowners' influence in the legislature prevented it from being brought to a vote. Two years later efforts to secure ratification of the federal child labor amendment also failed in the Georgia legislature, and women in the state then turned to efforts to strengthen state laws.[17]

Similar issues, all of them demonstrating the increasing influence of women, appeared in the other Southern states. In Arkansas, where as early as 1919 the suffrage organization had come out for minimum wages and maximum hours in all cotton mills, the federal child labor amendment was ratified by the legislature. Credit was given jointly to a woman legislator, the Arkansas Federation of Labor, and the women's organizations. The wife of the man who had led the floor fight against the amendment was

---

during the 1920's and was working behind the scenes with the women's groups. For contemporary analysis, see Nell Battle Lewis, "The University of North Carolina Gets Its Orders," *Nation,* CXXII (February 3, 1926), 114–15. Nora Houston of Virginia who was active in the effort to improve working conditions was also a painter and left at her death a dramatic painting of the Gastonia strike.

[15] North Carolina League of Women Voters, *Monthly News,* 1922–1926.

[16] Adele Clark Papers (Miss Clark, Richmond). Miss Clark helped organize the campaign. See also Eudora Ramsay Richardson, "Liberals in Richmond," *Plain Talk,* VI (February 1930), 213–19.

[17] Mrs. E. B. Chamberlain to Mrs. Solon Jacobs, October 25, 1922, and Report to Director of Southeastern Region, January 10, 1924, in League of Women Voters Papers, Georgia file.

reported to be delighted that he had failed; of her it was said, "she expressed the spirit of Arkansas women in politics."[18]

One result of the growing movement against the exploitation of women and children in the mills was an increasingly close association between Southern women and the labor movement. Lucy Randolph Mason, bluest of Virginia bluebloods, who was to become an organizer for the CIO, noted in 1930: "For a number of years many of us southern women have been concerned over the lack of social control in the development of southern industry. Vast numbers of southern women are becoming more acutely conscious of the need of safeguards, which have already been supplied by most of the states. . . ."[19] Association with labor unions actually had begun during the fight for suffrage when trade unions, along with the Farmers Alliances, were virtually the only male organizations to support woman suffrage. As early as 1910 the Georgia Suffrage Association reported holding its convention in the halls of "the Federation of Labor, *its true friend*."[20] Now, in the twenties, women's interests were in line with labor concerns, and they not only found a good press in liberal journals such as the *New Republic* but also co-operated with labor unions.[21]

Particularly important in deepening woman's concern for industrial labor was the work of the YWCA. Even before the first World War, the YWCA had undertaken to bring college students in touch with the facts of industrial life, and in the twenties a student-industrial movement flourished. Its legislative program included the abatement of poverty, abolition of child labor, a living wage as a minimum in every industry, an eight-hour day, and protection of workers from the hardships of continued unemployment. Through the YWCA, students at Randolph Macon were studying the problems of coal miners, while those at Converse delved into social legislation, and at Westhampton, unemployment. Girls from these and other colleges served on a regional committee for student-industrial co-operation, seeking, as they put it, to Christianize the social order.[22] Part of this program included a series of summer institutes for factory girls that by 1927 had evolved into the Southern Summer School for Women Workers in Industry, directed and financed by Southern women. The school grew steadily through the twenties and early thirties. The nature of its sympathies was evident in 1928 when strikers from the Marion Manufacturing Company

[18] Miss Earl Chambers to Marguerite Owen, October 2, 1924, *ibid.*, Arkansas file.

[19] Lucy R. Mason to Henry P. Kendall, December 31, 1930, in Lucy Randolph Mason Papers (Manuscripts Collection, Duke University Library, Durham, N. C.).

[20] Stanton and others (eds.), *History of Woman Suffrage*, VI, 125.

[21] There is ample evidence for this in League of Women Voters Papers, state files, and Mary O. Cowper Papers. Common interests made inevitably for co-operation.

[22] Gladys Bryson, student secretary, YWCA, to Lucy Somerville, March 23, 1923, in Somerville Family Papers (Woman's Archives, Radcliffe College Library, Cambridge, Mass.).

were invited to the campus to tell their story and were afterward joined by students and faculty in a march through Marion. It was the opinion of the *Nation* that "This small group of women . . . are playing an important part in the fight against economic slavery in the South."[23]

When unionization became a genuine possibility during the New Deal, a large proportion of the women graduates of the Summer School became active organizers. There is something appealing in the picture of a group of well-to-do Southern women, of ladylike mien, busy training labor organizers. Nor is there the least doubt, from the record, that they knew what they were doing. They were not innocent philanthropists taken in by hard-bitten radicals.[24]

The Southern Council on Women and Children in Industry, organized in 1931 to bring about a shorter working day and an end to night work in all the textile states, was another joint effort growing out of the experience of women in their separate states. The council hired Lucy Mason to organize their campaign. Calling to the colors a few progressive-minded mill-men who agreed with her objectives, she then set out to convert some of those who did not agree, recognizing clearly that pressure on the legislatures could not succeed without the support of some of the millowners.[25]

From a national point of view the concern for child welfare was reflected in the passage in 1921, largely due to the work of women over the nation, of the Sheppard-Towner Act for maternal and infant health. Nineteen of twenty-six Southern senators voted for the bill. In the House, 91 of the 279 votes in support of the bill came from the South and only 9 of 39 votes against it.[26] This support for a federal welfare program from Southern members of Congress is less impressive than the enormous amount of follow-up work that Southern women undertook to secure appropriation of the required matching funds from state legislatures and then to report on the actual results of the public health work thus instituted. It is not too much to say that the co-operative state work within the framework of the Sheppard-Towner Act brought about a revolution in maternal and infant health.[27]

In some ways the most intriguing of all the public activities of Southern women in the twenties was their racial work. The roots went back at

[23] Marion Bonner, "Behind the Southern Textile Strikes," *Nation*, CXXIX (October 2, 1929), 352.

[24] See Lucy P. Garner, "An Education Opportunity for Industrial Girls," *Journal of Social Forces*, I (September 1923), 612–13, and Alice M. Baldwin Papers (Manuscripts Collection, Duke University Library).

[25] Lucy Randolph Mason Papers, box 1.

[26] *Congressional Record*, 67 Cong., 1 Sess., 4216, 8036–37.

[27] This story is reflected in detail in League of Women Voters Papers, state files. See especially all the state-by-state reports on the operation of the law and the collection of letters from Texas women who benefited from it. Reports of the Children's Bureau also contain details of the actual workings of the law.

least to 1901 when Miss Belle Bennett encouraged the Woman's Board of Home Missions of the Methodist Episcopal Church, South, to undertake work among Negro girls and offered a personal contribution to that end. From that year forward the board annually appropriated money in behalf of work among Negroes. In 1910 another Methodist, Mary DeBardelben of Alabama, volunteered for missionary service, not in far-off lands but among Southern Negroes. In 1915 yet another Southern Methodist, Mrs. Lily H. Hammond, published a pathbreaking book in which she pleaded for a permanent burial of the "old Negro mammy" and some sensible attention to the needs of Mammy's daughters.[28]

The real breakthrough came in 1920 at an extraordinary meeting of Southern churchwomen in Memphis at which four Negro women spoke forthrightly of the needs of Southern Negroes. One of them told of having been forcibly removed by twelve white men from a Pullman car while on her way to Memphis. In the emotional stir of the moment, the ninety-odd white women, representing a number of churches, agreed that talk was not enough and constituted themselves the Woman's Department of the Commission on Inter-racial Cooperation. Headed by Mrs. Luke Johnson of Griffin, Georgia, and supported by leading women in every state, units of this organization set up interracial committees to attack common social and economic problems.

When the National League of Women Voters decided in 1924 to establish a Committee on Negro Problems with membership from every state that had more than fifteen per cent Negro population, members from eight Southern states accepted appointment. Many of these women had been active in their local interracial committees, of which there were eventually some eight hundred functioning in the South. In Tennessee white women organized a special citizenship school for Negro women. Many of the committeewomen took personal responsibility for their Negro fellow citizens, as did Mary Cooke Branch Munford of Richmond, who made a room of her house permanently available to Negroes for public meetings, or a busy doctor's wife in Alabama who waged a one-woman campaign for better Negro education. When the Richmond city council considered a segregation statute in 1929, it was Lucy Randolph Mason, almost single-handedly, who brought about its defeat.[29]

The most spectacular work in this field began in the thirties. It started

[28] Noreen Dunn Tatum, *A Crown of Service: A Story of Woman's Work in the Methodist Episcopal Church, South, from 1878–1940* (Nashville, 1960), 32, 65, 234; Lily Hardy Hammond, *In Black and White: An Interpretation of Southern Life* (New York, 1914). See also Wilma Dykeman and James Stokely, *Seeds of Southern Change: The Life of Will Alexander* (Chicago, 1961), 82–96.

[29] Norfolk *Journal and Guide,* February 2, 1929. See also Katherine Du Pre Lumpkin, *The Making of a Southerner* (New York, 1947) for evidence of the significance of the YWCA in breaking through traditional racial barriers.

with the organization in 1930, under the imaginative leadership of Jessie Daniel Ames, a Texas woman who had been active in a dozen reform movements, of the Association of Southern Women for the Prevention of Lynching. At its peak this organization had 40,000 small-town and rural churchwomen enrolled in an effort to put an end to the most spectacularly disgraceful aspect of the Southern race problem. While the federal anti-lynching law was blocked in the United States Senate, this band of Southern women took upon themselves the sometimes heroic responsibility of opposing any specific threat of a lynching in their own towns or counties.

The crusade against lynching was the most dramatic aspect of women's interracial work. Less visible, but of great significance, was the way in which groups of white and Negro women in the twenties were sitting down together to tackle common problems in an atmosphere of forthright discussion. Though a few Negro women were careful publicly to eschew any desire for social equality, most of them hammered away on equal rights in court, an end to segregation and discrimination in transportation, the Negro's need for the ballot, and every other sensitive issue that stood between whites and blacks in the South during this period of the resurgent Ku Klux Klan.[30]

Although women's interests tended to center upon measures that had a humanitarian element, especially those affecting disadvantaged groups and children, they devoted much time to more strictly political questions. After learning the mechanics of government, they turned their efforts to the improvement of governmental organizations. Studies of local and state governmental structure were published and used in schools and by other organizations. In Virginia in 1922 women's groups worked for an executive budget and improved election laws. A year later the state legislative chairman of the Virginia League of Women Voters reported that she was in daily attendance at budget hearings.[31] In 1924 her organization concentrated its attention on the improvement of tax administration and reported it had won an initial skirmish in the legislature by securing active consideration of the question despite orders from the Democratic machine that the subject was not to be raised. In the same legislature Virginia women voters worked for a bill to create a uniform fiscal year and were successful in their effort.[32] The League had also supported bills, that failed to pass,

[30] The story of women's interracial work is in Jessie Daniel Ames Papers (Mrs. Ames, Tryon, N. C.). Mrs. Ames pioneered the antilynching group and was for twelve years executive secretary of the Woman's Department of the Inter-Racial Commission. What is given here is a mere glimpse into a complex and fascinating story that deserves a chapter or a book all to itself.

[31] Nora Houston to Maud Wood Park, December 12, 1923, in League of Women Voters Papers, Virginia file.

[32] Miss M. E. Pidgeon to Belle Sherwin, 1924, *ibid.*

for civil service, creation of a conservation department, county government reform, and reforms in the state educational machinery.

Similar interests and similar campaigns developed in other states. Women in Georgia and Tennessee, after initial forays into the question of more efficient government, became convinced that the supreme obstacle lay in outmoded state constitutions; and in both states campaigns for constitutional reform were launched in the twenties and were eventually successful.[33] Kentucky women in 1937 began to work for home rule for cities, improvements in local charters, and the adoption of city manager government.

To an interest in the structure of government was added a concern for making government more democratic. Because of their long exclusion from politics, women were sensitive to the implications of "consent of the governed." It was they who invented the now commonplace idea of "getting out the vote." In some places women's work led to spectacular increases in the percentage of qualified voters going to the polls. In Alabama 54.4% of the qualified voters went to the polls in 1924 after women sponsored a get-out-the-vote campaign, compared to less than 30% in 1920. One county, where the women had been particularly active, got out 84.1% of its qualified voters.[34] Florida in the same year reported a 65.9% increase over 1920 in the qualified voters going to the polls.[35]

The poll tax was the subject of dual concern. Women's groups opposed the tax, but in the meantime they set out to collect money for the payment of poll taxes in order to increase the number of qualified voters. In 1925 Louisiana women collected $30,000 to this end. The work of North Carolina women for the Australian ballot, that finally succeeded in 1929, was part of the same interest in making the operation of government more democratic.

Close to home, yet a long way from women's traditional concerns, were two other political issues that developed strength in Southern women's groups in the twenties: government ownership of Muscle Shoals and the regulation of utility rates. Interest in both these questions developed from studies of the cost of living, and women in Alabama and Tennessee became enthusiastic supporters of what was to become the Tennessee Valley Authority. On these as on other questions the politically active women seem to have taken a pragmatic view without much concern for traditional free enterprise arguments.

In all their enterprises, political or social, women knew that the main

[33] *Ibid.*, Georgia and Tennessee files.
[34] Report on the Get Out the Vote Campaign, November 29, 1924, *ibid.*, Alabama file.
[35] Mrs. J. B. O'Hara to Ann Webster, September 2, 1924, *ibid.*, Florida file.

road to influence lay through political parties. Interest in partisan politics antedated suffrage, and unofficially some women had long taken an interest in party fortunes. It had been the accepted doctrine that the national suffrage organization should be nonpartisan since it hoped to get support from both parties for the national amendment. That this principle was occasionally honored in the breach is made clear when we find Jane Addams trying to recruit Jean Gordon of Louisiana for the Progressive party in 1912 or discover Mrs. Breckinridge on a speaking tour for the Democrats in 1916. A keen interest in party methods and organization had been one of the by-products of the highly organized national suffrage campaign.[36] Carrie Chapman Catt, the commanding general of the final suffrage drive, was intent that women should find their way not just to the outskirts but to the center of power in the political parties. At the Victory Convention in Chicago in 1920 she had told them:

> The next battle is going to be inside the parties, and we are not going to stay outside and let all the reactionaries have their way on the inside! Within every party there is a struggle between progressive and reactionary elements. Candidates are a compromise between these extremes. You will be disillusioned, you will find yourselves in the political penumbra where most of the men are. They will be glad to see you, you will be flattered. But if you stay long enough you will discover a little denser thing which is the umbra of the political party—the people who are picking the candidates, doing the real work that you and the men sanction at the polls. You won't be welcome, but there is the place to go. You will see the real thing in the center with the door locked tight. You will have a hard fight before you get inside . . . but you must move right up to the center.[37]

At the outset, a considerable number of Southern women set out to become active in party politics. Party organizations welcomed them, if not with enthusiasm at least with a realistic appreciation of their potential voting power. Some states began at once the custom that has since become standard of appointing a woman as vice-chairman of the state party committee. A considerable number of Southern women showed interest in running for elective office; and, though numerous obstacles lay between almost any woman and nomination, enough persisted so that by 1930 only Louisiana had yet to have women in the state legislature. But only a few, a

[36] See Carrie Chapman Catt and Nettie Rogers Shuler, *Woman Suffrage and Politics: The Inner Story of the Suffrage Movement* (New York, 1924) and Maud Wood Park, *Front Door Lobby,* Edna Lamprey Stantial, ed. (Boston, 1960).

[37] Mary Gray Peck, *Carrie Chapman Catt, a Biography* (New York, 1944), 325–26.

very few, Southern women seem to have made their way to that mysterious center of power to which Mrs. Catt had directed them.

One of these was Mrs. Nellie Nugent Somerville of Greenville, Mississippi, whose political influence preceded the Nineteenth Amendment. As soon as it was legal to do so she ran for the state legislature in a campaign that was a model of thorough organization and was elected. She had been observing party organization long enough to know the ropes, and she hoped the newly enfranchised women would be similarly observant. She advised them to be certain they had a hand in choosing county committees and reminded them: "It now becomes the duty of women voters to take lively interests in the details of political machinery. When any meeting or election is ordered by your political party be sure you take part in it."[38]

The chief obstacle to following such advice was the unwillingness of male politicians to promote women of independent mind and political skill. They preferred more amenable females, and hence the forthright and well-trained suffrage veterans often found themselves at odds with the entrenched politicians.[39] Mrs. Somerville herself managed to surmount the obstacles, and in 1924 Mississippi Democrats were divided into Somerville and Percy factions. At the showdown, hers won. She also served as a member of the committee on permanent organization of the 1924 Democratic National Convention and marshaled William G. McAdoo supporters in imposing array.[40] Her record in the legislature suggests that she understood the effective use of political power. When a bill she had initiated failed to pass, the fact was reported as news—as a rule anything she offered did pass—and her colleagues were frequently quoted in praise of her hard work and effectiveness as a lawmaker.[41]

Another politically minded woman who reached a position of genuine power in the party was Sue Shelton White of Tennessee, an independent court reporter, secretary to members of the Tennessee Supreme Court, and from 1920 to 1926 secretary to Senator Kenneth McKellar. In 1915 she drafted the first mother's pension law to be presented to the Tennessee legislature, finally passed in 1920. She went from Senator McKellar's office to practice law in Jackson, Tennessee, and was sufficiently effective in Democratic politics to be invited to work for the Democratic National

[38] Article in Jackson, Miss., *Woman Voter*, November 19, 1923. For the details of Mrs. Sommerville's campaign, see letters of her daughter, September 1923, in Somerville Family Papers.

[39] See analysis of first woman vice chairman of the Democratic National Committee, Emily Newell Blair, "Women in the Political Parties," American Academy of Political and Social Science, *Annals*, CXLIII (May 1929), 217–29.

[40] Clippings and note in Sommerville Family Papers.

[41] *Ibid.*, clippings. She had the additional distinction of providing the state with another successful woman politician, her daughter Lucy who followed her in the legislature in the 1930's and ultimately became a federal judge.

Committee. With Nellie Davis (Tayloe) Ross she helped lay the ground-work for the extensive women's program of the party during the early Franklin D. Roosevelt years. A fellow lawyer, who was general counsel of the Federal Social Security Board, said at her death:

> Sue knew politics from the inside and from the outside. Politics were more than a game to her, though I think she relished the intricacies of the game. She used her political acumen as an instrument for the pro-motion of the general welfare. And she wielded the instrument with a grace and effectiveness that delighted the wise and distressed the stupid.[42]

Mrs. Somerville and Miss White were exceptional rather than typical, but women in politics ranged from those who were effective politicians in their own right to those who blamed the men for not permitting them to gain nomination. The success stories make good reading, but the overall picture of women's efforts to exercise real influence in the political parties, South or North, was not one to gladden Mrs. Catt's heart. Sue White ana-lyzed the Southern situation in 1928 in a letter to Mary Dewson of the Democratic National Committee:

> Women have been discouraged by the rank and file of the party orga-nization. . . . We still have the old anti-suffrage attitude in the south, women have been indifferent, and their indifference has been preached to them, aided, abetted and encouraged. They have viewed politics as something they should stay away from. They have been told so and have believed it and the few feminists who have tried to push in have been slapped in the face. . . . And the few women who have been artificially reared up as leaders are not leaders of women and have been reared not to lead women but to fool them.[43]

Miss White's analysis was confirmed by Emily Newell Blair, the national vice-chairman of the Democratic party in the twenties. In Mrs. Blair's view, at the very beginning, competent women—the genuine leaders—had es-sayed party politics, but when they showed themselves unwilling to be rubber stamps they were replaced by women more willing to be led. These were the artificial leaders to whom Miss White referred.[44]

An increasing number of Southern women did undertake simple party work of the doorbell-ringing and envelope-stuffing variety—a trend that

[42] Jack Tate in Sue Shelton White Papers (Woman's Archives, Radcliffe College Library).
[43] Sue Shelton White to Mary Dewson, November 23, 1928, *ibid.*
[44] Blair, "Women in the Political Parties."

still continues. And whether they helped make policy or not, women voters affected the outcome of elections. Women claimed to have defeated James E. Ferguson and elected William P. Hobby governor of Texas in 1920. In Mississippi Henry L. Whitfield, former president of Mississippi State College for Women, was elected governor in 1923, largely through the efforts of alumnae of the college. South Carolina women thought they had a large hand in the defeat of Cole Blease. One South Carolina woman who worked through the whole campaign remarked innocently, "We made no partisan stand, we merely got out the vote." Tennessee Democrats, perhaps looking for a scapegoat, blamed the women for the Republican victory in Tennessee in the 1920 election. The women themselves claimed credit for the return of Cordell Hull to Congress three years later.[45]

Evidence of the increasing effectiveness of women voters may be deduced from the vituperative attacks leveled at them. In addition to the accusations that they were being used by Northern manufacturers, they were accused of being radical, unfeminine, of organizing Negro women, and of using "illegitimate pressure" to put across the measures of a "feminist block." David Clark, perhaps the South's bitterest enemy of child labor regulation, went so far as to claim that more babies died after the Sheppard-Towner Act was in operation than before. His *Textile Bulletin* attacked women harshly. The Associated Industries of Kentucky circulated a condemnation of "political women" reprinted from the Dearborn, Michigan, *Independent*. The Louisville *Herald* suggested the reason: "As we have said, the woman voter is making herself felt in ways not chartered for her. We will not go to the length of saying she is always welcome in these channels, but there are times when one may gauge the need of one's activity and curiosity by the ungracious manner of one's reception."[46]

Many of the women who undertook a more active role in Southern politics in the twenties had encountered this ungracious reception. But their motivation was deeply rooted. Those who had been trained during the two or three decades before suffrage were eager to move into a more active and effective political role in 1920. By then their goals had been formulated. Their underlying motivation is complex, but at least two main drives seem clear: first, the drive to assert themselves as individual human beings with minds and capacities that could be used; and, second, the drive to improve the world in which they lived. The balance of these motives varied from person to person. Some, like Lucy Mason, were primarily interested in social reform:

[45] These claims appear in letters and reports to the National Office of the League of Women Voters in League of Women Voters Papers. The information about Governor Whitfield is contained in Lucy Somerville Howorth to author, February 5, 1964.

[46] Louisville, Ky., *Herald*, May 9, 1923.

When I was fourteen, a missionary's sermon made me want to be a missionary myself. Later I recognized that religion can be put to work right in one's own community. It was this belief that took me into the Equal Suffrage League, and later the League of Women Voters, both of which were interested in labor and social legislation.[47]

Others thoroughly enjoyed the game of politics and the feeling of power that might occasionally go with it. Nearly all felt that significant reforms would be more easily achieved with women's help.

The Nineteenth Amendment changed a good many things, but it brought only a partial modification in the Southern culture pattern, and the difficulties in the way of women's full participation in public life were considerable. One major obstacle, in addition to the demands of home and family, was the flat opposition of many men. Equally important was the unwillingness of many women to assume and carry through large responsibilities. From the record it seems that numbers of women had a vague desire to "do something" but needed leadership in finding what to do and how to do it, and the leaders were never sufficiently numerous to tap all the potential resources. A good example, no doubt an extreme one, was a Virginia town of which it was reported that when a certain Miss Terry was at home the town was jumping with women's political activities but when she went to Europe all was quiet.

Around the handful of leaders there gathered a slowly growing number of supporters and workers, and when this support was effectively channeled specific goals were achieved. In almost every instance groups of men were working to the same ends, and frequently there was co-operation. It is impossible to say what would have happened without the women's efforts, but it does seem clear that in the two areas of race relations and factory regulation much less would have been accomplished without them.

Through it all the outward aspect of the Southern Lady was normally maintained as the necessary precondition of securing a hearing. For some women, this was a perfectly compatible role, so long as they could change its behavioral aspects. Others impatiently called for an end to pedestals, but even they found it more effective to operate within the ladylike tradition. The other side of the coin was that the image of the proper Southern Lady was used effectively as a weapon by those who objected to the substantive goals for which women were working, hoping thus to discredit the goals themselves.

No one would argue that the Southern states became a progressive paradise in the twenties, but it is impossible to study the history of the

[47] Lucy Randolph Mason, *To Win These Rights: A Personal Story of the CIO in the South* (New York, 1952), 4.

welfare movements of the time without being surprised by the degree to which the spirit of progressivism was still in flower, and the amount of hopeful optimism about the future of reform that animated women in the face of the general spirit of reaction which is said to have permeated political life. Professor George B. Tindall has adumbrated the "business progressivism" of Southern state governments in the twenties.[48] To the picture he drew must now be added the decided growth through the decade of the conception of state responsibility for public welfare, not in the old custodial sense, but in the newer sense of ameliorating the underlying conditions that created serious human problems. To the growth of this idea and its application in law, Southern women made a considerable contribution.

When all this has been said we are left with the most troublesome questions still unanswered. In spite of the impressive record of accomplishment, the high expectations of the women who had led the suffrage movement did not come to pass. What happened to the verve and enthusiasm with which the suffrage veterans set about to reorganize society? That it did not all vanish is evident from the Southern scene today, but that it did not lead to a clear-cut image of a New Woman to replace the Southern Lady is also evident. The numbers of women in public life, in proportion to the population, are probably no more today than in 1925. While the number of women in labor force climbs—some say alarmingly—the number of women in responsible jobs of leadership, policymaking, or in the professions is still not large. To these difficult and intriguing questions historians of women must now begin to turn their attention.

[48] George B. Tindall, "Business Progressivism: Southern Politics in the Twenties," *South Atlantic Quarterly,* LXII (Winter 1963), 92–106.

18

The Benighted South:
Origins of a Modern Image

George B. Tindall

Southerners and "other" Americans seem to share a basic affinity
for image-building. This prevailing habit of mind, though held in
common, seems more often than not to have taken the South as its
subject matter. Such a compulsion has worked over time to add
new facets and a new texture to a developing southern mythology.
A significant later addition to the longstanding vision of an Old
and a New South, for example, portrays a "benighted South"
predicated on bigotry, intolerance, superstition, and prejudice.
Newer and fresher southern stereotypes have been formulated in
the public mind depicting Dixie as intellectually and morally bankrupt, caught in the throes of cultural disintegration. These latest
patterns of explanation of the modern southern experience, asserts
George B. Tindall of the University of North Carolina, Chapel Hill,
are a product of the 1920s—keyed to the "South-baiting" of the
social critic H. L. Mencken. While unleashing diatribes against the
South reminiscent of the abolitionist crusades of the previous century, Mencken abrasively argued that the South of the 1920s represented a disturbing stage of cultural sterility, moral barbarism, and
blind prejudice. If anyone cared to doubt the malignancy and decay
of the South—a serpentine presence in the southern Eden—it stood
exposed in symbolic form for all to view during the famous Scopes
Trial of 1925. Scapegoats for this supposed atrophy of southern
intellect and sensibility were conveniently provided by fundamentalist clergy and the Ku Klux Klan—custodians of southern

George B. Tindall, "The Benighted South: Origins of a Modern Image," *The Virginia Quarterly Review*, 40 (1964), 281–294. Reprinted with permission of the
publisher and author.

cultural decay. Such indictments of the South, seeking to emphasize southern delinquencies and shortcomings, notes Professor
Tindall, fail to take sufficient account of important new departures
in education, literature, and industrial growth during the same
period. As such, the nuances of the twentieth-century southern experience have at best been obscured; at worst, they stand on the
verge of being prematurely relegated to historical oblivion.

We Southerners, Jonathan Daniels once said, are "a mythological people,
created half out of dream and half out of slander, who live in a still
legendary land." Most Americans, including Southerners, carry about with
them an assorted mental baggage of Southern mythology in which a variety
of elements have been assembled: the Jeffersonian image of agrarian
democracy, the progressive creed of the New South, the Vanderbilt Agrarian myth of the traditional South, the problem South of the regional sociologists, to mention a few. But the main burden of Southern mythology
is still carried in those unavoidable categories set by the nineteenth-century
sectional conflict: the romantic plantation myth of gentility on the one hand
and the obverse, if in many respects similar, abolitionist plantation myth
of barbarity on the other.

Both versions have had a remarkable longevity; both may yet be encountered in literature and popular thought; both have been adaptable
to new conditions; but somewhere along the road to reunion the abolitionist
version was outpaced by the myth of the New South and the popularity of
plantation romances. It was not until the 1920's that a kind of neoabolitionist image of the benighted South was compounded out of elements
both old and new into a mind-set that has influenced strongly the outlook
of the twentieth century.

The background for the newer and more complex image was what
Hamlin Garland called after a Southern visit in 1919 "an unlovely time
of sorry transition." As the postwar South of the 1920's surged into a
strange new world of urban booms and farm distress, it found itself on
a strange and unfamiliar terrain of diversity and change in which there
lurked a thousand hazards to the older orthodoxies. Reaction to the new
circumstances made it a time when, in Howard Odum's words, the South
was swept into a "state of mind similar to that commonly manifest in war
times. . . . During the Ku Klux era one was advised that it was better to
keep one's mouth shut on all debatable issues because one never knew
who was around."

The defensive temper of the 1920's, to be sure, was not altogether a

Southern phenomenon. Over the first two decades of the century there had been an increasing tendency to associate American nationalism with nativism, Anglo-Saxon racism, and militant Protestantism. The South was in the vanguards of the new development, with all the enthusiasm of a recent convert. By the 1920's nativism in the South had become a peculiar expression of sectionalism in terms of American nationalism. If the test of Americanism was native birth of Anglo-Saxon ancestry, it followed that the South was the "most American" of all regions. "One of the glories of the South," the Manufacturers Record boasted, "is that its foreign stock is so limited as compared with that of other sections." But if in adopting Anglo-Saxon nativism the white South was largely importing a creed that fulfilled ancient urges, it was soon developing to a new intensity the anti-Catholic and anti-Semitic corollaries and re-exporting nativism with the addition of certain historic Southern trappings in the new Ku Klux Klan.

Fundamentalism, the other great defensive movement of the day, had obvious similarities to the Klan. While there were no organic links between the two, more than one Klansman found his Anglo-Saxon nativism and his fear of the Roman menace reinforced from the Protestant pulpit. One of the classic tributes to the newest Chosen Race had been penned by Methodist Bishop Warren A. Candler of Georgia in his "Great Revivals and the Great Republic," which revealed the Anglo-Saxons to be divinely appointed for the advancement of evangelical religion in the world, a theme re-echoed time and again by preachers and revivalists. From there it was not far to sectionalism. Other regions, a Baptist divine noted, had lost "whatever there is of advantage in this unmixed Anglo-Saxon blood." Romanism had flooded their cities and had "invaded and despoiled the old patriotism and the old culture and political ideals." The logic was inescapable. "The hope of the world is America, the hope of America is evangelical religion of the most orthodox type, the hope of the American church is the Southern Evangelical churches. . . ."

Unfortunately, however, the serpent of rationalism had already entered the Southern Eden. The new temptation of evolution and the Higher Criticism had crept into the state universities, and Baptist leader Victor I. Masters complained that not even the Christian schools "have had altogether an easy time in safeguarding the class rooms from the miasmatic utterances of teachers who have been contaminated by the rationalistic and evolutionary imaginings of the New Religion."

With the dawning recognition that new theories were influencing the colleges and schools, even the pulpit, orthodoxy emerged into a new militancy with the fundamentalist movement, and by that mysterious process through which complex problems become simplified into symbolic issues, the defense of the fundamentalist faith came somehow to rest upon opposition to Darwinism. The movement found its peerless leader in

William Jennings Bryan, who in his lectures against Darwinism was already by 1920 on the high road to his great pyrrhic victory at Dayton, Tennessee.

It was probably the Scopes trial of 1925 more than any other single event that bore in upon the masses of Southerners the existence of a growing image of the benighted South that contrasted so starkly with the special images they had of themselves as democratic agrarians, as progressive builders and developers, as "the most American" of all Americans, as the defenders of the faith. By contrast they read or heard about the accounts of journalists attracted to the circus in Dayton, ranging from disappointment to ridicule, from the judgment by Joseph Wood Krutch that his native Tennessee was victimized chiefly by the timidity of its intellectuals and legislators to H. L. Mencken's columns cataloguing "morons," "hillbillies," "peasants," and the "degraded nonsense which country preachers are ramming and hammering into yokel skulls."

The image by then was already virtually complete, and it had been rapidly compounded out of multiple elements within less than a decade. After some years of relative neglect, the South had suddenly become an object of concern to every publicist in the country. "It is difficult now," Gerald W. Johnson wrote in 1924, "to find on the news stands a serious magazine without an article on some phase of life below the Potomac, or a discussion of one idea or another that has come out of the South." After the dissolution of the Wilsonian synthesis in 1920 it seemed that great torrents of abuse and criticism were suddenly released upon the region. In fact, the infidels had crossed the Mason-Dixon line to establish their headquarters in Baltimore, whence H. L. Mencken directed a great campaign of South-baiting. The sage of Baltimore, of course, was a man of catholic taste in his choice of targets. From the aristocratic heights of The Smart Set, The American Mercury, and the Sunpapers, he chronicled the doings of *Homo Boobiens* everywhere, but with a special solicitude for the Southern breed. Nearly all the major elements of his more fully developed image of the South were present in his first essay on the theme, "The Sahara of the Bozart," published in the New York Evening Mail in 1917 and later revised for Smart Set and "Prejudices"—but the emphasis at first was on the sterility of Southern culture. With characteristic glee he anointed one J. Gordon Coogler of South Carolina "the last bard of Dixie" and quoted his immortal couplet:

> Alas for the South! Her books have grown fewer—
> She never was much given to literature.

It was "amazing to contemplate so vast a vacuity," he wrote. "One thinks of the interstellar spaces, of the colossal reaches of the now mythical ether.

. . . It would be impossible in all history to match so complete a drying-up of civilization."

His genetic explanation of the Southern plight owed an interesting debt to the original plantation myth, and anticipated William Faulkner's saga of the Snopes family. Once there had been an aristocratic culture of the finest sort, his history went, but it had been left bleeding and helpless by the Civil War, which opened the way to the "lower orders" who had no more comprehension of the ancient faith "than any other like group of former plumbers, corner grocers, and crossroads lawyers." They were "eighth-rate men wearing the stolen coats of dead first-rate men. . . ." Their taste was "only a compound of elemental fears and appetites—chiefly the fears of ideas, and the appetite for security."

But the fundamental root of evil, and the most consistent target of Mencken's vilification, as time went by, was the peculiar clerical tyranny of "Baptist and Methodist barbarism" below the Potomac. "No bolder attempt to set up a theocracy was ever made in the world," he announced with typical hyperbole, "and none ever had behind it a more implacable fanaticism." The clerical will to power, culminating in the fundamentalist excesses of the 1920's, was also given a peculiarly Menckenesque history stemming from the Civil War. Numerous among the slackers and cowards, the preachers found themselves after the war the only survivors with any pretense of training. With little competition from the cultivated remnants of the Confederacy, they soon established a religious, cultural, and political hegemony. Ignorant even in their superiority to the "yowling yokels" over whom they held sway, they spread abroad their own obsessive fear of intelligence, the inquiring mind, or individual freedom. The climax came with prohibition, over which they gloated "in their remote Methodist Tabernacles as they gloat over a hanging." Intoxicated by that success, the Baptist and Methodist shamans of the Bible Belt proceeded next "to put down learning by the law." Professional defenders of the South, their antennae delicately tuned to sectional defamation, served with their responses only to publicize their tormentor and add to his bumptious gaiety. When Mencken wrote that he knew of New Yorkers who had been in Cochin China, Kafiristan, Paraguay, Somaliland, and even West Virginia, "but not one who has ever penetrated the miasmatic jungles of Arkansas," a former governor retorted with an unconsciously ludicrous letter offering statistics on agricultural production and a "two volume deluxe illustrated set of 'The Folklore of Arkansas'" as evidence of the state's cultural achievements. Mencken merrily gathered and published some of the prize castigations. "By cutting through six inches of fat and drilling through four inches of bone," Fred Sullens raged in the Jackson Daily News, "one might possibly find Mencken's brain cavity—but he would not find any

grey matter there." "This modern Attila!" Clio Harper cried in the
Arkansas Writer. "This brachycephalous Caliban! The Black Knight of
Slander! An intellectual Houyhnhnm!" All of which only inspired Mencken
to further heights of calumny against the South, the "bunghole of the
United States, a cesspool of Baptists, a miasma of Methodism, snake-
charmers, phoney real-estate operators, and syphilitic evangelists."

If Mencken was the guiding genius in creating the new image of the
benighted South, he was by no means its only architect. While Mencken
ran amok in Baltimore, other men of differing temperaments contributed
their own special perspectives. Two books significant in the developing
pattern were published in 1924. William Henry Skaggs, a young progressive mayor of Talladega in the 1880's, a leading Alabama Populist in
the 1890's, and subsequently a professional lecturer based in New York,
set forth in "The Southern Oligarchy" what he called in his subtitle, "An
Appeal in Behalf of the Silent Masses of Our Country Against the Despotic
Rule of the Few." In tones of righteous indignation, more redolent of
abolition than of Mencken, and in lengthy catalogs of Southern deficiencies
like the later fashion of regional sociologists, Skaggs handed down one of
the most thoroughgoing indictments of the region ever published, detailing
at length political corruption, landlordism, illiteracy, peonage, lynch law,
partisan and racial proscription, and a hundred other delinquencies. He
"brought to his work wide reading, a formidable array of statistics and
praiseworthy industry," one reviewer thought. "If he could have presented his material temperately he might have written a great and much
needed book." As it was, the book poured vitriol so "liberally upon . . .
the Southern princes, potentates and powers" that its impact was dissipated.

In contrast to Skaggs, Frank Tannenbaum, a young professor at Columbia University, brought together in his "Darker Phases of the South" a
slender collection of essays that constituted one of the most perceptive
social critiques of the times, more balanced and charitable in approach
than Skaggs' book but all the more damaging for its restraint. In successive
chapters he considered the Ku Klux Klan, mill villages, prisons, tenancy,
and the race question. The social setting for the development of the Klan
he described as one of "historical antecedents, passions, prejudices, hates,
loves, ennui, the need for constructing a defense mechanism against one's
own sins, the attempt to preserve as static what is becoming dynamic, the
craving for dramatization and excitement in the face of a dull and monotonous existence. . . ." Boasting of its racial purity, the South had segregated
and buried its Anglo-Saxons in the mill villages. The history of Southern
prisons was one long story of brutality, neglect, and indifference. The rural
South was afflicted with "a white plague—cotton," the source of poverty,
much of the race problem, soil exhaustion, laziness, peonage, ignorance,
and a dozen other shortcomings.

The grave social issues that troubled Skaggs and Tannenbaum became perennial topics for publicists and social scientists during the decade. For nearly a month in 1921, for example, the New York World ran a comprehensive exposé of the Ku Klux Klan, inadvertently contributing to its growth by the publicity. Although the Klan had become national in scope, its Southern origins gave it an important rôle in the pattern of the benighted South. The cotton mills from the beginning of the century had been through a cycle of criticism that firmly established the stereotype of the mill president as a greedy feudal baron. A second stage of attack in the 1920's, of which Tannenbaum's book is one example, dwelt upon the theme of the mill village and corporate control that threatened to develop a socially isolated and hereditary helot class. Though not unlike earlier mill villages in Old and New England, the Southern mill village, one writer says, took "its place in the eyes of the Nation as one in a long procession of peculiar characteristics of the South, along with slavery and cotton, sharecropping and low incomes, race problems and demagogic Democracy." The eternal race question had not yet been brought into the central focus of the image, but insofar as it appeared, it was in the most barbaric aspects. In the climate of a national consensus on white supremacy, the race issue of the 1920's was not an issue of segregation; it was an issue of lynching and peonage. In 1919 the National Association for the Advancement of Colored People sponsored a national conference on lynching that launched a drive for a federal anti-lynching bill and a publicity campaign, paralleled by efforts of the Commission on Interracial Co-operation, that lasted through a decade. In 1921 there came the first in a series of revolting disclosures of peonage and penal brutality, chiefly involving Negroes, when one John Williams on a farm near Covington, Georgia, murdered eleven Negroes in a vain effort to destroy the evidence that he was holding them in peonage. The episode of the "murder farm" was followed through the decade by other revelations of brutality toward prisoners both in convict lease camps and in state and county prisons.

In the South itself a fifth column of native Menckens and Tannenbaums contributed their own bit to the growing attack. Gerald W. Johnson of the Greensboro Daily News wielded perhaps the most trenchant style of the native critics both before and after he ascended unto the right hand of Mencken himself on the Baltimore Sun. "Too much has been said of the South's need for 'sympathetic criticism,' " Johnson complained. It needed no sympathy for bigotry, intolerance, superstition, and prejudice, but "criticism that is ruthless toward those things—bitter towards them, furiously against them—and sympathetic only with its idealism, with its loyalty, with its courage and its inflexible determination." But he found grounds for hope. The Ku Klux Klan had served the useful purpose "of rousing the intelligence of the South to a realization of the thralldom under which it has lain." Even Mencken had to admit that new rebels hatched out day by day. "The very heat of the fundamentalist and Ku Klux fury is hurrying them out of the egg."

Indeed, the incubator of the 1920's hatched out a sizable brood of Southern journalists who found an almost ridiculously simple formula for fame. Attack on the grotesqueries of the benighted South became for that decade a high road to the Pulitzer Prize. Three awards went for attacks on the Klan: in 1923 to the Memphis Commercial Appeal under C. P. J. Mooney; in 1926 to the Columbus Enquirer-Sun under Julian and Julia Collier Harris; and in 1928 to Grover C. Hall of the Montgomery Advertiser. Editorial prizes went in 1925 to Robert Lathan for an editorial in the Charleston News and Courier on the decline of Southern statesmanship and in 1929 to Louis I. Jaffe of the Norfolk Virginian-Pilot for an editorial campaign against lynching. And these were only the most celebrated among the vigorous journalists who had shaken off the inclination "to accept traditional romanticism as established fact."

Well before the end of the 1920's, then, most of the factors in the new image of the benighted South had fallen into place, and its influence ran deep. A philosopher and critic, Eliseo Vivas, who had a later change of heart, wrote of what at the time he took the South to be: "it was the Bible belt, the land of the Klu [sic] Klux Klan, and I knew, knew with the confidence of a good 'liberal,' that nothing but fundamentalism and intolerance could come out of the South. No one around me would have thought it possible to challenge this proposition. It was part of a system of idées reçues that constituted the then reigning orthodoxy of my group." "The legend of the barbarism of the South," Donald Davidson wrote in the 1930's, ". . . and of the vulgarity and dullness of the Middle West, for a good many years has governed the approach of the metropolitan East to the phenomena of life in the so-called hinterland. . . . The South—so the tale runs—is a region full of little else but lynchings, shootings, chaingangs, poor whites, Ku Kluxers, hookworm, pellagra, and a few decayed patricians whose chief intent is to deprive the uncontaminated, spiritualsinging Negro of his life and liberty. But what is more shocking, it is inhabited by believers in God, who pass anti-evolution laws; and more shocking still, it is in thought and deed studiously backward and antiprogressive . . . Over such pictures the East stormed, or shed crocodile tears, in the clever nineteen-twenties." Davidson's summary was almost definitively complete. About the only things omitted were the tyrannies of prohibition and the mill village.

Identifying the causes and consequences of this phenomenon presents an intricate puzzle for the historian, one that challenges his resources of analysis and objectivity. The historical context in which it developed offers one fundamental explanation. A Southern society that had remained comparatively static since Reconstruction suddenly felt itself caught up after World War I by the forces of change. The consciousness of change, the fears and defensiveness it aroused, gave increased power to what W. J. Cash called the "savage ideal" of intolerance and repression, heightening both its aggressiveness and visibility. But such times of transition are inevitably times of conflict. For better or for worse, the genie of modernism was out of the bottle, and the very ferocity of Ku Kluxery and fundamentalism was the ferocity of those who were fighting another lost cause.

As the growing band of critics and social scientists began turning over the rocks in the Sunny South, bringing its social ills out into the glare of daylight, the reform urge contributed significantly, if sometimes inadvertently, to the image of the benighted South. Even Mencken, who would have sunk into a purple dudgeon at the suggestion that he was associated with uplift, cannot wholly escape the charge. He was continually trying to nurture the critics and rebels of the New South.

Not least of all among the contemporary factors was the irreverent levity of the jazz age, finding its most bizarre expression in Mencken, an attitude of metropolitan sophistication that took jocular delight in baiting the clodhoppers, the Babbitts, and the Gantrys of the hinterland. The alienation of city and country ran deep in the 1920's, and took on a regional coloration that was reflected not only in the literature of the decade but in the curious presidential campaigns of 1924 and 1928.

Finally, and here one treads on an uneasy foundation of psychology, the historian must ask to what extent the image of the benighted South welled up from the subconscious depths. It had obvious polemical uses, but did it not also serve some secret function of national catharsis? Did it not create for many Americans (including even some Southerners) a convenient scapegoat upon which the sins of all might be symbolically laid and thereby expiated—a most convenient escape from problem solving?

To assay the consequences of the benighted image is even more troublesome than to identify its sources. It provoked a variety of responses in the South. The more defensive Southerners developed their own peculiar image of the benighted North, disfigured by slums, overrun by mongrel hordes that sullied the purity of the old Republic, and fatally corrupted by gangsters and their allies. Many editors of the "you're another" school bestirred themselves to toss stink bombs chiefly in the direction of Baltimore. But the pattern was broader than that. In Nashville and New York, Fugitive poets pondered the scene. "Was it possible," they asked, "that nobody in the South knew how to reply to a vulgar rhetorician like H. L. Mencken?" Was it not possible that the Southern heritage represented deeper values than either the boosters of the New South or its facile critics? And so for a small group of poets and their allies the trauma of Mencken and Dayton redirected their thinking toward the viable elements of the

Southern tradition, a new consciousness that soon issued in the Vanderbilt Agrarian movement.

Others rallied to the defense of their native region not in terms of tradition but in terms of progress. At Vanderbilt, whence the Agrarians held forth, Chancellor Kirkland announced that the answer to Dayton would be the building of new laboratories and Edwin Mims, head of the English department, hastily assembled a volume on "The Advancing South" that revealed "a veritable war of liberation" by "constantly enlarging groups of liberal leaders who are fighting against the conservatism, the sensitiveness to criticism, the lack of freedom that have too long impeded Southern progress. . . ." In Richmond, Virginius Dabney of the Times-Dispatch compiled in his book, "Liberalism in the South," the genealogy of a Southern liberal tradition which he traced back to Thomas Jefferson.

To many thinkers of the progressive school the situation raised the question of problems that called for constructive attention and rational planning. The result was a burgeoning interest in social science, the establishment in 1923 of institutes for research in social science at the Universities of Virginia, North Carolina, and Texas, a flood of monographs on regional problems from these and other universities, and ultimately a multitude of New Deal measures directed to the ills of "the nation's No. 1 economic problem."

Well before the Agrarian and regionalist movements got fully under way a regional literary movement had developed into what was already being called a renaissance before the end of the 1920's. It may be too much to claim, as Oscar Cargill does, that Mencken anticipated the movement and sought to cultivate it in his own backhanded manner. There can be little question, however, that within a few years, "like Aaron's rod Mencken's goad had proved itself a symbol of fertility."

In many respects, then, the image of the benighted South provoked positive reactions in the region: the rediscovery of tradition, the analysis of regional problems, a renaissance in literature, all growing at least in part out of the determination of Southerners to erase the deficiencies that had been so widely advertised. On the other hand one is led irresistibly to the conjecture that the image has functioned in some degree as a self-fulfilling prophecy. It established certain presuppositions about what is to be recognized as "typically" Southern. It established certain expectations about Southern behavior, and its widespread acceptance even in the South vitiated the courage and resolution of Southerners who would stand against the savage ideal.

While the image unquestionably has reflected certain elements of Southern reality, like all images it blinds the observer to those things that do not fit his mental picture. It has obscured certain important aspects of Southern diversity and dynamism behind a pattern of monolithic cussedness. The industrial and urban growth of the twenties, for example; the tremendous expansion of government services, particularly in highways and public schools; the interracial movement; the literary renaissance (which merely confirmed the benighted image for those preconditioned to accept it); the rise of universities and newspapers which inspired critical analysis of Southern problems—none of these would quite fit into the pattern.

But the image has lived on since the 1920's, reinforced by a variety of episodes from the Scottsboro trials to the Oxford riot, and not least of all by the lush growth of literature that covered Mencken's Sahara with Caldwell's "Tobacco Road," Faulkner's "Sanctuary," and various other flora of what Ellen Glasgow labeled the Southern Gothic and a less elegant Mississippi editor called the "privy school" of literature. In the words of Faulkner's character, Gavin Stevens, the North has suffered from a curious "gullibility: a volitionless, almost helpless capacity and eagerness to believe anything about the South not even provided it be derogatory but merely bizarre enough and strange enough." And Faulkner, to be sure, did not altogether neglect that market! Not surprisingly he was taken in some quarters for a realist, and the image of the benighted South long obscured the critics' recognition of his manifold merits.

That image has not been slain by new images of traditional agrarianism or the problem South, nor even by the region's rise from cultural aridity to literary predominance. In fact, it must be said that the twentieth-century South has not produced a positive and viable myth of its own identity powerful enough to challenge the image of the benighted South.

19

Southern Internationalism—
Myth and Reality

Charles O. Lerche, Jr.

While significant historical statements have been made which rather
clearly demonstrate decided pitfalls as regards the random use of
the label "isolationism," few have sought to apply the same critical
rigor to its antithesis—"internationalism." Such would seem to be
a particularly salient omission as regards the South. It traditionally
has been assumed that in the twentieth century, at least into the
post–World War II period, the South has been more addicted to
"internationalism" than any other region. Examining the interwar
period, particularly the League crisis of 1919 and the events leading to United States entry into World War II, Professor Charles
O. Lerche, Jr., late of the School of International Service, American
University, seeks to modify the South's position as the all-too-
convenient foil of the "isolationist" Midwest. Though granting the
South's "internationalist" image as appropriate in terms of her
commitment to free trade, her traditional support of the military,
and her sympathetic attitude toward northwestern Europe, Professor Lerche contends that myth enters when the region's foreign
policy posture is examined in terms of her motives for such actions.
In this regard, the South lacked a sense of "multilateralism"—
defined as an "appreciation of the interdependence of states and
peoples." When viewed from this perspective it can be seen that the
South acted out of decidedly parochial concerns; invariably, the
region's position on foreign policy matters was drawn through a
"southern filter." Nowhere was this more evident than in the area's

supportive response to Woodrow Wilson, the first southern president since the Civil War. Wilson's influence was both as "man and memory," and many southerners perceived his ultimate failures as but further installments on the "lost cause." Later, as the FDR presidency would demonstrate, the South again moved to support "internationalism," but it was a position always uniquely modified by the South's singular lack of enthusiasm for a foreign policy "multilateral" in nature.

A part of the working image of the American political process that has long been widely shared by most concerned, articulate, and mass media-sensitized Americans is that the South has long been the home of something they persist in calling "internationalism." The impression that south of the Mason-Dixon Line lives a people more aware of the responsibilities of the United States to the world community, more willing actively to support a policy designed to fulfill those responsibilities, and more inclined to participate personally in the implementation of those decisions with their money, their time, and their sons has had a firm grip on the imagination of much of the American body politic. Because this idea has won such wide acceptance and because the contemporary attitudes of Southerners in and out of Congress are so at variance with the image, the myth and the reality of the "traditional" Southern position must be examined before the deviations from this norm can be treated.

For many years, and especially since the era of 1939–1941 preceding the entry of the United States into World War II, casual political discourse has assumed the existence of deep splits within the American consensus on certain issues of foreign policy, largely in terms of the isolationism-internationalism antinomy. . . . As a starting point, it has been axiomatic that the seat of "isolationism" in the United States has long been in the Midwest, and that the excesses of the 1920's and the 1930's—the rejection of the League of Nations, the failure to enter the World Court, the Neutrality Acts, the equivocation during the Spanish Civil War, and so on—were more than anything else the results of the pernicious doctrines of isolationism as preached across the prairies and the plains. Offsetting this baleful influence to some extent, however, was the consistent (if often ineffective) counterforce of the South, whose spokesmen—according to the myth—consistently fought the good fight for a reasoned, pragmatic, yet ultimately idealistic American commitment to a working international order.

This version of history, which tends subtly to relegate the other sections of the United States to a relatively minor role as spectators of the battle between the major ideological opponents, received much of whatever empiric validation it may boast during two brief periods of recent American history: the League debate in 1919, and the immediately pre-war controversy that began in 1939 and climaxed at Pearl Harbor. In these two situations that mark the beginning and the end of the "interwar" era, there is little doubt that the Midwest (largely if not completely) and the South (also largely if not completely) took opposite sides and attempted to lead their respective camps. During 1940 and 1941, for example, the American First Committee (the holding company for all shades of isolationism, withdrawal, and non-participation in the war) became almost entirely a Midwestern organization, while it had virtually no supporters in the South. Southerners in Congress, on the other hand, were well ahead of any other regional delegation in their advocacy of measures of national defense, of proposals to aid the allies, and of early American entry into the war. All of these points are part of the record and cannot be gainsaid.

But myth-making requires oversimplification, and the actual position of Southern Congressmen and the attitudes among Southerners which provoked this regional posture were much more complex than they might seem to have been on the basis of the highly selective evidence usually advanced to support the general thesis of Southern multilateralism. The South's approach to foreign policy, like its approach to so many other issues of public affairs, has long been special. The unique ingredients in its own brand of "internationalism" clearly distinguish the traditional Southern view (or, more accurately, the view articulated by traditional Southern politicians) from the concepts of foreign affairs shared by the bulk of the leadership of the more complex societies in the Northeast, the Midwest, and the West.

Elements of the Southern Position

What are the data that lend credence to the myth of Southern internationalism? What was the traditional Southern outlook on world affairs that was held generally throughout the interwar years, was brought to a peak during World War II, and remained controlling in the postwar era up to the beginning of the first Eisenhower administration? Just what has the South done to deserve its reputation as an enlightened region on international affairs, always alert to advocate and support multilateralist foreign policy ventures?

Probably the most solid ingredient in the Southern approach to foreign affairs has been a consistent commitment to free trade as a general economic principle and low tariffs as a political goal. So strong has the Southern position long been on this point and so influential were Southerners in the councils of the Democratic party that for generations tariff policy was one of the very few legitimate differences that could be discovered between the two major political parties. The South's delegation in Congress after the Civil War (to say nothing of the violent Southern objections to Whig tariff policy in the first half of the nineteenth century) was always in the van of the continuing Democratic attempt to roll back the level of protectionism. The one-party system in the South, rooted though it might have been in the bitter memories of war, defeat, and occupation, nevertheless had this practical issue on which to feed for many years. The Republicans were the high-tariff party, and immediate Southern interest dictated the continuation of the region's historic identification with the low-tariff Democrats.

The Smoot-Hawley Tariff of 1930 was anathema to Southerners, but the Reciprocal Trade Program of 1934 almost immediately became a shining symbol to them. It was after all the work of Cordell Hull, himself a Democrat and a Southerner, and—whatever the limited results the program actually may have had—it was unquestionably a step in what the South conceived to be the right direction. Even today, when the magic of Roosevelt and the New Deal has tarnished in a very different South, the two monuments of that era that yet evoke fond memories are TVA and the Trade Agreements Program.

A second characteristic of the Southern approach to foreign policy for many years has been a consistently sympathetic attitude toward the symbolism of "a strong national defense" in general and toward virtually any and all specific proposals aimed at increasing or strengthening the armed forces. Always alert to the emotional impact of military power as an expression of national personality and will, Southerners in Congress have consistently been defenders of the armed forces and advocates of a greater place for them in American society.

Although the South, as cruelly injured by the depression of 1929 as any region of the country, went along with the early New Deal in its attempt to reduce the size and cost of the military establishment, it greeted President Roosevelt's rediscovery of military power with great enthusiasm and no little relief. With Southerners sitting in key positions on Congressional committees and with almost the entire Southern delegation united in support, the military measures looking toward the American entry into World War II were enthusiastically accepted. On seven important bills of this type between 1939 and 1941, Southern support outstripped that from any other region of the country: the fortification of Guam (1939), the revision of the Neutrality Acts (1939), the Lend-Lease Act (1941), the British Aid Bill (1941), the Draft Extension Act (1941), the Ship Seizure Bill (1941), and the repeal of the Neutrality Acts (1941). The strong Southern position on preparedness during this era, particularly in view of the intensity of the crisis of conscience which gripped so many Americans at the time, went far to shape the dominant Southern image of internationalism in the minds of an entire generation of Americans.

In the immediate postwar era, the South's orientation and commitment to affairs military did not diminish. Throughout the entire cold war period, to the limited extent to which there has been any serious Congressional conflict over the overall size of the nation's military establishment, Southerners by and large have been on the side of opposing any reduction and of demanding steady increases. The Armed Services Committees in both houses have for several Congresses been chaired by Southerners, and the same has been consistently true of the other committees and sub-committees strategic to the Pentagon. The South's deep dedication to national defense, it must be admitted, has both ideological and highly practical roots, and seems beyond either question or imminent change. To the extent that promotion of a large and powerful military establishment and the willingness to use it freely in support of national objectives is a component of an "internationalist" point of view, the South has been and may today claim to be highly qualified on this count.

A third ingredient in the traditional Southern position has been a relatively benign attitude toward northern and western Europe in general, and in particular toward Great Britain. Again, this leaning showed up most specifically during the two high points of Southern involvement in world affairs in the interwar years, at the end of World War I and on the eve of World War II. During the debate on the League of Nations, many Southerners voiced a clear Anglophilia and argued that the United States was and would remain in good hands so long as it remained closely allied with Britain. In the confusion of the war debt and depression eras the preoccupation lapsed, not to reappear in any major way until the fall of France and the Battle of Britain in 1940 forced the entire nation to re-examine its identification with Europe. Southerners, especially those most closely identified with the regional tradition, did not hesitate; from mid-1940 onward they were consistently in the vanguard of those arguing for extensive aid to the United Kingdom, not excluding American entry into the war.

The Southern preoccupation with Europe as the appropriate battleground for America continued throughout the war and projected itself almost unmodified into the cold war era. Southern support of the Truman Doctrine, the Marshall Plan, the North Atlantic Treaty Organization, and the United States military commitment in Europe during the late 1940's was almost complete and unquestioned. The student may search in vain for any Southern counterpart (at least prior to 1953) of the raucous Anglophobia and fear of Europe that dominated, for example, the pages of the *Chicago Tribune* and the public utterances of most Midwestern Republican Congressmen during this period.

It was not until the major focus of American policy began to swing away from Europe toward the non-western world that the marked Southern shift began. Although it is somewhat ahead of the story, it is nevertheless interesting to point out that even during the period of the great swing in Southern attitudes during the 1950's, only a very few Southern Congressmen voiced any qualms about the "mutual security"—that is, military assistance—aspects of foreign aid. Their objections tended to center on the increasing non-European orientation of the program and the dominant place in policy calculations gradually assumed by considerations of economic aid and development. A significant rebirth of Southern interest in aid programs took place when in 1962 and 1963 United States relations with Europe again became complicated by the issues of nuclear deterrence and the Common Market. This was a return to the familiar for many Congressmen from the South, and on these questions they had a ready-made tradition to guide their deliberations.

An economic commitment to a multilateral system of international trade, a preoccupation with military affairs, and a half-hidden sense of allegiance to Great Britain: these then were the traditional components of the Southern posture on world affairs. Do they add up to an acceptance of any abstract doctrine of "internationalism"? The proposition, even put in the most favorable terms, seems a doubtful one.

What is clearly lacking in the traditional Southern exegesis of foreign policy is . . . a sense of "multilateralism." There is nowhere in the Southern ethos any appreciation of the interdependence of states and peoples and the necessity facing the United States of adapting itself and its desires to the demands of a normally intractable environment. The point of constant reference of Southern spokesmen between 1919 and 1953 was in almost every case ostensibly "what is good for the United States," cast normally in terms xenophobic and unilateralist even when the rhetoric was the most flamboyant in calling for support of America's allies. The standardized image of "going it alone" even within the bounds of an international organization like the League of Nations or the United Nations was always implicit—and frequently explicit—in Southern discourse. There is in the traditional Southern outlook, in other words, no commitment to any generalized ideal of a world order; there is only the belief that complete fulfillment of American aspirations is possible in a world that can eventually be arranged to suit the purposes of the United States.

One is struck today by the naiveté and provincialism of even the most "internationalist" of the Southern spokesmen of the interwar period. Although they professed selfless dedication to the welfare of the United States and all its people, their working frame of analysis was forever and unquenchably Southern. Each of the issues that arose was evaluated in a peculiarly regional way and each found its resolution in Southern terms.

Foreign affairs, in other words, passed through a distinctly Southern filter and was finally reduced to the foreign policy of the South. The fact that in certain crucial periods the South and the remainder of the nation agreed on particular action programs should not mislead the observer into thinking that the South reached its conclusions in the same way or for the same reasons as did other parts of America.

The explanation for this divergence in foreign policy attitude is part and parcel of the special role that the South has played in American history. A different social order, a stubborn and anachronistic adherence to a rural-oriented economy, a constant and insoluble racial problem, a distinct political system based on one-party dominance, and a festering pessimism born of separation, defeat, and exclusion all contributed to the conditioning any Southern leader brought to his contemplation of world affairs. It would have required supermen to transcend their regional roots in order to adopt an enlightened and broad approach to international issues; the South, like the nation at large, does not breed an especially large supply of supermen, and of these only a few eventually find their way into Congress.

Sources of the Southern Position

Thus the elements in the traditional Southern position can be identified with certain long-standing strains in Southern political life. Several contributing factors led Southern leaders to take the position they did, forces indigenous to Southern life and deeply imbedded in the region's political code. Each of these—of which none is entirely dead today and of which several are still of major significance—played its own part in shaping the dominant attitude.

The economic internationalism intrinsic to the Southern position was legitimate and practical. Committed, alone among the major regions of the United States in the late nineteenth and twentieth centuries, to primary reliance upon cash-crop agriculture, the South had an immediate and continuing need for access to overseas markets. Exporting cotton and tobacco to Europe and importing European manufactures freed Southerners to some extent from the dominance of Northern industry and gave them a sense of being participants in a broader economic system. The Confederacy ultimately based its hopes for victory on the sovereign role of King Cotton in bringing about British intervention, and the South never wavered in its confidence that its capacity to produce certain agricultural products of guaranteed international demand was its own and the only available route to prosperity. Southern cotton and tobacco farmers, particularly the former, were throughout the bulk of the interwar period entirely without real price protection by the federal government and were, therefore, at the mercy of the world market. Up to the very eve of World War II, therefore, the South and its spokesmen were almost unanimous in eschewing protectionism and in insisting on the progressive liberalization of the terms and conditions of international trade.

But, even in dealing with such immediately practical and hard-headed matters as finding export markets for their cotton in an increasingly competitive system, the South remained incurably romantic and myth-ridden. The low-tariff position was a principle of faith and doctrine as much as it was the result of realistic calculation. Low tariffs were defended heatedly by many who had little or no appreciation of their real economic implications; it was sufficient for the quixotic Southerner to know that Northern manufacturers and Midwestern wheat farmers were on the other side. From this he could quickly deduce that they were, therefore, at bottom aiming at the further suppression and impoverishment of the South. A titillating air of unreality still clings to the official record of several of the tariff debates of the early years of this century. Many Southerners in Congress consciously evoked recollections of Shiloh and Chancellorsville as they encouraged each other to do battle with the forces of Northern bourgeois capitalism.

A second element, difficult to quantify but immediately obvious to anyone who becomes aware of the climate of Southern political discourse, is the impact of Woodrow Wilson as man and memory on Southern foreign policy attitudes. It is impossible accurately to verbalize the sense of pariahdom shared by politically sensitive Southerners during the long years from the Civil War to the election of Wilson. The region felt—with considerable justice—that after the war it had never been really readmitted to the inner circles of the national government where its sons had earlier bulked so large. The Republicans (at least after 1876) would have nothing to do with the South, and the national leadership of the Democrats, secure in the region's "solidity," saw no reason to make special concessions to a bloc of states already hopelessly committed to the party. The South's political frustration seemed complete.

Woodrow Wilson, although elected from New Jersey, was a Southerner by birth and rearing, and the South adopted him immediately as one of its own. When as President he showed a tendency to rely on Southern advisors and to listen sympathetically to Southern leaders, his victory over the South became complete. As the region's "first President since Jefferson Davis," Southerners gave him their hearts.

As a result, Southern support of Wilson was generous, undemanding, and in retrospect almost touching. Wilson, whose historic image in the North is that of a cold if liberal intellectual, emerges from Southern folklore as a romantic conservative, a true *beau ideal* of the Old South. And it is undeniable that his "New Freedom" domestic program made few embarrassing demands on Southern society while simultaneously serving to some extent to redress certain rankling injustices under which Southerners felt themselves burdened. In foreign policy, influenced as he was by such sons of the South as Colonel Edward House and Ambassador to Great Britain Walter Hines Page, Wilson approached his major crises completely in harmony with Southern predispositions. When the showdown finally came in the aftermath of the war, the South was prepared to go all the way with Wilson.

The fight for the League, and the eventual victory of the Senate Republicans both at the moment and in later years, quickly found their places as further installments in the history of the Lost Cause. The opposition to Wilson's grand design and to the Treaty of Versailles was in Southern eyes part of the continuing campaign against the South, and to argue in favor of the League was also to continue the struggle for the vindication of the peculiar values of Southern society. Very few of the dedicated battlers for the Covenant seem to have grasped the fact that Wilson's own image of the League as a body that would tie the hands of all sovereign states, including the United States, clashed directly with the regionalist and nationalist symbolism of the South. It was enough that a Southern President was demanding an international organization; no committed Southerner was interested in asking too many questions.

Since Wilson's fight became the South's fight as well, his ultimate repudiation was also accepted as a Southern defeat. The mythmakers thereupon went to work, and Wilson and the League became part of the interwar weaponry of Southern political leaders. Roosevelt, although welcomed as a Democrat, faced certain handicaps in winning Southern support: he was identified with the urban Northeast, he relied heavily for support upon organized labor, and he launched programs of reform that carried very disturbing implications for Southern society. Except for reciprocal trade, therefore, Southern acceptance of the Roosevelt foreign policy before 1938 was limited, cautious, and tentative.

The failure of the 1938 purge of conservative Southern Congressmen, the virtual abandonment of the reform phase of the New Deal after that date, and the approach of the war all changed the South's attitude toward Roosevelt and the President's own response. As the New Deal became engrossed in international crisis, the assumptions and the language of Wilsonianism again became common currency in the American body politic. To the South this was like coming home again, and its citizens responded almost unanimously.

The problems of World War II, whether of preparedness, prosecution, or settlement, were to the South a "second time around" on the issues of the age of Wilson. Finally, it seemed, the arguments of 1919 and 1920 were going to be repeated; this time, however, the side of reason, right, and justice was going to win. From the debate with the America First

Committee on through the ratification of the Charter of the United Nations, Woodrow Wilson played a major role as silent advisor and constant inspiration to most Southern leaders. Wilsonianism, and with it the South itself, was finally to be vindicated.

Closely connected in the long-term outlook of the South with the imagery of Wilson is the particular mythology of national party politics that has long been dominant in the South. During the long drought that began with the election of Lincoln and really endured until Franklin Roosevelt forged the new Democratic coalition in 1932, there were only two Democratic presidents. Under both Cleveland and Wilson, therefore, the South (playing such a major role in Democratic politics as it did) saw itself in the unusual position of being central to national affairs. The special significance attached to Wilson (and Roosevelt, at least immediately prior to and during the war) was in large if indefinite measure a function of his role as a Democratic president.

This would suggest that the Southern approach to foreign affairs owes a great deal to the pervasive effect of party regularity. It is a quirk of history that the first three Democratic presidents of this century—Wilson, Roosevelt, and Truman—all had their respective administrations capped by a major international war. Whatever thoughts this coincidence—never made overt, but today part of the folklore of American politics—might induce in other Americans, it has no way proved to be a difficulty for the Southern traditionalist. As successive Democratic presidents have been drawn into major wars, Southerners have followed unquestioningly.

There is a curious symmetry in the patterns formed by the administrations of Wilson and Franklin D. Roosevelt. Both presidents took office committed to domestic reform; both felt, on assuming office, that foreign affairs was of secondary importance. Both faced a series of international crises that gradually forced them to abandon the bulk of their domestic program in favor of deeper involvement in international affairs. Both achieved climax by military victory; the programs of both suffered postwar repudiation. The parallels are striking indeed.

Almost as interesting is the way in which the South's Congressional delegations throughout both periods reacted to the President. In neither case, for example, was the South's "internationalism" especially obvious (even to the Southerners themselves) until after the chief executive had made his own turnabout; in neither instance, furthermore, did the South ever go beyond the President in charting a positive course. The conclusion is easy to draw that just how far the Southern group was willing to go toward multilateralism in either case was determined more by what the President wanted in any situation than by independently-exercised Southern judgments on the merits of the case.

It was quite another matter, however, when Southern Democratic Congressmen were in positions of responsibility and leadership during periods when the White House was occupied by a Republican. Here the more revealing dimensions of the Southern thinking on foreign affairs can be found, freed as the Southerners were from the necessity of supporting a fellow Democrat. Here instances of partisan opposition—not a peculiarly Southern phenomenon by any means—are frequent; here also, however, can be found cases in which leading Southerners placed themselves behind Republican presidents who were following a course deemed satisfactory to the South. Perhaps the most striking recent example of this was the courageous and unremitting identification of Senator Walter George of Georgia with the Eisenhower foreign policy during the mid-1950's.

One anticipatory word might be said here about the decreasing effectiveness of party regularity in keeping Southerners in line behind a Democratic administration. The Democratic party, ever since the election of 1936, has not been dominated as it was for so long by Southern leadership and Southern ideas; on the contrary, the tendency has been quite in the other direction. Southerners, particularly since 1945, have found themselves increasingly at odds with a party leadership depending for so many of its votes on minority groups, organized labor, and urban party machines. A conservative coalition of Southern Democrats and Midwestern Republicans has largely dominated the House of Representatives ever since 1938 and has sporadically extended its influence to the Senate. Coincidentally, the rise of the Republican party in the South, although not spectacular, has been steady in the increasingly urbanized region.

All these factors have largely undermined the appeal of party solidarity to Southern Congressmen on any kind of issue, and on foreign policy in particular. The Kennedy administration, thoroughly and admittedly party-oriented and partisan in outlook, had in its three short years only limited success in winning Southern support for its foreign policy moves, and the 88th Congress elected in 1962 showed unmistakable signs of being even less amenable to this appeal than its immediate predecessor. No more graphic demonstration of the changes in Southern society that form the base of the argument in this study could be advanced than the tarnished symbolism of the Democratic party in the once-but-not-any-more solid South.

Another element in the Southern tradition that contributed to the region's composite foreign policy attitude is its philosophical view of violence. Also an exceptionally difficult concept about which to be specific, there is no doubt that Southern culture has long had a different attitude toward interpersonal violence than has had the remainder of the nation. Whether one analyzes the upper-class code of chivalry that still lingers on in many parts of the South or the cruder principles of man-to-man relations that govern poor-white (and poor-Negro) behavior, the phenomenon of violence bulks large.

Without attempting to speculate on the personality structure of Southerners—a fascinating but obviously inconclusive venture, at least in the present context—it is evident from the historical record that Southerners are willing to accept violence as a tolerable way to conduct international affairs much more readily than are most non-Southerners. Military establishments do not exist, the South insists, merely to provide satisfying careers for men with a strong sense of *noblesse oblige* (and, it may be cynically pointed out, relatively poor economic prospects in any other career); they should be used freely in the national interest. The United States maintains an army, a navy, and an air force in order to win victories over the nation's enemies and to accomplish the nation's objectives. For a president to neglect his duty to use military power with determination and courage is for him to fall short of what the American people should expect of their public servants.

Thus the military fixation of Southerners has a profound cultural root, and Southern conduct in a moment of crisis is highly predictable. During the prolonged crisis of the cold war Southerners have led not only in the steady escalation of the size, complexity, and expense of the armed forces of the United States, but also in the flaming rhetoric of the final "showdown" with communism, filled with gloomy but exciting forecasts of inevitable war.

A fairly abstruse point in this connection might help to throw the Southern approach to international violence into deeper perspective. Force is the only technique of true finality available to states in the international order. When a state goes to war, the correctness of its position and the persuasiveness of its public relations are substantially irrelevant; the only consideration that really matters is whether or not its will and its armed strength will be adequate to bring about victory on the battlefield and the submission of the enemy. In other words, in strict conceptual terms, violence in international politics may be viewed as the highest form of unilateralism, as the state seeks to have its way in the face of adamant and active opposition. The theory of warfare long accepted by sovereign states and the political order from which this elaborate doctrine depends both presuppose that in any military conflict there is always a winner and a loser, and furthermore, that the stakes of war themselves are of a sort that permit "victory" and "defeat" to be meaningful terms.

These abstractions lead to a concrete point. The extent to which Southerners are distinctive in their early and heavy reliance upon the calculus of violence in international affairs is a measure of the extent to which they are instinctively predisposed toward unilateral formulations of American policy choices. In war the unilateralist can see himself (and his nation as well) "taking arms against a sea of troubles" and reducing all the ambiguous and complex choices of politics to a simple we-or-they dichotomy. This is the unilateralist's view toward foreign policy matters of all sorts in any case—the United States against the world—and it is of special relevance in military crises only to the extent to which it is made explicit. No single proposition cuts so deeply into the image of Southern "internationalism" as the region's clear preference for military implementation of unilaterally-determined policies.

A word should also be said here about the regional Anglophilia to which some attention has already been paid. This visceral orientation seems to come from two sources, both today of markedly less influence than heretofore. The first is the South's remarkable immunity from the waves of immigration that rolled over American shores between 1860 and 1920. It must be admitted that during this era the South was much less attractive as a new homeland than were the rural Midwest or the urban East, nor was there much inclination in the South itself to welcome such immigrants as found their way there. In any case, at least until the onset of World War II, the South was ethnically the most homogeneous region of the United States, with a population (except, of course, for the Negroes) heavily Anglo-Saxon in origin, broken only occasionally by pockets of Latin (French or Spanish) influence. Although for most Southerners the British Isles were far away and long ago, the ethnic unity of the South contrasted so sharply with the diversity characteristic of most of the rest of the nation that it became a point of Southern pride to retain the memory of their British roots long after the notion had any social validity.

A second cause, less specific but of great value in developing the ideal of a "Southern way of life" as a combined palliative and stimulant to political action, was the fancied identity between the British and the Southern aristocratically-dominated social systems. Born in the days of the plantation aristocracy, the ideal of a propertied leisure class governing in the name of all for the common good had a profound and long-lasting effect on Southern attitudes generally. British upper-class sympathy with the Confederacy during the Civil War and British leadership in both world wars played their parts in contributing to the identification of Southern leadership with British traditions. Sympathy for and active support of British policy could thus easily be made into a matter of simple obligation rather than of complex and calculating policy.

A consequence of the South's racial homogeneity, however, was the region's leadership in the almost totally successful attempt to restrict immigration. Cultural isolation and political unsophistication led easily into a narrow xenophobia, and the national government's program to keep foreigners out received and still receives general approbation among Southerners. Strange disparities appear in the reasoning used, however; some

Southerners broaden their preoccupation with racial "purity" from the Negro to include Orientals, Slavs, Jews, and Latin Europeans in the general category of undesirables, while other Southerners are opposed to further immigration on the simple and pragmatic ground that immigrants are low-wage workers who take jobs away from natives. In either case, however, the result is the same: the picture of the United States as the haven for the oppressed is sharply conditioned by restrictions and limitations.

The Demagogic Aberration

Running alongside the traditional Southern approach to foreign policy as outlined above, sometimes coinciding but more often clashing with it, has been the second strain of Southern thought about international affairs. This has been more than anything else the voice of social and economic protest rooted in the discontent of the poor-white stratum of Southern society. Although as authentically Southern as the more orthodox attitude analyzed above, and although sharing a number of specific points of view with it, demagogic foreign policy pronouncements over the years have had a very different impact upon the political thinking of the South and ultimately the nation.

The phenomenon of protest, so central to the contemporary behavior of the South, is analyzed in some greater detail in Chapters VIII and IX. In this introductory discussion it is necessary only to clarify one or two of its salient features so that its aberrant foreign policy posture can be thrown into the sharpest possible contrast with the traditional points of view.

Probably the most important characteristic of demagogic protest in the South prior to World War II, at least in terms of international attitudes, was that it was a function of an activist climate of politics. The traditional foreign policy outlook of the Southern leadership elite was normally, as one writer put it, "laid athwart apathy" in the body politic and was viable only to the extent to which the masses of Southern citizenry did not feel themselves directly involved in the policies their own Congressmen were promulgating and supporting. As soon as individual awareness and identification replaced mass non-involvement among large numbers of voters, the easy upper-class formula of interventionism, militarism, and free trade became complicated and difficult to apply. The Southern demagogue of the interwar years, speaking for a social group ordinarily outside the scope of the Southern foreign policy consensus, had little patience with traditional formulas.

Protest was necessary to the demagogue because only in a crusade to rectify injustice as they saw it could the bulk of the Southern white population muster enough energy to go on the political warpath. Demagoguery was thus a result rather than a cause; no demagogue could hope to bulk large in the affairs of his community or his state without an aroused body of citizens mobilized behind him. Once he had his mass movement in operation and in hand, the peculiar dynamics of Southern politics made his importance inevitable and his victory probable.

The demagogue, in the course of feeding the appetites while continually sharpening the hostilities of his poor white, rural, unsophisticated, racist, and low-income constituency, tended to level his heavy guns at all "outsiders." The catalogue of his targets might be conceived as a set of concentric circles drawn around the rural South, with the Southern aristocrats receiving the first volleys and, as the range lengthened, other deviants such as the Northeastern United States, all large cities everywhere, all religions outside the narrow range of fundamentalist Protestantism, and all foreigners brought under fire. Thus the demagogue, in spite of his own exceptionally limited and parochial horizons, was almost inexorably drawn into the arena of foreign policy discussion.

Southern demagogues from the Populist Tom Watson of Georgia to the buffoon from Buncombe County, North Carolina, Robert Rice Reynolds, all preached a militant and obscurantist doctrine of total withdrawal and non-involvement in international affairs. Like their co-ideologists in the Midwest, they combined reformism with isolationism (in a literal sense, these are the only true *isolationists* in recent American history) and fused a demand for economic justice at home with a disavowal of the outside world, all in the grand tradition of American radicalism. The Southern demagogue differed from his Northern colleague primarily in his involvement in the issue of white supremacy, a key to the Southerner's political methodology but of virtually no relevance to the Northern rabble-rouser, except during the brief and ugly episode of the Northern Ku Klux Klan in the late 1920's.

The demagogues of the interwar South were in a real sense prosecuting a class war, and they spared no aspects of upper-class Southern life in their effort to set the poor whites against both the Bourbons and the Negroes simultaneously. This brought them into collision with the foreign policy symbols of Southern aristocracy, and the demagogue was openly Anglophobic, anti-Wilson, on occasion pacifist, and anti-League of Nations. No one can be certain today to what extent the foreign policies advocated by the demagogues of that era were sincere and the result of personal conviction, or were instead only convenient springboards from which to mount assaults against their local opponents. But the effect of this tactic is clear: audiences did not bother to question the demagogues' sincerity but tended instead to accept as revealed gospel their formulations of the nature of the world and the task of the United States.

In truth it is inaccurate to classify the demagogic aberration as a "for-

eign policy" position at all. Its overall effect was to deny the necessity of
the United States conducting anything like a real foreign policy in the world.
Consistently contradicting either the necessity or the desirability of American entry into world affairs, and projecting an image of a nation kept pure
and strong by turning its back on the temptations of diplomacy, the demagogue argued that the world could be kept forever from America's doorstep
if only the people remained alert and dedicated enough to see and avoid
the peril. The interventionist proclivities of the traditionalists and the Bourbons were devastatingly easy to portray as sinister plots to deliver the
United States (especially the rural South) to the mercy of London politicians and Anglophile New York (and Atlanta) bankers. Foreign affairs
was not a continuing responsibility of the national government, but was
instead a temporary process of exercising a finite set of devils, after which
therapeutic effort the nation could relax secure in its strength and prosperity.

In the face of overwhelming Southern support for World War II, some
of the prewar demagogues—notably Senator Reynolds—maintained their
true and radical isolationist position on into the era of active combat. This
was perhaps the truest test of demagogic consistency: if a leader of protest
was willing to fly in the face of his constituency's traditional support of
militarism and war, he was beyond doubt outside the pale of the Southern
norm even in its most generous dimensions. But by and large the demagogic
thrust in the interwar South had been largely stilled before the crisis of
1939–1941, and the voice of protest, although not stilled, did not ring
quite so loudly after the New Deal had begun to chip away at the discontent that was its source.

The South in the last years before World War II, in other words, had
returned almost completely to the stewardship of its traditional ruling class;
only a few of the old demagogues like Reynolds and Martin Dies were
functioning at the time of the fall of France. The region's response to the
threat of war was more in keeping with the long-term predilections of its
leaders than had been its overall outlook only some half-dozen years
earlier. The demagogic approach to foreign policy largely lapsed after the
mid-1930's, to reappear only in the aftermath of the school desegregation
decisions two decades later.

The Contemporary Shift

The firm grip of the traditionalist approach to world affairs that permitted
Southern Congressmen to vote for multilateralist measures continued un-
shaken throughout the war and the early stages of the cold war. There was
nothing surprising in the Southern response to the demands of World War

II itself, comporting so neatly as this great enterprise did with both the South's ego-image and the requirements of simple electoral politics. The traditionalists likewise greeted the United Nations warmly as a final if delayed vindication of Wilsonianism, but found little difficulty in combining the idealism of the United Nations with their simultaneous advocacy of a higher level of national defense expenditure than either President Truman or the majority of Congress accepted.

The onset of the cold war as well caused few problems for Southern leadership. Newly proud of their "conservatism" and with the exotic, baleful, and frightening specter of the Communist conspiracy to spur them on, the traditionalists found it simple to follow administration leadership into the programmatic implementation of the anti-Soviet campaign. Europe's centrality to at least the early phase, already noted, contributed to the ease with which the Wilsonian image of international co-operation in the United Nations was transmuted into a naked power struggle reminiscent of the titanic crusade against Hitler.

Disillusion began to set in even among the staunchest supporters of American cold-war policy when the struggle gave signs of being inconclusive and inordinately expensive. The Marshall Plan, originally accepted by the South as a one-time expedient to fill a temporary need, gave way to an apparently permanent Mutual Security Program; the Korean War, coming so close on the heels of the victory over the Nazis as to disconcert many normally military minded Southerners, reached its frustrating climax and dragged on in the slow agony of Panmunjom. The focus of American efforts shifted from Europe to strange battlefields in Asia, the Middle East, Latin America, and ultimately Africa. Gradually, the disinclination of successive administrations to seek final and complete victory as prohibitive in cost and unbearable in risk began to corrode many Southern attitudes, even as it was to do in other parts of the nation.

The regional disposition to support multilateralist efforts, never especially strong since it demanded a measure of perceptive "world-mindedness" that very few individual Southerners could muster, began to crumble in the face of time and bemusement. But even the frustrations of the Korean War, whatever their effect on the popular consensus, brought about no real Southern secession from the Congressional majority supporting the general line of American foreign policy. The time sequence argues that the true cause of the contemporary Southern shift is not to be found in the host of contradictions besetting the conduct of American foreign policy, however annoying the international environment might be. The breakaway of the South is the result of forces within Southern society itself rather than an outcome of any developments in international affairs.

Subsequent chapters recount an effort to determine what these forces were and are and to point out the direction in which they have and are yet moving the Southern mind. Fewer and fewer Southern Congressmen have been supporting the genuinely multilateralist aspects of current American policy, while more and more have been accepting the premises and and some of the conclusions of the more militant, demagogic brand of unilateralism. This is the major element in the contemporary Southern shift.

20

The Search for Southern Identity

C. Vann Woodward

Not unrelated to the quest for a central theme in southern history is the search for southern identity. With regard to the problem of identity, however, the American South has proven itself ambivalent —it has sought a distinct regional identification and the label of the "most American" of regions. Arguments supporting both positions have been drawn in terms of geography, race, climate, economics, and culture. C. Vann Woodward, one of the great specialists on the history of the South, here analyzes the South's "identity crisis" in terms of a regional heritage at variance with the myths of nationalism. A deft handling of "mythology" in both its regional and national manifestations allows Professor Woodward to draw attention to one of the grandest ironies of the collective southern experience. Juxtaposed against the American legends of success, victory, and innocence, Woodward contends the South's history has rather provided the region with the "un-American" fate of poverty, defeat, and guilt. Ironically, and in the end, the South would appear to be unique precisely because it *is* part of America. The South's unique and clearly identifiable qualities draw their significance only in terms of the American experience.

The time is coming, if indeed it has not already arrived, when the Southerner will begin to ask himself whether there is really any longer very much point in calling himself a Southerner. Or if he does, he might well wonder occasionally whether it is worth while insisting on the point. So long as

"The Search for Southern Identity" from *The Burden of Southern History*, by C. Vann Woodward. Baton Rouge: Louisiana State University Press, 1960. Reprinted by permission of the publisher.

he remains at home where everybody knows him the matter hardly becomes an issue. But when he ventures among strangers, particularly up North, how often does he yield to the impulse to suppress the identifying idiom, to avoid the awkward subject, and to blend inconspicuously into the national pattern—to act the role of the standard American? Has the Southern heritage become an old hunting jacket that one slips on comfortably while at home but discards when he ventures abroad in favor of some more conventional or modish garb? Or is it perhaps an attic full of ancestral wardrobes useful only in connection with costume balls and play acting—staged primarily in Washington, D.C.?

Asking himself some similar questions about the New England heritage, Professor George W. Pierson of Yale has come forth with some disturbing concessions about the integrity of his own region. Instead of an old hunting jacket, he suggests that we call New England "an old kitchen floor, now spatter-painted with many colors." He points out that roughly six out of every ten Connecticut "Yankees" are either foreign-born or born of foreign or mixed parentage, while only three have native forebears going as far back as two generations, and they are not necessarily New England forebears at that. "Like it or not," writes Pierson, "and no matter how you measure it—geographically, economically, radically or religiously, there is no New England Region today." It has become instead, he says, "an optical illusion and a land of violent contrast and change." And yet in spite of the wholesale and damaging concessions of his essay, which he calls "A Study in Denudation," he concludes that, "as a region of the heart and mind, New England is still very much alive."

One wonders if the Southerner, for his part, can make as many damaging admissions of social change and cultural erosion as our New England friend has made and come out with as firm a conclusion about the vitality of his own regional heritage. More doubt than assurance probably comes to mind at first. The South is still in the midst of an economic and social revolution that has by no means run its course, and it will not be possible to measure its results for a long time to come. This revolution has already leveled many of the old monuments of regional distinctiveness and may end eventually by erasing the very consciousness of a distinctive tradition along with the will to sustain it. The sustaining will and consciousness are also under the additional strain of a moral indictment against a discredited part of the tradition, an indictment more uncompromising than any since abolitionist times.

The Southerner may not have been very happy about many of those old monuments of regional distinctiveness that are now disappearing. He may, in fact, have deplored the existence of some—the one-horse farmer, one-crop agriculture, one-party politics, the sharecropper, the poll tax, the white primary, the Jim Crow car, the lynching bee. It would take a blind sentimentalist to mourn their passing. But until the day before yesterday there they stood, indisputable proof that the South was different. Now that they are vanished or on their way toward vanishing, we are suddenly aware of the vacant place they have left in the landscape and of our habit of depending upon them in final resort as landmarks of regional identification. To establish identity by reference to our faults was always simplest, for whatever their reservations about our virtues, our critics were never reluctant to concede us our vices and shortcomings.

It is not that the present South has any conspicuous lack of faults, but that its faults are growing less conspicuous and therefore less useful for purposes of regional identification. They are increasingly the faults of other parts of the country, standard American faults, shall we say. Many of them have only recently been acquired—could, in fact, only recently be afforded. For the great changes that are altering the cultural landscape of the South almost beyond recognition are not simply negative changes, the disappearance of the familiar. There are also positive changes, the appearance of the strikingly new.

The symbol of innovation is inescapable. The roar and groan and dust of it greet one on the outskirts of every Southern city. That symbol is the bulldozer, and for lack of a better name this might be called the Bulldozer Revolution. The great machine with the lowered blade symbolizes the revolution in several respects: in its favorite area of operation, the area where city meets country; in its relentless speed; in its supreme disregard for obstacles, its heedless methods; in what it demolishes and in what it builds. It is the advance agent of the metropolis. It encroaches upon rural life to expand urban life. It demolishes the old to make way for the new.

It is not the amount of change that is impressive about the Bulldozer Revolution so much as the speed and concentration with which it has come and with which it continues. In the decade of the forties, when urbanization was growing at a swift pace on the country as a whole, the cities of the South's fifty-three metropolitan areas grew more than three times as fast as comparable cities in the rest of the country, at a rate of 33.1 percent as compared with 10.3 percent elsewhere. For every three city dwellers in the South at the beginning of that decade there were four at the end, and for every five farm residents there were only four. An overwhelmingly rural South in 1930 had 5.5 millions employed in agriculture; by 1950, only 3.2 millions. A considerable proportion of these Southerners were moving directly from country to suburb, following the path of the bulldozer to "rurbanization" and skipping the phase of urbanization entirely. Rural Negroes, the most mobile of all Southerners, were more likely to move into the heart of the urban areas abandoned by the suburban dwellers. In the single decade of the forties the South lost a third of its rural-farm Negro population. If the same trend were continued through the present decade, it would reduce that part of the colored population to about one-fifth of the Negroes living in the region.

According to nearly all of the indices, so the economists find, economic growth of the South in recent years greatly exceeds the rate maintained in the North and East. The fact is the South is going through economic expansion and reorganization that the North and East completed a generation or more ago. But the process is taking place far more rapidly than it did in the North. Among all the many periods of change in the history of the South it is impossible to find one of such concentration and such substantive impact. The period of Reconstruction might appear a likely rival for this distinction, but that revolution was largely limited to changes in legal status and the ownership of property. The people remained pretty much where they were and continued to make their living in much the same way. All indications are that the bulldozer will leave a deeper mark upon the land than did the carpetbagger.

It is the conclusion of two Southern sociologists, John M. Maclachlan and Joe S. Floyd, Jr., that the present drive toward uniformity "with national demographic, economic, and cultural norms might well hasten the day when the South, once perhaps the most distinctively 'different' American region, will have become in most such matters virtually indistinguishable from the other urban-industrial areas of the nation."

The threat of becoming "indistinguishable," of being submerged under a national steamroller, has haunted the mind of the South for a long time. Some have seen it as a menace to regional identity and the survival of a Southern heritage. Premonitions of the present revolution appeared during the industrial boom that followed the First World War. Toward the end of the twenties two distinctive attempts were made by Southerners to dig in and define a perimeter of defense against further encroachment.

One of these entrenchments was that of the twelve Southerners who wrote *I'll Take My Stand*. They sought to define what they called "a Southern way of life against what may be called the American or prevailing way," and they agreed "that the best terms in which to represent the distinction are contained in the phrase, Agrarian *versus* Industrial." Agrarianism and its values were the essence of the Southern tradition and the test of Southern loyalty. Their credo held that "the whole way in which we live, act, think, and feel," the humanist culture, "was rooted in the agrarian way of life of the older South." They called for "anti-industrial measures" which "might promise to stop the advances of industrialism, or even undo some of them."

Even in 1930 the agrarians were prepared to admit "the melancholy fact that the South itself has wavered a little and shown signs of wanting to join up behind the common or American industrial ideal." They admonished waverers among the younger generation that the brave new South they contemplated would "be only an undistinguished replica of the usual industrial community."

Three decades later the slight "wavering" in the Southern ranks that disturbed the agrarians in 1930 would seem to have become a pell-mell rout. Defections came by the battalion. Whole regiments and armies deserted "to join up behind the common or American industrial ideal." In its pursuit of the American Way and the American Standard of Living the South was apparently doing all in its power to become what the agrarians had deplored as "only an undistinguished replica of the usual industrial community." The voice of the South in the 1950's had become the voice of the chamber of commerce, and Southerners appeared to be about as much absorbed in the acquirement of creature comforts and adult playthings as any other Americans. The twelve Southerners who took their stand in 1930 on the proposition that the Southern way stands or falls with the agrarian way would seem to have been championing a second lost cause. If they were right, then our questions would have already been answered, for the Southerner as a distinctive species of American would have been doomed, his tradition bereft of root and soil. The agrarian way contains no promise of continuity and endurance for the Southern tradition.

Two years before the agrarian pronouncement appeared, another attempt was made to define the essence of the Southern tradition and prescribe the test of Southern loyalty. The author of this effort was the distinguished historian, Professor Ulrich B. Phillips. His definition had no reference to economic institutions but was confined to a preoccupation with race consciousness. The essential theme of continuity and unity in the Southern heritage, wrote Professor Phillips, was "a common resolve indomitably maintained" that the South "shall be and remain a white man's country." This indomitable conviction could be "expressed with the frenzy of a demagogue or maintained with a patrician's quietude," but it was and had been from the beginning "the cardinal test of a Southerner and the central theme of southern history."

Professor Phillips' criterion of Southernism has proved somewhat more durable and widespread in appeal than that of the agrarians. It is not tied so firmly to an ephemeral economic order as was theirs. Nor does it demand—of the dominant whites, at least—any Spartan rejection of the flesh pots of the American living standard. Its adherents are able to enjoy the blessings of economic change and remain traditionalists at the same time. There are still other advantages in the Phillipsian doctrine. The traditionalist who has watched the Bulldozer Revolution plow under cherished old values of individualism, localism, family, clan, and rural folk culture has felt helpless and frustrated against the mighty and imponderable agents of change. Industrialism, urbanism, unionism, and big government conferred or promised too many coveted benefits. They divided the people and won support in the South, so that it was impossible to rally unified opposition to them.

The race issue was different. Advocates and agents of change could be denounced as outsiders, intruders, meddlers. Historic memories of resistance and cherished constitutional principles could be invoked. Radical prejudices, aggressions, and jealousies could be stirred to rally massive popular support. And with this dearly bought unity, which he could not rally on other issues, the frustrated traditionalist might at last take his stand for the defense of all the defiled, traduced, and neglected values of the traditional order. What then is the prospect of the Phillipsian "cardinal test" as a bulwark against change? Will it hold fast where other defenses have failed?

Recent history furnishes some of the answers. Since the last World War old racial attitudes that appeared more venerable and immovable than any other have exhibited a flexibility that no one would have predicted. One by one, in astonishingly rapid succession, many landmarks of racial discrimination and segregation have disappeared, and old barriers have been breached. Many remain, of course—perhaps more than have been breached —and distinctively Southern racial attitudes will linger for a long time. Increasingly the South is aware of its isolation in these attitudes, however, and is in defense of the institutions that embody them. They have fallen rapidly into discredit and under condemnation from the rest of the country and the rest of the world.

Once more the South finds itself with a morally discredited Peculiar Institution on its hands. The last time this happened, about a century ago, the South's defensive reaction was to identify its whole cause with the one institution that was most vulnerable and to make loyalty to an ephemeral aspect which it had once led in condemning the cardinal test of loyalty to the whole tradition. Southerners who rejected the test were therefore forced to reject the whole heritage. In many cases, if they were vocal in their rejection, they were compelled to leave the South entirely and return only at their peril. Unity was thus temporarily achieved, but with the collapse of the Peculiar Institution the whole tradition was jeopardized and discredited for having been so completely identified with the part abandoned.

Historical experience with the first Peculiar Institution ought to discourage comparable experiments with the second. If Southernism is allowed to become identified with a last ditch defense of segregation, it will increasingly lose its appeal among the younger generation. Many will be tempted to reject their entire regional identification, even the name "Southern," in order to dissociate themselves from the one discredited aspect. If agrarianism has proved to be a second lost cause, segregation is a likely prospect for a third.

With the crumbling of so many defenses in the present, the South has tended to substitute myths about the past. Every self-conscious group of any size fabricates myths about its past: about its origins, its mission, its righteousness, its benevolence, its general superiority. But few groups in the New World have had their myths subjected to such destructive analysis as those of the South have undergone in recent years. While some Southern historians have contributed to the mythmaking, others have been among the leading iconoclasts, and their attacks have spared few of the South's cherished myths.

The Cavalier Legend as the myth of origin was one of the earlier victims. The Plantation Legend of ante bellum grace and elegance has not been left wholly intact. The pleasant image of a benevolent and paternalistic slavery system as a school for civilizing savages has suffered damage that is probably beyond repair. Even the consoling security of Reconstruction as the common historic grievance, the infallible mystique of unity, has been rendered somewhat less secure by detached investigation. And finally, rude hands have been laid upon the hallowed memory of the Redeemers who did in the Carpetbaggers, and doubt has been cast upon the antiquity of segregation folkways. These faded historical myths have become weak material for buttressing Southern defenses, for time has dealt as roughly with them as with agrarianism and racism.

Would a hard-won immunity from the myths and illusions of Southern sectionalism provide some immunity to the illusions and myths of American nationalism? Or would the hasty divestment merely make the myth-denuded Southerner hasten to wrap himself in the garments of nationalism? The danger in the wholesale rejection of the South by the modern Southerner bent on reaffirming his Americanism is the danger of affirming more than he bargains for.

While the myths of Southern distinctiveness have been waning, national myths have been waxing in power and appeal. National myths, American myths have proved far more sacrosanct and inviolate than Southern myths. Millions of European immigrants of diverse cultural backgrounds have sought and found identity in them. The powerful urge among minority groups to abandon or disguise their distinguishing cultural traits and conform as quickly as possible to some national norm is one of the most familiar features in the sociology of American nationalism. European ethnic and national groups with traditions far more ancient and distinctive than those of the South have eagerly divested themselves of their cultural heritage in order to conform.

The conformist is not required nor expected to abandon his distinctive religion. But whether he remains a Protestant, a Catholic, or a Jew, his religion typically becomes subordinate or secondary to a national faith. Foreign observers have remarked that the different religions in America resemble each other more than they do their European counterparts. "By every realistic criterion," writes Will Herberg in his study of American religious sociology, "the American Way of Life is the operative faith of the American people." And where the mandates of the American Way of Life conflict with others, they take undisputed sway over the masses of all religions. Herberg describes it as "a faith that has its symbols and its rituals, its holidays and its liturgy, its saints and its sancta," and it is common to all Americans. "Sociologically, anthropologically, if one pleases," he writes, the American Way of Life "is the characteristic American religion, undergirding American life and overarching American society despite all indubitable differences of region, section, culture, and class." Differences such as those of region and section, "indubitable" though he admits them to be, he characterizes as "peripheral and obsolescent."

If the American Way of Life has become a religion, any deviation from it has become a sort of heresy. Regionalism in the typical American view is rather like the Turnerian frontier, a section on the move—or at least one that should keep moving, following a course that converges at not too remote a point with the American Way. It is a season's halt of the American caravan, a temporary encampment of an advancing society, eternally on the move toward some undefined goal of progress. If the encampment of regionalism threatens to entrench or dig in for a permanent stand, it comes to be regarded as "peripheral and obsolescent," an institutionalized social lag.

The same urge to conformity that operates upon ethnic or national minorities to persuade them to reject identification with their native heritage or that of their forebears operates to a degree upon the Southerner as well. Since the cultural landscape of his native region is being altered almost beyond recognition by a cyclone of social change, the Southerner may come to feel as uprooted as the immigrant. Bereft of his myths, his peculiar institutions, even his familiar regional vices, he may well reject or forget his regional identification as completely as the immigrant.

Is there nothing about the South that is immune from the disintegrating effect of nationalism and the pressure for conformity? Is there not something that has not changed? There is only one thing that I can think of, and that is its history. By that I do not mean a Southern brand of Shintoism, the worship of ancestors. Nor do I mean written history and its interpretation, popular and mythical, or professional and scholarly, which have changed often and will change again. I mean rather the collective experience of the Southern people. It is in just this respect that the South remains the most distinctive region of the country. In their unique historic experience as Americans the Southerners should not only be able to find the basis for continuity of their heritage but also make contributions that balance and complement the experience of the rest of the nation.

At this point the risks of our enterprise multiply. They are the risks of spawning new myths in place of the old. Awareness of them demands that we redouble precautions and look more cautiously than ever at generalizations.

To start with a safe one, it can be assumed that one of the most conspicuous traits of American life has been its economic abundance. From early colonial days the fabulous riches of America have been compared with the scarcity and want of less favored lands. Immense differentials in economic welfare and living standards between the United States and other countries still prevail. In an illuminating book called *People of Plenty,* David Potter persuasively advances the thesis that the most distinguishing traits of national character have been fundamentally shaped by the abundance of the American living standard. He marshals evidence of the effect that plenty has had upon such decisive phases of life as the nursing and training of babies, opportunities for education and jobs, ages of marriage and childbearing. He shows how abundance has determined characteristic national attitudes between parents and children, husband and wife, superior and subordinate, between one class and another, and how it has molded our mass culture and our consumer oriented society. American national character would indeed appear inconceivable without this unique experience of abundance.

The South at times has shared this national experience and, in very recent years, has enjoyed more than a taste of it. But the history of the South includes a long and quite un-American experience with poverty. So recently as 1938, in fact, the South was characterized by the President as "The Nation's Economic Problem No. 1." And the problem was poverty, not plenty. It was a poverty emphasized by wide regional discrepancies in living standard, per capita wealth, per capita income, and the good things that money buys, such as education, health, protection, and the many luxuries that go to make up the celebrated American Standard of Living. This striking differential was no temporary misfortune of the great depression but a continuous and conspicuous feature of Southern experience since the early years of the Civil War. During the last half of the nineteenth and the first half of the twentieth centuries, when technology was multiplying American abundance with unprecedented rapidity, the South lagged far behind. In 1880 the per capita wealth of the South, based on estimated true valuation of property, was $376 as compared with $1,186 per cápita in the states outside the South. In the same year the per capita wealth of the South was 27 percent of that of the Northeastern states. That was just about the same ratio contemporaneously existing between the per capita wealth of Russia and that of Germany.

Generations of scarcity and want constitute one of the distinctive historical experiences of the Southern people, an experience too deeply embedded in their memory to be wiped out by a business boom and too deep not to admit of some uneasiness at being characterized historically as a "People of Plenty." That they should have been for so long a time a "People of Poverty" in a land of plenty is one mark of enduring cultural distinctiveness. In a nation known around the world for the hedonistic ethic of the American Standard of Living, the Southern heritage of scarcity remains distinctive.

A closely related corollary of the uniquely American experience of abundance is the equally unique American experience of success. During the Second World War Professor Arthur M. Schlesinger made an interesting attempt to define the national character, which he brought to a close with the conclusion that the American character "is bottomed upon the profound conviction that nothing in the world is beyond its power to accomplish." In this he gave expression to one of the great American legends, the legend of success and invincibility. It is a legend with a foundation in fact, for much can be adduced from the American record to support it and explain why it has flourished. If the history of the United States is lacking in some of the elements of variety and contrast demanded of any good story, it is in part because of the very monotonous repetition of successes. Almost every major collective effort, even those thwarted temporarily, succeeded in the end. American history *is* a success story. Why should such a nation not have a "profound conviction that nothing in the world is beyond its power to accomplish"? Even the hazards of war—including the prospect of war against an unknown enemy with untried weapons—proves no exception to the rule. The advanced science and weaponry of the Russian challenger are too recent to have registered their impact on the legend. The American people have never known the chastening experience of being on the losing side of a war. They have, until very recently, solved every major problem they have confronted—or had it solved for them by a smiling fortune. Success and victory are still national habits of mind.

This is but one among several American legends in which the South can participate only vicariously or in part. Again the Southern heritage is distinctive. For Southern history, unlike American, includes large components of frustration, failure, and defeat. It includes not only an overwhelming military defeat but long decades of defeat in the provinces of economic, social, and political life. Such a heritage affords the Southern people no basis for the delusion that there is nothing whatever that is beyond their power to accomplish. They have had it forcibly and repeatedly borne in upon them that this is not the case. Since their experience in this respect is more common among the general run of mankind than that of their fellow Americans, it would seem to be a part of their heritage worth cherishing.

American opulence and American success have combined to foster and encourage another legend of early origin, the legend of American innocence. According to this legend Americans achieved a sort of regeneration of sinful man by coming out of the wicked Old World and removing to an untarnished new one. By doing so they shook off the wretched evils of feudalism and broke free from tyranny, monarchism, aristocracy, and privilege—all those institutions which, in the hopeful philosophy of the Enlightenment, accounted for all, or nearly all, the evil in the world. The absence of these Old World ills in America, as well as the freedom from much of the injustice and oppression associated with them, encouraged a singular moral complacency in the American mind. The self-image implanted in Americans was one of innocence as compared with less fortunate people of the Old World. They were a chosen people and their land a Utopia on the make. Alexis de Tocqueville's patience was tried by this complacency of the American. "If I applaud the freedom which its inhabitants enjoy, he answers, 'Freedom is a fine thing, but few nations are worthy to enjoy it.' If I remark on the purity of morals which distinguishes the United States," complained Tocqueville, " 'I can imagine,' says he, 'that a stranger, who has been struck by corruption of all other nations, is astonished at the difference.' "

How much room was there in the tortured conscience of the South for this national self-image of innocence and moral complacency? Southerners have repeated the American rhetoric of self admiration and sung the perfection of American institutions ever since the Declaration of Independence. But for half that time they lived intimately with a great social evil and the other half with its aftermath. It was an evil that was even condemned and abandoned by the Old World, to which America's moral superiority was supposedly an article of faith. Much of the South's intellectual energy went into a desperate effort to convince the world that its peculiar evil was actually a "positive good," but it failed even to convince itself. It writhed in the torments of its own conscience until it plunged into catastrophe to escape. The South's preoccupation was with guilt, not with innocence, with the reality of evil, not with the dream of perfection. Its experience in this respect, as in several others, was on the whole a thoroughly un-American one.

An age-long experience with human bondage and its evils and later with emancipation and its shortcomings did not dispose the South very favorably toward such popular American ideas as the doctrine of human perfectibility, the belief that every evil has a cure, and the notion that every human problem has a solution. For these reasons the utopian schemes and the gospel of progress that flourished above the Mason and Dixon Line never found very wide acceptance below the Potomac during the nineteenth century. In that most optimistic of centuries in the most optimistic part of the world, the South remained basically pessimistic in its social outlook and its moral philosophy. The experience of evil and the experience of tragedy are parts of the Southern heritage that are as difficult to reconcile with the American legend of innocence and social felicity as the experience of poverty and defeat are to reconcile with the legends of abundance and success.

One of the simplest but most consequential generalizations ever made about national character was Tocqueville's that America was "born free." In many ways that is the basic distinction between the history of the United States and the history of other great nations. We skipped the feudal stage, just as Russia skipped the liberal stage. Louis Hartz has pointed up the complex consequences for the history of American political thought. To be a conservative and a traditionalist in America was a contradiction in terms, for the American Burke was forever conserving John Locke's liberalism, his only real native tradition. Even the South, in its great period of reaction against Jefferson, was never able fully to shake off the grip of Locke and its earlier self-image of liberalism. That is why its most original period of theoretical inspiration, the "Reactionary Enlightenment," left almost no influence upon American thought.

There is still a contribution to be derived from the South's un-American adventure in feudal fantasy. While the South was not born Lockean, it went through a Lockean phase in its youth. But as Hartz admits, it was "an alien child in a liberal family, tortured and confused, driven to a fantasy life." There *are* Americans, after all, who were not "born free." They are also Southerners. They have yet to achieve articulate expression of their uniquely un-American experience. This is not surprising, since white Southerners have only recently found expression of the tragic potentials of their past in literature. The Negro has yet to do that. His first step will be an acknowledgment that he is also a Southerner as well as an American.

One final example of a definition of national character to which the South proves an exception is an interesting one by Thornton Wilder. "Americans," says Mr. Wilder, "are abstract. They are disconnected. They have a relation, but it is to everywhere, to everybody, and to always." This quality of abstraction he finds expressed in numerous ways—in the physical mobility of Americans, in their indifference or, as he might suggest, their superiority to place, to locality, to environment. "For us," he writes, "it is not *where* genius lived that is important. If Mount Vernon and Monticello were not so beautiful in themselves and relatively accessible, would so many of us visit them?" he asks. It is not the concrete but the abstract that captures the imagination of the American and gives him identity, not the here-and-now but the future. " 'I am I,' he says, 'because my plans characterize me.' Abstract! Abstract!" Mr. Wilder's stress upon abstraction as an American characteristic recalls what Robert Penn Warren in a different connection once described as "the fear of abstraction" in the South, "the instinctive fear, on the part of black or white, that the massiveness of experience, the concreteness of life, will be violated; the fear of abstraction."

According to Mr. Wilder, "Americans can find in environment no confirmation of their identity, try as they may." And again, "Americans are disconnected. They are exposed to all place and all time. No place nor group nor movement can say to them: we are waiting for you; it is right for you to be here." The insignificance of place, locality, and community for Thornton Wilder contrasts strikingly with the experience of Eudora Welty of Mississippi. "Like a good many other [regional] writers," she says, "I am myself touched off by place. The place where I am and the place I know, and other places that familiarity with and love for my own make strange and lovely and enlightening to look into, are what set me to writing my stories." To her, "place opens a door in the mind," and she speaks of "the blessing of being located—contained."

To do Mr. Wilder justice, he is aware that the Southern states constitute an exception to his national character of abstraction, "enclaves or residual areas of European feeling," he calls them. "They were cut off, or resolutely cut themselves off, from the advancing tide of the country's modes of consciousness. Place, environment, relations, repetitions are the breath of their being."

The most reassuring prospect for the survival of the South's distinctive heritage is the magnificent body of literature produced by its writers in the last three decades—the very years when the outward traits of regional distinctiveness were crumbling. The Southern literary renaissance has placed its writers in the vanguard of national letters and assured that their works will be read as long as American literature is remembered. The distinguishing feature of the Southern school, according to Allen Tate, is "the peculiar historical consciousness of the Southern writer." He defines the literary renaissance as "a literature conscious of the past in the present." The themes that have inspired the major writers have not been the flattering myths nor the romantic dreams of the South's past. Disdaining the polemics of defense and justification, they have turned instead to the somber realities of hardship and defeat and evil and "the problems of the human heart in conflict with itself." In so doing they have brought to realization for the first time the powerful literary potentials of the South's tragic experience and heritage. Such comfort as they offer lies, in the words of William Faulkner, in reminding us of "the courage and honor and hope and pride and compassion and pity and sacrifice" with which man has endured.

After Faulkner, Wolfe, Warren, and Welty no literate Southerner could remain unaware of his heritage or doubt its enduring value. After this outpouring it would seem more difficult than ever to deny a Southern identity, to be "merely American." To deny it would be to deny our history. And it would also be to deny to America participation in a heritage and a dimension of historical experience that America very much needs, a heritage that is far more closely in line with the common lot of mankind than the national legends of opulence and success and innocence. The South once thought of itself as a "peculiar people," set apart by its eccentricities, but in many ways modern America better deserves that description.

The South was American a long time before it was Southern in any self-conscious or distinctive way. It remains more American by far than anything else, and has all along. After all, it fell the lot of one Southerner from Virginia to define America. The definition he wrote in 1776 voiced aspirations that were rooted in his native region before the nation was born. The modern Southerner should be secure enough in his national identity to escape the compulsion of less secure minorities to embrace uncritically all the myths of nationalism. He should be secure enough also not to deny a regional heritage because it is at variance with national myth. It is a heritage that should prove of enduring worth to him as well as to his country.

21

The Great Confrontation: The South and the Problem of Change

John Hope Franklin

Man has invariably found his past experience and present condition somewhat less perfect than he imagined it might be. Undaunted, however, he usually has sought a state of faultless excellence through the psychological manipulation of the past or the future. He has found it possible, then, to extrapolate visions of individual and social perfection from the imagined glories of the historic past or to suggest that utopia stands on the verge of becoming. Americans are no strangers to such a process, having developed a particular ideological bias in support of such mythical ventures and fictions. In a variation on this theme, and unlike many societies which consistently point to the far horizon as the abode of utopian dreams, the American South has long been convinced that it indeed discovered, and for a time savored, a golden age of perfection. Such a time, when things were *different,* was the South of ante-bellum days. It is just such a preserved memory that John Hope Franklin, John Matthews Manly Distinguished Service Professor of History at the University of Chicago, here attempts to analyze. By artfully controlling its legendary past, and summarily announcing that the pure and perfect society had already arrived, the South's fund of historical experience has served as a convenient touchstone. The region's greatest energies have thus been expended in preserving, as a historical antique, her gilded past. As a result, Professor Franklin contends that the South has too often failed to

John Hope Franklin, "The Great Confrontation: The South and the Problem of Change," *Journal of Southern History,* 38 (February 1972), 3–20. Copyright 1972 by the Southern Historical Association. Reprinted by permission of the Managing Editor.

accommodate itself to fundamental change—as reflected by the correlated experience of women and blacks. As both groups can attest, the South has been more a believer in civil and human *rites* than rights. And though such imitations of grandeur may at times be appealing—in the words of Wilbur Cash, "perpetually suspended in the great haze of memory . . . colossal, shining, and incomparably lovely"—they fail to take due account of the myths and fallacies which serve as the substructure of the South's supposed perfection. Both the South's past and present stand frustrated and obscured by its myths.

The vision of the New World as the utopia of their dreams—or as the challenge to create one—seized all Europeans who decided to cast their lot with what was, perhaps, the most remarkable overseas venture in the history of mankind.[1] Not every New World settler came of his own volition, of course. There were the kidnapped orphans and derelicts from Britain's streets and tippling houses, the debtors from scores of Europe's jails, and the hapless Africans whose "most sacred rights of life & liberty" were violated by a "cruel war against human nature itself."[2] Regardless of their background or antecedents, all who came were soon caught up, in one way or another, in the relentless drive to find or create an Eden that would completely satisfy the aspirations of its people. Indeed, many would project "visions of liberation and perfection in the vacant spaces of the New World."[3]

The search for the perfect society was everywhere. New Englanders believed that they were approaching utopia as they developed a set of religious and economic institutions whose centralized control tolerated neither variations nor aberrations. Those in the Middle Atlantic area saw in their very diversity the key to a prosperous and peaceful future. In the South the remarkable success of a staple economy built on a reliable and durable labor system gave white settlers the opportunity to establish and maintain a social order free of the anxieties that plagued some of their neighbors to the North. It appeared to most of those in authority and

[1] The view of the New World as a liberating and regenerating force has been discussed by many writers. See the summary statement in David Brion Davis, *The Problem of Slavery in Western Culture* (Ithaca, 1966), 4–7.

[2] This was among the indictments against the king that did not appear in the final draft of the Declaration of Independence. Carl L. Becker, *The Declaration of Independence: A Study in the History of Political Ideas* (New York, 1942), 180–81.

[3] Davis, *Problem of Slavery*, 4.

leadership that only the refinements were necessary to forge a state of existence that would be lasting and satisfying.

But utopia was not quickly or easily attained—not for everybody or, indeed, for anybody. Soon, religious misfits were challenging authority in New England, stimulating in due course a whole body of restless souls who would expand into new areas to attempt what they had failed to accomplish in their first New World homes. Pennsylvanians and New Yorkers soon discovered that their vaunted pluralism was not entirely satisfactory; and they also began the westward trek. Even residents in the South, unhappy with limited profits or unable to compete in a slave economy, looked beyond the mountains to the new Southwest for new worlds to conquer. Those remaining behind seemed no happier after the dissidents departed than before. They continued to seek some new arrangement in their economy, some modification in their religious practices or in their relationships with their fellows that would be more satisfying. In some areas they began to industrialize, to embrace or at least witness the emergence of new religions, and even to free their slaves.

These new arrangements created as many problems as they solved. Industrialization required capital that was not always available. The former slaves of the "free" states, although not overwhelming in numbers, were new competitors in the free labor markets and their troublesome presence raised questions about their place in the social order. The new religions and the modernization of the old religions caused anxious moments of soul-searching and raised doubts regarding the stability of human and even divine institutions. The quest for the perfect society seemed never ending.

There was, however, one region—the South—where, thirty years before the Civil War, the search for utopia came to a grinding halt. If the quest of all southerners for perfection had been less vigorous, it was nevertheless more fortuitous; for they had discovered what they regarded as the components of a perfect civilization. In due course they became the zealous guardians of what they had discovered.

It was in the context of the sectional controversy that white southerners sharpened their conception of the perfect society; and by the time they defined it they discovered that they had achieved it. In the North the Transcendentalists advanced the idea of the perfectibility of man, but the emphasis was on how imperfect the social order was. In the South there was rather general agreement on the depravity of man, but the real emphasis was on how perfect the social order was. In a dozen areas the northern reformers sought to bring about change. They called for equal rights for women, the recognition of labor as an equal partner with management or capital in the economy, democratization of the schools, and above all, the abolition of slavery. Some were quite specific about such things as prison reform, pacifism, and religious pluralism, while others registered no confidence in the social order by retreating into communitarian settlements such as Icaria in Iowa or Zoar in Ohio.

In the South things could hardly have been better. The economic system was, for all practical purposes, perfect. As one writer claimed, slavery was the force that "beautifully blends, harmonizes, and makes them [capital and labor] as one. . . . This union of labour and capital in the same hands, counteracts . . . all those social, moral, material, and political evils which afflict the North and Western Europe."[4] Observed from any angle—whether it be the perfect distribution of labor by means of the slave system or the inevitable cooperation of the indolent with the industrious or the most effective utilization of the soil and other resources—the South's economic system was as close to perfection as one could hope for or even want.

The South's political system was, in the eyes of white southerners, a remarkable achievement. White men, relieved of the cares and the drudgery of manual toil, were free to give their attention to the problem of governance. It was, as James Henry Hammond put it, a harmony of the South's political and social institutions. "This harmony gives her a frame of society, the best in the world, and an extent of political freedom, combined with entire security, such as no other people ever enjoyed upon the face of the earth."[5] It was sheer folly, the slavocracy insisted, to argue that the essential element of a republic was the perfect political equality of all persons. On the contrary, Representative Thomas L. Clingman insisted, inequality was a significant element of the constitutional republican form.[6] As far as slavery was concerned, the Constitution itself recognized slavery and the inequality of persons. That fact was extremely important to the southern position. As William Pinkney pointedly asked in 1820, "if it be true that all the men in a republican Government must help to wield its power, and be equal in rights . . . why not all the *women*?"[7] No, the South's political system was the ideal system, even if it did not, and perhaps *because* it did not, extend equality to blacks or to women!

The role of the white woman in southern life was defined with a precision that made it almost legal. There were, of course, some legal restrictions on women such as their inability to sue or be sued alone or to own property separate from their husbands or to dispose of property they

---

[4] "American Slavery in 1857," *Southern Literary Messenger*, XXV (August 1857), 85.

[5] *Congressional Globe*, 35 Cong., I Sess., 961–62 (March 4, 1858).

[6] *Ibid.*, 30 Cong., 1 Sess., Appendix, 43–44 (December 22, 1847).

[7] *Annals of Congress*, 16 Cong., 1 Sess., 414 (February 15, 1820).

owned before marriage without the permission of their husbands.[8] But the southern woman's role as defined by custom and tradition was one infinitely more exacting than the requirements of the law. For she had to fulfill the queenly role in what Anne Firor Scott has called "The Image," while having to perform the dozens of tasks in the rather unattractive everyday life that was "The Reality." Thus "She was timid and modest, beautiful and graceful," she was " 'the most fascinating being in creation . . . the delight and charm of every circle she moves in.' " But she was also a submissive creature "whose reason for being was to love, honor, obey, and occasionally amuse her husband, to bring up his children and manage his household."[9] It could be a grim and drab business, especially when isolation from friends and insulation from many of her husband's activities doomed her to an accommodation that made the image supremely difficult to live up to.

One facet of the insulation must have been extremely painful; and that was the manner in which her lord and master, by his own conduct, defined the role of the black woman. The nocturnal visit—or, for that matter, the emboldened daytime visit—to the slave cabin, the regular trips to Charleston or Mobile or New Orleans when it was "not convenient" to have other members of the family accompany him, and the regular appearance of mulatto babies on the plantation took their toll in the capacity of the mistress to live up to expectations. But the other woman's lot must have been at least as difficult. "When she is fourteen or fifteen," one of them said, "her owner, or his sons, or the overseer, or perhaps all of them, begin to bribe her with presents. If these fail to accomplish their purpose, she is whipped or starved into submission to their will."[10]

When Frederick Law Olmsted visited Richmond in the autumn of 1855 he was "surprised at the number of fine-looking mulattoes, or nearly white colored persons" that he saw. "Many of the colored ladies were dressed not only expensively, but with good taste and effect, after the latest Parisian mode." About a fourth of those whom Olmsted observed "seemed . . . to have lost all distinguishingly African peculiarity of feature, and to have acquired, in place of it, a good deal of that voluptuousness of expression which characterizes many of the women of the south of Europe."[11] The

---

[8] Guion Griffis Johnson, "The Changing Status of the Southern Woman," in John C. McKinney and Edgar T. Thompson, eds., *The South in Continuity and Change* (Durham, 1965), 421.

[9] Scott, *The Southern Lady: From Pedestal to Politics, 1830–1930* (Chicago and London, 1970), 4.

[10] [Harriet B. Jacobs], *Incidents in the Life of a Slave Girl,* edited by Lydia Maria Child (Boston, 1861), 79.

[11] Olmsted, *A Journey in the Seaboard Slave States* (New York, 1856), 18, 28.

wife of one planter "found it impossible to long keep a maid . . . for none could escape the licentious passions of her husband, who was the father of about one-fourth of the slaves on his plantation, by his slave women."[12] Another "watched her husband with unceasing vigilance; but he was well practised in means to evade it."[13] Small wonder one mistress was beside herself with rage, when a visitor mistook one of the girl servants for a member of the slaveholder's family and addressed her with appropriate familiarity.[14] But the half million mulattoes in the United States by 1860 were an integral part of the perfect society to which the white southerner had become so attached and committed.[15]

The white southerner's social order was one in which his own sense of superiority was constantly nurtured by the subordination to which he subjected all blacks. It mattered not whether the blacks were slave or free—although their natural lot was, of course, as slaves—they existed for the sole purpose of gratifying the needs, desires, even the ego, of the whites. It was so important to the white elite to maintain the southern social order that they enlisted every white, regardless of economic or social status, in its support.[16] Color became the badge of distinction, and every white man could be proud of his own racial distinction. "We have among us," Judge Abel P. Upshur declared, "but one great class, and all who belong to it have a necessary sympathy with one another; we have but one great interest, and all who possess it are equally ready to maintain and protect it."[17]

A sense of racial superiority became at once a principal defense of slavery and an obsession with it as the "cornerstone" of southern civilization. "[P]ublic liberty and domestic slavery were cradled together," Robert Toombs declared.[18] This view complemented James Henry Hammond's argument that Africans had the requisite vigor, docility, and fidelity to perform the "drudgery of life" while the whites preoccupied themselves with "progress, civilization, and refinement."[19] Others, in large numbers, lent their philosophical speculations and their scientific "findings" to further

[12] John Thompson, *The Life of John Thompson, a Fugitive Slave* (Worcester, 1856), 31.

[13] [Jacobs], *Incidents,* 49.

[14] Lewis and Milton Clarke, *Narratives of the Sufferings of Lewis and Milton Clarke* (Boston, 1846), 20.

[15] U.S. Bureau of the Census, *Negro Population, 1790–1915* (Washington, 1918), 208.

[16] See, for example, James D. B. De Bow, *The Interest in Slavery of the Southern Non-Slaveholder* (Charleston, 1860).

[17] Upshur, "Domestic Slavery," *Southern Literary Messenger,* V (October 1839), 685.

[18] Quoted in William S. Jenkins, *Pro-Slavery Thought in the Old South* (Chapel Hill, 1935), 291.

[19] *Cong. Globe,* 35 Cong., 1 Sess., Appendix, 71 (March 4, 1858).

justification of the inevitable lot of Negroes as slaves. Physiologically they were inferior, emotionally they were juvenile, and intellectually they were hopelessly retarded. Fortunately for them, the argument went, they were the chattel of an aristocracy characterized by talent, virtue, generosity, and courage.[20]

The fact that more than one-tenth of all Negroes in the United States were free and that some of them were most accomplished in the economic and intellectual spheres did not shake the confidence of white southerners in their perfect society that refused to recognize blacks as persons worthy of any respectable social status. Free Negroes were pariahs, and the whites enacted laws to confirm it. The fact that the annual crop of runaways was regularly increasing created an apprehension that whites successfully concealed. A slave who ran away was afflicted with a disease called "drapetomania," which could be cured by flogging; or he was the victim of the evil designs of abolitionists, which could be dispelled by more stringent laws and direct action.[21] The fact that there were slave revolts and rumors of them merely confirmed the demented and immoral character of some of the slaves which could best be dealt with by constant surveillance. In any case, slavery was a great missionary institution, "one arranged by God." As Bishop Stephen Elliott of Georgia put it, "we are working out God's purposes, whose consummation we are quite willing to leave in his hands."[22]

White southerners did not leave such matters altogether in God's hands. If their religious institutions were ordained by God, they were, in turn, built and managed by man and with a view toward refining and sustaining the perfect society. In forging what one observer has called "a southern religion" the whites made certain that the orthodoxy of their churches, regardless of denomination, was in perfect harmony with the southern social order.[23] The churches condemned all signs of social instability such as intemperance, gambling, divorce, and dancing. Indeed, some religious groups objected to any and all programs of reform, holding to the view that their mission was to save souls rather than rehabilitate society.

Under the circumstances this was a better stance, even if some idealists preferred to advocate social change. As the leading politicians and planters

[20] William Stanton, *The Leopard's Spots: Scientific Attitudes Toward Race in America, 1815–59* (Chicago, 1960); and Jenkins, *Pro-Slavery Thought.*

[21] S. A. Cartwright, "Diseases and Peculiarities of the Negro," in James D. B. De Bow, ed., *The Industrial Resources, etc., of the Southern and Western States* (3 vols., New Orleans and Washington, 1853–1856), II, 322.

[22] Quoted in Jenkins, *Pro-Slavery Thought,* 217–18.

[23] Joseph H. Fichter and George L. Maddox, "Religion in the South, Old and New," in McKinney and Thompson, eds., *The South in Continuity and Change,* 359–60.

would look with suspicion if not scorn on those who criticized things as they were, it was scarcely prudent to challenge them. Better still, it proved to be the better part of wisdom to speak out for the status quo. Thus, the leading clergymen not only rationalized slavery as an institution whose severity was mitigated by the influence of Christianity, but some of them defended it with incomparable zeal. Slavery was not a sin, they told its critics, for it conformed to the highest code known to man and was based on divine revelation.[24] Indeed, it was the abolitionists who were sinful, for they refused to recognize the explicit sanctions of slavery in the Scriptures.[25] In the course of the slave controversy the southern clergy did not fail to provide their political leaders with every conceivable moral and religious defense of the institution that they could possibly use.

Thus, southerners, believing that their social system was the best that had evolved, must have been immensely pleased by the actions of their religious leaders in breaking off from their northern brethren. By 1845, when southern Baptists followed the example of the Presbyterians and Methodists in setting up their own sectional denominations, slavery had become as much a part of the religious orthodoxy of the South as the Creation in the Book of Genesis or Armageddon in the Book of Revelations. The work of promoting and defending slavery, when entrusted to the southern clergy, could not have been in safer hands. It was left for James Henley Thornwell, the brilliant Presbyterian minister and philosopher, to put the matter succinctly when he said that slavery was "one of the conditions in which God is conducting the moral probation of man— a condition not incompatible with the highest moral freedom, the true glory of the race, and, therefore, not unfit for the moral and spiritual discipline which Christianity has instituted."[26]

By 1860 it was sheer folly to criticize the social order that the white southerners had developed. They had succeeded where others had failed; and they were unwilling to countenance any suggestion for change. They insisted that it was the North that needed to change. Yet, it was the North that was pressing for change in the South. With his characteristic sneer, George Fitzhugh observed that the "invention and use of the word Sociology in free society, and of the science of which it treats, and the absence of such word and science in slave society, shows that the former is afflicted with disease, the latter healthy."[27] The North's radical movements, such as communism, socialism, and anarchism, were a clear indica-

---

[24] A classic statement of the case is in Thorton Stringfellow, "The Bible Argument: or, Slavery in the Light of Divine Revelation," in E. N. Elliott, ed., *Cotton Is King, and Pro-Slavery Arguments* (Augusta, Ga., 1860), 459–521.

[25] *Ibid.*, 461, 496–97.

[26] Thornwell, *The Rights and the Duties of Masters* (Charleston, 1850), 43–44.

[27] Fitzhugh, *Sociology for the South, or the Failure of Free Society* (Richmond, 1854), 222.

tion of its failure. If slavery was more widely accepted, man would not need to resort "to the unnatural remedies of woman's rights, limited marriages, voluntary divorces, and free love, as proposed by the abolitionists."[28]

If the South was unwilling to make any significant concessions toward change during the antebellum years, it saw no reason why defeat at the hands of the North during a bloody Civil War should justify or provide any reason for change. To be sure, the slaves had been set free, the Confederacy had collapsed, and southern agrarianism had proved no match for the northern industrial juggernaut. But that was sheer might, which was not necessarily right. "They say *right* always triumphs," Emma LeConte wailed in 1865, "but what cause could have been more just than ours?"[29] Such southerners were not prepared to accept the changes that came in the wake of the Civil War.

Emma LeConte apparently spoke for many. While white southerners were compelled to recognize the most obvious results of the war, such as the end of the legalized institution of slavery, they were willing to make few concessions regarding the place of blacks in the social order or, indeed, the existence of a new social and political order. The attempts to nullify the effects of the Reconstruction amendments and the moves at the first opportunity—in 1865 and again at the time of the overthrow—are clear indications that they would resist change with all the resources at their command. The hue and cry over the importance of preserving the integrity of the South's political institutions was never so loud as when whites were vowing to keep blacks from holding office, regardless of ability, training, or experience. By the end of the century the virtually total disfranchisement of blacks indicated how successfully southern whites had resisted change.

That the postwar readjustments were essentially a realignment to prevent revolutionary or even significant change can be seen in the superficial adjustments that white southerners made to the "new order." They would accept the former slaves as free agricultural workers, but only on terms that made a mockery of freedom. Sharecropping and peonage made it possible for the leaders of the old order to subject masses of poor whites to a new form of degradation and to keep most Negroes in a state of involuntary servitude.[30] They would accept industrialization, but only on their own terms. This would assure them that the new industry would operate

[28] Fitzhugh, *Cannibals All! or, Slaves Without Masters* (Richmond, 1857), 97–99.

[29] LeConte, *When the World Ended: The Diary of Emma LeConte*, edited by Earl S. Miers (New York, 1957), 90.

[30] The convict lease system and peonage are among the forms of involuntary servitude discussed in C. Vann Woodward, *Origins of the New South, 1877–1913* ([Baton Rouge], 1951), 212–15; George B. Tindall, *The Emergence of the New South, 1913–1945* ([Baton Rouge], 1967), 212–13; and Stetson Kennedy, *Southern Exposure* (Garden City, N.Y., 1946), 48–77.

along lines that were strikingly similar to the plantation system. The new factories were largely if not exclusively for whites; and when blacks were employed, they would have their "place" on the lowest rung on the employment ladder, with no hope of climbing up. The Negro factory worker, who could not even approach the pay window to receive his inferior wage until all whites had been paid, knew that whites would stop at nothing in their determination to degrade him.[31]

We now know that the romantic picture of woman's role in the antebellum South was more imaginary than real. In the years following the war more southern white women everywhere openly played the role that many had covertly played before the war.[32] The census continued to describe them as "keeping home" while, in fact, they were managing farms and plantations, teaching in the local schools, working in factories, and entering numerous service occupations.[33] Meanwhile, their black counterparts shared the lot consigned to all former slaves, happily with some lessening in the exploitation of them as mistresses or concubines.

Regardless of race or color, the gallant men of the South did not greet the changing role of women with enthusiasm. Some regarded it as an affront to their own masculinity, while others were certain that it was an advance herald of the doom of their way of life. If women persisted in their quest for equality, they would undermine some of the most important foundations of civilization. Only men, said Georgia's Senator Joseph E. Brown, could deal with "the active and sterner duties of life," such as farming, road building, attending public assemblages, and voting.[34] Leave such matters as voting to men, and the future of society would be in safe hands. Furthermore, if white women gained the franchise, black women voters would follow in their wake, and such a calamity was too terrible to contemplate. Surely, this must have been in the minds of some of the women who themselves opposed their own enfranchisement.[35]

And during the antebellum years the southern churches had learned their role well, so well in fact that they continued to function as principal bulwarks against change in the postwar years. Southern clergymen remained vigorous and vocal proponents of the Confederate cause, while their "churches became centers of conservative political sentiment and of resistance both to the invasion of northern culture and to the doctrine of the New South."[36] They did much to insulate the South from social as well

---

[31] J. C. Wood to J. O. Wilson, secretary, American Colonization Society, February 9, 1903, American Colonization Society Records, Series I, Vol. 292 (Manuscript Division, Library of Congress, Washington, D. C.).

[32] Woodward, *Origins of the New South*, 226–27.

[33] Scott, *Southern Lady*, 106–33.

[34] *Congressional Record*, 49 Cong., 2 Sess., 980 (January 25, 1887).

[35] Scott, *Southern Lady*, 169–70.

[36] Fichter and Maddox, "Religion in the South," 360.

as religious change by opposing church unity, a liberal theology, and a new role for religious institutions in the social order.

Southern churches could differ, almost violently, over such matters as immersion as opposed to other forms of religious induction, but they were not in conflict over the prime role of the church in preparing its children of God for the next world. Not only should its members be content with the world as it was, but they should be aggressive defenders of the social order as God ordained it. "Organized religion in the South became," as Hodding Carter put it, "the mighty fortress of the *status quo* . . ."[37] It seems fruitless to argue that the churches merely reflected the views of their communicants or even that they shaped the views of their communicants. What is important is that the conflict between the position of the church on religious and social questions was indistinguishable from the position of other southern institutions. It stood against change as firmly as any other.

It was in the area of race relations that the South of the postwar years was more committed to stability—a euphemism for the status quo—than in any other area. And since the threat of change appeared to be greater, what with Radicals enfranchising the freedmen and enacting civil rights laws, the active, vehement resistance to change was greater. That is why southern whites became active in 1865 in defining the place of Negroes in southern life and continued to do so until the definition had extended to every conceivable aspect of life. The way to make absolutely certain that the status of blacks would not change was to institutionalize and legalize their subordinate and degraded place in southern life.

If the place of blacks was to be subordinate, whites argued, they must not be permitted to participate in the affairs of government. The move that began in 1865, only to be rather mildly interrupted for a few years during Reconstruction, was resumed in the 1870s and virtually completed by the end of the century.[38] If their place was to be degraded, whites reasoned, they must be separated on all means of transportation, in all places of public accommodation, in schools, churches, hospitals, orphanages, poorhouses, jails, penitentiaries, and cemeteries.[39] They were to receive no address of courtesy but were always to extend it to whites of any age or status. Their oath in the court was to be taken on a separate

[37] Carter, *Southern Legacy* (Baton Rouge, 1950), 30.

[38] William A. Mabry, *Studies in the Disfranchisement of the Negro in the South* (Durham, 1938); Vernon L. Wharton, *The Negro in Mississippi, 1865–1890* (Chapel Hill, 1947); and Paul Lewinson, *Race, Class, & Party* (London, New York, and other cities, 1932) are among the many works that deal with the new legal status of Negroes in the postwar years.

[39] John Hope Franklin, "History of Racial Segregation in the United States," American Academy of Political and Social Science, *Annals*, CCCIV (March 1956), 1–9; and Charles S. Johnson, *Patterns of Negro Segregation* (New York and London, 1943).

Bible, and they were never to challenge the claims or assertions of whites.[40] The enforcement of these laws and customs was the responsibility of all whites, who could resort to violence with impunity to prevent any breach whatsoever.

As the South entered the twentieth century it was as deeply committed to its social order as it had ever been; and it was as determined to resist change as it had been a half century earlier. But the resistance would be more difficult, for the forces of change were everywhere, and they seemed to be sweeping everything before them. If the forces were all powerful and all pervasive, then the South would perhaps be forced to adopt what Wilbur J. Cash called a "revolution in tactics," without yielding significant ground on important matters.[41] It would thus be in a position to force the new dispensation to accommodate itself to the South's social order, rather than the other way around.

When progressivism called for a greater role for government in the regulation of many aspects of life, the South's leaders responded with their own special brand of progressivism. Indeed they took the initiative in the promotion of direct primary elections, but they made certain that the increased democracy would be for whites only.[42] The great movement to extend education swept over most of the South, but the widespread practice of discriminating against Negroes in the expenditure of public funds detracted from the movement as a truly progressive one.[43] In more than one state the reform movement was carried forward on a wave of race-baiting and race-hating, with the clear understanding that the benefits of reform, whether they were political or economic, would not breach the line that separated the races.

One of the most effective obstacles to the success of women's suffrage was the specter of race. There were, of course, the expected arguments in 1917 and 1918 that the proposed constitutional amendment permitting women to vote was "against the civilization of the South."[44] And there were some courageous southern suffragettes who *demanded* the vote. But by 1917 no leading southern member of the House of Representatives and no southern member of the Senate had declared for women's suffrage.

[40] Bertram W. Doyle, *The Etiquette of Race Relations in the South: A Study in Social Control* (Chicago, 1937).

[41] Cash, *The Mind of the South* (New York, 1941), 183.

[42] Woodward, *Origins of the New South*, 372–73.

[43] Louis R. Harlan, *Separate and Unequal: Public School Campaigns and Racism in the Southern Seaboard States, 1901–1915* (Chapel Hill, 1958), 248–69.

[44] See the communication from Caroline Patterson, president of the Georgia Association Opposed to Woman Suffrage, to Frank Clark, January 4, 1918, U. S. Congress, House of Representatives, Committee on Woman Suffrage, 65 Cong., 2 Sess., *Extending the Right of Suffrage to Women: Hearings on H. J. Res. 200, Jan. 3–7, 1918* (Washington, 1918), 327.

There persisted the argument, developed in the previous century, that the suffrage amendment would open the door to voting by Negro women and, perhaps, even Negro men. "Remember that *woman suffrage,*" one southerner cried, "means a reopening of the entire *negro suffrage* question, loss of State rights, and another period of reconstruction horrors, which will introduce a set of female carpetbaggers as bad as their male prototypes of the sixties."[45] Indeed, the connection in the minds of many southerners between race and women's suffrage was so strong that the suffragists themselves devoted much attention to the task of dispelling the connection. They did so by assuring southern whites that if they enfranchised women they could continue to disfranchise blacks![46]

Despite fierce opposition by many southerners, including some women, to the changing role of women, the march toward freeing southern women from some of the trammels of the nineteenth century seemed inexorable. In time they would sit in a few seats of power such as the governor's chair in Texas, in one Arkansas seat in the United States Senate, and on the North Carolina Supreme Court. Some of them would reject the tired and largely false claim that blacks had been lynched to protect their virtue and would call for civilized conduct to replace the barbarism of the rope and faggot.[47] But as the status of southern women improved, there remained the lag between blacks and whites of the so-called weaker sex; and few raised their voices in the effort to close the gap in wages, in educational opportunities, and in the general esteem of southern chivalry.

The secularization of life in general tended to undermine the effectiveness of southern organized religion and to challenge age-old orthodoxies and fundamentalist doctrines. It would be incorrect, however, to assume that the conservative character of southern religion disappeared altogether or that southern churches were easily adjusting to social and economic change. All too often Protestant churches in the South became centers of refuge for the most conservative social and political forces and, as in earlier years, led the resistance to change.[48]

Nowhere was the resistance to change more pronounced than in the opposition of southern religious groups to theories that challenged the literal interpretation of the Holy Scriptures. They vigorously opposed the

[45] Quoted in A. Elizabeth Taylor, *The Woman Suffrage Movement in Tennessee* (New York, 1957), 112.

[46] Elizabeth C. Stanton *et al.*, eds., *History of Woman Suffrage* (6 vols., New York and other cities, 1881–1922), V, 463.

[47] Wilma Dykeman and James Stokely, *Seeds of Southern Change: The Life of Will Alexander* (Chicago, 1962), 143–52.

[48] The conservative character of southern churches is discussed in Kenneth K. Bailey, *Southern White Protestantism in the Twentieth Century* (New York, Evanston, and London, 1964), 1–24. For a discussion of the southern churches and race see David M. Reimers, *White Protestantism and the Negro* (New York, 1965), 25–50.

teaching of what they called atheism, agnosticism, and Darwinism.[49] In Texas Governor Miriam A. Ferguson, in denouncing Darwinism, said that she would not let "that kind of rot go into Texas text-books."[50] In Tennessee a young high school teacher was found guilty of teaching evolution and was saved from punishment only by a technicality. In several states in the 1920s the Bible Crusaders put up a vigorous, if unsuccessful, fight to eliminate Darwinism from the public schools.[51] In all these efforts southern religious groups manifested a fierce and fearsome hostility to change.

In the antebellum years the fight for the freedom of the slaves was spearheaded by northern white abolitionists, although both slaves and free Negroes did much more for freedom than has generally been conceded.[52] In the post-Reconstruction years the fight for racial equality and human dignity was waged largely by blacks, with only an infrequent assist by whites. In the twentieth century the struggle to destroy every vestige of racial distinction passed through several stages, with whites—largely in the North—giving greater assistance on some occasions than on others.

In their struggle for complete equality blacks, whether in the South or in the North, could be fairly certain to receive northern white assistance in matters of transportation, voting, education in general, and in the enjoyment of places of public accommodation. They could not be nearly as certain of such support in matters of employment, housing, security in their persons, and equal education in the urban ghetto. In that sense the resistance to significant change in race relations could be as vigorous in the North as in the South.[53]

But if northern whites could react crudely and even violently to the pressures of the new masses of blacks in the urban ghettoes, they were merely catching up with a problem that southerners had faced for centuries. They were less prepared to meet it, for although they had always consigned Negroes to an inferior place in their society, they had been smug in their satisfaction that the numbers were insignificant and the "problem" correspondingly minor.[54] They had much to learn, and they became apt,

[49] Tindall, *Emergence of the New South*, 204.

[50] Quoted in Maynard Shipley, *The War on Modern Science: A Short History of the Fundamentalist Attacks on Evolution and Modernism* (New York and London, 1927), 174.

[51] The fight is summarized in Bailey, *Southern White Protestantism*, 72–91.

[52] Benjamin Quarles, *Black Abolitionists* (London, Oxford, and New York, 1969).

[53] Gilbert Osofsky, *Harlem: The Making of a Ghetto: Negro New York, 1890–1930* (New York, 1966) and Allan H. Spear, *Black Chicago: The Making of a Negro Ghetto, 1890–1920* (Chicago and London, 1967) deal with white resistance to change in two northern cities.

[54] Gilbert Osofsky, "The Enduring Ghetto," *Journal of American History*, LV (September 1968), 243–55.

even eager students of the southern method of dealing with the problem of race.

Even as Negroes left the South in increasing numbers between 1910 and 1950 white southerners discovered that the nationalizing of the race problem did not relieve them of having to confront the significantly changing status of those blacks who remained. Negroes wanted better jobs and equal pay. They wanted to vote and hold office. They wanted to desegregate public transportation and the schools. They wanted to eradicate every vestige of second-class citizenship, and they insisted that there could be no compromise with the high principles that were the birthright of *all* Americans.[55]

For white southerners this was the most serious challenge to their social order since the Civil War. They had always conceived of their "perfect society" in terms of the subordination of Negroes. Now that it was once again challenged, they would respond characteristically by that remarkable combination of praising things as they were and resisting the change that they abhorred. The South had devoted centuries to building its civilization, they insisted. Except for a few malcontents and those exposed to outside subversive influences, Negroes in the South were not only better off than elsewhere but were happy with their condition. "Go down South where I live," John E. Rankin told the House of Representatives in 1948. That is "where more Negroes are employed than anywhere else in the country, where they enjoy more happiness, more peace, more prosperity, more security and protection than they ever enjoyed in all history."[56]

But change was taking place so rapidly that there was scarcely time to celebrate the old order. Two world wars and a New Deal had facilitated the South's industrial revolution. Government, federal and state, had introduced social controls and social programs that poverty and privation forced the South to accept. The successful drive of southern women to liberate themselves from their long entrapment was greatly accelerated by changes and reforms in the political and economic spheres. Even religious institutions felt the winds of change and responded with various forms of accommodation. And in all these changes white southerners asked the age-old question, "How will it affect the blacks?" It was an affirmation of V. O. Key's assertion that "Whatever phase of the southern . . . process one seeks to understand, sooner or later the trail of inquiry leads to the Negro."[57]

Not only were these numerous developments affecting the blacks in a

[55] Rayford W. Logan, ed., *What the Negro Wants* (Chapel Hill, 1944). See also the "Publisher's Introduction" by W. T. Couch, in which he expressed disagreement with most of the contributors to the volume.

[56] *Cong. Record,* 80 Cong., 2 Sess., 4543 (April 15, 1948).

[57] V. O. Key, Jr., *Southern Politics in State and Nation* (New York, 1949), 5.

dozen different ways, but specific developments in the area of race relations overshadowed other disquieting events. Some southern white leaders observed what was happening on the racial front in utter disbelief, while others regarded it as their greatest challenge that must be confronted and combated. In the process some of their responses were as graceless as they were reprehensible.

When President Harry S. Truman issued executive orders and recommended legislation to protect Negroes in their enjoyment of civil rights, Senator Richard B. Russell, Jr., of Georgia condemned the moves as steering this country toward a "police state" and threatened to introduce legislation looking toward the removal of blacks from the South.[58] In 1947 a federal district court judge, J. Waties Waring, ruled that the Democratic primary of South Carolina could not exclude Negroes from participating in its elections. Immediately, a South Carolina member of the House of Representatives, W. J. Bryan Dorn, wailed that it opened the way for Communists to vote in the Democratic primary.[59] Another representative from South Carolina, L. Mendel Rivers, predicted that the decision would cause bloodshed, and he seriously considered the possibility of instituting impeachment proceedings against Judge Waring.[60] The return of Harry Truman to the White House in 1948 and the refusal of the United States Supreme Court to review the Waring decision effectively subdued the confrontation that Russell and Rivers and company sought to bring about.

White southerners all across the region attempted to meet the changes that blacks sought in the field of education by launching a massive program to equalize the facilities and programs in white and Negro schools. If they approached success in this ploy, it was effectively undermined by the Supreme Court decision in 1954 that declared legally segregated schools unconstitutional. The South's response was varied, but the major response was rejection of the law of the land. Its leading members of the United States Congress—more than one hundred of them—signed a manifesto that praised the "separate but equal" decision of 1896 as "founded on elemental humanity and commonsense" and condemned the 1954 decision as an "unwarranted exercise of power by the Court" that "planted hatred and suspicion where there has been heretofore friendship and understanding."[61]

The signatories of this "Declaration of Constitutional Principles" were

---

[58] Atlanta *Constitution*, July 27, 1948; Charleston *News and Courier*, July 28, 1948.

[59] *Cong. Record*, 80 Cong., 2 Sess., Appendix, 4654–55 (July 27, 1948).

[60] Charleston *News and Courier*, August 5, 6, 1948.

[61] *Cong. Record*, 84 Cong., 2 Sess., 4515–16 (March 12, 1956).

among the South's most respected and influential leaders. In declaring that they would "use all lawful means to bring about a reversal" of the decision, they vowed to "refrain from disorders and lawless acts." But Senator Harry F. Byrd, Sr., was already developing a plan of "massive resistance" that in due course would compromise the principles of law and order to which he and his colleagues claimed to be committed.[62]

While it is not possible to assess the impact of the southern manifesto on subsequent developments, there can be no gainsaying that it set the stage and tone for the resistance that followed during the next decade or so. The search for alternatives to desegregated schools led to a veritable spate of maneuvers ranging from pupil placement to the closing of some public schools and the establishment of private all-white schools. The path of massive resistance led to the establishment of white citizens' councils and violent confrontations with blacks who had resorted to various forms of protest and demonstration against noncompliance with the decisions in their communities.

It is not the interracial confrontations, important and tragic as they were, that are of prime significance in this discussion. It is the South's confrontation with change, its response in defending what it regarded as a perfect society, that is instructive. The massive resistance, the fire hoses, police dogs, and the electronic cattle prods were, in a real sense, a desperate but futile confrontation with the inexorable forces of change. It all added up to the hopeless defense of a position that, in terms of the nation's laws and its expressed social philosophy, was illogical and indefensible.

The futility of this defense lay in the failure to take into account the myths and fallacies that were the basis of the white South's conception of its perfect society. It failed to recognize the inherent inconsistencies and contradictions in its argument that it could enjoy a social order that was founded on the exploitation of a group that was an integral part of that social order. It failed to see that in arrogating to a few the privileges and rights that belonged to the many, it was depriving itself of the resources that could do so much to create the social order that had, for so long, proved elusive. Its inflexibility had resulted in driving out much of its best talents, white as well as black, that could not flourish or even survive where confrontation with change meant unreasoned and unreasonable resistance to free expression and experimentation. It had also resulted in the development of techniques to defy and circumvent both law and custom. Its obsession was to maintain a government, an economy, an arrangement of the sexes, a relationship of the races, and a social system that had never existed,

[62] J. Harvie Wilkinson III, *Harry Byrd and the Changing Face of Virginia Politics, 1945–1966* (Charlottesville, 1968), 113–54.

as Paul M. Gaston has suggested, except in the fertile imagination of those who would not confront either the reality that existed or the change that would bring them closer to reality.[63]

One would hope that a region whose experience and talents had proved to be so ample in so many ways—in the creative arts, in certain aspects of the science of government, and in the capacity to transform so many phases of its economic order—might yet be able to confront fundamental changes in its social order. For only by such confrontation, tempered by a healthy recognition of the importance of change, can the South expect to survive as a viable and effective unit in the body politic and to point the way toward the ordering of a truly vital social organism where men and women, black and white, can live together in their common search for a better society.

[63] Gaston, *The New South Creed: A Study in Southern Mythmaking* (New York, 1970).

22

Tolerating the South's Past

Francis Butler Simkins

To follow the dictates of the "scientific historians," that is, to reconstruct the southern past as it acually happened (*wie es eigentlich gewesen*), is almost impossible given the fact that the splendid legacy of its history is in many ways a "reality" too elusive to be totally explained in objective terms. Indeed, the South's "semi-invisible" past—its myth-saturated history—must be granted as great a measure of concern as its more visible "past politics." Clearly, one must remain attentive to both "history as actuality" and "history as perceived"—to both definitions of myth prescribed for this work. Since the South is, in many ways, the product of an overactive imagination, both regional and national, southern history must be told both in terms of distorted historical inaccuracies and the subtle peculiarities of the southern mind which work to "fuse concept and emotion into an image." Thus, the distinction between a *historical* and a *fictitious* South becomes a particularly difficult one. Reemphasizing this significant dichotomy, Francis Butler Simkins, late of Longwood College, Farmville, Virginia, here forwards further commentary on the South—both of history and historical memory. Any intellectually coherent statement on the South's past, argues Professor Simkins, necessitates a dual perspective: one view focused on the "facts" of the southern experience, the other keyed to the elemental "truth" contained in southern legend. The southerner, and for that matter anyone who would wish to share his experience, must function in a state of controlled ambiguity. Though seduced and fascinated by a legendary South of the mythic imagination, one need not forfeit a tough-minded commitment to

Francis Butler Simkins, "Tolerating the South's Past," *Journal of Southern History*, 21 (February 1955), 3–16. Copyright 1955 by the Southern Historical Association. Reprinted by permission of the Managing Editor.

scholarly integrity. In striking contrast to John Hope Franklin who
contends that the South's impulse for the mythical has served to
frustrate her ability to accommodate change, Professor Simkins
seeks not only to tolerate but to heed as real the "legends, the
underlying prejudices and superstitions, of the people." One must
be ever vigilant, counsels Simkins, not to fall complete victim to
"the danger of equating facts with truth."

The Age of Enlightenment represented the Middle Ages as a Gothic night
—an interlude of ignorance and superstition when men were enveloped in
a cowl, oblivious to the wonders of knowledge, and concerned only with
escape from the miseries of this world and of hell. Voltaire said that Dante
was considered a great poet because no one read him and that a Gothic
cathedral was a monument to the stupidity of its builders. The humility of
holy men and the faith of the Catholic offended the egotism, skepticism,
and common sense of the leaders of the Enlightenment.

Historians of the nineteenth and twentieth centuries have thrown aside
the conceits of those who went before them and have learned to appraise
the medieval age in terms of its own values. It is now recognized as a
period when the Christian church and an imaginative architecture flowered,
when artists were humble enough to glorify God rather than themselves,
and when universities, chivalry, and vernacular literatures had their
beginnings.

The reputation of the region of the United States below the Potomac
today suffers from the same forces from which the Middle Ages suffered at
the hands of historians during the Enlightenment. The historians of the
South often do not grasp the most elementary concept of the sound historian: the ability to appraise the past by standards other than those of the
present. They accept a fanatical nationalism which leaves little room for
sectional variations, a faith in Darwinian progress which leaves no room
for static contentment, and a faith in the American dream of human equality which leaves little room for one person to get ahead of another except
in making money. In theory at least, our historians refuse to tolerate the
concept of "all sorts and conditions of men" of which *The Book of Common Prayer* speaks.

Growing out of the uncritical acceptance of the creed of contemporary
Americans by the historians of the South are certain concrete dogmas.
Among them are: the church and the state should be separate, but not the
school and the state; school but not church attendance should be compulsory; universal education is better than folk culture; political democracy

is better than aristocracy; freedom is better than slavery; nationalism is better than provincialism; urban standards are better than rural standards; small farms are better than plantations; the larger the number of voters the better the commonwealth; and the two-party system is better than the harmony of one party.

I am not asking the abandonment of any of these dogmas as bases for action in the world of today. These dogmas make up the American Dream on which much of American prosperity and hope is based. I am asking that Southern historians not hide the fact that their ancestors did not put these dogmas into practice in the aspects of their lives which explain their regionalism. I am also asking that Southern historians not accuse their ancestors of being stupid or unreasonable when they did not do so.

The friendly historians of the region who accept the ideal of human equality seem ashamed of the degree to which the South has not attained this ideal. In defense of their beloved region, the hopeful among them find evidences of the struggle of the lower classes for a greater degree of equality. They present the followers of Nathaniel Bacon as yeomen farmers rebelling against an oligarchy of planters. They give credence to many rumors of slave insurrections, and they often envisage the common people rising against political oligarchies. Their faith in the benefits of two political parties has led them to predict, for the past eight decades, the breakup of the solid South and the coming of a state of rectitude like that of New York or Illinois. They are apologetic over the existence in the South of the sharpest social distinction in all America: that between the white man and the Negro. They hail breaks in the color line as forecasts of the good times a-coming.

Their attitude when proclaimed by publicists and politicians may be justified as part of the policy of accommodation to the dominant ideals of the ruling part of the United States. But such diplomacy applied to the issues of the past convicts historians of naïveté or what the French and the Germans call Anglo-Saxon hypocrisy.

Those who accept national unity as the ultimate goal of all Americans find it difficult to defend a region whose chief distinction is that it attempted to destroy that unity. The friendly historian often chooses states' rights or secession as the theme of his writings. Then, when he starts writing, he deplores the existence of the things which, if they had never existed, would have deprived him of his theme. He joyously emphasizes the existence of minorities who adhered to the national rather than the sectional cause. He gives the honors to such nationalists as Andrew Jackson and Andrew Johnson instead of to such divisionists as John Randolph and John C. Calhoun. He seems almost to get his inspiration from William T. Sherman who felt justified in imposing a cruel punishment upon the South because it tried to destroy the national unity.

Why do not our historians take their cue from Sinclair Lewis when he condemns America to an esthetic hell because most of its provinces have succeeded in ironing out their provincial differences? Why are they not proud of the fact that Lewis' criticisms apply least of all to the South? If this were not true, the South would not be worth writing about. So let the historians take for themselves the task of understanding and appreciating the sectional variations.

There is a reality about the South which historians with egalitarian standards find hard to understand or appreciate. This reality is that many of the so-called advances in equality turn out to be imaginary. Freedom, for example, to the early Georgians meant revolt against the tyranny of foreign despots who wanted to prohibit slavery and large estates as a means of preventing the colony from having the social and economic inequalities of the other Southern colonies. The so-called rising of the Virginians in the American Revolution against oppressors turns out to be, in the light of modern researches, the struggle of an aggresive aristocracy against an official oligarchy, with the common man following noisily the leadership of his social betters. There is much that is artificial and sentimental in Virginia's greatest political philosopher advocating the equality of man and at the same time owning slaves, living in a house which Europeans would call a palace, and tolerating a political machine more oligarchical than that of Harry F. Byrd.

A paradox of Southern history is that progress in political democracy was often followed by the desire of the newly enfranchised to destroy certain aspects of equality. Those who got the vote under the Jacksonian reforms of the 1830's were not displeased when their leader was transformed into a planter and a Southern gentleman; and when a catty journalist in our day accused Rachel Jackson of smoking a pipe, there was resentment among the descendants of the original Jacksonians. The Jacksonian reforms were followed by the strengthening of the slave code and the disfranchisement of the free persons of color. The freer exercise of the suffrage by the common white man in the 1890's was followed by the Jim Crow laws and the disfranchisement of most of the Negroes.

The Southern Negro has never got much beyond the rhetorical stage in his enthusiasm for closing the social gap which has separated him from the Southern whites. As a slave, he never carried out a general rising against his masters. The equalities which after the Civil War were supposed to be his never got beyond a narrow political stage. One of the reasons for this is that the Negro never made a determined demand for social equality. In withdrawing from the white churches he surrendered an element of social intimacy with the white man which he had experienced under slavery. In our day he has been invited to attend white churches, but in many cases he does not want to accept this invitation. The most exalted of outside interventionists in the social arrangements of the South recently restored to the Negro the suffrage, but he turned around and joined the political party of the white oligarchy.

Much is written by our historians concerning the Negro's discontent with his caste status and concerning the progress he has made in changing this status. It cannot be denied that there is some reality in these assertions, but it is often forgotten that the white man has more often been discontented with the Negro than the Negro with the white man. Those of us who, through the years, have known Southern life intimately are familiar with the constant complaints leveled against the exasperating race. The white man has been able to act on his complaints more effectively than the Negro has on his. In recent decades the white man, for example, sharpened the color line and took business and residential opportunities away from the black man.

It is time that historians who explain or defend the South recognize the existence of social hierarchy in their section. They can be sympathetic toward it without being illogical, remembering that arguments advanced for social gradations by Plato are as logical as arguments advanced to the contrary. They should realize that the arguments of Jefferson Davis and James D. B. De Bow in favor of the gradations in slave society had more influence on the nonslaveholding whites than did the arguments advanced by Hinton R. Helper and other enemies of Southern social practices. They should know that the color line was created to sustain the most important fact in Southern history. Two biologically aggressive races have dwelt together in large numbers for 385 years without the ruling race losing its integrity of blood. Without this fact there would be no South in the social or psychological sense; the region between the Potomac and the Rio Grande would be just a geographical expression.

The historian of the South should accept the class and race distinctions of his region unless he wishes to deplore the region's existence. He should display a tolerant understanding of why in the South the Goddess of Justice has not always been blind, why there have been lynchings and Jim Crow laws, why the legend of the Cavaliers exists, and why, as William Alexander Percy puts it, "Even today from Virginia to Texas ten thousand crepuscular old maids in ghostly coveys and clusters" seek to trace their ancestors. Our historian should stop trying to prove that the maidens of the Old South did not always have wasp waists and stand on colonnaded porches attended by bandannaed mammies who did not have wasp waists. At least one Southern historian, Francis P. Gaines, has retired from the iconoclastic task of trying to prove that the Old South was not what it is supposed to have been. He has become the keeper of the tomb of the knight whom not even our most energetic fact-finder has accused of being unworthy of the company of King Arthur.

A logical consequence of the disparagement of the sectional values is that the leader who tried hardest to break the national unity has fared so badly at the hands of his biographers. They condemn Jefferson Davis as a prolonged conspirator against the Union. But the facts show that as late as 1860 he, as a United States senator, was advocating appropriations for the army he was to fight in less than a year. A proper sympathy for the sectional values would perhaps lead to a condemnation of Davis because he did not become a conspirator against the Union soon enough. Unlike Caesar or Hitler, Davis was not one of the great revolutionists of history; he was too honorable for that. Unlike William L. Yancey and R. Barnwell Rhett, he was slow in understanding that the North was in a revolutionary conspiracy against the Constitution as he interpreted it and could be answered effectively only by counterrevolution. Allen Tate, the poet, is the only biographer who condemns Davis for not understanding that the aim of the plutocratic democracy of the North was to crush his beloved Southland.

Davis should be praised for at last recognizing the forces arrayed against his section and then heroically defending its concept of truth and justice. Despite physical weaknesses, he maintained a proud but ragged nation for four years against the powers of wealth, progress, and patriotism. After defeat he did not repent.

For his failure to repent, historians will not forgive Davis. He did not respond to the new wave of nationalism which came after the Civil War. He was no pragmatist, no evolutionist. Until his death he remained in spirit the slavemaster, the soldier who found greatest virtue in continuing the battle charge after the enemy has inflicted a grievous wound, and remained the scholastic who accepted the Bible and the Constitution just as they are written. He was as optimistic in his devotion to the antique values of the South as was Don Quixote to the antique values of an older land. If the historians of the South were as tolerant of our past as are the European historians of theirs, they would confer on the defeated President of the Confederacy as many honors as have been conferred on the famous Spanish knight.

Friendly Southern historians bolster the pride of the section by exaggerating the ways in which the South approximated the achievements of the North. Ignoring the Negro third of the population, they emphasize the degree to which the Old South achieved political democracy and universal education. Remembering prejudices against the large landowner, they emphasize the role of the yeoman farmer in Southern agriculture. Ignoring the prejudices of the section against foreigners, they make much of isolated cases of foreigners who found the South congenial. And, in refutation of the assertion that the region has been a Sahara of talent, long lists have been compiled of Southerners who played eminent roles in the building of the nation.

The candid observer must admit that, according to the urban standards of the North and of Europe, Frederick Law Olmsted's harsh judgment on the paucity of Southern culture has remained sound for most of the hundred years since this nosy New Englander wrote. Perhaps the reason the *Dictionary of American Biography* has articles on only 724 natives of Virginia compared with articles on 1,763 natives of Massachusetts is that Southerners have been indifferent to those in their midst who have had latent talents in music, sculpture, painting, and the other arts. Here in the South Carolina of my youth the only art we recognized was English and Northern literature. We read Walter Scott and James Fenimore Cooper; we did not read William Gilmore Simms. We recognized native greatness only in war and in politics.

It is true that in recent years the South has learned to recognize native eminence in literature and in business. But a Southern book to be acceptable to Southerners must first hit the New York sounding board. Our distinguished businessmen are often dependent on Wall Street to promote and finance the South's industrial expansion. For mechanical inventions, the most creative of American achievements, the South has been utterly dependent upon the North. Its people do not invent or manufacture the machinery which makes possible Southern industry. Industrially the section is still as colonial as Asia or South America.

Our historians should explain or justify these supposed deficiencies of the South by showing that its genius is rural, not urban; that the larger the cities grow the more countrified they become because of the rural origin of their newer inhabitants. Our historians should also explain that our townsmen build country-style houses, that they have little or nothing to contribute to the urban amenities, and that they support few good restaurants, theaters, orchestras, or book stores. As in the days of the English traveler George W. Featherstonbaugh, they talk of hogs, horses, and cows when they are not talking about the mechanical contrivances Northerners have sold them.

The true Southerner should take pride in the fact that his section's fame is based on tobacco, hogs, rice, and cotton, and that its greatest man is the country gentleman with his cult of hospitality, his sense of leisure, his neglect of the passion for trade, his capacity to refurbish old mansions and to build new ones in imitation of the old, and his creative interest in the rehabilitation of antique furniture. In his capacity as a farmer the Southern gentleman has been creative from the days of John Rolfe and George Washington down to the day of our professors of agriculture and of our merchant-farmers. Our professors of agriculture perfect new seeds and varieties of animals; our merchant-farmers establish farms with green pastures which serve as models for professional farmers. If the South has had an internal revolution since 1865, it is in a type of endeavor in which the people have adhered most firmly to the traditions of their ancestors. The revolution has been in agriculture.

Southern historians, trapped by the belief that education is a cure-all, have exaggerated the accomplishments of formal schooling. They like to prove that Sir William Berkeley was inaccurate when he said that there were no free schools in seventeenth-century Virginia. They are dazzled that today we have "a triumphant 'progressive' education which progresses even faster than the North." They gloss over the defects of our much-praised educational system. They should remember that our public schools have affronted the American dogma of the universality of education, treating the Negroes differently from other people and at one time prohibiting them from going to school. They should realize that we of the South indulged to a greater degree than other people in "the education that does not educate" in the sense of changing people, presumedly for the better, in the arts of living and in outlook on life.

The historians would be wise to admit the defects of Southern education as measured by the proclaimed goals of American public schools; indeed they might be skeptical of these goals. They might admit that Berkeley was not a complete fool when he inveighed against schools and presses. The defender of this seventeenth-century gentleman can find comfort in high scholarly authority of the twentieth century. Arnold J. Toynbee wrote in 1947: "The bread of universal education is no sooner cast upon the water than a shoal of sharks [the presslords] arises from the depths and devours the children's bread under the educator's very eyes." Southern historians should realize that the faith in the rule of the educated common man has brought us no nearer the millennium than were our ancestors in the eighteenth century.

Southern historians agree with Montesquieu that a political structure should "fit the humor and disposition of the people," and yet they judge the educational achievements of a rural people by standards imported from Prussia by way of New England. In New England the Prussian-type school was loaded with antislavery sentiments and with notions of social reform repulsive to a region of Christians not dominated by hopes of earthly perfection. The leveling tendencies of the new schools ran counter to the Old South's conception of hierarchy. Their content was more suited for those who needed guidance for town life than for a people whose chief task was to subdue a wilderness and to establish farms.

Someone should tell that the South's resistance to formal schooling did not grow out of laziness or stupidity. This resistance was a vital part of the region's attempt to survive as a social and cultural entity. The South unconsciously fought against the idea that the school be allowed to iron out provincial differences in order to make the Southern states into undifferentiated units of the republic. Southerners have preserved their folkways and ancestral superstitions. Thereby they have avoided the fate of the people of Hawaii, a people who have deliberately escaped their ancestral heritage in order to be Americanized through the public schools. Such a people lack creative originality.

Our chroniclers of the past should quit being ashamed of the cloud of illiteracy which once hung over their province. They should wake up to the fact that the unschooled Uncle Remus was among the wisest Southerners. They have stressed to such a degree the benefits of the schools that they have neglected the triumphs of informal training outside the school. This informal education was good because it was useful. Our colonial and frontier ancestors put the arts of subduing the wilderness first; they learned to use the ax and the rifle extremely well. With some justice they regarded formal education as an adornment of the upper classes.

The dark spot on Southern civilization of denying formal education to the slaves can be wiped out by an understanding of what was accomplished in the so-called school of the plantation in which the barbarian captive from Africa was Anglicized. This was a type of training more effective than anything the South has experienced since. The slave was so well inoculated with Anglo-American culture that almost all elements of his African background disappeared. The Negro imbibed the rich heritage of European folklore and became so skilled in English handicrafts and in the intricate practices of plantation agriculture that he was perhaps better educated in the industrial arts than those Negroes who have lived since the time of Booker T. Washington.

The acceptance by our historians of the national faith in equality has led them to neglect the constructive role of class distinctions and aristocracy in Southern culture. The masses of the South imitate the classes with so much enthusiasm that most of the section's approved practices and attitudes are of upper-class origin. I can think of only two popular social diversions of lower-class origin. They are jazz music and corn whisky. The aristocratic pretensions of all classes are so strong that everybody thinks of himself as a gentleman. Wilbur J. Cash observes that the yeoman farmers of the Old South adopted from the plantation aristocracy "a kindly courtesy, a level-eyed pride, an easy quietness, a barely perceptible flourish of bearing, which for all its obvious angularity and fundamental plainness was one of the finest things the Old South produced." And the Jeeter Lesters, for all their ignorance and barbarism, possessed aristocratic attitudes, hating manual toil and taking on, as Cash says, "a sort of unkempt politeness and ease of port, which rendered them definitely superior to their peers in the rest of the country."

A majority of Southerners believes that the nearest approach to heaven this side of the grave is that aristocratic perfection known as the Old South. This was not only the belief of Walter Hines Page's "mummies," but also of such innovators as Daniel A. Tompkins, Ben Tillman, and Tom Watson. One finds it in the writings of such divergent persons as Thomas Nelson Page and William Faulkner. Then it was, so runs the legend of the Old South, that the Virginia Gentleman lived in a feudal splendor that was justified by the belief that he had ancestors from the novels of Walter Scott; that the Mississippi Gentleman's comparable splendors were justified by the belief that he had Virginia ancestors. These beliefs are supplemented by the assertion that the Confederate soldier because he was always brave was also always virtuous. The fact that all classes in the South cherish the aristocratic concept has brought about a unity of spirit which results in a friendly tie between the masses and the classes.

A host of Southern historians would prove, through the collection of multitudes of facts, that things were not what they were supposed to have been. Census reports are used to prove that the number of planters who owned a hundred slaves was small; that plantation houses were more often like factories than like Walter Scott's castles; that beautiful maidens were then not more numerous than they are now. Some historians are at pains to prove that the ancestors were not Virginia gentlemen and that the ancestors of the ancestors were not knights. Numerous investigators accuse the colonial Virginians of being ordinary persons. James Branch Cabell, with a vicious glee, befouls the nests of the ancestors of the ancestors by creating a repulsive age of chivalry.

Some Southern historians would change a belief which both friend and foe have taught us to think was the essence of the Old South. They tell us that the distinctions between aristocracy and humble folk were not so great as was once supposed; thereby would they take away from the aristocracy many of the distinctions of superior position. They tell us that the poor whites were not so numerous as was once supposed and that there was a substantial middle class which had no reason to feel inferior to the planter aristocracy. On the other hand, others, touched by twentieth-century concepts of human welfare, would let us know that the glory and glamor of the ante-bellum aristocracy was paid for by the humbling of the masses of both races.

A small shelf of books has been written by Southerners proving that all Confederate soldiers were not brave and loyal Christian gentlemen; that in fact many of them were seditionists, draft dodgers, and deserters. To add to the disillusionment, Vann Woodward advances the belief that many of the brave and loyal veterans of the Confederate army did not possess common honesty. In page after page of interesting but disillusioning data, he parades paladins of the Confederacy from John B. Gordon to Basil Duke as a second generation of scalawags who robbed the land they professed to love.

This revision of Southern legends is factually correct, based as it is upon much research in manuscripts and other original documents. But it carries with it the danger of equating facts with truth. The facts that can be unearthed by research in as complex a subject as human behavior are so infinite in extent that one set of facts can be unearthed to refute another set of facts. The masters of research, for example, have for a generation or two been digging up data to prove whether or not the gentry of Virginia are descended from King Charles' Cavaliers. The evidence is so varied, and the English and Southern methods of computing aristocratic descent so different, that the reader has not yet been able to draw conclusions.

Sometimes Southern historians forget that what is often important to Southerners is not what actually happened but what is believed to have happened. Southerners want their historians to do them concrete good by revealing or creating ancestors for them. An ironic fact about Southern historical writing is that the only practitioners of the craft able to make a living from their efforts are the genealogists. Their unique vice or virtue is that they are able to dig up useful ancestors where there may have been none before. Such discoveries give a person of declining fortunes a satisfaction not unlike the consolations of religion or philosophy. Such discoveries, on the other hand, give persons of energy and ambition something with which to justify their assumptions of social and civic worth.

Disillusioning researches in the records of the South's past have not generally impressed the Southern people. This sort of revelation must go unheeded if the South is to survive as a cultural entity.

Donald Davidson says that the key to Southern literary greatness is not the literature of protest but "the literature of acceptance." Obedience to this standard, Mr. Davidson believes, is why the Southern imaginative literature of our times is appreciated by the critics and the reading public. William Faulkner, Eudora Welty, and Robert Penn Warren write in the most modern manner; at times their stories are sordid. They tell everything good and bad about the South. They only reject what Davidson calls "the false knowledge" of ignoring or deploring aspects of Southern life and character. They are not, like so many of our historians, narrow democrats and nationalists who measure the South's past by the values of educated Americans of today.

The standards of factual accuracy demanded of the Southern historian are so exacting that he is often frightened out of writing a book because he must face the holy terror of having his factual errors exposed by well-intentioned reviewers. A strange sense of reticence prevents him from telling a tale which may be a revelation of the truth about the teller and his people. Think of the fate of one of our historians if he were to join Faulkner in asserting that our mulattoes were descendants of Yankee soldiers and carpetbaggers. The Southern novelist is more concerned with the meaning of events than with the technical accuracy of their recording. He heeds the legends, the undying superstitions and prejudices of the people. His willingness and ability to use these in his tales is where his genius lies.

Southern historians often ignore the poor whites, rationalize them out of existence, or treat them as fit subjects for social-welfare programs. The novelists, on the other hand, portray them without apology or gratuitous sympathy and endow them with pride and humor. William Faulkner gives us a mob of country folk too chivalric to push aside a lady guard in order to lynch a Negro.

Religion as a constructive force in Southern life is generally unappreciated by our historians except for what it has done for education and social progress. Christian Fundamentalists are scolded for their capture of the Southern mind in the early nineteenth century and for their interference in science and politics in the twentieth century. The great Baptist church is tactfully ignored because, perhaps, it is an example of the union of Southern democracy with absolutism too indelicate and lusty for believers in Jeffersonian democracy. On the other hand, the novelists possess an affecting sympathy for the traditional religion. Ellen Glasgow in *Vein of Iron* and William Faulkner in *Light in August,* for example, demonstrate a tender understanding of Southern clergymen who were persecuted by their congregations.

Vann Woodward in *Origins of the New South* complains of the lack of understanding among Southern historians of the strain of violence which runs through Southern history. If measured at all by our historians, it is in terms of civics textbooks. Violence, on the other hand, is a dominant theme in Southern fiction. There murderous gentlemen and outlaws are presented with compassion and explained in terms of grand tragedy.

The historian of the South should join the social novelist who accepts the values of the age and the section about which he writes. He should learn to identify truth with legend and with faith as competently as he has learned to identify truth with facts. By mixing sympathy, understanding, and a bit of kindness with his history, he might attract the people about whom he writes to read his books. And this could be done without sacrificing scholarly integrity.

Not all historians who rise above the level of scholarly compilations are ashamed of the peculiar standards of their section. Some of them write "the literature of accommodation." The Southern historian who has won the greatest applause writes of the heroes of the Confederacy without arguing whether or not they were quixotic. The best recognized historian of the Old South pictures plantation life without assuming that it was a grand mistake. Another historian examines the literature on the poor whites without moralizing against them because they were not as thrifty as their social betters. A recent historian of the New South joins William Faulkner in exposing the true tragedy of the South. It was not the defeat at Appomattox but the truckling of both scalawag and Bourbon, both materialist and idealist, to alien values.

23

The South, America's Will-o'-the-Wisp Eden

Charles P. Roland

Perhaps the clearest demonstration that myth remains a significant imperative of the southern mind is the South's historically persistent belief that she stands on the verge of becoming a New World Eden. Indeed, if hopes could have made it so the South would have achieved the millennium decades ago. As noted by Charles P. Roland of the University of Kentucky, the myth of southern millennialism has been revisited many times. A vision of the full-flowering of southern achievement seems to have had its genesis in pre-colonial times, and to have enjoyed sustained and positive reinforcement ever since. To be sure, recurrent notions of southern economic fulfillment have never suffered for lack of apologists. In this sense, Henry Grady and Walter Prescott Webb have functioned as latter-day Sir Walter Raleighs. The frustrations of poverty—the blatant correlation between economic deprivation and the southern experience—have thus too often been obscured by augurings of an imminent stage of "conspicuous consumption" for the total South. Utopian images to the contrary, the Southland has consistently remained "the nation's economic problem No. 1." The great irony in this regard, of course, is that the South is purported to have a particularly keen sense of her historical past. The southerner, we are told, *remembers*. He has a "historical consciousness" seldom shared by his fellow Americans. But despite this supposed affinity for history—this remembrance of things past—the South, regarding

Charles P. Roland, "The South, America's Will-o'-the-Wisp Eden," *Louisiana History,* 11 (1970), 101–119. Reprinted by the permission of the Louisiana Historical Association.

her economic realities, seems to suffer a fitful case of "historical amnesia." Frustrated utopias seem to have fed rather than diminished the clear image of the South as a beckoning El Dorado.

In an address to the leaders of the Democratic Party in New Orleans, Louisiana, during the 1964 presidential campaign, President Lyndon Johnson summoned a vision of a future Southland flowing with milk and honey. "I want us to put behind the problems of the past and turn toward the promise of the future," he said. "For Louisiana, and for the South, the meaning of our victory [in the forthcoming presidential election] will be a fresh burst of progress, not a new spate of problems." Calling upon the South to forget both the Mason-Dixon line and the color line in her pursuit of prosperity, and to accept the counsel of Robert E. Lee that she lay aside old animosities and rear her sons to be Americans, the President cast a tempting horoscope for the region. "From the tip of Texas to the tip of Florida," he declared, "this crescent of the Gulf offers one of the great opportunities of the Western World. . . . I see a day when New Orleans will stand as a queen city on this crescent—a center of trade with the world—a center of culture for the nation—a terminal for waterways reaching into the heart of America . . . a good and gracious city for your families to call home." Then in conclusion, "We are not going to lose that tomorrow in division over things of the past."[1]

True enough, President Johnson spoke these words as a politician seeking votes. Yet, after full allowance is made for political motives, his remarks still have the ring of sincerity. One observer aptly said of him, "He dreams of a South rid at last of its ancient racial grievances entering a new age of abundance and gracing the whole nation with a fresh flowering of Southern achievement."[2]

Indeed, President Johnson would have been alien to an abiding current of American thought if he had not believed in the promise of an abundant South. Since the first camp was pitched by Englishmen on Roanoke Island almost four centuries ago, Southern citizens and observers alike have been predicting that the region was just about to become the garden spot of the universe. "The air is temperate and wholesome there," wrote a chronicler of Sir Walter Raleigh's venture upon Roanoke Island, "the soil is fertile. . . .

[1] New Orleans *Times Picayune*, October 10, 1964. This essay was originally presented by the author in an address sponsored by the Institute of Southern Culture, Longwood College, Farmville, Va., and is published here with the permission of that organization.
[2] *Ibid.*

and in a short time the planters may raise . . . commodities . . . [that] will enrich themselves and those who trade with them."[3]

The happy theme of Southern bounty pervaded the literature of all her early settlements. "Virginia equals, if not exceeds all others in goodness of climate, soil, health, rivers, plenty, and all necessaries and conveniences of life. . . ." wrote a booster of the mother colony of the South. He believed that the very temperament of the Virginians was superior to that of other colonists. "If New England be called a receptacle of dissenters, and an Amsterdam of religion," he said, "Pennsylvania the nursery of Quakers, Maryland the retirement of Roman Catholicks, North Carolina the refuge of runaways, and South Carolina the delight of Buccaneers and pyrates, Virginia may be justly esteemed the happy retreat of true Britons and true churchmen for the most part; neither soaring too high nor drooping too low, consequently should merit the greater esteem and encouragement."[4]

The Carolinas also were said to abound in all resources needed for the production of wealth;[5] and the marvels of Georgia prompted one admirer to turn poet in his effort to do them justice. He wrote:

> The Spring, which but salutes us here,
> Inhabits there, and courts them all the Year;
> Ripe Fruits and Blossoms on the same Tree live;
> At once they promise what at once they give.
> So sweet the Air, so moderate the Clime,
> None sickly lives, or dies before his Time.
> Heav'n sure has kept this Spot of Earth uncurst,
> To shew how all Things were created first.[6]

The supreme example of such visions was John Law's use of an overflowing horn of plenty to symbolize the inexhaustible riches said to be awaiting emigrants to Louisiana.

At the end of the colonial era, the South bade fair to fulfill her promise of prosperity for all. A gracious plantation society throve along the tide-

---

[3] Thomas Hariot, *A Brief and True Report of the New Found Land of Virginia* (London, 1855), quoted in Stefan Lorant, *The New World* (New York, 1946), 276–77.

[4] Hugh Jones, *The Present State of Virginia*, edited by Richard L. Morton (Chapel Hill, 1956), 83.

[5] John Lawson, *Lawson's History of North Carolina*, edited by Frances Latham Harris (Richmond, 1952), 80–178; Newton D. Mereness (ed.), *Travels in the American Colonies* (New York, 1916), 397–401.

[6] Pat. Tailfer and others, *A True and Historical Narrative of the Colony of Georgia*, edited by Clarence L. Ver Steeg (Athens, Ga., 1960), 12.

water section, while the yeomanry of the Piedmont and back country enjoyed a rude plenty. The severing of ties with England in the Revolution opened a fair prospect of increased well-being by sweeping away the planters' debts, which, almost like heirlooms, had been handed down from father to son; by confiscating and distributing the great estates of many wealthy Tories; by removing all restrictions on westward expansion; and by freeing the planters to sell their produce in the markets of the entire world.

Then an event occurred that kindled the highest hopes yet held for Southern affluence, an event that altered all the subsequent history of the region. In 1795 Eli Whitney invented the cotton gin, and the South began that great transition which ultimately would establish her as a "Kingdom of Cotton" from the Atlantic seaboard to the plains of Texas.

Southerners among the Founding Fathers trusted the laws of nature, if left free of governmental tampering, to bring the South into a rich agricultural destiny. "Our revenues once liberated by the discharge of the public debt," wrote Thomas Jefferson from his retirement at Monticello, "and its surplus applied to canals, roads, schools, etc., and the farmer will see his government supported, his children educated, and the face of his country made a paradise. . . . The path we are now pursuing leads directly to this end, which we cannot fail to attain unless our administration should fall into unwise hands."[7]

Immediately after the War of 1812 a group of nationalistic young Southern political figures, led by John C. Calhoun of South Carolina and Henry Clay of Kentucky, briefly abandoned the earlier Southern fear of governmental interference, and embraced economic nationalism as the source of Southern plenty. Supporting a bill in 1816 to establish tariff rates that would succor domestic industries, Calhoun argued that prosperity was the result of a combination of agriculture, manufactures, and commerce. "When our manufactures are grown to a certain perfection," he said, "as they soon will be under the fostering care of government, we will no longer experience the evils [of the recent war]. The farmer will find a ready market for his surplus produce; and what is almost of equal consequence, a certain and cheap supply of all his wants. His prosperity will diffuse itself to every class in the community."[8]

But the South quickly veered away from Calhoun's economic nationalism. Within a decade, Calhoun himself had turned against the tariff; from the mid-1830's to the Civil War, the South placed its highest hopes of

[7] Thomas Jefferson to Dupont de Nemours, April 15, 1811, in Andrew A. Lipscomb and "Others" (eds.), *The Writings of Thomas Jefferson* (20 vols., Washington, 1904), XIII, 39.

[8] Quoted in Robert L. Meriwether, *The Papers of John C. Calhoun* (2 vols., Columbia, 1959), I, 350.

riches upon slavery and cotton, and an open world market. To many Southerners of this period the economic millennium seemed almost to have arrived: they glowed with anticipation and pride as they expanded their plantations, purchased additional slaves, and built new and more ornate mansions. Senator James H. Hammond of South Carolina voiced the aspirations and the boast of the plantation South when in 1857 he claimed that the wealth and strength of the entire nation—indeed, of the entire world—rested upon Southern agriculture, and concluded with the ringing proclamation, "Cotton is King."[9]

The faith expressed by Senator Hammond found its ultimate manifestation in the movement for Southern independence. Addressing a convention of delegates from the slave states in Nashville, Tennessee, in 1850, the South Carolina lawyer and political thinker, Langdon Cheves, cried "Unite, and you shall form one of the most splendid empires on which the sun ever shone [with] a soil the most fruitful, and a climate the most lovely. . . ."[10] Ten years later the city of Charleston greeted the South Carolina secession convention with paintings of wharves piled high with cotton and a harbor bristling with masts—visions of the blessings expected of Southern nationhood.[11]

The Civil War itself stimulated a diversification of Southern agriculture and an expansion of Southern industry. A Manufacturing and Direct Trade Association of the Confederate States was organized, with the famed factory master of the Old South, William Gregg, as president. Southern editors hailed the burgeoning mines and factories as harbingers of a self-sufficient South. Chattanooga called herself the "Pittsburgh of the South"; other communities assumed comparable suggestive titles.[12] The Confederacy seemed about to fulfill the hopes of one of her citizens, a prominent Louisiana sugar planter, who had predicted that she would achieve "prosperity . . . as permanent as earthly things may be."[13]

Such a happy end was not to come. Long before the collapse of the ill-starred Confederacy, these dreams of affluence had vanished in a nightmare of privation.

There were many all along who vehemently rejected the Old South's articles of faith. Northern and European abolitionists condemned the institution of slavery as severely on economic grounds as on moral principles. The most thorough and perceptive of the outside critics of the Old South,

[9] *Congressional Globe,* 35th Congress, 1st Session, Appendix, 70.

[10] Quoted in Rollin G. Osterweis, *Romanticism and Nationalism in the Old South* (New Haven, 1949), 133.

[11] Charles P. Roland, *The Confederacy* (Chicago, 1960), 5.

[12] *Ibid.,* 69.

[13] A. Franklin Pugh Plantation Diary (Louisiana State University Archives, Baton Rouge, La.), January 17, 1861.

Frederick Law Olmsted, concluded that slavery was an economic millstone around the region's neck.[14]

The few remaining Southern abolitionists agreed with the Northern critics. "Lawyers, merchants, mechanics, laborers," wrote Cassius M. Clay of Kentucky, "How many clients do you find among [the slaves]? How many goods do you sell, how many hats, coats, saddles, and trunks do you make? . . . All our towns dwindle, and our farmers lose, in consequence [of slavery], all home markets. . . . A home market cannot exist in a slave state."[15] The most disparaging book written by an antebellum Southerner, Hinton R. Helper's *The Impending Crisis of the South,* indicted slavery for the impoverishment of the entire white farmer and laboring population of the South. "The North has surpassed [the South] in everything," concluded Helper, "and is going farther and farther ahead of her every day. . . . The downward tendency of the South can be arrested only by the abolition of slavery." Remove this curse, he urged, and the section would reap the blessing that God Almighty had promised to the ancient Israelites on a comparable occasion. "And the Lord shall guide thee continually and satisfy thy soul in drought, and make fat thy bones; and thou shalt be like a watered garden, and like a spring of water, whose waters fail not."[16]

Though Olmsted's and Helper's books were repudiated by the Old South almost as vehemently as *Uncle Tom's Cabin* was, their central theme —that all of the region's material ills were caused by slavery—ultimately would become a truism on the lips of all critics of the Southern economy.

This theme provided the North in the Civil War with a war aim almost as compelling as that of the preservation of the Union or the emancipation of the slaves. Once the blight of slavery was removed, reasoned Northern leaders, the South would blossom forth into a New England below the Potomac or a Northwest below the Ohio. "The lands of the South will rapidly appreciate to double, treble, quadruple their former values," prophesied the New York *Tribune.* "Idleness will give way to Industry."[17] Not only would the downtrodden Southern poor whites and the freed slaves quicken to the energizing Northern touch; the South would receive also a transfusion of vigorous Northern blood as multitudes of victorious soldiers would remain to enjoy her fertile soil and salubrious climate. "Schools and

[14] Frederick L. Olmsted. *A Journey Through the Seaboard Slave States* (2 vols., New York, 1856), I, 213–15; and *Our Slave States: A Journey Through Texas* (3 vols., New York, 1837), II, xiii–xviii.

[15] Eugene D. Genovese, "The Significance of the Slave Plantation for Southern Economic Development," *Journal of Southern History,* XXVIII (November, 1962), 457.

[16] Hinton R. Helper, *The Impending Crisis of the South* (New York, 1860), 33–34, 412.

[17] New York *Tribune,* December 24, 1864.

churches will be multiplied under Northern inspiration and example," predicted one Yankee observer; "industry, production, and intelligence will follow our arms, and when our forces withdraw instead of leaving a desolate country behind them, they will point to it as a blooming and regenerated Eden."[18] This was an inspiring vision: the Garden freed of the serpent, and its inhabitants and their rescuers sharing its fruit undisturbed!

Radical Reconstruction after the Civil War was, at least in part, an effort to translate into reality these Northern visions of a purged and prosperous South. Hand in hand with the mischievous schemes of Reconstruction went innumerable plans for industrializing the defeated region, for rebuilding its railroads, redistributing its land, diversifying its agriculture, overhauling its tax and fiscal structure, uplifting its poor—both black and white—vitalizing its educational system, and purifying its churches. Along with the crooks and adventurers among the Northern newcomers were countless ex-soldiers who were sincerely sympathetic toward the stricken country, who were genuinely attracted to its soil, climate, and people, and who earnestly believed in its future. Within months after the war's end, Louisiana alone was estimated to be playing host to 50,000 Northern men engaged in lumbering, planting, and a great variety of other business activities. Inflated as this estimate doubtless is, it nevertheless indicates the promise of wealth which the South held in the minds of the conquerors.[19] The authors of what the Southern people have traditionally regarded as being the foulest crimes ever committed against their section—Carpetbaggery and Negro rule—were beguiled by the image of an opulent South.[20]

Optimism soon yielded to disillusionment as the Reconstruction experiment ran afoul of the realities of Southern life and the weaknesses of human nature. Corruption and incompetence, both real and imagined, united with the South's implacable hostility toward the freed Negroes and with the apathy of the North to bring about the overthrow of Reconstruction and to make its very name a hiss and a byword on the American tongue. Yet, even in abandoning Reconstruction, its protagonists did not give up

[18] Milwaukee *Sentinel*, February 2, 1864. For comparable statements, see Columbus *Ohio State Journal*, November 23, 1861; Terre Haute *Daily Express*, September 16, 1862; Dubuque *Daily Times*, September 28, 1862; New York *Tribune*, August 25, December 25, 1863, January 23, December 24, 1864; Indianapolis *Daily Journal*, January 24, 1865; *Congressional Globe*, 37th Congress, 2nd Session, 1495, 2196; *ibid.*, 3rd Session, 630; *ibid.*, 38th Congress, 1st Session, 1188; *ibid.*, 2nd Session, 484–85.

[19] John T. Trowbridge, *The Desolate South, 1865–1866*, edited by Gordon Carroll (New York, 1956), and (Toronto, 1956), 212.

[20] John Hope Franklin, *Reconstruction after the Civil War* (Chicago, 1961), 127–51; Francis Butler Simkins and Robert H. Woody, *South Carolina during Reconstruction* (Chapel Hill, 1932), 147–223, 266–311; Hodding Carter, *The Angry Scar* (Garden City, 1959), 310–21.

all hope of an abundant South. Writing in 1875, and urging that Southern political and social affairs be left in Southern hands, Charles Nordhoff of the New York *Herald* said: "The South contains the greatest body of unreclaimed soil on this continent. Louisiana seems to me to have elements of wealth as great as California. Georgia has a great future as a manufacturing state, and will, I believe, within a few years tempt millions of Northern and European capital into her borders to engage in manufacture. Alabama now exports iron to Europe—in small quantities, to be sure—and her coal-fields and iron ores will make her the rival of Pennsylvania at no distant date. . . ."[21] And so it went for the entire region. Nothing could altogether blot out the vision of Southern plenty.

But the South emerged from Reconstruction almost as lifeless economically as she had been immediately after Appomattox. Plantation homes still lay in ruins, railroads were scarcely passable, towns were deserted and stores empty: the region's per capita wealth was reckoned at about 35 percent of that of the rest of the nation. "Fifteen years have gone over the South," wrote a perceptive Northern journalist, "and she still sits crushed, wretched, busy displaying and bemoaning her wounds."[22]

Not all Southerners, however, sat in the ashes of despair. Even while outside observers shook their heads over the apparently incurable lethargy and poverty of the region, a group of young Southern economic evangelists were beginning to preach a fresh hope and to exhort their people to a renewed faith. The heaven of their economic religion was called the New South.

An energetic young Georgian, Henry W. Grady, editor of the Atlanta *Constitution,* was the most compelling spokesman of this movement. Multitudes, both North and South, were converted to the New South persuasion through Grady's facile pen and tongue. Born in 1851, the son of a well-to-do merchant who had lost his life in the Confederate army, and reared amid the abortive efforts of Reconstruction to industrialize and revitalize the South, Grady combined the heritage, the experience, the personal qualities, and the timeliness required to lead a great transition in Southern outlook. His vision of the South's future was that of a community blending the virtue and grace of the Old South, minus its weaknesses, with a vigor and industry copied from the triumphant North. Grady glorified the South's past and extolled those forces that had produced a Washington, a Jefferson, a Clay, and a Calhoun; he spoke with reverence of the men who had supported the Lost Cause, and declared that the New South ought to stand

---

[21] Charles Nordhoff, *The Cotton States in the Spring and Summer of 1875* (New York, 1876), 23.

[22] C. Vann Woodward, *Origins of the New South, 1877–1913* (Baton Rouge, 1951), 107–11.

dumb and motionless rather than deny the greatness of Generals Lee and Jackson. But, he asserted, the New South rejoiced over the destruction of slavery and the preservation of the Union. The New South, as he put it, was the Old South under new conditions.[23]

Grady especially deplored the economic colonialism of the Old South— her dependence upon the North for manufactured wares and foodstuffs. His travesties for exposing this colonialism—his description of a prewar Georgia funeral, and his analysis of the ills of single-crop agriculture—have become Southern classics of a sort. The marble headstone for the Georgia funeral came from Vermont, said Grady, though the grave was dug through solid marble; the pine coffin came from Cincinnati, though the cemetery lay beside a pine forest; the iron nails, screws, and shovels came from Pittsburgh, though a mountain of iron ore overshadowed the graveyard; the wagon used as a hearse came from South Bend, Indiana, though hard wood and metals abounded in Georgia; the clothing on the body came from Cincinnati, though cotton fields spread in every direction about the burial ground. "[Georgia], so rich in undeveloped resources, furnished nothing for the funeral except the corpse and the hole in the ground," Grady declared, "and probably would have imported both of those if it could have been done."[24]

Once, while traveling through a particularly rich agricultural area in Pennsylvania, said Grady, he inquired the source of the remarkable prosperity. "Tobacco," was the reply. Later, traveling through a particularly poor agricultural section of North Carolina, Grady inquired the cause of such poverty. "Tobacco," was the reply. The difference was, he said, that in Pennsylvania tobacco was made the crown and money crop of a diversified agriculture, while in North Carolina tobacco was the sole crop, and the growers were obliged to purchase all foodstuffs and household necessities at premium prices.[25] "Develop Southern industry and diversify Southern agriculture," was Grady's repeated exhortation to the South.

Other voices were almost as powerful as Grady's in preaching the Gospel of the New South. Daniel A. Tomkins of South Carolina invoked the South's industrial past as an inspiration to an industrial future. Convinced by studying the federal census records of 1810 that the South Atlantic states had then produced more manufactured wares than New England and New York combined, and that slavery and cotton had sidetracked this promising career, Tomkins devoted his life to speaking, writing, investing, and laboring to build up in the South a new cotton textile industry that would rival the industry of New England. Sidney Lanier, the Georgia poet,

[23] Henry W. Grady, *The New South* (New York, 1890), 146–47.
[24] *Ibid.*, 188–89.
[25] *Ibid.*, 208–09.

called for a revolution in Southern farm tenure and agricultural methods. Walter Hines Page of North Carolina—and later, New York—supported a score or more of programs for what he called the "rebuilding of old commonwealths." Francis W. Dawson, Charleston publicist and capitalist, urged his people to "bring the cotton mills to the cotton fields." Richard H. Edmonds through the columns of the Baltimore *Manufacturers Record,* Henry Watterson in the pages of the Louisville *Courier-Journal,* Major E. A. Burke of New Orleans by means of press and public addresses, and a host of lesser figures in newspapers about the countryside, all sang the praises of a burgeoning industrial and commercial South.[26]

Grady and his fellow believers were convinced that the advent of the New South was at hand, and that it would fulfill all of the promises of affluence which had so long tantalized the region. In 1890, after quoting and endorsing a wide selection of authorities who said that the South was just about to become the center of the nation's industry, Grady exclaimed in rhapsody: "Surely, God has led the people of the South into this unexpected way of progress and prosperity. . . . The industrial system of the South responds, grows, thrills with new life, and it is based on sure and certain foundations. For it is built at the field, by the mine, in the field— from which come the cheapest and best and fullest supply of cotton, iron and wood!. . . The industries of other sections—distant from the source of supply—may be based on artificial conditions that in time may be broken. But the industrial system of the South is built on a rock—and it cannot be shaken!"[27] To which the South resounded with "amens."

The half-century following the appearance of Grady and his associates was a period of vast change for the section. In the Piedmont South arose a cotton textile industry that did indeed rival that of New England; at Birmingham arose an iron and steel industry that threatened the supremacy of Pittsburgh; in the cotton country arose a flourishing cotton oil industry; and in Louisiana and Texas arose one of the world's richest petroleum and chemical industries. Even the pine barrens of the South became a source of wealth with the discovery of ways to make paper out of soft pulpwood. At the same time, Southern agriculture throve as new methods and fertilizers enabled small farmers to compete with planters in growing cotton, and as great numbers of husbandmen turned their capital and efforts to the production of cattle, fruit or vegetables. The prophecies of a New South seemed indeed to have come true.

[26] George T. Winston, *A Builder of the New South: Being the Story of the Life Work of Daniel Augustus Tomkins* (New York, 1920), 20–73, 84–94, 349–67; Sidney Lanier, *Retrospects and Prospects* (New York, 1899), 104–35; Walter Hines Page, *The Rebuilding of Old Commonwealths* (New York, 1902), 107–53; Broadus Mitchell, *The Rise of Cotton Mills in the South* (Baltimore, 1921), 77–159; Woodward, *Origins of the New South,* 144–48.

[27] Grady, *The New South,* 193–95, 206–07.

The major prophets of this epoch—the Gradys, Tomkinses, and Daw-sons—were followed by a series of minor prophets who offered fresh and expanded visions of the coming Utopia in the Southland.[28] An English observer in 1910 captured the spirit of this group when he wrote: "[This] great agricultural, industrial, and educational revival is rapidly transmuting the South from a ghost-haunted region of depression and impoverishment into one of the most eagerly progressive, and probably one of the wealthiest, of modern communities."[29] Seventeen years later, a distinguished Southern scholar—Professor Edwin Mims of Vanderbilt University—summed up these optimistic analyses of the region's affairs in a book bearing the significant title, *The Advancing South*. Professor Mims foresaw a South balancing diversified agriculture with diversified industry, and crowning her economic victories with comparable intellectual and artistic triumphs. If the people of the twentieth-century South would but prove true to their New South forebears, he concluded, "the time is not far off when scholarship, literature and art shall flourish, and when all things that make for the intellectual and spiritual emancipation of man shall find their home under Southern skies."[30]

Although the New South philosophy did not go entirely unchallenged at any time, the major critical appraisal of it on its own terms—that is, the South's economic well-being—appeared only when the Great Depression of the 1930's obliged all Americans to re-examine the premises of their social and economic beliefs. President Franklin D. Roosevelt's National Emergency Council, including a group of selected Southern scholars, laid bare the economic facts of life in the New South. In spite of all efforts to catch up with the rest of the nation, the council concluded, the South was still woefully behind. Her per capita annual income was hardly more than half of that of the nation as a whole; her agriculture was the most archaic and wasteful in the nation; her industry the most colonial; her out-migration of human talent the most crippling; her citizens generally the poorest housed, clothed, and fed; her sick the least adequately treated; and her children the least effectively educated. "The South," declared the President after receiving the report, "is the nation's economic problem No. 1."[31]

Realistic as it was in analyzing the region's shortcomings, the council did not repudiate the ancient vision of an opulent South. Its exposition of Southern possibilities sounded like a paraphrase of Henry W. Grady's

---

[28] Hilary A. Herbert, *Why the Solid South?* (Baltimore, 1890), 430–42; Philip A. Bruce, *The Rise of the New South* (Philadelphia, 1905), 472.

[29] William Archer, *Through Afro-America: An English Reading of the Race Problem* (New York, 1910), xiv.

[30] Edwin Mims, *The Advancing South* (New York, 1927), 20–79, 80–112, 315–16.

[31] Arthur Goldschmidt, "The Development of the U. S. South," *Scientific American* (September, 1963), 225; National Emergency Council, *Report on Economic Conditions of the South* (Washington, 1938), 8.

rhetoric.[32] But the South could not achieve this goal unaided, reasoned the council. The federal government must come to the region's assistance by spending federal funds on Southern public works and services, by encouraging industries to move south, by providing favorable credit facilities to farmers and home builders, and by removing discriminatory taxes and freight rates.[33]

The epoch of President Roosevelt's New Deal and of World War II, with its aftermath of booming prosperity for the entire nation, has given the South the greatest affluence of its history. Most of the implicit recommendations of the National Emergency Council have been carried out: TVA, rural electrification, soil conservation, and farmers' and home builders' credit have long been in effect. Government price support has vastly increased the farmers' income. Discriminatory taxes on Southern cotton oil products, such as margarine, and prejudicial freight rates against Southern manufacturers have long been gone. The munitions and armaments industries of World War II, and the thriving aluminum, synthetics, and petrochemical industries of the post-war years have changed the base of the southern economy from agriculture to industry. Cotton has been dethroned and reduced to the ranks of the minor nobility.[34]

Finally, the most persistent of all problems affecting the region's economy—that of racial accommodation—has been attacked pointblank. All players in the Southern drama have sought a solution to this difficulty as a key to the fulfillment of their dreams of Southern betterment. The Old South sought a solution in slavery; the abolitionists sought it in emancipation; the Radicals of Reconstruction sought it in political equality for the freedmen; the New South sought it in white supremacy and racial segregation.

Ever since the overthrow of Reconstruction, however, a minority of white Southerners has insisted that segregation and suppression of the Negro retard the South economically even as they debase her morally. In the late nineteenth century, Louisiana novelist George Washington Cable said this discreetly in a book entitled *The Negro Question;* the Virginia industrialist Lewis Harvie Blair said it vehemently in a book entitled *Prosperity of the South Dependent on the Elevation of the Negro.*[35] Although President Roosevelt's National Emergency Council recommended no spe-

[32] National Emergency Council, *Report on Economic Conditions of the South,* 5–8.

[33] Goldschmidt, "The Development of the U. S. South," *Scientific American* (September 1963), 228.

[34] John S. Ezell, *The South Since 1865* (New York, 1963), 438–39; Thomas D. Clark, *The Emerging South* (New York, 1961), 55–56.

[35] George Washington Cable, *The Negro Question* (New York, 1890), 51–53; C. Vann Woodward, "A Southerner's Answer to the Negro Question," *The Reporter* (February 27, 1964), 41–44.

cific program to solve this problem, it did again call attention to the crippling effects of Negro deprivation on the general Southern welfare.[36]

Beginning with the United States Supreme Court's school desegregation decision in 1954, and culminating in the passage by Congress of the civil rights acts of the 1960's the federal government—both applauded and assisted, and damned and resisted—has sought to solve the Southern racial problem by fiat and persuasion, and, when necessary, by coercion.

This cluster of Southern developments—economic and social—since World War II has brought forth a fresh chorus of voices ringing with optimism over the section's future.[37] A prime example of this trend appeared in an address entitled "The South's Call to Greatness: Challenge to All Southerners," by a renowned Texas historian, the late Professor Walter P. Webb. After cataloging the South's unmatched natural resources—her coastlines, rivers, water power, climate, fertile soil, and metal and mineral deposits—Professor Webb then reviewed the region's great recent gains in industry, agriculture, per capita income, bank deposits, and ownership of corporate stock. The South, he asserted, was "on the threshold of a new era. Chance and circumstance [had] conspired to offer [her] a great opportunity." He concluded by endorsing the words of a modern Southern industrialist, who said: "The conscientious, level-headed citizens of the South may one day hold the destiny of America in their hands."[38]

One would be foolish indeed to deny that since the Civil War, and especially during and since World War II, the South has taken giant strides in industry and prosperity. A century ago the South possessed less than 10 percent of the nation's industry and her per capita annual income was less than half that of the nation as a whole; today the South possesses better than 20 percent of the nation's industry and her per capita annual income is roughly 80 percent of that of the nation as a whole.

But figures and statistics are not infallible. Indeed, every prophet of Southern opulence since the days of Sir Walter Raleigh has enlisted arithmetic to support his optimism. Perhaps one ought to consider the line on a certain comic card which reads, "The hurrier I go, the behinder I get." If the application of this absurdity exaggerates the economic plight of the South—and admittedly it does do so—it at least suggests a comparable problem. It is instructive, and at the same time frustrating, to consider how

---

[36] National Emergency Council, *Report on Economic Conditions of the South,* 19–20.

[37] Ezell, *The South Since 1865,* 451; Clark, *The Emerging South,* 121–23; Goldschmidt, "The Development of the U. S. South," *Scientific American* (September 1963), 228–29.

[38] Walter P. Webb, "The South's Call to Greatness: Challenge to All Southerners," an address to the Seventh Annual Conference, The Texas Council for Social Studies, San Marcos, Texas, June 29, 1959.

much the Southern economy, notwithstanding its remarkable gains, has remained the same. For the South still lags seriously behind the rest of the nation economically. A statement issued in 1964 by the Federal Department of Health and Welfare is strikingly reminiscent of the report of President Franklin D. Roosevelt's National Emergency Council thirty years ago. The Welfare Department named Tunica County, Mississippi, as the poorest spot in the nation, then went on to list among the ten states with the highest number of impoverished families the following states of the South: Mississippi, Arkansas, South Carolina, Alabama, Tennessee, North Carolina, Kentucky, Georgia, and Louisiana.[39] In 1967 the annual income of the average citizen of Florida, the South's richest state according to personal per capita income, was more than $1,000 below that of Connecticut, the nation's richest. In 1968 the annual income of the average citizen of Mississippi, the South's poorest state, was more than $1,200 below the national average.[40] Thus the South remains the nation's economic problem No. 1.

The achievement of genuine economic parity by the South would seem to require a drastic alteration in the very nature of her society and economy, and to a degree, in the nature of the national economy as well. For the Southern economy remains highly colonial. The happy statistics on Southern industry do not reveal that it is still primarily extractive—concerned with drawing out the oil, mineral ores, timber, and farm products of the South to provide fuel, metal, and fiber for the national industrial machine. Or that Southern industry is disproportionately crude, leaving the fabrication of the finished, and therefore more expensive, products to be done outside of the region. Or that a great part of Southern industry is held by national corporations that are chiefly owned and managed by outsiders.[41]

Perhaps most serious of all, the figures on Southern progress do not expose the general weakness of the Southern educational system, which is expected to serve as the very incubator of a truly superior industry and economy. Notwithstanding strenuous efforts by the Southern population to create a strong school system, the high birth rate of the region combines with the relative lack of wealth to keep its schools behind those of other sections of the country. An eminent student of the South has recently said, "The South needs some first-rate universities and graduate schools to attract and hold the best students and the best professors it produces. At present, the region does not have a one of the ten or fifteen best universities

[39] New Orleans *States-Item*, November 24, 1964.

[40] *Survey of Current Business* (April 1968), 14.

[41] C. Vann Woodward, "The New South Fraud Is Papered by Old South Myth," Washington *Post*, July 9, 1961.

in the country."[42] The same criticism can be made of the South's elementary and secondary schools. Nor, apparently, is the educational gap being closed. Only a short time ago the United States associate commissioner of education reported that the South's public schools are losing ground instead of gaining, in relation to those elsewhere. "The present generation of Southern students is more disadvantaged than was my generation," he declared.[43]

Three quarters of a century ago Henry W. Grady used the story of a Georgia funeral to dramatize the colonial nature of the Southern economy. Let us do the same today. Suppose Grady were to return to a funeral in the present South. Would he find everything changed? Admittedly many things would be different; but many would also be the same. Chances are that he would find the corpse today dressed in a suit made in Chicago, transported in a hearse made in Detroit, and buried in a casket made in St. Louis. Moreover, Grady would find a number of innovations in economic colonialism that have been added since his day. The bereaved family of the present would be calmed by tranquilizer pills made in Philadelphia, and supported by insurance payments from a company in Hartford where most of the life savings of the departed one had been invested. Perhaps the supreme irony of the modern Southern funeral would be that the very commodities imported for the occasion—the hearse, the clothes, and the casket—had been made by the hands of Southern-born laborers now living outside of their native region.

The South has persistently been the nation's greatest economic enigma —a region of want in the midst of boundless natural riches. It has been, and remains today, a land becoming and not a land become—a garden spot that beckons only to recede like a mirage when approached. It is America's will-o'-the-wisp Eden.

[42] *Ibid.*
[43] Quoted in New Orleans *States-Item,* December 19, 1964.

Suggestions for Further Reading

The works indicated below, in addition to those from which the selections in the body of the book have been drawn, bear a particular relevance to southern history in its mythic context. The list is extensive, but certainly not all-inclusive. Acquaintance with the following materials should give the reader a basic grasp of the mythical content of the southern past. More importantly, the citations can be viewed as yet further evidence of the viability of "myth" as an approach through which the "reality" of the southern experience might better be judged.

Adams, Richard P. "Faulkner and the Myth of the South." *The Mississippi Quarterly,* 14 (1961).

Alexander, Thomas B. "Persistent Whiggery in the Confederate South, 1860–1877." *The Journal of Southern History,* 27 (1961).

Amacher, Anne Ward. "Myths and Consequences: Calhoun and Some Nashville Agrarians." *South Atlantic Quarterly,* 59 (1960).

Boorstin, Daniel J. "The Vision and the Reality." In *The Americans: The Colonial Experience.* New York: Random House, 1966.

Bradford, M. E. "What We Can Know for Certain: Frank Owsley and the Recovery of Southern History." *Sewanee Review,* 78 (1970).

Bridenbaugh, Carl. *Myths and Realities: Societies of the Colonial South.* New York: Atheneum, 1963.

Brooks, Cleanth. "Faulkner and History." *The Mississippi Quarterly,* 25 (1972).

Cann, Marvin L. "The End of a Political Myth: The South Carolina Gubernatorial Campaign of 1938." *The South Carolina Historical Magazine,* 72 (1971).

Clendenen, Clarence C. "President Hayes' 'Withdrawal' of the Troops—An Enduring Myth." *The South Carolina Historical Magazine,* 70 (1969).

Cole, Wayne S. "America First and the South." *The Journal of Southern History,* 22 (1956).

Cords, Nicholas and Patrick Gerster, eds. "The Mythology of the South." In *Myth and the American Experience.* Beverly Hills and New York: Glencoe/Macmillan, 1973.

Danoff, Clarence H. "Four Decades of Thought on the South's Economic Problems." In Melvin Greenhut and W. Tate Whitman, eds., *Essays in Southern Economic Development.* Chapel Hill: University of North Carolina Press, 1964.

Davenport, F. Gavin, Jr. *The Myth of Southern History: Historical Consciousness in Twentieth-Century Southern Literature.* Nashville: Vanderbilt University Press, 1970.

————. "Thomas Dixon's Mythology of Southern History." *The Journal of Southern History,* 36 (1970).

Davis, Michael. *The Image of Lincoln in the South.* Knoxville: The University of Tennessee Press, 1972.

DeConde, Alexander. "The South and Isolationism." *The Journal of Southern History,* 24 (1958).

Degler, Carl. "There Was Another South." *American Heritage,* 11 (1960).

————. "The South in Southern History Textbooks." *The Journal of Southern History,* 30 (1964).

Dillon, Merton L. "Three Southern Antislavery Editors: The Myth of the Southern Antislavery Movement." *Eastern Tennessee Historical Society Publication,* No. 42 (1970).

Donald, David. "The Scalawag in Mississippi Reconstruction," *The Journal of Southern History,* 10 (1944).

————. "The Confederate as a Fighting Man." *The Journal of Southern History,* 35 (1959).

Dykeman, Wilma. "The Southern Demagogue." *The Virginia Quarterly Review,* 33 (1957).

Eaton, Clement. *The Waning of the Old South Civilization.* New York: Pegasus, 1969.

Engerman, Stanley L. "The Antebellum South: What Probably Was and What Should Have Been." *Agricultural History,* 44 (1970).

Fishwick, Marshall. "Robert E. Lee: The Guardian Angel Myth." *Saturday Review* (March 4, 1961).

Floan, Howard R. *The South in Northern Eyes, 1831–1861.* Austin: University of Texas Press, 1958.

Gaines, Francis Pendelton. *The Southern Plantation: A Study in the Development and Accuracy of a Tradition.* (New York: Columbia University Press, 1924.

Gara, Larry. *The Liberty Line: The Legend of the Underground Railroad.* Lexington: The University Press of Kentucky, 1967.

Genovese, Eugene D. *In Red and Black: Marxian Explorations in Southern and Afro-American History.* New York: Vintage Books, 1971.

Govan, Thomas P. "Was the Old South Different?" *The Journal of Southern History,* 21 (1955).

Grantham, Dewey, W., Jr. "Politics Below the Potomac." *Current History,* 35 (1958).

————. "The Southern Bourbons Revisited." *South Atlantic Quarterly,* 55 (1961).

————. "South to Posterity." *Mid-West Quarterly,* 8 (1966).

————. "Regional Imagination: Social Scientists and the American South." *The Journal of Southern History,* 34 (1968).

————, ed. *The South and the Sectional Image: The Sectional Theme Since Reconstruction.* New York: Harper & Row Publishers, 1967.

Green, Fletcher M. "Listen to the Eagle Scream: One Hundred Years of the Fourth of July in North Carolina." *North Carolina Historical Review,* 31 (1954).

————. "The South and Its History." *Current History,* 35 (1958).

————. *The Role of the Yankee in the Old South.* Athens: University of Georgia Press, 1973.

Gross, Seymour L., and Eileen Bender. "History, Politics and Literature: The Myth of Nat Turner." *American Quarterly,* 24 (1972).

Hansen, Vagn K. "Jefferson Davis and the Repudiation of Mississippi Bonds (1842): The Development of a Political Myth." *Journal of Mississippi History,* 33 (1971).

Havard, William C. "The Burden of the Literary Mind: Some Meditations on Robert Penn Warren as Historian." *South Atlantic Quarterly,* 62 (1963).

Herskovits, Melville. *The Myth of the Negro Past.* Boston: Beacon Press, 1958.

Hofstadter, Richard. "Ulrich B. Phillips and the Plantation Legend." *Journal of Negro History,* 29 (1944).

Karanikas, Alexander. *Tillers of a Myth: Southern Agrarians as Social and Literary Critics.* Madison: University of Wisconsin Press, 1966.

Keyserling, Hermann. "The South—America's Hope." *Atlantic Quarterly,* 144 (1929).

Mayo, Bernard. *Myths and Men.* New York: Harper & Row Publishers, 1963.

McWhiney, Grady. *Southerners and Other Americans.* New York: Basic Books, Inc., 1973.

McWhiney, Grady and Francis Simkins. "The Ghostly Legend of the KKK." *Negro History Bulletin,* 14 (1951).

Mowry, George E. *Another Look At the Twentieth-Century South.* Baton Rouge: Louisiana State University Press, 1973.

Nash, Gary B. "The Image of the Indian in the Southern Colonial Mind." *The William and Mary Quarterly,* 29 (1972).

Noggle, Burl. "Variety and Ambiguity: The Recent Approach to Southern History." *Mississippi Quarterly,* 16 (1963–64).

Osterweis, Rollin G. *Romanticism and Nationalism in the Old South.* New Haven: Yale University Press, 1949.

Owsley, Frank L. and Harriet C. Owsley. "The Economic Basis of Society in the Late Ante-Bellum South." *The Journal of Southern History,* 6 (1940).

Potter, David M. *The South and the Sectional Conflict.* Baton Rouge: Louisiana State University Press, 1968.

Payne, Ladell. "Willie Stark and Huey Long: Atmosphere, Myth or Suggestion." *American Quarterly,* 20 (1968).

Rock, Virginia J. "The Making and Meaning of 'I'll Take My Stand': A Study in Utopian Conservatism." Unpublished Ph.D Dissertation: University of Minnesota, 1961.

Rozwenc, Edwin C. "Captain John Smith's Image of America." *William and Mary Quarterly,* 16 (1959).

Rubin, Louis D. "The Historical Image of Modern Southern Writing." *The Journal of Southern History,* 22 (1956).

———. "The South and the Faraway Country." *The Virginia Quarterly Review,* 38 (1962).

Scarborough, William K. *The Overseer: Plantation Management in the Old South.* Baton Rouge: Louisiana State University Press, 1966.

Scott, Anne Firor. "The 'New Women' in the New South." *South Atlantic Quarterly,* 61 (1962).

———. "The Progressive Wind from the South, 1906–1913." *The Journal of Southern History,* 29 (1963).

———. *The Southern Lady: From Pedestal to Politics.* Chicago: University of Chicago Press, 1970.

Sellers, Charles G., Jr., ed. *The Southerner as American.* Chapel Hill: University of North Carolina Press, 1960.

Simkins, Francis B. "The Everlasting South." *The Journal of Southern History,* 13 (1947).

———. "The South." In Merrill Jensen, ed., *Regionalism in America.* Madison: University of Wisconsin Press, 1951.

Smiley, David L. "The Quest for the Central Theme in Southern History." *South Atlantic Quarterly,* 71 (1972).

Sosna, Morton. "The South Old and New: A Review Essay." *The Wisconsin Magazine of History,* 55 (1972).

Spruill, Julia Cherry. *Women's Life and Work in the Southern Colonies.* New York: W. W. Norton & Co., 1973.

Stampp, Kenneth M. "The Tragic Legend of Reconstruction." In *The Era of Reconstruction.* New York: Alfred A. Knopf, 1965.

———. "Rebels and Sambos: The Search for the Negro's Personality in Slavery." *The Journal of Southern History,* 37 (1971).

Stephenson, Wendell Holmes. "The South Lives in History." *Historical Outlook,* 23 (1932).

Tate, Allen. "Faulkner's 'Sanctuary' and the Southern Myth." *The Virginia Quarterly Review,* 44 (1968).

Tindall, George B. *The Disruption of the Solid South.* New York: W. W. Norton & Co., 1973.

Trelease, Allen W. "Who Were the Scalawags?" *The Journal of Southern History,* 29 (1963).

Vandiver, Frank E. "The Confederacy and the American Tradition." *The Journal of Southern History,* 28 (1962).

Ver Steeg, Clarence L. "Historians and the Southern Colonies." In Ray A. Billington, ed., *The Reinterpretation of Early American History.* San Marino, California: The Huntington Library, 1966.

Ward, John William. *Andrew Jackson: Symbol for an Age.* New York: Oxford University Press, 1962.

Warren, Robert Penn. *The Legacy of the Civil War: Meditations on the Centennial.* New York: Alfred A. Knopf, 1964.

Whitridge, Arnold. "The John Brown Legend." *History Today,* 7 (1957).

Williams, D. Alan. "The Virginia Gentry and the Democratic Myth." In Quint, Albertson, and Cantor, eds., *Main Problems of American History.* Rev. ed. Homewood, Illinois: The Dorsey Press, 1972.

Woodward, C. Vann. "The Antislavery Myth." *The American Scholar,* 31 (1962).

————. "Southern Mythology." *Commentary,* 42 (1965).

————. *The Strange Career of Jim Crow.* New York: Oxford University Press, 1966.

Wright, Louis B. "Intellectual History and the Colonial South." *William and Mary Quarterly,* 16 (1959).

————. *The Dream of Prosperity in Colonial America.* New York University Press, 1965.

Zinn, Howard. *The Southern Mystique.* New York: Alfred A. Knopf, 1964.

Index

PRINTED IN U.S.A.